TALMUD ESER SEFIROT
The Study of the Ten Sefirot

Volume One

Rav Yehuda Leib Ashlag (Baal Hasulam)

LAITMAN
KABBALAH
PUBLISHERS

TALMUD ESER SEFIROT
The Study of the Ten Sefirot
Volume One
Preliminary Edition

Laitman Kabbalah Publishers, 2022
Copyright [c] 2022 by Laitman Kabbalah Publishers
1057 Steeles Avenue West, Suite 532
Toronto, ON M2R 3X1, Canada
All rights reserved.

Contact Information
E-mail: info@kabbalah.info
Website: www.kabbalah.info

Toll free in USA and Canada: 1-866-LAITMAN
1057 Steeles Avenue West, Suite 532, Toronto,
ON, M2R 3X1, Canada

ISBN: 9798362063894

Translation: Chaim Ratz
Content Editing: Shaul Dar
Editing and Proofreading: Mary Miesem
Cover Design: Inna Smirnova
Printing and Post Production: Uri Laitman

FIRST EDITION: November 2022
First printing

CONTENTS

VOLUME 1

PART ONE

Restriction and line, containing two chapters

CHAPTER ONE

Explains the issue of the first restriction, when the light of Ein Sof became restricted in order to emanate the emanated beings and create the created beings; containing five issues:

1. Before the restriction, Ein Sof filled the entire reality. 2. The reason for creation was the revelation of His Names and Appellations. 3. The restriction of the light around the middle point. 4. The space that remained after the restriction was circular. 5. Because the light of Ein Sof was even, the restriction was also even. This is the meaning of the circle.

Before the restriction Ein Sof filled the entire reality

1. Know that before the emanated beings were emanated and the created beings created (1), an upper, simple light (2) had filled the entire reality (3). There was no vacant place (4), such as empty air (5) and space (6), but everything was filled with that simple, boundless light (7).

   It did not have a quality of Rosh, or Sof (8), but it was all one, simple light (9), completely even (10), called light of Ein Sof (20).

Inner Light

We must remember that the entire wisdom of Kabbalah is founded on spiritual matters that do not take up time or space. They are not subject to change or absence and all the changes that are spoken of in this wisdom do not imply that the first form becomes absent and is replaced by a different form. The above change rather implies an additional form, while the first does not move from its place, as absence and change are corporeal conducts.

It is difficult for beginners, for they perceive matters by means of corporeal boundaries of time, space, change and exchange. However, the authors only used those as signs to point to their upper roots.

For this reason, I will make an effort to give every word its spiritual identity, detached of space, time and change. It is upon the readers to memorize the meaning of these words thoroughly, for it is impossible to repeat them every time.

1. The issue of spiritual time is explained thoroughly in Inner Observation Chapter 9, item 33.

2. It refers to the light that expands from the Creator Himself. Know that all the names and appellations that appear in the wisdom of Kabbalah are not at all in the Creator Himself, but only in the light that expands from His self. However, we cannot utter even a single word regarding His self, for the rule is that anything we do not attain, we do not know its name. Remember that and you will not fail.

3. It is seemingly perplexing, for it speaks of the time before the worlds were created. Thus, which reality exists here, that the upper light should fill? The thing is that all the worlds and the souls that exist and that are destined to be created with all their incidents until the end of their correction are all included in Ein Sof in their full measure and glory.

   Thus, there are two rudiments we should discern in the reality before us: 1) They are fixed and exist in Ein Sof with their full measure and glory. 2) How they are arranged and cascade and are renewed before us after the first restriction in the five worlds: Adam Kadmon, Atzilut, Beria, Yetzira, Assiya.

   The ARI writes that the upper light that extends from His self "had filled the entire reality," meaning the entire reality of the first rudiment, relating to their existence in Ein Sof before the restriction. He tells us that the upper light filled them entirely, until they had no vacant place left where correction and perfection could be added whatsoever.

4. It means that before the worlds were created there was only Ein Sof. There was no "vacant place," meaning a place of dearth that would qualify for corrections because the upper light filled that place. It left no room for the lower ones to distinguish themselves and add something to His completeness.

   Because of the restriction there came about a wanting and a vacant place for the corrections. However, do not be mistaken to think that the book speaks of a corporeal place.

5. This does not refer to corporeal air whatsoever; but there is a spiritual light that is called by that name. There are two qualities of light in each complete Partzuf: light of Hochma and light of Hassadim.

   Light of Hochma is the Partzuf itself, meaning its vitality. Light of Hassadim only operates as clothing light over the light of Hochma in the Partzuf since light of Hochma cannot permeate the Partzuf if it does not wear the light of Hassadim first.

   However, sometimes, when the Partzufim [pl. of Partzuf] are in Katnut, they do not have more than light of Hassadim. You should know that that light of Hassadim is called "air" or "wind" (as well as "spirit"). In itself, without light of Hochma, it is called "empty air," meaning devoid of light of Hochma. Then it waits for light of Hochma to clothe it and fulfill it.

The ARI tells us that before the worlds were created, meaning in Ein Sof, such empty air did not exist in reality at all, because there was not any dearth there.

6. To understand that word, you must first know the essence of a spiritual vessel. Since the emanated being receives its vitality from the Emanator, it necessarily implies that it has a desire and yearning to receive that abundance from Him.

Know that the amount of that desire and yearning is the entire substance that exists in the emanated being. Thus, everything that exists in the emanated being that is not that substance, no longer relates to its substance, but to the abundance that it receives from the Emanator.

Furthermore, this substance determines the Gadlut and the level of each emanated being, each Partzuf, and each Sefira. The expansion of the upper light from the Emanator is certainly immeasurable, but it is the emanated being that limits the abundance, for it receives no more and no less than its measure of desire to receive. This is the criterion in spirituality, because there is no coercion there; it depends entirely on the desire.

For this reason, we call this will to receive the "vessel of reception" of the emanated being. It is regarded as its substance and the reason that it stopped being regarded as an emanator and was denominated as an emanated being. The emanated being is defined by a substance that does not exist in the Emanator whatsoever, for there is absolutely no will to receive in the Emanator, because from whom would He receive?

Now we will explain how there are four degrees in this substance, from Katnut to Gadlut (of reception). The fourth degree, being the Gadlut of the reception, is complete only in Ein Sof, before the worlds were created. It is the only one that was subject to the restriction, and we will clarify henceforth that it was emptied of every abundance that she had from Ein Sof and remained a vacant space. This is what the ARI means when he says that before the world was created, meaning in Ein Sof, this vacant space did not exist.

7. This means that there is nothing that the lower ones can add to it by means of their actions.

8. The terms Rosh and Sof will be explained below.

9. Meaning without discriminating small and great, everything is even.

10. Where there is no refinement and thickness by which the degrees are set. These discriminations were established only with the renewal of the restriction.

20. We should ask: since we have no attainment in Ein Sof, how then do we know Him by name? After all, each name designates the attainment that we attain in Him, according to the definition of that name. We cannot excuse ourselves by saying that the name merely points to the negation of attainment, for then we should have named Him "Unattainable."

The thing is that that name indicates the entire difference between Ein Sof and all the worlds beneath it. The restriction took place after Ein Sof. Thus, in every place this force awakens, it restricts the light and that ends the illumination in that place.

Hence, any Sof and Sium in any illumination in any Partzuf come solely from the restriction. Moreover, all the beings and their various fillings in the worlds come about and are innovated because of that Sof and Sium.

It is called Ein Sof because the restriction does not apply there, indicating that there isn't any ending there whatsoever. With that we can deduce that this light is simple and completely even, for one depends on the other.

The reason for creation was the revelation of His Names and Appellations

2. When it rose upon His simple desire (30) to create the worlds and emanate the emanated beings to bring the perfection of His deeds, His names and appellations to light, which was the reason of the creation of the worlds,

Inner Light

30. We need not wonder how there is a desire in Ein Sof, who is higher than any notion, to which we can say, "**rose upon His simple** desire." You should comprehend what has been said above that in every emanated being there is by necessity a will to receive the abundance from the Emanator.

However, in Ein Sof it is a "simple desire" because He is One and His Name One. The light in Ein Sof is called He and the will to receive is called His Name, and they are simple unity without any form of separation.

However, we should not resemble the unity and separation discussed here with corporeal unity and separation that are distinguished by motion, nearness and distance. That is because the spiritual essence does not take up any space.

Having said that, you should know that separation in spirituality occurs only by means of disparity of form. Thus, if one spiritual thing acquires an additional form that is unlike its current form, it stops being one and becomes two separate entities. Their distance from each other is measured by the oppositeness of their forms.

Just as corporeal entities connect and separate through proximity and remoteness, so spiritual entities connect and separate according to their difference and equivalence of form. The disparity of form separates them from one another, and the equivalence of form brings them together. Remember that for it is the key element to this wisdom.

Now you will understand the meaning of the aforementioned words "He is One and His Name One," and the simple unity we are so meticulous about in Ein Sof. Indeed this unity is of the wonders of His almightiness.

We have witnessed the difference between the Emanator and the emanated being that was caused by the form of that will to receive that exists in the emanated being and not in the Emanator. Because of that disparity of form, the emanated being became separated from the Emanator and acquired its own separate name, meaning emanated being, and not emanator.

The above explanation might mislead us into thinking that light of Ein Sof, called "He," is not entirely adherent with Ein Sof, called "His Name," meaning the will to receive the light and the abundance, called "He." That is because the upper light that extends from Himself, called "He," has but one attribute—to bestow—and none of the form of the will to receive.

However, Ein Sof, called "His Name," which does have a will to receive, is therefore different from the upper light, which has no will to receive whatsoever, as has been explained, and we know that disparity of form separates. However, the Midrash and the ARI tell us that it is not so. Instead, He is One and His Name One in Simple Unity, means that there is no difference between them.

Although there is necessarily a difference of form between "He" and "His Name," it is nevertheless completely inactive there. We do not understand it, but it is undoubtedly so. It is said about that, that there is no perception or thought in Ein Sof whatsoever, since this matter is above our mind (will be discussed further in the next item).

The restriction of the light around the middle point

3. **Ein Sof then restricted Himself (40) in His middle point (50), in the very middle, restricted that light, and drifted (60) to the sides around that middle point (70).**

Inner Light

40. You already know the meaning of He is One and His Name One. Although there is disparity of form with respect to the will to receive incorporated in Ein Sof, that still does not create any differentiation between that and the upper light, and they are in simple unity.

Still, this disparity of form has become the reason and the cause for the creation of the worlds, "to bring the perfection of His deeds, His names and appellations to light," as the ARI says here. The creation of the worlds and their cascading down to this world, created and renewed the possibility to give room for work in Torah and Mitzvot not in order to receive, but only to bestow contentment upon the Maker.

It is then that the souls become able to invert the form of the will to receive in them, which separates them from the Emanator, into the form of the will to bestow contentment upon Him, which is what He wants (see item 90). This is the equivalence of form with the Emanator, called adhesion and unification. It is so because then they have already been stripped from the form of the will to receive and acquired the form of the will to bestow, being the form of the Emanator Himself.

You already know that equivalence of form makes the spirituals become one. For this reason, the worlds return to their previous condition.

This is the meaning of the ARI's words, "When it rose upon His simple desire to create, etc." "It rose" means that He increased the refinement and adhesion by diminishing the measure of the will to receive imprinted in him in order to equalize the form with the upper light.

The will to receive in Ein Sof, called Malchut of Ein Sof, or "His Name," did not have any dearth in adhesion with the upper light because of its disparity of form. However, it embellished himself in order to equalize its form with the upper light and depart from the great will to receive, called "phase four," so as to cleave more strongly to the upper light.

The proximity of the form makes for adhesion. It is expressed in the words "it rose," meaning Malchut of Ein Sof, being a simple desire, rose and cleaved to the upper light, meaning diminished her will to receive.

This is the meaning of the words of the ARI, "Ein Sof then restricted Himself." It has already been explained above (item 6) that the entire measure of His abundance and light and the height of the emanated being are measured by the amount of the will to receive in him.

Thus, since the above Malchut of Ein Sof restricted herself and diminished her will to receive, the light and the abundance departed due to the diminishing of the desire. This is the meaning of the restriction. The ascent of the desire caused the departure of the abundance and the light from there.

50. It is perplexing, for since there is neither Rosh nor Sof there, how is there middle? Moreover, are we dealing with a corporeal matter here? The thing is that it has already been explained that there is necessarily a will to receive in Ein Sof too. However, it is a simple desire, without discriminations of great and small, because the will to receive there is not regarded as a disparity of form that makes any separations. Consequently, it is in no way inferior to the upper light.

You should know that the upper light must expand via four degrees before it uncovers that will to receive in its fullest and permanent measure in the emanated being. The reason for it is that the will to receive is incorporated in the expansion of light from the root, and by that the light is considered to have departed from the Emanator and acquired its own name, meaning expansion from the Emanator.

As long as this disparity of form of the will to receive was not incorporated in it, it was still regarded as an emanator and not as expansion that departed and shifted from the Emanator. That is because the only difference in spirituality is the disparity of form (see item 6 and Inner Observation).

However, as much as this desire became disclosed by the force of the emanated being, it still was not permanent in the emanated being. It means that the emanated being must yearn to receive the abundance before it is considered that the will to receive appeared by the force of the emanated being himself.

This yearning can only be when he does not have the abundance, for only then is it possible to want it in a way that the will to receive will be uncovered through his own strength. It is then that the vessels of reception are completed permanently.

You should also know that any expansion of light from the Emanator must consist of a will to bestow, just as it consists of a will to receive. Otherwise, the Emanator and the emanated being would have been in oppositeness of form, meaning a total separation, and the oppositeness of form would then depart them from one another as the west departs from the east.

Thus, each light that expands from the Emanator must be incorporated of a will to bestow as well, so that the emanated being will have proximity of form with the Emanator. When the will to bestow appears in the emanated being, a great light extends to him from the Emanator, related to that awakening. This light is always referred to as light of Hassadim.

The first expansion from the Emanator, in which the will to receive is incorporated, is always referred to as light of Hochma, or the light of His self. You should memorize these two types of lights.

The second light, being light of Hassadim, is much lower than the first light, being light of Hochma. That is because it is extended by the intensification and the awakening of the emanated being by his own force, as he wants to equalize his form with the Emanator, for which reason he intensifies himself and awakens toward the will to bestow.

However, the first expansion, being light of Hochma, extends directly from the Emanator and the emanated being has no part in its extension. For this reason, it is much higher than it.

For this reason, the light of Hochma is regarded as the emanated being's self and vitality. The light of Hassadim is only regarded as light for corrections, for the completion of the emanated being.

Now you will understand the four phases and degrees that must be in every emanated being. First, the light expands from the Emanator as the light of Hochma, containing only the "will to receive." This is phase one.

Then, the will to bestow intensifies in that light, and it extends light of Hassadim. This intensification is regarded as phase two. Then this light of Hassadim expands intensively (will be explained below), and this is phase three.

After the above three phases fully emerge, the force of the will to receive incorporated in the first expansion reawakens and draws light of Hochma once more. This completes the permanent will to receive in the Partzuf that appears as yearning, when there weren't light of Hochma in the Partzuf but light of Hassadim, after phase three, when the emanated being could yearn for light of Hochma.

It is this yearning that determines the will to receive in him, and completes his vessels of reception, which was absent in the first expansion. For this reason, the vessels of reception are completed only in this phase four, also called the second intensification.

Once phase four was completed in Ein Sof, the restriction occurred in her, meaning the departure of the will to receive from phase four, causing the departure of the light of Ein Sof from there.

This completes the explanation of the four phases that must exist in every emanated being. Phase one is called the first expansion, or Hochma; phase two is called the first intensification, or Bina; phase three is called the second expansion, or Zeir Anpin; phase four is called the second intensification, or Malchut.

The two expansions are regarded as males, for they are abundance that extends from the Emanator. The first expansion is abundance of light of Hochma, and the second expansion is abundance of light of Hassadim. The two intensifications are regarded as two females, for they are an awakening of the emanated being and the intensification of the desire by his own power.

The first intensification is the awakening in the emanated being for the will to bestow, which becomes the root for the light of Hassadim, and the second intensification is the awakening of the emanated being for the will to receive, which becomes the complete vessel of reception in the Partzuf. It is always referred to as phase four.

This phase four is called "The Middle Point" in Ein Sof. It is that which the ARI refers to when he says, "restricted Himself in His middle point." It is called by that name for it is a vessel of reception for the light of Ein Sof, which is immeasurable and boundless.

For this reason, it is like a point in the interior and the middle of that light, while the light revolves around it and cleaves to it from all around immeasurably. Only thus can it sustain the upper light immeasurably and boundlessly.

However, in the vessels of reception after the restriction and below, meaning in the lower emanated beings, there are vessels that hold their light within them, in their internality. It means that the walls of the vessels, being their four phases, place a boundary and a measurement on the light inside them, because of their thickness.

However, in Ein Sof, where light and vessel are in simple unity, meaning He is One and His Name One (see item 30), the vessel does not limit that light that it holds. Hence, the light in it is regarded as Ein Sof.

Now we have thoroughly explained the issue of the middle point in Ein Sof. We have shown that it does not refer to a corporeal and tangible place and area, but phase four, which is incorporated in Ein Sof, is called by that name to indicate its simple unity with the upper light. Also, the restriction in that middle point has already been explained above (see item 40).

60. The term "spiritual distance" has already been explained in item 30. It has also been explained that there weren't any distance between Ein Sof and the middle point, meaning between the light and the vessel.

However, after it restricted the light from the middle point, it uncovered a disparity of form from the light. That is because the light hasn't any will to receive, but the point is indeed a will to receive, which differs from the light. Because their form is different, they are as far apart from each other as is the difference between them. This is what the ARI meant in the word "drifted."

70. The above-mentioned four phases are also called "four sides." The ARI tells us that although the restriction was only in the middle point, meaning phase four, the light nonetheless departed from all four phases as well. It happened because there is no partial in spirituality, and thus it departed from the three phases as well.

The space that remained after the restriction was circular

4. **Then there was a vacant place (80), air, and an empty space, from the very middle point.**

Behold, this restriction was even around that empty middle point (90), in such a way that that place of space was circular on every side, completely even (100). It had not a shape of a square, a perpendicular angle, for Ein Sof too had restricted Himself like a circle, even on all sides.

Inner Light

80. Has already been explained in items 4 and 5.

90. Meaning without discriminations of great and small. We should not wonder about that, since the disparity of form in the middle point had already been exposed by the departure of the light from it. Consequently, the smaller measurements were necessarily recognized as well, one smaller than the other.

For example, phase three is more refined than the middle point because the measure of her will to receive is less than phase four. Similarly, phase two is more refined than phase three because her measure of will to receive is smaller than phase three, and phase one is the most refined of all, for she has the least will to receive, rendering her disparity of form the least apparent.

Thus, we have a differentiation of great and small in the degrees. In that case, why does the ARI say that the restriction was even around that point? The answer is that the restriction did not turn the middle point into a Sof [end/conclusion]. In other words, if the light had left the point because of her disparity of form, then it would certainly become a Sof, meaning the lowest degree.

Then we would also regard the three preceding phases as more important than the middle point, as one above the other. However, it was not so, for the restriction did not occur due to the disparity of form in the point. This cannot be, for we are still concerned with Malchut of Ein Sof, in which there is no disparity of form between her and the light; they are both in simple unity, meaning He is One and His Name One.

The restriction occurred only because His simple desire wished to create the worlds, etc. (see item 40). It means that He wanted that equivalence of form which is destined to appear by the creation of the worlds, meaning the form of reception in order to bestow contentment to the Maker.

There is a great virtue in that: on the one hand, it is complete bestowal, because the desire is only to bestow contentment upon the Maker and not at all for one's "self." That makes the form completely equal with the upper light of the Emanator, and in complete adhesion with Him.

On the other hand, it is possible to deepen and increase the vessel of reception indefinitely and eternally. That is because now the form of reception does not produce any disparity of form, as it comes from within the will to bestow.

Our sages have said that with an important personality, if she gives the matrimony capital, and he says, "With this I thee sanctify," then she is sanctified. It is written in the Torah "and giveth it in her hand," meaning it is the husband who is to give the matrimony capital.

However, because he is important, the pleasure she receives from him is exactly the same as giving. An important person who receives money from her is similar to him giving her money. It is written in the Torah "and giveth it in her hand," because he receives only in order to bestow contentment to the woman, to honor her with his reception.

We learn from the above that the primary reason for the restriction was the desire for the new form of reception in order to bestow that is destined to appear by the creation of the worlds (see item 40). However, it was not at all by reason of the thickness she felt in the middle point, for there were no thickness and difference there at all.

Hence, the middle point did not become a Sof because of the restriction. Thus, it is impossible to distinguish a small matter from a great one. That is why the ARI writes that the restriction was "completely even."

100. It means that there was some image that had to have been made by reason of the restriction, though the restriction was even (as explained above thoroughly), and not because of any disparity of form. After the restriction and the departure of the light from that middle point, it became apparent that the upper light is unfit to cleave to it because of her form of the increased reception.

Because that became known she fell from the degree she had had in Ein Sof, and was now regarded as Sof, meaning the lowest possible thickness. Only that middle point remained a vacant space, unfit to clothe the light (see item 6), and the three former phases in virtue and refinement were still fit to clothe the light even after the restriction.

We have explained above (previous item) that she did not become a Sof for the above reason. This is the meaning of the precision of the ARI when he says that "that place of space was circular on every side, completely even." He wishes to say that it is not an actual Sof, but is like the Sof in a circular picture, whose Sof is in the middle.

You can compare these four phases to four circles one within the other, like onionskins. The central circle is phase four, surrounded by phase three, surrounded by phase two, surrounded by phase one. This way there is no up or down, right or left.

For example, phase one is above all of them in its one half, and below all of them in its other half, and so it is in all the phases. Therefore, there is not up or down, right or left here. There is no difference between their virtue, and they are all completely even.

It has already been explained (above item) that the reason for the restriction was not the disparity of form. This is also the meaning of the precision of the ARI "circular on every side, completely even."

Because the light of Ein Sof was even, the restriction too was even.
This is the meaning of the circle

5. **The reason was that since the light of Ein Sof was completely even, it had to have restricted itself evenly on all sides, and not restrict itself on one side more than on the others.**

It is known in the wisdom of geometry that there is none so even an image as the image of the circle (200)**. However, this is not the case with the square** (300)**, with the bulging perpendicular angle, the triangle** (400)**, and all the other images. For this reason, the restriction had to have the form of a circle.**

200. Has already been explained in the previous item.

300. If there had been a differentiation of up and down, right and left there, it would appear in the image of a square, which contains these four sides, being the four names of these phases. However, it was not so, but in the form of a circle, which does not have these discernments.

400. Indicating a degree that has but three phases, lacking phase four, meaning three sides – up, right and left. It lacks the bottom side, hence the name triangle.

CHAPTER TWO

Explains how the light of Ein Sof extended a line to the worlds that were emanated and created in the place of the space that was restricted; containing five issues:

1. A line extended from Ein Sof into the space. 2. The beginning of the line touches Ein Sof, not its Sium [same as Sof (end/conclusion)]. 3. The light of Ein Sof expands to the worlds through the line. 4. All the worlds are in the place of that space that has been restricted. 5. Prior to the restriction there was He is One and His Name One, and the mind cannot attain Him.

A line extended from Ein Sof into the space

1. After the above restriction there remained a place of space and vacant, empty air in the middle of that light of Ein Sof$_{(1)}$. Then there was a place for the emanated beings and the created beings and the formed beings and the made beings.

   Then, one straight line extended from the light of Ein Sof$_{(2)}$, from His circular light$_{(3)}$ from above downward$_{(4)}$, and hung down into that space.

Inner Light

1. Do not be misled into the thought that the restriction of the light from the middle point caused any changes in Ein Sof. There is no change and absence in spirituality, and all the more so in such a sublime place.

   The above restriction became a new essence, in addition to Ein Sof. Thus, Ein Sof remained in its entire simple unity as before the restriction, as He is one and His Name One.

   The restriction on the middle point is perceived as a new world that came out, from which the light departed and left an empty space as we've explained above. It is in the place of that space that all the worlds were emanated.

2. We should not perceive this act in its superficial meaning, as a human act, where one does one thing, and then another, while no longer performing the first act. There is no greater materialization than that, because He is not subject to change and episodes.

It is written: "I the Lord do not change." We are not discussing His self, but only the light that expands from Him. However, because there is no change and incident and motion in His self, and He is in complete and utter rest, so must be the light that expands from Him, as long as it does not reach the emanated being, meaning as long as it did not clothe the vessels.

Only then does it come to exit His self and become an emanated being that is renewed and receives from Him. We have already explained that this renewal revolves primarily on the vessel of the emanated being, meaning the will to receive in the emanated being. Although this desire is spiritual, it is none-theless a new form and an "incident," since it is not necessitated in Himself.

However, the light that clothes it is not new, for it extends from Himself as existence from existence. The actuation of the upper light is according to the measure of the vessel, meaning the vessel is affected and receives from the upper light as an innovation, which is necessarily an incident.

You should know that all the innovations and the cascading of degrees regard only impact on the vessel and its reception from the upper light, for only that is subject to change and multiplication. However, the light itself is always in complete rest, as it expands from His self. Understand that well and remember every single word of it for the rest of the study in this wisdom.

According to the above, you can thoroughly understand that the upper light does not stop shining for the created beings even for a moment. It is not subject to change and innovations, but is in complete rest. The whole issue of the restriction and the aforementioned departure of the light regard only the influence on the vessel and its reception, meaning the middle point.

In other words, although the upper light does not stop shining, the vessel did not receive any of its illumination because it diminished itself. It diminished its will to receive, so as not to receive in its phase four, being the middle point, but only in its three preceding phases, whose will to receive is frailer, and where the will to bestow dominates (see item 50).

Thus, the upper light was not affected by the restriction and did not change its way. Just as it illuminated in Ein Sof, so it illuminated during the restriction and after the restriction and in all the worlds, even in world of Assiya. It did not stop shining for a minute, but it is the vessels that make all those changes, for they only receive according to their measure, being the measure of their will to receive.

Now you can understand what the ARI meant by the words, "one straight line extended from the light of Ein Sof." It means that the place of the space itself, meaning the vessel that had been emptied of the light of Ein Sof itself, caused the extension of the line from Ein Sof, by reason of the diminution that was renewed in its will to receive.

The measure of its current reception, after the restriction of its phase four, is called line, meaning relating to its previous reception in phase four that filled the entire place. However, now that she does not have that great will to receive, but only the previous three phases of the desire, whose will to receive is frail. It is regarded as that vessel not receiving more of the light of Ein Sof, but only one line of light.

The entire place of the vessel remains empty and vacant from light because that minute light that she receives now is not enough to fulfill the entire place of the vessel. That happened because of the wanting of phase four that diminished it.

We see that the upper light was not at all stopped by the restriction, and did not change so as to extend the light as one line. Instead, this whole great change happened because of the vessels of reception that were diminished and became unable to receive from the light of Ein Sof more than a very small measure, called line, according to the measure of her desire. That is because she does not want more than that measure.

3. We have already explained the meaning of the circular image (Chap 1, item 100). He tells us that even after the restriction, the upper light remained in the form of a circle, meaning without discrimination of degrees. Its four phases are of equal virtue (there), and the reason is (above item) that the upper light is not subject to change and incidents. These above occurrences of innovations are only with respect to the vessels.

4. Do not forget that we are not discussing corporeal terms whatsoever. Instead, the more refined is called higher, and the thicker is called lower. Anything that can be perceived as expansion of light from the Emanator and its permeation in the emanated being is regarded primarily as a renewal of the disparity of form that exists in the emanated being. In other words, it refers to the will to receive that does not exist in the Emanator and was renewed in him.

Because of that, the emanated being is considered to be far, thick, low, and inferior to the Emanator. It is the disparity of form from the Emanator that does all that and separates him from being an emanator to an emanated being.

You should also know that this disparity of form, namely the will to receive, does not appear at once, but is conceived slowly, over four phases. Its form is complete only in phase four.

It therefore turns out that the entire form of its will to receive is very frail, meaning the first phase of the four phases. This phase is regarded as the closest to the Emanator, more important, more refined and higher, because her disparity of form is not as great as in the three phases that follow.

phase two, whose desire is greater than phase one, is regarded as farther from the Emanator, thicker, lower and indeed inferior to phase one. Finally, phase four is the farthest from the Emanator, lower, thicker and more inferior to all of them.

That is why the ARI writes that the line extends from above downward, meaning from the first phase to the fourth [and not all the way], which is the lowest. The above matter of above and below was renewed with the emergence of the line. Before the line illuminated, meaning during the restriction, there was no up or down there (see Chap 1, item 100).

However, after she received the light merely as a line, meaning not in all four phases, but only in her first three phases, phase four remained dark, without light. Only now did it become known that phase four is low, thick and inferior, and that the three preceding phases are erected on top of her, according to their refinement and proximity to the Emanator. However, during the restriction, when the light left all four phases at once, that discernment among the degrees had not yet occurred.

The beginning of the line touches Ein Sof, not its end

2. **The upper beginning of the line(5) extended from Ein Sof Himself and touched it(6), although the conclusion of that line, down at its end(7), does not touch the light of Ein Sof.**

Inner Light

5. Meaning the first Behina of the four phases (see above item).

6. Phase one, being the Upper Rosh, is the closest to Ein Sof, meaning to the Emanator. For this reason, she is regarded as touching Him, because the disparity of form in phase one is not apparent enough to separate it from the Emanator.

7. "Down at its end" implies phase four, the farthest and lowest of them all (Chap 2, item 4). She does not receive the upper light and is therefore regarded as not touching the light of Ein Sof and as separated from it.

The Light of Ein Sof expands to the worlds through the line

3. **The Light of Ein Sof extended and expanded down through that line.**

All the worlds are in the place of that space that has been restricted

4. **He emanated and created and made and formed (8) all the worlds in that place of that space.**

Inner Light

8. It implies the four worlds called Atzilut, Beria, Yetzira, Assiya, which contain all the inner innumerable worlds. These four worlds extend from the four above phases: Atzilut from phase one; Beria from phase two; Yetzira from phase three and Assiya from phase four.

Prior to the restriction there was He is One and His Name One, and the mind cannot attain Him

5. **Prior to these four worlds (9), the Ein Sof was He is One and His Name One (10), in wondrous and concealed unity. Not even the angles that are close to Him (20) have the might and the attainment of Ein Sof, for there is not a created mind that can attain Him, for He has no place, no boundary, no name (30).**

Inner Light

9. Called Atzilut, Beria, Yetzira, Assiya (see above item), which contain all the worlds. Before all that, meaning before the restriction, these four phases were considered to be one above the other (see Chap 2, item 4), but as Simple Unity (Chap 1, item 30). The meaning of simple unity is that there is no differentiation of degrees or between the light and the vessel, but He is One and His Name One (see Chap 1, item 30).

10. "He" implies the upper light. "His Name" implies the will to receive that is necessarily there (see Chap 1, item 30). His Name is desire (in *Gematria*), implying the will to receive.

20. This means that now, after the worlds have been created, even the angles, which are spiritually the closest creations, do not have attainment in Ein Sof.

30. Since in Ein Sof it is He is One and His Name One, and since there is no place and vessel apparent there at all, no mind of a created being can attain Him, for there is no attainment without a vessel.

TABLE OF QUESTIONS FOR THE MEANING OF THE WORDS

Note: Forgetting the meaning of a word regarding some issue is worse than erasing that word from the issue. This is because the alien perception would blur the matter entirely. Hence, accustom yourself through the Table of Questions and Answers, until you can answer them by heart without trouble.

1. What is Light
2. What are Light and Vessel
3. What is Circular Light
4. What is Simple Light
5. What is Light of Hochma
6. What is Light of Hassadim
7. What is Empty Air
8. What is Afterwards
9. What is Middle
10. What is One
11. What is Creator
12. What is Adhesion
13. What is Equivalence
14. What is Expansion
15. What is Refined
16. What is Time
17. What is Darkness
18. What is Hochma
19. What is Space
20. What is Before and After
21. What is Unique and Unified
22. What is Unification
23. What are Right and Left
24. What is Maker

INNER OBSERVATION

First, we must know that when dealing with spiritual matters, which have no concern with time, space or motion, and moreover when dealing with Godliness, we do not have the words by which to contemplate and express. Our entire vocabulary is taken from sensations of imaginary senses. Thus, how can they assist us where sense and imagination do not reign?

For example, if you take the subtlest of words, namely "lights," it nonetheless resembles and borrows from the light of the sun or an emotional light of contentment. Thus, how can they be used to express Godly matters? They would certainly fail to provide the reader with anything true.

It is even truer in a place where these words should disclose the negotiations in the wisdom in print, as is done in any research of wisdom. If we fail with even a single inadequate word, the reader will be instantly disoriented and will not find his hands or legs in this whole matter.

For this reason, the sages of the Kabbalah have chosen a special language that we can call "the language of the branches." There is not an essence or a conduct of an essence in this world that does not derive from its root in the upper world. Moreover, the beginning of every being in this world starts from the upper world and then hangs down to this world.

Thus, the sages have found an adequate language without trouble by which they could convey their attainments to each other by word of mouth and in writing from generation to generation. They have taken the names of the branches in this world, where each name is self-explanatory, as though pointing to its upper root in the system of the upper worlds.

That should appease your mind regarding the perplexing expressions we often find in books of Kabbalah, and some that are even foreign to the human spirit. It is because once they have chosen this language to express themselves, namely the language of the branches, they could no longer leave a branch unused because of its inferior degree. They could not avoid using it to express the desired concept when our world suggests no other branch to be taken in its place.

Just as two hairs do not feed off the same foramen, so we do not have two branches that relate to the same root. It is also impossible to exterminate the object in the wisdom that is related to that inferior expression. Such a loss would inflict impairment and great confusion in the entire scope of the wisdom, since there is no other wisdom in the world where matters are so intermingled through cause and effect, reason and consequence as in the wisdom of Kabbalah, where matters are interconnected and tied to each other from top to bottom like one long chain.

Thus, there is no freedom of will here to switch or replace the bad names with better ones. We must always provide the exact branch that points to its upper root and elaborate on it until the accurate definition is provided for the scrutinizing readers.

Indeed, those whose eyes have not been opened to the sights of heaven, and have not acquired the proficiency in the connections of the branches of this world with their roots in the upper worlds are like the blind scraping the walls. They will not understand the true meaning of even a single word, for each word is a name of a branch that relates to its root.

Only if they receive an interpretation from a genuine sage who makes himself available to explain the matter in the spoken language, which is necessarily like translating from one language to another, meaning from the language of the branches to the spoken language, only then he will be able to explain the spiritual term as it is.

This is what I have troubled to do in this interpretation, to explain the ten Sefirot as the Godly sage the Ari had instructed us, in their spiritual purity, devoid of any tangible terms. Thus, any beginner may approach the wisdom without failing in any materialization or mistake. With the understanding of these ten Sefirot, one will also come to examine and know how to comprehend the rest of the issues in this wisdom.

CHAPTER ONE

"Know that before the emanated beings were emanated and the created beings created, an upper simple light had filled the whole of reality" (*Tree of Life*, 1:1). These words require explanation: How was there a reality that the simple light had filled before the worlds were emanated? Also, the matter of the ascent of the desire in order to be restricted so as to bring to light the perfection of His deeds. It is implied in the book that there was already some deficiency there.

Also, the issue of the middle point in Him, where the restriction occurred, is also quite perplexing, for he had already said that there is neither beginning nor end there, so how is there a middle? Indeed these words are deeper than the sea, and I must therefore elaborate on their interpretation.

There is not one thing in the whole of reality that is not contained in Ein Sof. The contradicting terms in our world are contained in Him in the form of One, Unique, and Unified.

1) Know that there is not an essence of a single being in the world, both the ones perceived by our senses and the ones perceived by our mind's eye, that is not included in the Creator, for they all come to us from Him, and can one give that which is not in him?

    This matter has already been thoroughly explained in the books, but we must understand the concepts that are separated or opposite for us, such as the term "wisdom" is regarded as different from the term "sweetness," as wisdom and sweetness are two separate terms. Similarly, the term "operator" certainly differs from the term "operation." The operator and its operation are necessarily two separate concepts. It is even more so with opposite terms such as "sweet" and "bitter"; these are certainly discerned as separate.

    However, in Him, wisdom, pleasure, sweetness and acerbity, operation and operator, and other such different and opposite forms are all contained as one in His simple light. There are no differentiations among them whatsoever, as is the term "One, Unique, and Unified."

    "One" indicates a single evenness. "Unique" implies that everything that extends from Him, all these multiplicities, are in Him as single as His self. "Unified" shows that although He performs the multiple operations, one force performs all these, and they all return and unite in the form of One. Indeed, this one form swallows all the forms that appear in His operations.

This is a very subtle matter and not every mind can tolerate it. Nachmanides explained to us the matter of His uniqueness, as "One, Unique, and Unified." These are his words in his commentary on *The Book of Creation*, Chapter 1, 47: There is a difference between One, Unique, and Unified: When He unites to act with one force, He is called "Unified." When He divides to act His act, each part of Him is called "Unique." When He is in a single evenness, He is called "One." Thus far his pure words.

Interpretation: "Unites to act with one force" means that His operations differ from each other and He seems to be doing good and bad. At that time, He is called "Unique" since all His different operations have a single outcome: doing good.

We find that He is unique in every single act and does not change by His different operations. "When He is in a single evenness," meaning "One," it points to His self, for in Him, all the opposites are in "single evenness," as written above. It is as Maimonides wrote, "In Him, the one who knows, the known and the knowledge are one, for His thoughts are far higher than our thoughts, and His ways from our ways."

Two discernments in bestowal: before it is received and after it is received.

2) We should learn from those who ate the manna. Manna is called "bread from heaven" because it did not materialize when clothing in this world. Our sages said that each one tasted in it everything he wanted.

This means that it had to have contained opposite forms: One person tasted it as sweet and another tasted it as acrid and bitter. Thus, the manna itself had to have contained both opposites together, for can one give what is not in him? Thus, how can there be two opposites in one subject?

It is therefore necessary that it is simple and devoid of both flavors, but is only included in them in a way that the corporeal receiver might discern the taste that one wants. Likewise, you can understand that anything spiritual is unique and simple in itself, but contains all the myriad forms in the world. When it comes to corporeal, limited receiver, the receiver makes in it a separate form from all the myriad forms united in that spiritual essence.

We should therefore always distinguish two discernments in His bestowal: The first is the form of the essence of that upper abundance before it is received, when it is still an inclusive, simple light. The second is that after the abundance has been received, for by this it acquired one separate form according to the properties of the receiver.

How can we perceive the soul as a part of Godliness?

3) Now we can come to understand what the Kabbalists wrote about the essence of the soul: "The soul is a part of God above and is not at all changed from the Whole, except in that the soul is a part and not the Whole." It is like a stone that is carved from a mountain. The essence of the mountain and the essence of the stone are the same and there is no distinction between the stone and the mountain, except that the stone is a part of the mountain, and the mountain is the Whole, thus far the essence of their words.

These words seem utterly perplexing, and the most difficult is to understand how it is possible to discern a difference and a part in Godliness to the point of resembling it to a stone that is carved from a mountain. The stone is carved from the mountain by an ax and a sledgehammer. But in Godliness, how and what would separate them from one another?

The spiritual is divided by disparity of form, as the corporeal is divided by an ax.

4) Before we come to clarify the matter, we shall explain the essence of the separation in spirituality: Know that spiritual entities become separated from one another only by disparity of form. In other words, if one spiritual entity acquires two forms, it is no longer one, but two.

Let me explain it in souls of people, which are also spiritual: It is known that the form of the spiritual law is simple. Certainly, there are as many souls as there are bodies, where the souls shine. However, they are separated from one another by the disparity of form in each of them, as our sages said, "As their faces are not the same, their opinions are not similar." The body can discern the form of the souls and tell if each specific soul is a good soul or a bad soul, and likewise with the various forms.

You now see that as a corporeal matter is divided, cut, and becomes separated by an ax and motion that increase the distance between each part, a spiritual matter is divided, cut, and separated by the disparity of form between each part. According to the measure of disparity, so is the distance between each two parts, and remember this well.

How can there be disparity of form in creation with respect to Ein Sof?

5) We are still not content. In this world, in souls of people, in relation to the soul, of which it was said to be a part of God above, it is still unclear how it is separated from Godliness to the point that we can call it "a Godly part." We should not say "by disparity of form," since we have already said that Godliness is simple light that contains the whole abundance of forms and opposite forms in the world in His simple uniqueness, as in "one, unique, and unified." Hence, how can we depict disparity of form in the soul, making

it different from Godliness, rendering it distinct, to acquire a part of Him there?

Indeed, this question applies primarily to the light of Ein Sof [infinity/no end] prior to the restriction, for in the reality before us, all the worlds, upper ones and lower ones, are discerned by two discernments: The first discernment is the form of this entire reality as it is prior to the restriction. At that time, everything was without a boundary and without an end. This discernment is called "the light of Ein Sof." The second discernment is the form of this entire reality from the restriction downward. Then everything became limited and measured. This discernment is called the four worlds Atzilut, Beria, Yetzira, Assiya.

It is known that there is no thought or perception whatsoever in His self, and there is no name or appellation in Him, anything that we do not attain, how can we define it by a name? Any name implies attainment, indicating that we have attained it as that name. Thus, it is certain that there is no name or appellation whatsoever in His self, and all the names and appellations are but in His light which expands from Him. The expansion of His light prior to the restriction, which had filled the whole of reality, without a boundary or an end, is called Ein Sof. Thus, we should understand how the light of Ein Sof is defined in and of itself, and has departed from His self to the point that we may define it by a name, as we have said about the soul.

Explanation of the words of our sages: "Hence, work and labor have been prepared for the reward of the souls, for 'One who eats that which is not one's own is afraid to look upon one's face.'"

6) To somewhat understand this sublime place, we must go into further detail. We shall research the axis of the entire reality before us and its general purpose. Is there an operation without a purpose? And what is that purpose for which He has invented this entire reality before us in the upper worlds and in the lower worlds?

Indeed, our sages have already instructed us in many places that all the worlds were created only for Israel, who observe Torah and Mitzvot [commandments], etc., and this is well known. However, we should understand this question of our sages, who asked about it: "If the purpose of the creation of the worlds was to delight His creatures, why did He create this corporeal, turbid, and tormented world? Without it, He could certainly delight the souls as much as He wanted, so why did He bring the soul into such a murky and filthy body?"

They explained it with the verse, "One who eats that which is not one's own is afraid to look upon one's face." This means there is a flaw of shame in any free gift. To spare the souls this blemish, He has created this world where there is work, and they will enjoy their labor in the future, for they take their whole reward in return for their work, and are thus spared the blemish of shame.

What is the connection between working seventy years and eternal delight, as there is no greater free gift than this?

7) These words of theirs are perplexing through and through. First bewilderment: Our primary aim and prayer is "Spare us the treasure of a free gift." Our sages said that the treasure of a free gift is prepared only for the greatest souls in the world.

Their answer is even more perplexing: They said that there is a great flaw in free gifts, namely the shame that encounters every receiver of a free gift. To mend this, the Creator has prepared this world, where there is work and labor, so as to take the reward for their work and labor in the next world.

But their answer is very odd. What is this like? It is like a person who says to his friend, "Work with me for just one moment, and in return, I will give you every pleasure and treasure in the world for the rest of your life." There is indeed no greater free gift than this, since the reward is utterly incomparable with the work, for the work is in this world, a transient, worthless world compared to the reward and the pleasure in the eternal world, for what value is there to the passing world compared to the eternal world? It is even more so with regard to the quality of the labor, which is worthless compared to the quality of the reward.

Our sages said, "The Creator is destined to bequeath each and every righteous 310 worlds, etc." We cannot say that the Creator gives some of the reward in return for their work, and the rest as a free gift, for then what good would that do? The blemish of shame would remain in the rest of the gift! Indeed, their words are not to be taken literally, for there is a profound meaning here.

The whole of reality was emanated and created with a single thought. It is the operator; it is the very operation; it is the sought-after reward, and it is the essence of the labor.

8) Before we delve into the explanation of their words, we must understand His thought in creating the worlds and the reality before us. His operations did not come to be by many thoughts, as is our way, for He is one, unique, and unified. And as He is simple, His lights, which extend from Him, are simple and unified, without any proliferation of forms, as it is written, "My thoughts are not your thoughts, neither are your ways My ways."

Therefore, understand and perceive that all the names and appellations, and all the worlds, upper and lower, are all one simple, unique, and unified light. In the Creator, the light that extends, the thought, the operation, the operator, and anything the heart can think and contemplate are in Him one and the same thing.

Thus, you can judge and perceive that this entire reality, upper ones and lower ones as one, in its final state of the end of correction, was emanated and created with a single thought. That single thought performs all the operations; it is the essence of all the operations, the purpose and the essence of the labor. It is by itself the very perfection and the sought-after reward, as Nachmanides wrote, "one, unique, and unified."

The matter of the restriction explains how an incomplete operation emerged from the perfect operator.

9) The ARI elaborated on the matter of the first restriction in the first chapters of this book. This is a very serious matter as it is necessary that all the corruptions and all the various shortcomings extend and come from Him.

It is written, "the maker of light and creator of darkness," but then the corruptions and the darkness are the complete opposite of Him, so how can they stem from one another? Also, how could they come together with the light and the pleasure in the thought of creation?

We cannot say that they are two separate thoughts; God forbid that we should even think that. Thus, how does all this extend from Him down to this world, which is so filled with scum, torment, and filth, and how do they exist together in the single thought?

CHAPTER TWO

Explaining the thought of creation.

10) Now we shall come to clarify the thought of creation. Certainly, "The end of the work is in the preliminary thought." Even in corporeal humans, with their many thoughts, the end of the work is in the preliminary thought. For example, when one builds one's house, we understand that the first thought in this engagement is the shape of the house in which to dwell.

Therefore, it is preceded by many thoughts and many actions until this shape that he had predesigned is completed. This shape is what appears at the end of all his operations. Thus, you see that "The end of the work is in the preliminary thought."

The end of the work, which is the axis and the purpose for which all these were created, is to delight His creations, as it is written in *The Zohar*. It is known that His thought ends and acts immediately, for He is not a human, who is impelled to act. Rather, the thought itself completes the entire work at once.

Hence, we can see that as soon as He thought about creation, to delight His created beings, this light immediately extended and expanded from Him in the full measure and form of the pleasures He had contemplated. It is all included in that thought, which we call "the thought of creation," and understand this thoroughly since it is a place where they instructed to be concise. Know that we call this thought of creation "the light of Ein Sof [infinity/no end]" since we do not have a single word or utterance in His essence to define Him by any name at all, and remember this.

The will to bestow in the Emanator necessarily begets the will to receive in the emanated, and it is the vessel in which the emanated being receives His abundance.

11) The Ari said that in the beginning, an upper simple light had filled the whole of reality. This means that since the Creator contemplated delighting the created beings and the light expanded from Him and seemingly departed Him, the desire to receive His pleasure was immediately imprinted in this light.

You can also determine that this desire is the full measure of the expanding light, meaning that the measure of His light and abundance is as the measure of His desire to delight, no more and no less.

For this reason, we call the essence of that will to receive, imprinted in this light through the power of His thought, by the name, "place." For instance, when we say that a person has a stomach big enough to eat a pound of bread, while another person cannot eat more than half a pound of bread, which place are we talking about? It is not the size of the intestines, but the measure of the appetite. You see that the measure for the place of the reception of the bread depends on the measure and the desire to eat.

It is all the more so in spirituality, where the desire to receive the abundance is the place of the abundance, and the abundance is measured by the intensity of the desire.

The will to receive contained in the thought of creation brought it out of His self to acquire the name Ein Sof.

12) By this we can learn why the light of Ein Sof departed from His self, in which we cannot utter any word, and became defined by the name "light of Ein Sof." It is because of this above discernment that the will to receive from His self is included in this light. This is a new form that is not included whatsoever in His self, as from whom would He receive? This form is also the full measure of this light. Examine this well for it is impossible to elaborate here.

Prior to the restriction, the disparity of form in the will to receive was indiscernible.

13) In His almightiness, this new form would not have been defined as a change from His light, as it is written in *Pirkey de Rabbi Eliezer*, "Before the world was created, there were He is one and His name One."

"He" indicates the light in Ein Sof, and "His name" implies the "place," which is the will to receive from His self, contained in the light of Ein Sof. He tells us that He and His name are one. "His name" is Malchut of Ein Sof, being the desire, namely the will to receive that has been imprinted in the entire reality contained in the thought of creation. Prior to the restriction, no disparity of form and difference from the light was discerned in it, and the light and the "place" are truly one. Had there been any difference and deficiency in the place compared to the light of Ein Sof, there would certainly have been two discernments there.

Restriction means that Malchut of Ein Sof diminished the will to receive in her. Then the light disappeared because there is no light without a vessel.

14) This is the meaning of the restriction, that the will to receive that is contained in the light of Ein Sof, called Malchut of Ein Sof, which is the thought of creation in Ein Sof, which contains the whole of reality, embellished herself

to ascend and equalize her form with His self. Hence, she diminished her will to receive His abundance in phase four in the desire. Her intention was that by so doing, the worlds would be emanated and created down to this world.

In this manner, the form of the will to receive would be corrected and return to the form of bestowal, and that would bring her to equivalence of form with the Emanator. Then, after she had diminished the will to receive, consequently, the light departed from there, for it is already known that the light depends on the desire, and the desire is the place of the light, for there is no coercion in spirituality.

CHAPTER THREE

Explanation of the origin of the soul.

15) Now we shall explain the matter of the origin of the soul. It has been said that it is a part of God above. We asked, "How and in what does the form of the soul differ from His simple light until it separates it from the Whole?" Now we can understand that there really is a great disparity of form in it. Although He contains all the conceivable and imaginable forms, still, after the above said, you find one form that is not contained in Him, namely the form of the will to receive, as from whom would He receive?

However, the souls, whose creation came about only because He wanted to delight them, which is the thought of creation, were necessarily imprinted with this law of wanting and yearning to receive His abundance. This is where they differ from Him, since their form has changed from His. It has already been explained that a corporeal essence is separated and divided by the force of motion and remoteness of location, and a spiritual essence is separated and divided by disparity of form. According to the measure of disparity of form from one another, so is the measure of the distance between them. If the disparity of form comes to complete oppositeness, from one extreme to the other, they become completely severed and distinct, to the point where they can no longer suckle from one another, for they are regarded as alien to each other.

CHAPTER FOUR

After the restriction and the screen that were made on the will to receive, it became unfit to be a vessel of reception and departed from the system of Kedusha [holiness]. In its stead, the Reflected Light serves as a vessel of reception, and the vessel of the will to receive was given to the system of Tuma'a [impurity].

16) After the restriction and the screen that were placed on that vessel called "will to receive," it was canceled and departed from the system of Kedusha. In its stead, the reflected light became the vessel of reception, (as it is written in Part 3).

Know that this is the whole difference between ABYA of Kedusha and ABYA of Tuma'a. The vessels of reception of ABYA of Kedusha are from the reflected light that is established in equivalence of form with Ein Sof, while ABYA of Tuma'a use the will to receive that was restricted, being the opposite form from Ein Sof. That makes them separated and cut off from the "Life of Lives," namely Ein Sof.

Man feeds on the yeast of the Klipot [shells], and thus uses the will to receive as they do.

17) Now you can understand the root of the corruptions that were incorporated promptly in the thought of creation, which is to delight His created beings. After the cascading of the five general worlds, Adam Kadmon and ABYA, the Klipot appeared in the four worlds ABYA of Tuma'a, too, as in "God has made them one opposite the other." In that state, the turbid, corporeal body is set before us, of which it was said, "For the inclination of a man's heart is evil from his youth." This is so because its entire nursing from its youth is from the yeast of the Klipot. The whole matter of Klipot and Tuma'a is the form of the desire only to receive that they have, and they have nothing of the will to bestow.

By this they are opposite from Him, for He has no will to receive whatsoever, and all He wants is to delight and bestow. This is why the Klipot are called "dead," since their oppositeness of form from the Life of Lives severs them from Him and they have nothing of His abundance.

Hence, the body, too, which feeds on the yeast of the Klipot, is also severed from life and is filled with filth. And all of this is because of the will to only receive and not to bestow that is imprinted in it. Its desire is always open to receive the whole world into its stomach. This is why "The wicked, in their lives, are called 'dead,'" since their fundamental disparity of form from their root, where they have nothing of the quality of bestowal, severs them from Him and they become truly dead.

Although it seems that the wicked, too, have the form of bestowal when they give charity, etc., it has been said about them in The Zohar, "Any grace that they do, they do for themselves, as their aim is primarily for themselves and for their own glory."

But the righteous, who engage in Torah and Mitzvot [commandments] not in order to receive reward but to bestow contentment upon their Maker, thus refine their bodies and invert their vessels of reception to the form of bestowal.

It is as our teacher said, "It is known and revealed," etc., "and I did not enjoy even with the little finger" (*Ketubot* 104). This makes them completely adhered to Him, for their form is identical to their Maker without any disparity of form. Our sages said about the verse, "Say unto Zion: 'You are My people.'" It was interpreted in the "Introduction of The Book of Zohar," Item 67, that you are with Me in partnership. This means that the righteous are partners with the Creator, since He started creation, and the righteous finish it by turning the vessels of reception into bestowal.

The whole of reality is contained in Ein Sof and extends existence from existence. Only the will to receive is new and extends existence from absence.

18) Know that the whole matter of innovation that the Creator had innovated with this creation, which our sages said He elicited existence from absence, applies only to the form of the desire to enjoy imprinted in every created being. Nothing more was innovated in creation, and this is the meaning of "maker of light and creator of darkness." Nachmanides interpreted the word "Creator" as indicating a novelty, meaning something that did not exist before.

You see that it does not say, "create light," since there is no innovation in it by way of existence from absence. This is because the light and everything contained in the light, all the pleasant sensations and conceptions in the world, extend existence from existence. This means that they are already included in Him; hence, there is no innovation in them. This is why it is written, "The maker of light," indicating that there is no innovations or creation in it.

However, it is said of the darkness, which contains every unpleasant sensation and conception, "and creator of darkness." This is because He invented them literally existence from absence. In other words, it does not exist in His reality whatsoever, but was rather innovated now. The root of all of them is the form of the "will to enjoy" included in His lights, which expand from Him.

Initially, it is only darker than the upper light, and is therefore called "darkness" compared to the light. But finally, the Klipot [shells/peels], Sitra Achra [other side], and the wicked cascade and emerge because of it, which cuts them off entirely from the root of life.

This is the meaning of the verse "Her legs descend to death." "Her legs" indicate the end of something. He says that in the end, death cascades from the legs of Malchut—the desire to enjoy that exists in the expansion of His light—to the Sitra Achra and to those that feed off her and follow her.

Because we are branches that extend from Ein Sof, the things that are in our root are pleasurable to us, and those that are not in our root, are burdensome and painful.

19) We can ask, "Since this disparity of form of the will to receive must be in the created beings, for how else would they extend from Him and shift from being Creator to being created beings?" This is only possible by the above-mentioned disparity of form.

Furthermore, this form of the will to enjoy is the primary essence of creation, the axis of the thought of creation. It is also the measure of the delight and pleasure, as we have said above, for which it is called a "place."

Thus, how can we say about it that it is called "darkness" and extends to the discernment of death, since it creates separation and interruption from the Life of Lives in the receiving lower ones? We should also understand what is this great anxiety that comes to the receivers because of the disparity of form from His self and why the great wrath about it.

To explain this subtle matter sufficiently, we must first clarify the origin of all the pleasures and sufferings felt in our world. Know this: It is known that the nature of every branch is equal to its root. Therefore, the branch desires, loves, and covets every conduct in the root, and does not tolerate and hates any conduct that is not in the root.

This is an unbreakable law that applies to every branch and its root. Because He is the root of all His creations, everything in Him and that extends from Him directly is pleasurable and pleasant to us, for our nature is close to our root. Also, everything that is not in Him and does not extend to us directly from Him, but is rather opposite to creation itself, will be against our nature and will be hard for us to tolerate.

For example, we love rest, and vehemently hate movement, to the point that we do not make even a single movement if not to find rest. This is because our root is motionless and restful; there is no movement in Him whatsoever. For this reason, it is against our nature and hated by us.

Similarly, we love wisdom, power, wealth, and all the virtues because they are contained in Him, who is our root. We hate their opposites, such as folly, weakness, poverty, ignominy, and so on, since they are not at all in our root, making them despicable, loathsome, and intolerable to us.

We should still examine how can there be any extension that does not come directly from Him, but from the opposite of creation itself. It is like a wealthy man who called on a poor fellow, fed him and gave him drinks, and granted him silver and gold every single day, and each day more than the day before.

Note that this man simultaneously tastes two distinct flavors in the great gifts of the rich man: On the one hand, he tastes immeasurable pleasure due to the abundance of his gifts. On the other hand, it is hard for him to tolerate the abundant benefits and he is ashamed when receiving it. This matter causes him intolerance due to the abundant gifts showered on him every time.

It is certain that his pleasure from the gifts extends to him directly from the wealthy benefactor, but the impatience that he felt in the presents did not come from the wealthy benefactor, but from the very essence of the receiver—the shame awakened in him because of the reception and the free gift. The truth is that this, too, comes to him from the rich man, of course, but indirectly.

Because the will to receive is not in our root, we feel shame and intolerance in it. Our sages wrote that in order to correct this, He has "prepared" for us labor in Torah and Mitzvot in this world, to invert the will to receive into a desire to bestow.

20) From all the above-said, we learn that all the forms that extend indirectly to us from Him present a difficulty for our patience and are against our nature. By this you will see that the new form that was made in the receiver, namely the desire to enjoy, is not in any way inferior or deficient compared to Him. Moreover, this is the primary axis of His creation. Were it not for this, there would be no creation here at all. However, the receiver, who is the carrier of this form, feels the intolerance due to his "self" since this form does not exist in his root.

By this we have succeeded in understanding the answer of our sages that this world was created because "One who eats that which is not one's own is afraid to look upon one's face." This seems very perplexing, but now their words feel very pleasant to us, for they refer to the matter of disparity of form of the desire to enjoy, which necessarily exists in the souls, since "One who eats that which is not one's own is afraid to look upon one's face." That is, any receiver of a present is ashamed when receiving it due to the disparity of form from the Root since the root does not have that form of reception. In order to correct this, He created this world where the soul comes and clothes a body. Through engagement in Torah and Mitzvot [commandments] in order to bring contentment to his Maker, the soul's vessels of reception are inverted into vessels of bestowal.

Thus, for herself, she did not want the distinguished abundance, yet she receives the abundance in order to bring contentment to her Maker, who wishes for the souls to enjoy His abundance. Because she is cleansed from the will to receive for herself, she is no longer afraid to look upon her face, and this reveals the complete perfection of the created being. The need and necessity for the long cascading to this world will be explained below, that this great labor of turning the form of reception into the form of bestowal can only be conceived in this world.

The wicked lose twofold, and the righteous will inherit twofold.

21) Come and see that the wicked lose twofold for they hold both ends of the rope. This world is created with absence and emptiness of all the good abundance, and in order to acquire possessions we need movement. It is known that profusion of movement pains man, for it is an indirect extension from His essence. However, it is also impossible to remain devoid of possessions and good, for this, too, is in contrast with the root, since the root is filled abundantly. Hence, we choose the torment of movement in order to acquire filling with possessions.

However, because all their possessions and property are for themselves alone, and "he who has a hundred wants two hundred," it follows that "One does not die with half one's wishes in one's hand." Thus, they suffer from both sides: from the pain of increased motion, and from the pain of deficiency of possessions, half of which they lack.

But "The righteous in their land will inherit twofold." In other words, once they turn their will to receive into a desire to bestow, and what they receive is in order to bestow, they inherit twofold. Not only do they attain the perfection of the pleasures and a variety of possessions, they also acquire the equivalence of form with their Maker. Thus, they come to true adhesion and are also at rest since the abundance comes to them by itself, without any movement or effort.

CHAPTER FIVE

The thought of creation compels every item in reality to stem from one another until the end of correction.

22) Now that we have been rewarded with all the above, we will have some understanding of His uniqueness, that His thoughts are not our thoughts, and all the abundance of matters and forms we perceive in this reality before us is united in Him in a single thought, being the thought of creation to delight His creations. This singular thought encompasses the whole of reality in perfect unity through the end of correction, for this is the whole purpose of creation, and this is the operator, like the force that operates in the operated. This is because what is merely a thought in Him is a binding law in the created beings. Because He contemplated delighting us, it necessarily occurred in us that we receive His good abundance.

It is the operation. This means that after this law of the will to receive pleasure has been imprinted in us, we define ourselves by the name "operation." This is so because through this disparity of form, we stop being Creator and become a created being, and from being the Operator we become the operation.

This is the labor and the work. Due to the force that operates in the operated, the will to receive increases in us as the worlds cascade until we become a separated body in this world, opposite in form from The Life of Lives, who does not bestow outside of itself at all, which brings death to the bodies and every kind of torment and labor to the soul.

This is the meaning of the work of the Creator in Torah and Mitzvot. Through the illumination of the line in the restricted place, the holy names—Torah and Mitzvot—extend. By laboring in Torah and Mitzvot in order to bestow contentment upon the Maker, our vessels of reception gradually turn into vessels of bestowal, and this is the whole sought-after reward.

The more uncorrected our vessels of reception, the more we cannot open our mouths to receive His abundance, for fear of disparity of form, as in "One who eats that which is not one's own, is afraid to look upon one's face," as this was the reason for the first restriction. However, when we correct our vessels of reception to work in order to bestow, we thereby equalize our vessels with their Maker and become fit to receive His abundance unboundedly.

Thus, you see that all these opposite forms in the whole of creation before us, namely the form of operator and operated, the form of the corruptions and corrections, and the form of the labor and its reward are all included in His singular thought. In simple words, it is "to delight His created beings," precisely that, no less and no more.

The whole variety of concepts is also included in that thought, both the concepts in our holy Torah, and those of external teachings. All the many creations and worlds and various conducts in each and every one stem from this singular thought, as I will explain below in their proper place.

Malchut of Ein Sof means that Malchut does not place any Sof [end] there.

23) According to the above, we can understand what is presented in *Tikkuney Zohar* [part of *The Zohar*] regarding Malchut of Ein Sof, for which the doors trembled from the cries of the doubtful that it was possible to recognize a Malchut in Ein Sof? For if we can, it means that there are the first nine Sefirot there, too! From our words, it becomes very clear that the will to receive that is necessarily included in the light of Ein Sof is called Malchut of Ein Sof. However, Malchut did not place a boundary and an end on the light of Ein Sof there because the disparity of form due to the will to receive had not yet become apparent in her. This is why it is called Ein Sof, meaning that Malchut does not put a stop there. Conversely, from the restriction downward, an end was made in each Sefira and Partzuf by the force of Malchut.

CHAPTER SIX

It is impossible for the will to receive to appear in any essence, except in four phases, which are the four letters of HaVaYaH.

24) Let us elaborate a little on this matter, to fully understand the end that occurred in Malchut. First, we will explain what the Kabbalists have determined and is presented in *The Zohar* and the *Tikkunim*, that there is no light, great or small, in the upper worlds or in the lower worlds that is not arranged in the order of the four-letter name HaVaYaH.

This goes hand in hand with the law presented in *Tree of Life*, that there is no light in the worlds that is not clothed in a vessel. I have already explained the difference between His self and the light that expands from Him, that it is only due to the desire to enjoy that is contained in His expanding light, being a disparity of form from His self, for He does not have this desire.

This defines the expanding light by the name "emanated being" because due to this disparity of form, the light emerges from being the Emanator and becomes an emanated being. It is also explained that the desire to enjoy included in His light is also the measure of the greatness of the light. It is called the "place" of the light, meaning it receives its abundance according to its measure of will to receive and craving, not less and not more.

It also explains that this matter of the will to receive is the very innovation that was generated in the creation of the worlds by way of making existence from absence. This is so because this form alone is not included in His self whatsoever, and the Creator has only now created it for the purpose of creation. This is the meaning of "and creates darkness," since this form is the root of the darkness due to the disparity of form in it. For this reason, it is darker than the light that expands within her and because of her.

Now you see that any light that expands from Him instantly consists of two discernments: The first discernment is the expanding light itself, before the form of "desire to enjoy" appears in it. The second discernment is after the form of "desire to enjoy" appears in it, at which time it becomes coarser and somewhat darker due to the acquisition of disparity of form.

Thus, the first discernment is the light, and the second discernment is the vessel. For this reason, any expanding light consists of four phases in the impression on the vessel. This is because the form of the will to receive, called "a vessel to the expanding light," is not completed at once, but by way

47

of operator and operated. There are two discernments in the operator and two discernments in the operated. They are called "potential" and "actual" in the operator, and "potential" and "actual" in the operated, which make up four discernments.

The will to receive is set in the emanated being only through its awakening to receive of its own accord.

25) Because the vessel is the root of the darkness, as it is opposite from the light, it must therefore be activated slowly, gradually, by way of cause and consequence. This is the meaning of the verse: "The water conceived and begot darkness" (*Midrash Rabbah*, *Shemot*, Chapter 22).

The darkness is a result of the light itself and is operated by it, as in conception and birth, meaning potential and actual. This means that the will to receive is necessarily included in any expanding light. However, it is not regarded as a disparity of form before this desire is clearly set in the light.

The will to receive that is included in the light by the Emanator is not enough for this. Rather, the emanated being itself must independently reveal the will to receive in him, in practice, meaning of his own choice. This means that he must extend abundance through his own will, more than the measure of the light of the expansion in him by the Emanator.

After the emanated being is operated by its own choice by increasing the measure of its desire, the yearning and the will to receive become fixed in it, and the light can clothe this vessel permanently.

It is true that the light of Ein Sof seemingly expands over all four phases, reaching the full measure of the desire by the emanated being itself, being phase four, since it would not emerge from His self anyhow and acquire a name for himself, meaning Ein Sof.

However, in His almightiness, the form did not change at all because of the will to receive, and no change is distinguished there between the light and the place of the light, which is the desire to enjoy; they are one and the same thing.

It is written in *Pirkey de Rabbi Eliezer*, "Before the world was created, there was He is one and His name One." It is indeed difficult to understand this double reference "He" and "His name." What has His name got to do there before the world was created? It should have said, "Before the world was created, He was one."

However, this refers to the light of Ein Sof, which precedes the restriction. Even though there is a place there and a will to receive the abundance from

His self, it is still without change and distinction between the light and the "place."

"He is one" means the light of Ein Sof. "His name is one" means the desire to enjoy included there without any change whatsoever. Understand what our sages implied, that "His name" is desire in Gematria, meaning the "desire to enjoy."

All the worlds in the thought of creation, called "the light of Ein Sof," and what contains the receivers there is called Malchut of Ein Sof.

26) It has already been explained regarding "The end of the work is in the preliminary thought," that it is the thought of creation, which expanded from His self in order to delight His creations. We have learned that in Him, the thought and the light are one and the same thing. It therefore follows that the light of Ein Sof that expanded from His self contains the whole of reality before us through the end of the future correction, which is the end of the work. In Him, all the creations are already complete with all their perfection and joy that He wished to bestow upon them. This reality, which is complete sufficiently, is called "the light of Ein Sof," and that which contains them is called Malchut of Ein Sof.

CHAPTER SEVEN

Although only phase four was restricted, the light left the first three phases as well.

27) It has already been explained that the middle point, which is the comprehensive point of the thought of creation, namely the will to enjoy in it, embellished itself to enhance its equivalence of form with the Emanator. Although there is no disparity of form in His Almightiness from the perspective of the Emanator, the point of the desire felt it as a kind of indirect extension from His essence, as with the allegory about the rich man. For this reason, she diminished her desire from the last phase, which is the complete Gadlut [greatness/adulthood] of the will to receive, to increase the adhesion] by way of direct extension from His essence.

Then the light was emptied from the entire place, meaning from all four degrees that exist in the place. Even though she diminished her desire only from phase four, it is the nature of the spiritual that it is indivisible.

Afterwards, he re-extended a line of light from the first three phases, and phase four remained a vacant space.

28) Afterwards, the light of Ein Sof extended once more to the place that was emptied. It did not fill the entire place in all four phases, but only three phases, as was the desire of the point of restriction. Hence, the middle point that has been restricted remained empty and hollow since the light illuminated only through phase four, but not all the way, and the light of Ein Sof stopped there.

We will henceforth explain the matter of the incorporation of the phases in one another applied in the upper worlds. Now you see that the four phases are incorporated in one another in such a way that within phase four itself there are all four phases, too. Thus, in phase four, too, the light of Ein Sof reached the first three phases in it, and only the last phase in phase four remained empty and without light.

CHAPTER EIGHT

Hochma is called "light," and Hassadim, "water." Bina is called "upper water," and Malchut, "lower water."

29) Now we will explain the meaning of the four phases of cause and consequence, necessary to complete the form of the will to receive, as in "The water conceived and begot darkness." There are two discernments in the light in Atzilut. The first discernment is called "light," which is Hochma, and the second discernment is called "water," which is Hassadim.

The first discernment extends from above downward without any assistance from the lower one. The second discernment extends with the help of the lower one, hence the name "water," for it is the nature of the light, whose foundation is above, and the nature of the water, whose foundation is below.

There are also two discernments in the water itself: upper water, by phase two in the four phases, and lower water, by phase four in the four phases.

Explanation of the expansion of the light of Ein Sof into the four phases in order to reveal the vessel, which is the will to receive.

30) For this reason, any expansion of the light of Ein Sof consists of ten Sefirot since the light of Ein Sof, which is the root and the Emanator, is called Keter. The light of the expansion itself is called Hochma, and this is the full measure of expansion of the light from above, from Ein Sof. It has already been said that the will to receive is incorporated in every expansion of light from above. However, the form of the will to receive does not actually become apparent before the desire awakens in the emanated being to extend more light than the measure of its expansion.

Thus, because the will to receive is included as potential immediately in the light of the expansion, the light is compelled to bring the potential to the actual. Consequently, the light awakens to extend additional abundance more than the measure of its expansion from Ein Sof. By this, the will to receive appears in practice in that light and acquires the form of the innovation through a slight disparity of form, for by this it becomes darker than the light, since it grew coarser by the new form.

Also, this part, which has become coarser, is called Bina. This is the meaning of "I am Bina [understanding], mine is the Gevura [strength]." In truth, Bina is a part of Hochma, meaning the actual light of expansion of Ein Sof. However, because she increased her desire and drew more abundance than the measure of the expansion in her from Ein Sof, she thus acquired disparity of form and grew slightly coarser than the light. Thus, she acquired her own name which is the Sefira Bina.

The essence of the additional abundance that she extended from Ein Sof by the power of the intensification of her desire is called "light of Hassadim," or "upper water." This is because this light does not extend directly from Ein Sof like the light of Hochma, but through the assistance of the emanated being who intensified the desire. Hence, it merits its own name, to be called "light of Hassadim" or "water."

Now you find that the Sefira Bina consists of three discernments of light: The first discernment is the light of Bina itself, which is a part of the light of Hochma. The second is her growing coarser and the disparity of form in her, acquired by the intensification of the desire. The third discernment is the light of Hassadim that came to her through her own extension from Ein Sof.

However, this still does not complete the entire vessel of reception, since the essence of Bina is the light of Hochma, which is very exalted, a direct expansion from the light of Ein Sof. Consequently, only the root for the vessels of reception and the operator for the operation of the vessel appeared in Bina.

Afterward, that same light of Hassadim that she extended through the power of her intensification extended from her once more, and some illumination of Hochma was added. This expansion of light of Hassadim is called Zeir Anpin, or HGT.

This light of expansion also increased its desire to extend a new abundance, more than the measure of illumination of Hochma in its expansion from Bina. This expansion is also regarded as two phases because the light of the expansion itself is called ZA or VAK, while the intensification in it is called Malchut.

This is how we come by the ten Sefirot: Keter is Ein Sof; Hochma is the light of the expansion from Ein Sof; Bina is the light of Hochma that intensified in order to increase abundance, by which it grew coarser. ZA, which consists of HGT NHY, is light of Hassadim with illumination of Hochma that expands from Bina, and Malchut is the second intensification to add illumination of Hochma more than there is in ZA.

The four phases in the desire are the four letters HaVaYaH, which are KHB TM.

31) This is the meaning of the four letters in the four-letter Name: The tip of the Yod is Ein Sof, meaning the operating force included the thought of creation,

which is to delight His creations, namely the vessel of Keter. Yod is Hochma, meaning phase one, which is the potential in the actual that is immediately contained in the light of the expansion of Ein Sof. The first Hey is Bina, meaning phase two, regarded as the actualization of the potential, meaning the light that has grown coarser than Hochma.

Vav is Zeir Anpin or HGT NHY, meaning the expansion of light of Hassadim that emerged through Bina. This is phase three, the potential for revealing the operation, the bottom Hey in HaVaYaH. It is Malchut, meaning phase four, the complete manifestation of the act in the vessel of reception that has intensified to extend more abundance than its measure of expansion from Bina. This completes the form of the will to receive and the light that clothes its vessel, being the will to receive that is completed only in this fourth phase and not before.

Now you can easily see that there is no light in the upper ones and lower worlds that is not arranged under the four-letter Name, being the four phases. Without it, the will to receive that should be in every light is incomplete, for this desire is the place and the measure of that light.

The letters Yod and Vav of HaVaYaH are thin because they are discerned as mere potential.

32) This might surprise us, since Yod implies Hochma and Hey implies Bina, and the entire light itself that exists in the Ten Sefirot is in the Sefira of Hochma, while Bina, Zeir Anpin, and Malchut are merely garments with respect to Hochma. Thus, Hochma should have taken the greater letter in the four-letter Name.

The thing is that the letters of the four-letter Name do not imply or indicate the measure and amount of light in the ten Sefirot. Instead, they indicate measures of impression of the vessel. The white in the parchment of the scroll of Torah implies the light, and the black, being the letters in the scroll of Torah, indicates the quality of the vessels.

Thus, because Keter is only discerned as the root of the root of the vessel, it is implied only in the tip of the Yod. Hochma, which is the potential that has not appeared in practice, is implied by the smallest of the letters, namely the Yod.

Bina, in which the potential is carried out in practice, is indicated by the widest letter, the Hey. Since ZA is only the potential for revealing the act, it is implied by a long and thin letter, which is the Vav. Its thinness indicates that the essence of the vessel is still concealed in it in potential, in hiding.

The length of the line indicates that at the end of its expansion, the complete vessel appears through it.

Hochma did not manage to reveals the complete vessel through her expansion, for Bina is still an incomplete vessel; rather, it is the operator of the vessel. This is why the leg of the Yod is short, implying that it is still short and did not reveal a complete vessel through the force concealed in it and through its expansion.

Malchut, too, is implied by the letter Hey, like Bina, which is a wide letter, appearing in its complete form. It should not surprise you that Bina and Malchut have the same letters because in the world of correction they are indeed similar and lend their vessels to one another, as in the verse, "And they two went."

Chapter Nine

Spiritual movement means a new change of form.

33) We should still explain the meaning of time and movement that we come across in almost every word in this wisdom. Indeed, you should know that spiritual movement is not like tangible movement from place to place. Rather, it refers to a new form. We denominate every new form by the title "movement." That innovation, meaning a new change of form that has occurred in the spiritual, unlike its general preceding form in that spiritual, is regarded as having been divided and distanced from that spiritual. It is considered to have emerged with its own name and authority, by which it is exactly like a corporeal being that some part departed from it and moves about from place to place. Hence, the new form is called "movement."

"Spiritual time" means a certain number of new changes of form that stem from one another. Former and latter mean cause and consequence.

34) Concerning the spiritual definition of time, understand that for us, the whole concept of time is only a sensation of movements. Our imagination pictures and devises a certain number of consecutive movements that it senses one by one and interprets them as a certain amount of "time." Thus, if one had been in a state of complete rest with one's environment, he would not even be aware of the concept of time. So it is in spirituality: A certain amount of new forms is regarded as "spiritual movements" which are intermingled in one another by way of cause and consequence, and they are called "time" in spirituality. Also, "before" and "after" always mean "cause and consequence."

CHAPTER TEN

The entire substance that is attributed to the emanated being is the will to receive. Any addition in it is attributed to the Emanator.

35) Know that the will to receive in the emanated being, it has been clarified that it is its vessel. Know also that it is all the general substance attributed to the emanated being. It follows that all that exists besides it is attributed to the Emanator.

The will to receive is the first form of every essence. We define the first form as "substance" because we have no attainment in the essence.

36) Although we perceive the will to receive as an incident and a form in the essence, but how do we perceive it as the substance of the essence? Indeed, it is the same with essences that are near us. We call the first form in the essence by the name "the first substance in the essence" since we have no attainment or perception whatsoever in any substance, as all of our five senses are completely unfit for it. The sight, hearing, smell, taste, and touch offer the scrutinizing mind mere abstract forms of "incidents" of the essence, formulating through collaboration with our senses.

For example, if we take even the smallest, microscopic atoms in the smallest elements of any essence, which are separated through a chemical process, they, too, are merely abstract forms that appear that way to the eye. More precisely, we distinguish and discern them by the ways of the will to receive and to be received that we find in them.

Following these operations, we can distinguish and separate these various atoms to the very first matter of that essence. However, even then they would be no more than forces in the essence and not a substance.

Thus, you find that even in corporeality, we have no other way to understand the first matter, except by assuming that the first form is the first matter, which carries all other incidents and forms that follow it. It is much more so in the upper worlds, where tangible and imaginary do not apply.

TABLE OF QUESTIONS FOR TOPICS

82. Why didn't the restriction create a Sof?

83. Why did the light depart from all the phases during the restriction?

84. Why weren't the four phases mentioned as four degrees one below the other during the restriction and before the appearance of the line?

85. Why did phase four not become coarse immediately at the restriction of the light, and all four phases remained equal?

86. Which phase remains empty of light?

87. When will phase four also be filled with upper light?

88. What caused the creation of the worlds?

89. What is the desired purpose of Torah and good deeds?

90. What is the power of the disclosure of the Holy Names?

91. How do the Holy Names reveal?

92. What is the End of Correction?

93. What is the root of every corruption?

94. Why is it not possible to turn a vessel of reception into a vessel of bestowal except here in this world, and not in the Upper Worlds?

95. What are the two phases of the light?

96. What does the expansion of the light from the emanator contain?

97. Which light appears with the intensification of the will to bestow?

98. Which two lights are included in every emanated being?

99. Why is light of Hassadim inferior to light of Hochma?

100. When is the vessel of reception completed?

101. What is the difference between one who receives within and one who receives without, as in Ein Sof?

102. What are Sefirot of circles?

103. Why are the degrees in circles not regarded as being one below the other before the appearance of the line?

104. Is there is evil in the will to receive by the nature of its creation?

105. What does "Indirect extension" from the emanator mean?

1. Light (Part 1, Inner Observation, 18)

   Everything in the worlds that exists as "existence from existence," which is everything but the substance of the Kelim (see items 2 and 24).

2. Light and vessel (Part 1, Chap 1, Inner Light, 6)

   The will to receive in the emanated being is called vessel; and the abundance that he receives is called light.

3. Circular Light (Part 1, Chap 1, Inner Light, 100)

   A light that makes no discernment of degrees.

4. Simple light (Part 1, Chap 1, Inner Light, 30)

   A light that contains within it the Kli to the point that the light and the vessel are indistinguishable.

5. Light of Hochma (Part 1, Chap 1, Inner Light, 50)

   A light that extends to the emanated being in the first expansion, being the general vitality and self of the emanated being.

6. Light of Hassadim (Part 1, Chap 1, Inner Light, 5)

   A light that clothes the light of Hochma and extends to the emanated being at the first intensification.

7. Empty Air (Part 1, Chap 1, Inner Light, 5)

   It is light of Hassadim before it is clothed in light of Hochma.

8. Afterwards (Part 1, Inner Observation, 34)

   That which stems from its previous phase. (See item 20).

9. Middle (Part 1, Chap 2, Inner Light, 2)

   See item 39.

10. One (Part 1, Chap 2, Inner Light, 1)

    The upper light that expands from Himself is One and as simple as Himself. As it is in Ein Sof, so it is in the world of Assiya, without any change and addition of form whatsoever, and that is why it is called One.

11. Creator (Part 1, Inner Observation, 18)

    The name Creator relates solely to the actual innovation, meaning the "existence from absence," which is the substance of the Kelim, defined as the "will to receive" in every essence. It was necessarily absent from Himself prior to creation.

12. Adhesion (Part 1, Chap 1, Inner Light, 30)

    It is equivalence of form that brings the spirituals together and attaches them to one another, while disparity of form separates them from one another.

13. Equivalence (Part 1, Chap 1, Inner Light, 10)

When there is no discernment whatsoever among the four phases of the will to receive it is said that they are even and equal.

14. Expansion (Part 1, Chap 1, Inner Light, 1)

Light that stems from the emanator to the emanated being is called expansion of light. In fact, the upper light is not affected in any way by that. It is like lighting one candle from another, when the first is not lessened by it. The name only indicates the reception of the emanated being.

15. Refined (Part 1, Chap 1, Inner Light, 90)

Phase one in the will to receive is regarded as more refined than the three phases that follow her.

16. Time (Part 1, Inner Observation, 34)

It is a certain sum of phases that cascade from one another and are mingled with one another by an order of cause and consequence, such as days, months and years.

17. Darkness (Part 1, Inner Observation, 24)

Phase four in the desire, which does not receive the upper light inside her by the power of the restriction, is regarded as the root of the darkness.

18. Hochma (Part 1, Chap 1, Inner Light, 50)

It is the light of the emanated being's self and vitality (see item 5).

19. Space (Part 1, Chap 1, Inner Light, 6)

Phase four of the desire that became empty of light is regarded as darkness compared to the light. With respect to the vessel she is regarded as a space because Phase four was not deprived from the emanated being in itself by the restriction, but there is an empty air in it, without light.

20. Before and After (Part 1, Inner Observation, 34)

When speaking of a relationship of cause and consequence of the emanated beings, we express the cause by the term "Before" and the consequence of that consequence by the term "After." (see item 16).

21. Unique and Unified (Part 1, Inner Observation, 1)

Unique indicates the upper light that shines and rules all the various degrees in their different forms to the extent that it makes them equalize with His unique form. Unified indicates the end of that rule, meaning after He had already equalized and brought their form to be as unique as He is (see item 14).

22. Unification (Part 1, Chap 1, Inner Light, 6)

Two different phases that have equalized with one another in their form unite into one (see item 12).

23. Right and Left

Sometimes, an inferior degree ascends to an equal level with the superior, when the superior needs her for her own completion. In that state, the inferior is regarded as the "left" and the superior as the "right."

24. Maker (Part 1, Inner Observation, 18)

The title "Maker" relates specifically to the pouring of the light into the worlds, which means everything but the substance of the Kelim (see above items 11 and 1).

25. Vessel (Kli) (Part 1, Chap 1, Inner Light, 6)

The will to receive in the emanated being is the vessel.

26. Above (Part 1, Chap 2, Inner Light, 3)

Equivalence of form of the inferior with the superior is a "rise above."

27. Emanator

Any cause is regarded as the emanator of the effected degree. The title emanator contains both the extension of the light and the vessel that receives the light.

28. Origin of the Soul (Part 1, Inner Observation, 15)

The will to receive that was imprinted in the souls is what separates them and "carves" them off from the upper light. That is because it is the disparity of form that separates in spirituality (see item 12). The issue of the origin of the soul refers to the transition between world of Atzilut and world of Beria, which will be explained in its place.

29. Below (Part 1, Chap 2, Inner Light, 3)

The one of a lesser virtue is regarded as being "below."

30. Unified

See definition of Unique and Unified

31. Malchut of Ein Sof (Part 1, Inner Observation, 14)

It is the will to receive that is necessarily there.

32. From Above Downward (Part 1, Chap 2, Inner Light, 3)

Meaning from phase one to phase four. Phase four that was left without light is regarded as being "below" all the other degrees. The frailer the will to receive, the higher one is considered to be. Therefore, phase one is regarded as the "highest" of all.

33. Fulfilling (Part 1, 1)

Where there is no deficiency whatsoever and where an addition to the wholeness that exists there is inconceivable.

34. Above, Below (Part 1, Chap 2, Inner Light, 3)

The more important is regarded as "Above," and the worse as "Below."

35. Place (Part 1, Inner Observation, 11)

The will to receive in the emanated being is the "Place" for the abundance and the light in it.

36. Square (Part 1, Chap 1, Inner Light, 200)

It is a degree that consists of all four phases of the desire.

37. Triangle (Part 1, Chap 1, Inner Light, 400)

It is a degree with only the first three phases of the desire.

38. Touching (Part 1, Chap 2, Inner Light, 5)

If the disparity of form of the degree from the root is not so apparent as to separate from the root, it is regarded as "touching" the root. The same applies between each two adjacent degrees.

39. Middle Point (Part 1, Chap 1, Inner Light, 50)

This is the name of phase four in Ein Sof. She is named after her unification with the light of Ein Sof.

40. Sof (Part 1, Chap 1, Inner Light, 20)

The Sof and the Sium of every emanated being is done by the detaining force in phase four, where the upper light stops shining because she does not receive it.

41. Circle (Part 1, Chap 1, Inner Light, 100)

When there are no discriminations of above and below among the four phases of the will to receive, it is considered as a circle (like an image of a corporeal circle, where there is no discernment of up or down). Because of that, the four phases are regarded as concentric circles one inside the other, where it is impossible to distinguish up from down.

42. Upper (Part 1, Chap 2, Inner Light, 3)

It is the more important.

43. Separation (Part 1, Inner Observation, 12)

Two degrees without any equivalence of form on any side are regarded as completely separated from one another.

44. Vacant (Part 1, Chap 1, Inner Light, 4)

This is a place that is prepared to receive correction and wholeness.

45. Simple (Part 1, Chap 1, Inner Light, 9)

Where there are no discernments of degrees and sides.

46. Restriction (Part 1, Chap 1, Inner Light, 40)

One who conquers one's desire. In other words, one who detains oneself from receiving and does not receive despite one's great desire to receive, is regarded as restricting (performing a restriction) one's desire.

47. Line (Part 1, Chap 2, Inner Light, 1)

Indicates a discernment of up and down that was not there before. It also designates a much frailer illumination than before.

48. Near (Part 1, Chap 1, Inner Light, 3)

The closer one's form is to another, the closer they are considered to be.

49. Rosh (Part 2, Chap 2, Inner Light, 6)

That part in the emanated being that is the most like the root is called Rosh.

50. Wind (Part 1, Chap 1, Inner Light, 5)

Light of Hassadim is called wind.

51. Desire

See item 45.

52. Name (Part 1, Inner Observation, 5)

The Holy Names are descriptions of how the lights that they imply are attained. The name of the degree designates the conduct of attainment in that degree.

53. Toch (Part 1, Chap 1, Inner Light, 50)

One who receives inside is regarded as the light being measured and limited in the vessel. However, one who receives outside is not regarded as placing any boundary on the light that one receives.

54. Movement (Part 1, Inner Observation, 33)

Any new form is regarded as a spiritual movement, for it is separated from the previous form and acquires a name of its own. It is like a part that is separated from a corporeal object that moves and exits its earlier place.

TABLE OF ANSWERS FOR TOPICS

55. What terms are absent in the wisdom of Kabbalah?

From the beginning to the end of the wisdom there is not even a single word that relates to any tangible or imaginary term, such as space, time, motion and so on.

Also, there is no absence in spirituality, and any change of form does not mean that the first form is absent. Instead, the first form remains in its place unchanged at all and the disparity of form that has now been acquired is added to the first form.

(The beginning of Inner Light)

56. What is the ordinary language in the wisdom of Kabbalah?

This language is a "Language of Branches" that points to their Upper Roots. That is because "You haven't even a single blade of grass below that has not a root above."

Therefore, the sages of the Kabbalah have put together a language that is equipped to imply through the branches and teach of the Upper Roots.

(Inner Light, page 1 and the beginning of Inner Observation, item 1)

57. What separates and discriminates in the wisdom of Kabbalah?

The disparity of form distinguishes and departs the spirituals from one another.

(Inner Light, item 30)

58. What is the origin of the "will to receive?"

The will to bestow in the upper light necessitates the existence of the will to receive in the emanated being.

(Inner Observation, item 11)

59. What makes the light exit the emanator and become an emanated being?

This innovated part stopped being regarded as the Emanator and became an emanated being because of the form of the will to receive that was innovated with the upper light, since it wants to bestow.

(Inner Observation, item 11 & item 15)

60. What is the first substance of every emanated being?

The new form that emerged existence from absence, meaning the "will to receive" that is in every essence, is the "first substance" of every emanated being and every essence. Moreover, everything that exists in the emanated being or in the essence that is more than that substance, is regarded as light and abundance that extends from the upper light "existence from existence" and not at all as an emanated being and a created being.

It is not surprising that a form becomes a substance, because it is so in corporeality as well. Our conduct is to regard the first form of the essence as the first substance. That is because there is no attainment whatsoever in any matter in the entire reality, since our senses perceive only incidents in the matter, which are forms that incarnate and manifest in the first substance.

(Inner Observation, item 35)

61. **From which time is it regarded as an emanated being?**

It stops being an Emanator and becomes an emanated being right at the beginning of the formation of the will to receive in the emanated being, called phase four in the desire.

(Inner Light, Part 1, Chap 2, item 3)

62. **Has a spiritual that accepted a disparity of form, by which a part of it departed and became a different phase, lost anything because of that?**

There is no absence or loss in spirituality. The part that departs because of the change of form does not diminish or lessen the upper light in any way; rather, it is like lighting one candle from another; the first is not lessened whatsoever. Thus, any change of form is an addition to the first.

(Inner Observation, Part 2, regarding the integration of Ten Sefirot in every Sefira)

63. **How and in whom are there many forms and changes in the worlds?**

All the changes and the multiplications are carried out only by the impact of the light on the vessels that receive it. However, the upper light in and of itself remains in complete rest, meaning unchanged and without any innovation.

(Inner Light, Part 1, Chap 2, item 1)

64. **How are innovation and movement depicted in the light?**

There is no movement, meaning innovation, in the upper light. Instead, the part that the emanated being receives from the upper light is what becomes "innovated" and multiplies (like lighting a candle from another without the first lessening), according to the new forms in the vessels.

Each receives according to the degree of its own desire, which changes from to the other and cascades from one to the other incessantly and immeasurably.

(Inner Light, Part 1, Chap 2, item 1)

65. **How are all the opposites and the multitude of forms that extend from Him to the worlds contained in His simple unity?**

See Inner Observation item 18 and item 29.

66. **By whom and by what is the line extended from Ein Sof?**

The screen is a detaining force that was placed on phase four after the restriction to prevent her from receiving inside. That is what caused the emergence of the line from Ein Sof, because the upper light is never subject to change, and it shines after the restriction as it did before the restriction.

However, now the above screen caused the upper light to be received only in the three phases of the desire whose measure is very small compared to the reception in phase four in Ein Sof. For that reason it received only a thin line of light compared to the measure of the light in Ein Sof.

(Inner Light, Part 1, Chap 2, item 1)

67. **Has anything changed in Ein Sof after the restriction as well?**

Although phase four in Ein Sof restricted herself, still there is no issue of putting on a form or taking one off in the absence of the first, as it is in corporeality. Instead, there is an issue of a new form that is added to the first, without the first form changing at all, as there is not absence in anything spiritual.

Thus, this entire innovation of the departure of the light and the detaining force that was performed in phase four to avoid receiving light inside her is regarded as a new and distinguished world. It is added to the light of Ein Sof, which remained as it was without any change. You should infer from that regarding every new form in spirituality.

(Inner Light, Part 1, Chap 2, item 1)

68. **When has the coarseness in phase four been uncovered?**

When the line that comes from Ein Sof was detained from shining in phase four by the screen. Because she remained without light, the coarseness in her became apparent.

(Inner Light, Part 1, Chap 2, item 3)

69. **What are the four phases in the will to receive?**

First the light from the emanator expands as light of Hochma, being the general vitality that belongs to that emanated being. Inside it there is phase one in the will to receive, called the first expansion or phase one

After that the will to bestow increases in that light, which in turn draws light of Hassadim from the emanator. This is called the first intensification, or phase two.

Afterwards that light of Hassadim performs a great expansion, namely with illumination of Hochma. This is called the second expansion or phase three.

After that the will to receive that is included in the light from the first expansion intensifies and completes the measure of the will to receive. This is called the second intensification or phase four.

(Inner Light, Part 1, Chap 1, item 50)

70. **What are the four letters of HaVaYaH?**

The Yod of HaVaYaH is the first expansion of the light, called phase one (see item 69). The first Hey of HaVaYaH is the first intensification in the light, called phase two. The Vav is the second expansion or the light, called phase three, and the last Hey of HaVaYaH is the second intensification in the light, called phase four.

(Inner Observation, item 31)

71. **What is the upper beginning of the line that touches Ein Sof?**

See item 49.

72. **What is the single thought that contains all the forms and the opposites in the entire reality?**

It is the thought "to delight His created beings."

(Inner Observation, item 22)

73. **Where do the sages of the Kabbalah begin to engage?**

Kabbalah speaks only of the expansion of the light from Himself, though in Himself, we haven't any word or uttering.

(Inner Light, Part 1, Chap 1, item 2)

74. **What are the two primary rudiments that contain everything?**

The first rudiment is that the entire reality before us is already set and exists in Ein Sof in its utter perfection. This is called the light of Ein Sof.

The second rudiment is the five worlds called Adam Kadmon, Atzilut, Beria, Yetzira, Assiya, which cascade from Malchut of Ein Sof after the restriction. Anything that exists in the second rudiment extends from the first rudiment.

(Inner Light, Part 1, Chap 1, item 3 and Inner Observation, item 5)

75. **What is the meaning of "He is One and His Name One?"**

"He" indicates the light in Ein Sof. "His Name" implies the will to receive in Ein Sof, called Malchut of Ein Sof. "One" indicates that there is no disparity of form whatsoever detected there between the light, which is "He" and the vessel, which is "His Name." Rather, it is all light.

(Inner Light, Part 1, Chap 1, item 30 and Inner Observation, item 13)

76. **What is the name "Ein Sof?"**

Before the restriction, the name Ein Sof implies that there is no Sof or Sium (end) there whatsoever, since phase four receives the light as well. Thus, in that place there is no reason to stop the light and form a Sof and Sium.

(Inner Light, Part 1, Chap 1, item 20)

77. **What extends from the will to receive that is contained in Ein Sof?**

The creation of the worlds and their entire contents. It restricted itself in phase four in order to uncover the worlds down to this world, where it is possible to turn the form of reception into a form of bestowal.

(Inner Light, Part 1, Chap 1, item 90 and Inner Observation, item 17)

78. **What is the reason for the restriction of the light?**

Malchut of Ein Sof regarded the equivalence of form with her Maker as embellishment, which could only be achieved by the creation of the worlds. That is why she restricted herself.

(Inner Light, Part 1, Chap 1, item 40 and Part 1, Chap 1, item 90)

79. **Which kind of reception would be regarded as bestowal?**

Reception only because it gives contentment to the giver.

(Inner Light, Part 1, Chap 1, item 90)

80. **What is the purpose of the restriction?**

To turn the form of reception into the form of bestowal.

(Inner Light, Part 1, Chap 1, item 90)

81. **Why did the light leave the middle point and never returned?**

See Inner Light Part 1, Chap 1 item 40 and Inner Observation item 22.

82. **Why didn't the restriction create a Sof?**

The restriction was not because of the disparity of form that appeared in the will to receive that wanted to correct it. It was only because of the embellishment, without any necessity and coercion.

83. **Why did the light depart from all the phases during the restriction?**

Because there is no some (part) in spirituality.

(Inner Light, Part 1, Chap 1, item 70)

84. **Why weren't the four phases mentioned as four degrees one below the other during the restriction and before the appearance of the line?**

Before the illumination of the line phase four did not regard herself as thick and low (see item 83). For that reason there is no issue of the impact she has on the degrees.

(Inner Light, Part 1, Chap 1, item 90)

85. **Why did phase four not become coarse immediately at the restriction of the light, and all four phases remain equal?**

Because the restriction did not occur due to a disparity of form.

(Inner Light, Part 1, Chap 1, item 90)

86. **Which phase remains empty of light?**

Only phase four.

(Inner Light, Part 1, Chap 2, item 3)

87. **When will phase four also be filled with light?**

When the vessels of reception acquire the form of bestowal.

(Inner Light, Part 1, Chap 1, item 40)

88. **What caused the creation of the worlds?**

The will that is necessarily there had a desire to embellish itself and resemble the form of the light completely, and that became the "cause" for the creation of the worlds.

(Inner Light, Part 1, Chap 1, item 90)

89. **What is the desired purpose of Torah and good deeds?**

To make the vessels of reception work in order to bestow.

(Inner Observation, item 22)

90. **What is the power of the disclosure of the Holy Names?**

Their power is specifically to turn the form of reception into bestowal.

(Inner Light, Part 1, Chap 1, item 90)

91. **How do the Holy Names reveal?**

By laboring in Torah and good deeds.

(Inner Light, Part 1, Chap 1, item 40)

92. **What is the end of correction?**

The turning of the form of reception into a form of bestowal.

(Inner Light, Part 1, Chap 1, item 40)

93. **What is the root of every corruption?**

The disparity of form of the will to receive from the emanator.

(Inner Observation, item 18)

94. **Why is it not possible to turn a vessel of reception into a vessel of bestowal except here in this world, and not in the Upper Worlds?**

Corruption and correction in the same carrier exist only in this world.

(Inner Observation, item 20)

95. **What are the two phases of the light?**

Light of Hochma and light of Hassadim.

(Inner Light, Part 1, Chap 1, item 50)

96. **What does the expansion of the light from the emanator contain?**

The will to bestow and the will to receive.

(Inner Light, Part 1, Chap 1, item 50)

97. **Which light appears with the intensification of the will to bestow?**

Light of Hassadim.

(Inner Light, Part 1, Chap 1, item 50)

98. **Which two lights are contained in every emanated being?**

Light of Hochma and light of Hassadim.

(Inner Light, Part 1, Chap 1, item 50)

99. **Why is light of Hassadim inferior to light of Hochma?**

Because it is extended by the intensification of the desire of the emanated being.

(Inner Light, Part 1, Chap 1, item 50)

100. **When is the vessel of reception completed?**

When phase four of the desire appears, which is the great will to receive.

(Inner Light, Part 1, Chap 1, item 50)

101. **What is the difference between one who receives within and one who receives without, as in Ein Sof?**

The one who receives within can only hold within a limited amount of light, because of the limitation of the vessel. When receiving without, the vessel does not limit the light that it holds, and it is without ration.

(Inner Light, Part 1, Chap 1, item 50)

102. **What are Sefirot of circles?**

When there is no differentiation of above and below among the four phases in the desire, they are regarded as four circles one within the other, like onionskins.

(Inner Light, Part 1, Chap 1, item 100)

103. **Why are the degrees in circles not regarded as being one below the other before the appearance of the line?**

Because the restriction did not occur because of the inferiority of the disparity of form.

(Inner Light, Part 1, Chap 1, item 100)

104. **Is there evil in the will to receive by the nature of its creation?**

There is no inferiority in it by the nature of its creation, nor would it appear in it had it not been restricted.

(Inner Observation, item 19)

105. **What does "Indirect extension" from the Emanator mean?**

See Inner Observation, item 19.

PART TWO

Circles and Straightness, Containing Two Chapters

CHAPTER ONE

Explains the ten Sefirot of circles that appeared after the restriction, the light of Ein Sof that surrounds them, and all the light of the Sefirot of circles that is given to them through the line. It contains eleven subtopics:

1. The line is like a thin pipeline. 2. The expansion of the light of Ein Sof into the space. 3. The expansion unfolded slowly. 4. The circle is not attached to Ein Sof, but is connected to it through the line. 5. The light of Ein Sof surrounds and influences the circle from afar. 6. The line is called Adam Kadmon. 7. The order of expansion of the ten Sefirot of the circles. 8. The line connects all the circles. 9. Each world and each Sefira consist of ten inner Sefirot. Within each Sefira, there are ten additional Sefirot, and so on and so forth endlessly. 10. The Sefirot of circles envelop each other like onionskins. 11. The closer the circle to Ein Sof, the higher and better it is considered. Because this world is at the middle point, the farthest from Ein Sof, it is utterly corporeal.

The line is like a thin pipeline

1. **This line $_{(1)}$ is like $_{(2)}$ one thin pipeline $_{(3)}$, where the water of the upper light $_{(4)}$ of Ein Sof expands and extends to the worlds in that place of space and air.**

Inner light

1. The line that extends from the light of Ein Sof into the space after the restriction (see Part 1, Chap 2, item 2).

2. The vessels of the ten Sefirot of straightness are called a pipeline, or pipelines, because they confine the routes of the light that travels through them with great accuracy and control. They guarantee it will expand only through certain routes in those vessels.

   They are like a pipeline that channels the water that travels through it accurately. They extend and continue from it in the same shape as inside the pipeline. If it is narrow, the water is narrow; if it is wide, so is the current, and it never changes.

   For this reason, the lights that travel through those pipelines are called ten Sefirot of straightness. It is so because they expand in straightness (also honesty) and justly by the same rules as these pipelines.

This means that the more refined the vessel is, the greater the importance of the light that clothes it. This rule is unchanging because of the strong influence of the pipelines on them.

This power of control in the above pipelines is there because any desire in the upper degree is a compelling force in the lower degree, which is created by it. Therefore, the restriction on phase four, which is a free choice in the vessels of circles, becomes a compelling force in the vessels of straightness created by them. This force is called screen.

This is the meaning of the words in *The Zohar* (*Tikkunim*): "Invert *ratzon* [desire] and you will find *tzinor* [pipeline]." This means that when the pipeline is a screen, a controlled restriction, meaning when it detains its will to receive in phase four by the power of the upper one that controls it, it is the opposite of the substance of the vessel itself, namely the will to receive. That is because it detains itself from using its desire.

That is why they implied, "Invert Ratzon [desire] and you will find Tzinor [pipeline]." It means that the pipeline is opposite to the desire for it compels its desire and does the opposite of what it wants.

That is why you can find in all the teachings and the writings that when they want to denominate and emphasize the departure of the light from phase four, they call it restriction.

When we want to emphasize the power of the restriction that is added by the light of the line that did not expand to phase four, we define it as screen, which is a detaining force that prevents the light from reaching phase four.

When we discuss the vessel in general, meaning the vessel and the screen together, we define it as a pipeline. When discussing the light, the vessel, and the screen together, meaning the light that is clothed in the measure of the pipeline, it is defined as a line. And when we discuss a vessel that does not have a screen, we denominate it by the name circle.

3. The ARI's precision with regards to the word "one" emphasizes the correction of the three lines that was performed in the world of Atzilut. It tells us that in the world of Adam Kadmon this correction is still absent, and there is only one line.

The reason for it is that the correction of the three lines occurred afterwards, in the world of Atzilut. This correction extends from the association of the quality of mercy with the quality of judgement. Here, however, we are concerned with the world of Adam Kadmon, where this association has not yet taken place. That is why there is only one line here.

The entrance of the light into the vessel of reception of the emanated is called expansion (see Table of Answers, Part one, item 14). It has already been clarified that the vessel of reception in this emanated being is called pipeline.

4. There is a specific value that discriminates between the degrees of the birth of the Partzuf. In that birth, the four phases of the desire are called by the names: light, water, firmament, and one hundred blessings (or one hundred gates). It happens because the lights change their places. Because of that displacement, the light takes the form of water.

   The ARI tells us that the root of this state occurred with the appearance of the line: The light that expands as a line is considered to be water with regards to the upper light. For this reason he states precisely: "The water of the upper light of Ein Sof." With the expansion of the upper light into the thin pipeline, the value of the light was greatly lessened from its value in Ein Sof, and it is therefore considered as water.

Expansion of the light of Ein Sof into the space. The expansion occurred slowly

2. **When the light of Ein Sof extended as a straight line (5) into the above space, it did not expand (6) and extend all the way down at once, but rather expanded slowly.**

   I wish to say that in the beginning, the line of light began to expand, and right at the beginning (7) of its expansion as a line, it expanded and extended and became like one wheel, (8) round on all sides.

Inner light

5. A light that expands gradually, according to the laws of the four phases, meaning from refined to coarse and stops at phase four, is called a straight line.

6. Do not be mistaken and interpret the terms, "at once" and "slowly" that are used here, as times, for it is known that spirituality is above time. Therefore, "all the way down at once" means that there is no change of degrees. The term "slowly" refers to an order of degrees. He wishes to say that it follows the order of the four known phases, as he will explain henceforth.

7. This is the root of the expansion that was innovated, called a line. Because it is a new emanated being, it has a specifically designated root that shines upon it as its innovation. That illumination is called the Sefira of Keter of the line.

From this Keter, the light of Ein Sof expands to the line by way of the above four phases: phase one is called Hochma; phase two is called Bina; phase three is called Zeir Anpin; and phase four is called Malchut.

The ARI says with regards to this order that it expanded "slowly." He says that Keter expanded first, Hochma next, and then Bina, Zeir Anpin etc. (see Answers Table part one, item 8, the meaning of the word, "afterwards").

8. For the meaning of the word circle see Answers Table part one, item 41, and also Part One, chapter one, item 100. When the light of the line dresses in a circle, it is called a wheel.

The circle is not adhesive with Ein Sof, but is connected to it through the line.

3. **This circle was not adhesive [9] with the light of Ein Sof that surrounds it from all sides. That is because if it adheres to it [10], it will return to its prior state, and will be annulled in the light of Ein Sof. In that case, its power will not be apparent at all, and everything will be only the light of Ein Sof as in the beginning.**

   Hence, this circle is adjacent to the circle Ein Sof and is not in adhesion with it. The connection and adhesion of that emanated circle with the emanating Ein Sof [20] is done primarily through that line [30], through which light from Ein Sof descends, extends and influences in that circle.

Inner light

9. That means that the entire light that is found in the circles comes only from what they receive from the line, which is regarded as a new illumination. Since that light has only three phases, it differs from the light of Ein Sof that encircles in the form of circular light.

   That is why the ARI writes that it is not in adhesion with the light of Ein Sof. This means that the form of the circular light of Keter of the circles is not the same as the light in Ein Sof. It is so because equivalence of form means adhesion in spirituality (see Part 1, Table of Questions, item 12 and Part 1, Chap 2, Inner light item 1), and the term "cause" means the causing element.

10. If its illumination had been in all four phases as is light Ein Sof, its form would have been the same and in adhesion with Ein Sof. In that state it would be totally annulled in Ein Sof and completely indistinguishable.

20. The light that expands from Ein Sof to the emanated being is called direct light. This light is tied to the emanated being by a clothing of reflected light that rises from the screen upward through a coupling by striking (this will

be explained later). This is called attachment because this reflected light that rises from the screen of phase four, from the straight line, holds and captures the upper light in the circle.

Thus, in a place where the reflected light does not clothe the upper light, the emanated being regards it as absent, because it cannot attain it without this clothing called reflected light. It is like a candle made of tallow; although its lighting force comes primarily from the tallow, still that light is not connected with it, but with the wick. When the wick burns down, the light burns out, although there is still a lot of tallow left.

30. The reason for it is that there is no screen in the circles that can raise reflected light. Without it the emanated being cannot connect with the upper light.

We learned that the vessel of the line is called a pipeline, and that it is much lower than the vessels of the circles that appeared with the first restriction, before the line appeared. That is why the ARI tells us that although the vessels of the circles are much higher than the line, they do not receive any light by themselves. Instead, they must receive all the light through the much lower line, for the above reason.

The light of Ein Sof surrounds and imparts to the circle from afar

4. **Ein Sof encircles and surrounds it from all sides (40) because it is also like a circle around it and far from it (50). The illumination of Ein Sof in the emanated beings must come only through this line. If the light had come to them through their surroundings as well, the emanated beings would have been like the Emanator Himself (60), without boundary (meaning unlimited) and ration (meaning unrestricted) (70).**

Inner light

40. We distinguish two kinds of light in each Sefira: inner light and surrounding light. The light that is clothed inside the Sefira is called inner light, and the light that cannot clothe inside it because of the boundary there, is considered to be remaining in its root. In that state the Sefira receives from it only an illumination from afar, called surrounding light.

The ARI tells us that although the circles are far from Ein Sof, meaning that there is a great disparity of form between them, still they receive from it an illumination from afar, called surrounding light. That light shines in two manners, namely in general and in particular. The term encircling relates to the general surrounding light, and the term surrounding relates to the particular surrounding light.

50. He tells us that this surrounding light that the circles receive from Ein Sof shines and surrounds them from all sides, meaning from all four phases. This means that even phase four, where the inner light does not shine, still receives an illumination from afar by means of the surrounding light from Ein Sof.

The reason for it is because Ein Sof "is also like a circle." This means that the light of Ein Sof is called circular light because it does not discriminate between the phases, and shines and fills phase four as well. Therefore, its illumination reaches phase four of the circles as well, though from afar.

60. See answer 10.

70. The restriction and the screen that were placed on phase four, so she would not receive light inside, puts a boundary on the light. It limits its expansion, which stops on the boundary of phase four. What the emanated being does receive in general, diminished by the restriction, is called a ration.

The order of expansion of the ten Sefirot of circles.
The line is called Adam Kadmon

5. That first circle is the closest to Ein Sof (80), and is called Keter of Adam Kadmon.

Afterwards this line continued to expand, extended a little and became round once more (90), turning into a second circle (100) within the first circle. This circle is called the circle of Hochma of Adam Kadmon (200).

Then it expanded further down, became round once more, and formed a third circle within the second circle. It is called the circle of Bina of Adam Kadmon (300).

It continued to expand and become round in the same manner, finally reaching the tenth circle, called the circle of Malchut of Adam Kadmon (400).

Thus we explained how the ten Sefirot (1) were emanated as ten circles, one within the other (2).

Inner light

80. We must understand the discernments in the names of the ten Sefirot. Sometimes we refer to them as four phases, sometimes we call them Yechida, Haya, Neshama, Ruach, Nefesh, and sometimes we refer to them as Keter, Hochma, Bina, Zeir Anpin (consisting of six Sefirot of its own), and Malchut.

When we refer specifically to the vessels, meaning only to the substance of the emanated being, we define the names of their ten Sefirot by means of the four phases in the will to receive. When we refer specifically to the light that clothes these vessels, we call them Nefesh, Ruach, Neshama, Haya, Yechida.

Lastly, when we refer specifically to the vessels, but want to emphasize the records of the lights that they contain when they are emptied of their lights, we then refer to them as Keter, Hochma, Bina, Zeir Anpin, and Malchut.

The origin of the above ten vessels, Keter, Hochma etc., is back in the world of restriction, before the emergence of the line, after the departure of the light of Ein Sof from the ten Sefirot, when the vessels remained devoid of lights, and they are called ten circles.

It is known that although the light departed from them, there still remained a record in each and every circle from the light that it had. In other words, a very small illumination from the entire previous light was left in every vessel. This illumination produces in the vessel a yearning, so it will not rest and will not be at peace until it draws once more all that light it had before, both in quantity and quality.

This illumination is called a record. Know that the content of the names of the ten Sefirot, Keter, Hochma, etc. define primarily the records of the light that remained in the ten vessels.

From this you learn that there is not a single desire in the worlds, or even a slight awakening of a desire, both in the upper ones as well as in the lower ones, that is not rooted in these ten Sefirot of circles. It is true even with respect to the corporeal still, vegetative, animate and speaking. However, it is clearly impossible for any desire to awaken in some essence, if a sufficient fulfillment for that desire did not appear before.

We have already clarified thoroughly in the Part 1 of this book, that the will to receive is not the first reason for the light, or for its fulfillment, as people think. Quite the contrary, the light and the fulfillment are the reason for the desire. The will to bestow that is necessarily included in the upper light created the will to receive in the emanated being, because a desire in the upper one becomes a compelling force in the lower one.

Thus, the upper light became the reason for the occurrence of the four phases of the will to receive in the emanated being. These phases are the roots of all the desires that appear in the worlds.

Therefore, how can a desire appear without a reason, meaning without that upper light that begets it? It is tantamount to stating that there is some being in the world without a father and a mother that begot it.

You must also know that the entire reality and all the creations that are destined to come into the worlds, already exist in Ein Sof. Moreover, they exist there in their full glory and perfection, as it is destined to appear in the worlds.

Thus you evidently see that all the desires that are destined to appear, already appeared and were revealed in Ein Sof. They appear there in their perfect, complete state, and it is the completeness and the fulfillment, namely the upper light, that begot and revealed these desires. It turns out that the filling of the desire precedes the occurrence of the desire that is related to that fulfillment, and indeed causes it.

Now you can thoroughly understand the issue of the records that remained in the ten Sefirot of circles after the restriction and the departure of the perfection and the fulfillments that were in the above four phases that are called ten circles. These records mean that all the desires that filled them when they were in Ein Sof, and that they now lost, remained thoroughly imprinted and "recorded" in them.

For this reason, they necessarily remained longing and yearning for the fulfillments and the perfection that they had. This is what we call records.

We said above that there cannot be any occurrence of a desire of any kind, both in the upper worlds and in the corporeal world, that is not rooted in the ten Sefirot of circles. There are two roots that precede the existence of all the worlds after the restriction: The first is when every desire already exists in its full glory and grandeur. This is the reality that exists in Ein Sof. The second is when all the desires are completely emptied of the fulfillment that was related to them in Ein Sof. This root is called the world of restriction. All the vessels and the substance of the creations extend from the world of restriction. This means that they are only empty vessels and desires that have lost their fulfillments, and all the fulfillments of these desires extend from Ein Sof.

Remember these roots well, for they are among the most necessary to remember as we continue to engage in this wisdom.

90. Do not be misled into the interpretation that the word extends refers to a place and an area. Rather, anything that gains coarseness is considered as an extension from above downward, because the refined is considered to be above, and the coarse is considered to be below.

This is evaluated according to the closeness of form to phase four: the closer to phase four, the greater the coarseness it is considered to have, and the farther from it is regarded as being more refined. "Extends a little" implies that it gained some coarseness, and the word extends relates to the light of the line.

This issue of extension appears because in each and every Sefira, there are ten inner Sefirot, both in the ten Sefirot of circles and in the ten Sefirot of straightness.

When the ten Sefirot of Keter first emerged, the line appeared only with its three upper Sefirot. These are called Rosh of Keter of straightness, and their illumination expanded to the Sefira of Keter of circles, which consist of ten Sefirot as well.

These ten Sefirot of Keter of circles surround only the first three Sefirot of the ten Sefirot of Keter of the line. After that, meaning after the ten Sefirot of circles were fully completed, the line extended a little and expanded further down, meaning produced its seven lower Sefirot in order to complete the Keter with ten Sefirot of straightness.

Thus, these seven lower Sefirot of Keter of line extended downward, meaning became coarser than the ten Sefirot of Keter of circles. The reason that there are no Sefirot of circles around these seven lower Sefirot is that the circles are higher than them, meaning more refined, and you already know that higher means more refined.

You can understand the reason for it according to the above explanation (item 30) that the Sefirot of the circles precede and are much more important than the Sefirot in the line. That is because there is no screen in the circles, and this screen in the Sefirot of the line stands in the middle of each Sefira, meaning in the last phase of the Rosh of the Sefira.

In other words, it stands at the last phase of the first three Sefirot of the ten Sefirot of straightness. These Sefirot exist in each and every Sefira of straightness, and are called the Rosh of that Sefira.

It turns out that our statement that the screen is incorporated in the Sefirot of the line is true only in the seven lower Sefirot of each Sefira below the screen. However, in the upper three, called the Rosh, there is no screen, because they are above it.

Thus, these upper three are completely identical to all the ten Sefirot of circles in that they do not have a screen. For this reason, they stand at the same phase, and you find that the ten Sefirot of each Sefira of circles are the cause of the three upper Sefirot of each Sefira of the line.

However, the seven lower Sefirot of each Sefira of the line are much worse than the circles. Because worse is also regarded as lower, they are regarded as being lower than all the ten Sefirot of circles. There is not a single phase of circles that can be in the place of these seven Sefirot, because of the importance of the circles.

Thus it has been thoroughly explained how there is a vacant space between each two Sefirot of circles, the size of the seven Sefirot of the Sefira of straightness that stands there. That is because all ten Sefirot of circles of the Sefira of Keter surround only the first three Sefirot of Keter of the line.

However, the seven lower Sefirot of the Keter of line extend lower than every ten Sefirot of Keter of circles. At the end of these seven Sefirot of Keter of the line, the first three Sefirot of Hochma of the line begin to emerge, surrounded by the ten Sefirot of Hochma of circles.

Thus, between the last phase of Keter of circles and the first phase of Hochma of circles, there is a vacant space. That is where the seven lower Sefirot of Keter of the line are, meaning where the circles do not surround them. It is likewise between Hochma and Bina too, and between each two Sefirot.

100. We must be very careful here, so as not to be confused with imaginary descriptions of space and area in the straightness and the circle, which might trip us into this notion by a slip of the tongue.

As we continue, you should remember that straight illumination means that the light enters vessels that have a screen on phase four, and that rounding illumination means that the light enters vessels that do not have a screen on phase four.

You should bear in mind that although there is no screen on phase four in the vessels of circles, still phase four cannot receive any illumination from there after the first restriction. It is so because all the light in the circles must come from the illumination of the line, which is a straight illumination (see item 30), and the light of the line does not shine in phase four at all, since it is drawn from the power of the screen.

Thus, the absence of light in phase four of circles is not because of the vessels, since they have no screen at all. Rather, it is because of the first restriction that operates on them. Because the first restriction is not regarded as a disadvantage, all four phases of the vessels of circles are of equal degree, without any differentiation of small and great. Instead, the darkness that exists in phase four is due to the light that is received from the line, and does not shine there, as aforementioned.

Now you can understand that after the circles received the light through the line, there came about a differentiation of small and great in their degrees, and also in the ten Sefirot of circles. Zeir Anpin became greater and more important than phase four, namely Malchut, since there is no light in Malchut while in Zeir Anpin there is light as it is phase three.

Similarly, the Sefira of Bina of circles has a greater light than Zeir Anpin, since it is farther from phase four than Zeir Anpin, being that she is phase two. Thus, you should remember that all these degrees are created not by the vessels, but by the light of the line that they receive.

200. It has already been explained with regards to the names of the four phases, whose root, namely the will to bestow that is included in the upper light, is called Keter. The beginning of the expansion to the emanated being, meaning phase one, is called Hochma, phase two is called Bina, phase three is called Zeir Anpin (or the six Sefirot: Hesed, Gevura, Tifferet, Netzah, Hod, Yesod), and phase four is called Malchut.

It has also been explained that only when we speak of the first substance in them, we denominate them by the names of the four phases and their root. However, if these four phases are already included in the records, as they were in the world of restriction, they are called Keter, Hochma, etc.

Now we will explain why they are called by these names: The root is called Keter [crown] because it is not clothed inside the vessels of the emanated being, but rather surrounds and crowns it from outside its own vessels. The word Keter comes from the word surrounding. Phase one is called Hochma because the wisdom of the Torah extends from her, and all the various kinds of wisdoms that exist in the world, in their final form. Our sages have already defined that name well, when they said, "Who is wise? He who sees the outcome." This means that at first glance upon a thing, the wise knows the outcome and the consequence of it. It means that he sees all the future effects that will emerge from it, to the last upshot of it.

For example, when you say that the doctor is very wise, it means that the doctor can vividly see all the possible implications that can come out of any illness. Also, when examining some remedy, he fully perceives all the ramifications of that remedy on the body of the sick.

Similarly, one who is wise in the conducts of nature, when observing some natural being, sees all the consequences that that being brings when it connects to the general reality. It is the same in every other kind of wisdom. It turns out that the meaning and definition of the name "wise," or "wisdom," refers solely to the ability to know the outcome of every detail and item in reality, to the last upshot.

From this you can also come to know the true meaning of the name Bina: All the power of Hitbonenut [lit. scrutiny/observation] so as to see the outcome of every item in reality, both in the holy Torah and in externality, extends from the Sefira of Bina, hence the name: Bina.

The name Malchut [kingship] indicates absolute authority through force and coercion that extends from it, much like one fears the king, hence the name: Malchut. The names of the rest of the Sefirot will be explained in their appropriate places.

Now we might ask: Bina should have come before Hochma, because the examination of the future and the desire to know it comes first. Moreover, they produce and cause the final perfection, meaning the knowing of the result in advance, called Hochma [wisdom].

Indeed, I have already explained to you that the order of the emanation of the worlds is the opposite of how we understand it: The fulfillment of the desire comes first and causes the appearance of the desire (see item 80). The perfection precedes and causes the appearance of the imperfection, for thus the degrees cascade and descend from Ein Sof, restriction after restriction, down to this world, the most corrupted.

300. See answer 200.

400. The first world, emanated after the restriction, is called the world of Adam Kadmon. It is also called the world of Keter. The four worlds: Atzilut, Beria, Yetzira, Assiya, clothe this Adam Kadmon.

1. Although they are but four degrees, meaning the above four phases, they still have ten Sefirot. This is because phase three, called Zeir Anpin or Tifferet, consists of six Sefirot, called: Hesed, Gevura, Tifferet, Netzah, Hod, Yesod. The reason for it will be explained in its appropriate place.

You should be aware of the precision in *Sefer Yetzira* [*Book of Creation*], Chapter 1, section 4. It states as follows: "Ten and not nine." This is something noteworthy indeed, for it has already been explained that all the illuminations of the Sefirot of the upper light, even in the circles which are completely even, do not shine in phase four, namely Malchut.

The name Sefira indicates light and vessel only when they are together, meaning when the upper light is clothed in the vessel. However, a vessel without light is not called by that name, for the name Sefira designates glowing and brightness.

Accordingly, it would have been plausible to think that Malchut isn't a Sefira at all, since the upper light does not shine in her. For this reason, the author of *Sefer Yetzira* indicates and states precisely, "They are ten Sefirot and not nine," because Malchut too is regarded as a Sefira.

The reason is that any connection of the upper light with the ten Sefirot happens specifically through the reflected light that Malchut raises by the power of the screen in her, from below upward (see item 20).

Thus, it is quite the contrary: Malchut is the most notable of the ten Sefirot, for without her, the light would not connect with the upper nine Sefirot. For this reason, Malchut is regarded as being all light (this will be explained further in its place).

2. (See Part 1, Inner light, Chapter 1, item 100)

The line connects all the circles together

6. **What connects all the circles together (3) is that thin line that expands from Ein Sof and passes (4) and descends (5) and extends (6) from one circle to the next, down to the very last of them (7).**

    The light and the abundance that each of them needs extends through that line.

Inner light

3. You have already learned that there is a cessation and a vacant place between each Sefira in the ten Sefirot of circles, as the size of the seven Sefirot of the illumination of straightness in that Sefira (see item 90).

    However, there is no cessation at all in the ten Sefirot of the line. They begin at Ein Sof and expand to the middle point, which is phase four, called Malchut, the lowest point there is.

    Thus, there is no cessation whatsoever between the first ten Sefirot that expanded from Ein Sof as a straight line, also called ten Sefirot of Adam Kadmon. That is why the ARI says that the Sefirot of the line connect the ten Sefirot of circles as well. The seven lower Sefirot in each Sefira of straightness connect the ten Sefirot in the upper Sefira of circles with the ten Sefirot of the lower Sefira of circles.

    The illumination of the ten Sefirot of Hochma of circles that receive from the upper three of Hochma of straightness necessarily passes through the seven lower Sefirot of the Sefira of Keter of straightness. That is because GAR of Hochma of straightness must receive from the seven Sefirot of Keter of straightness, and impart to the ten Sefirot of Hochma of circles.

In the end, the seven lower Sefirot of Keter of straightness connect the ten Sefirot of Keter of circles with the ten Sefirot of Hochma of circles. The same conduct applies between Hochma and Bina and so on and so forth.

4. The line, which is an illumination of straightness, seemingly breaks through the tops of the circles, passes through the circles, descending and extending downward to the Sium, meaning to the middle point. However, this is certainly not about a place and an area.

To understand this, we must know that there is no occurrence of light in the worlds, both the upper ones and the lower ones, that does not extend from Ein Sof above the restriction. It must cascade and pass through all the degrees and worlds between that world, where the receiver of the revelation of that light is in, and Ein Sof above the restriction.

You already know that there is no absence in the spiritual. Thus, it is impossible to say that that appearance, meaning the renewed light that cascades down through the degrees, becomes absent in the first degree when it moves to the next, and becomes absent in the second when it comes to the third, as corporeal objects do when they move from place to place.

This is utterly impossible because there is no absence in spirituality. Instead, it necessarily stays in each degree as it passes through it. Moving between the degrees is like lighting one candle from another, where the first does not diminish its light in any way.

Thus, the appearance of the light that comes to a certain degree in the world of Assiya, is first given to all the degrees in the worlds between Ein Sof above the restriction and the receiver that is in the world of Assiya.

It turns out that the illumination of the straight line must pass through the vessels of circles because the vessels of circles preceded the line; they appeared immediately with the restriction. However, the vessels of straightness appeared later, with the line, which is why this illumination that passes between them never leaves there, as we have mentioned "There is no absence in the spiritual."

You should also know that regarding the cascading of the light from place to place, there are two manners of remaining in the places of the passing: The first is "Permanent stay": This means that it mingles and connects with the light that is already in the degree, and they become one, as though they were always one. And there is a second manner, which is only a "passing stay," meaning that it does not mingle and unite with the light of that place and they become one. Instead, it exists there as a discernment of its own.

The ARI tells us that the light of the line that passes through the degrees of circles is not from the manner of a "permanent stay," but from the manner of a "passing stay." This teaches us that it does not mingle with the light of the circles to form one discernment, but is there as a discernment of its own. This is the meaning of the ARI's precision regarding the word "passes."

The reason for it is that the light in the line comes before the light in the circles, because the circles receive their lights only from the light of the line. That is why the light of the line is far more important than the light of the circles, and that is why it does not mingle with the light of circles.

The light of the line is called the light of Ruach, and the light of the circles is called the light of Nefesh.

5. Any expansion of the upper light to the emanated being is regarded as a descent. It means that as it expands it also becomes coarser. You already know that the more refined is regarded as above, and the coarser is regarded as below. Because the light gains coarseness as it expands, it also descends from above downward.

   The reason for the increased coarseness that the light gains because it expands is that it expands by the order of the four phases: It begins with phase one until it comes and strikes the screen in phase four. It gains coarseness because phase one is the most refined, then comes phase two, and so on until phase four, the coarsest (see Part 1, Chap 1, item 50).

6. The illumination of straightness is expressed in the word "extends" and the illumination of circles in the words "becomes round" (see item 90).

7. Meaning phase four in the circles, called the "middle point." It is also called "the material sphere in this world."

   The phase of Atzilut in the world of Adam Kadmon expanded first to this world. However, after the second restriction had been performed, called the world of Nekudim, the Sium of Atzilut Adam Kadmon rose to the point of the next world, whose place is considered to be above the world of Beria, as we will explain in its place.

   Each world and each Sefira consist of ten inner Sefirot. Inside each Sefira there are another ten inner Sefirot, and so on and so forth. The Sefirot of circles envelop each other like onionskins

7. **Each and every world has its own ten Sefirot. Each and every Sefira in each and every world consists of its own inner ten Sefirot (8). They are like onion-skins, one within the other (9), as in pictures of wheels in geometry books.**

Inner light

8. You can understand the reason for the above incorporation of the Sefirot according to the famous rule that "there is no absence in spirituality," and any light that passes from one place to another retains its place forever in every phase it passes through (see item 4). Because each inferior Sefira emanates from a higher Sefira by way of cause and effect, the inferior one is considered to be passing through the superior one.

Consequently, all the Sefirot are necessarily incorporated in each other. For example, when the first two Sefirot appear, namely Keter and Hochma, the light of Hochma is compelled to exit Ein Sof, from which everything is extended. Afterwards, the light of Hochma must pass through the Sefira of Keter before it reaches the Sefira of Hochma, because Keter caused its emergence.

Because the Sefira of Hochma passed there, it acquired its place there, and now there are two Sefirot in Keter, namely Keter and Hochma. Similarly, after all ten Sefirot of the upper light emerged from above downward to Malchut, all nine Sefirot below Keter were compelled to pass through Keter. It is so because it was the first reason for the emergence of them all.

Hence, they all acquired their place there, as there is no absence in the spiritual. It means that all nine lower Sefirot are necessarily present in Keter itself, too, since they passed through there.

By the same principal there are also nine Sefirot in Hochma, because the eight Sefirot below it were compelled to pass through her, as in Keter. Also, there are eight Sefirot in Bina for the above reason, and seven Sefirot in Hesed and so on. In Malchut there is only one because she is the lowest.

We also know that Malchut raises ten Sefirot of reflected light from her upward, which clothe the ten Sefirot of the upper light, called the ten Sefirot of direct light. This reflected light is called the light of Malchut, because she has no other light.

This reflected light is referred to in all the places as ten Sefirot that rise from below upward (see Inner Observation, Part 2, Chap 6, item 66). It is written there that Malchut is regarded as the Keter of those ten Sefirot, because she is the reason for their emergence.

The one adjacent to her is called Hochma, and the third degree from her is called Bina, etc. In this manner, the more refined is also the smaller, until the real Keter receives only the Malchut of this reflected light.

From this you can deduce that these ten Sefirot from below upwards are all found in Malchut, because they pass through Malchut, as Malchut is their root. Thus, all of them acquired their place in Malchut, and you find that Malchut too consists of ten Sefirot.

Nine Sefirot pass through Yesod of reflected light, and thus there are ten Sefirot in Yesod: one from the upper light from above downward, and nine Sefirot of reflected light from below upward, which must pass through it.

The same manner applies in the ten Sefirot of Hod: two Sefirot from above downward, meaning the light of Hod and the light of Yesod that passes through it, and eight Sefirot from below upward. The same applies to the ten Sefirot of Netzah: three from above downward, and seven from below upward. The rest adhere to the same pattern.

Finally, after the emergence of the ten Sefirot of the upper light and the ten Sefirot of the reflected light, each of them necessarily contains ten complete Sefirot. The same pattern applies to every single inner item in them and every single item in the inner items, and so on and so forth, indefinitely. This manner of the above-mentioned incorporation is necessary, and there is nothing more to add here, and look in Inner Observation, where we elaborated on the subject extensively.

9. Meaning every upper one surrounds its lower one from all sides equally, without any discrimination of degrees (see above item 50).

The closer the circle to Ein Sof, the higher and finer it is considered. Because this world is at the middle point, the farthest from Ein Sof, it is utterly corporeal

8. **In each and every circle within each and every world in the space, the closer** (10) **it is to the light of Ein Sof, the higher and finer it is. You find that this earthly, material world, is the middle point, inside all the circles, within the middle of that entire space and the vacant air.**

It is also utterly distanced from Ein Sof, farther from all the worlds. That is why it is so corporeal and utterly materialized, although it is the middle point, inside all the circles.

Inner light

10. You already know that the term "close" does not refer to a place, but to proximity of form. You also know that there are four phases of disparity of form, which consist of the ten Sefirot of circles from Ein Sof to the middle point.

    The middle point is phase four, the coarsest of them all, and the first circle, called Keter, is regarded as instilling the root of these above four phases. Naturally, the circle of Keter is the most refined of all the circles as its form is the closest to Ein Sof. Phase one, which is slightly coarser, is farther from Ein Sof than Keter.

    Phase two is even coarser and is therefore farther from Ein Sof than phase one. Finally, the middle point, which has more coarseness than all of them, is regarded as the farthest from Ein Sof.

    We should not wonder about what we have said above (in Part 1, Chap 1, item 100), that there is no above and below in the circles, because here we refer to the circles after they received the illumination of the line inside them. It is that which created in them the above and below and all the other characteristics of the line.

CHAPTER TWO

Explains the ten Sefirot of straightness, their emergence and evolution and what they contain. This chapter contains seven issues:

1. The order of the emergence of the ten Sefirot of straightness. 2. The five parts in the soul of the lower Adam: Nefesh, Ruach, Neshama, Haya, Yechida. 3. There is surrounding light, inner light, external vessel and inner vessel in both the circles and the straightness. 4. The light of circles is the light of Nefesh, and the light of straightness is the light of Ruach. The circles were emanated first, and the straightness next. 5. Arich Anpin of circles shines for Abba and Ima of the circles in the form of windows, from the three lines – right, left and middle in him. The light extends from them to all the circles, and therefore, every detail that is in the straightness also exists in the circles. 6. Adam Kadmon extends from Ein Sof until the end of Atzilut, contains all the worlds, and we are not permitted to delve into it. 7. We do not delve into the circles, but only into the straightness;

The order of the emergence of ten Sefirot of straightness

1. **Now we will explain the second discernment of the ten Sefirot, being the light of straightness, which is similar to three lines in the form of the upper Adam. The circles expand from above downward through the aforementioned line, which also expands in straightness from above downward, from the beginning of the upper top (1) of the highest circle, to below the bottom of the end of all the circles from above downward. It consists of ten Sefirot, like the image of a straight Adam (2), upright (3), consisting of 248 organs (4) depicted as three lines: right, left and middle. He consists of ten Sefirot overall, and each and every Sefira is divided into ten inner Sefirot and so on and so forth indefinitely.**

Inner light

1. In each world or Sefira, the Keter is regarded as the top of that world or Sefira. Malchut in each world or Sefira is regarded as the bottom of that world or Sefira. The upper circle is the Sefira of Keter, and the top of that Keter is the Keter of the ten Sefirot of that Keter.

2. The clothing of the Mochin is called Tzelem [image, semblance], from the word Tzel [shade]. The illumination of straightness, which consists of the first

three Sefirot, is called Adam, because it receives GAR clothed in Tzelem. This is a long issue and here is not the place to elaborate on it.

3. The Rosh of every Sefira and Partzuf consists of the first three Sefirot: Keter, Hochma, Bina. The seven lower Sefirot: Hesed, Gevura, Tifferet, Netzah, Hod, Yesod, Malchut in each Sefira and Partzuf are regarded as the Guf of that Sefira and Partzuf.

When they are in the right order, meaning when the lights of GAR are in the vessels of GAR and the lights of ZAT are in the vessels of ZAT, the Partzuf is considered to be in an "upright" state. However, if the lights of Guf are clothed in the vessels of GAR instead of clothing the lights that should clothe there, then that Partzuf is not considered to be "upright."

It is so because in that state, the Rosh is not more important than the Guf, since even the Rosh uses only the lights of the Guf. This state is called the lowering of the Rosh, in which the Rosh is on the same level as the Guf.

4. There are 248 discriminations of Hesed in the upper Partzuf, from which extend 248 organs in the lower ones (elaborated in the *Mishnah, Ohalot*).

Five parts in the soul of the lower Adam: Nefesh, Ruach, Neshama, Haya, Yechida

2. **There are five types of light in the lower Adam (5): Nefesh, Ruach, Neshama, Haya, Yechida (6). They form five levels (7), one above the other. This is the meaning of the five repetitions of the verse, "Bless the Lord, O my soul, etc." as mentioned in Masechet Berachot (page 10, 71), which represent the five phases of the soul.**

Inner light

5. There is not an essence in all the worlds, both in the Upper Worlds, as well as in this world, that do not consist of the above ten Sefirot, being the four above mentioned phases and their root. That is what he means by saying that these five phases are also found in the lower Adam of this world.

6. The vessels in the ten Sefirot are called: Keter, Hochma, Bina, Zeir Anpin, and Malchut, and the lights in them are called: Yechida, Haya, Neshama, Ruach, Nefesh. It is written (Midrash Raba, 82, 26), that the light of Yechida clothes the vessel of Keter, and the light of Haya clothes the vessel of Hochma, the light of Neshama clothes the vessel of Bina and the light of Ruach clothes the vessel of Zeir Anpin. The light of Nefesh clothes the vessel of Malchut.

7. You have already learned that the degrees are differentiated according to their refinement and coarseness. The term "above" refers to a greater refinement than the "lower" degree.

There is surrounding light, inner light, external vessel and inner vessel in both circles and straightness

3. **Each of the ten Sefirot of circles has all the above discernments, namely lights and vessels (8). The light is divided (9) into inner light and surrounding light, and the vessel is divided (10) into externality and internality. The ten Sefirot of straightness in the image of Adam have all those discernments too.**

Inner light

8. The lights are NRNHY and the vessels are KHB ZON.

9. The spiritual division happened due to the disparity of form that was innovated there (see Part 1, Chap 1, item 30). Higher than another means more refined than the other, and lower than another implies being coarser than the other. It is in the disparity of form of this coarseness that one is separated and exits from the other, becoming lower than him.

It is known that the lights are imparted from any upper one to its lower one. Because of that, the lower one must receive the abundance in its highest and most refined phase, while the upper one imparts the abundance only from its lowest and coarsest phase.

Thus, the form of the light that comes from the upper one equalizes with the form of the vessel in the lower one, since the coarsest and crudest phase in the upper one is equal to the finest and most refined phase in the lower one. It turns out that the lower one cannot receive all the light that belongs to it, but only a very small part, as much as its most refined vessel can receive. Its other phases, which are not that refined, must remain without their appropriate light, because of their disparity of form from the upper one that imparts to them.

For this reason, we find that the light that belongs to the lower one is divided into two phases: The first is the small amount of light that it receives from the upper one inside its uppermost vessel. That kind of light that it receives is called the inner light in the lower one. The second is the full amount of light that belongs to the phases that remain in the lower one and cannot receive due to their disparity of form from the upper one. That full amount is regarded as remaining in the upper one and not descending to the lower one. It is called surrounding light because it surrounds the lower one, meaning shines on it from afar, though it is not clothed in it; rather it is a diminished and far illumination. This distant illumination can purify the coarseness in the lower one until all the phases in the lower one equalize in form with the upper one. Then it will be able to receive the full measure of the light that belongs to it. This state is called the entrance of surrounding lights. It means that the surrounding lights entered and clothed the vessels of the lower one that were refined, turning all of them into inner light.

10. Because the lights were divided into inner light and surrounding light there are now two kinds of reception in the vessel. They are: reception inside the vessel, and reception in the externality of the vessel (see Part 1, Table of Topics, item 102).

The inner light is received inside the vessel, and the surrounding light that refines it from its coarseness is regarded as received through the externality of the vessel, meaning without clothing inside the vessel.

This division of the vessel to internality and externality is determined according to the coarseness and refinement in the vessel. That is because only its coarseness is worthy of receiving the inner light, because the vessel of reception of the emanated being consists primarily of phase four.

Indeed, the first three phases are not qualified to receive, but cause phase four to appear. For this reason, each vessel is regarded as having its own four phases in the vessel, and the light appears primarily in its phase four. That is why she is called the internality of the vessel and its interior, where the abundance is found.

The three phases that only make phase four appear in the vessel, while they do not receive themselves, are regarded as encircling phase four from the outside. It is like the coarseness of a wall of a corporeal vessel that consists of four layers, one surrounding the other. Everything is received only in the interior of the vessel, meaning in the interior crust, while the other three crusts of the walls of the vessel only strengthen the interior crust so that it has the strength to tolerate its filling.

We should understand spirituality in much the same way, namely that phase four is the primary phase that holds the abundance in the vessel. The first three phases are the reasons for the appearance of the full power of phase four, until she is suitable to hold the abundance, while for themselves they are not qualified to sustain the inner light.

They are called the externality of the vessel because they are excluded from receiving the inner light. Phase three is the externality of phase four; phase two is the externality of phase three; phase one is the externality of phase two and surrounds all the other phases.

Outside all of them there is yet another external phase, without any coarseness, which is the root of all four phases in the vessel. Know that this totally refined phase is the vessel of reception for the surrounding light. The reason for it is that its wondrous purity enables it to receive the illumination of the surrounding light, although it comes from afar.

We now learned about the division of the vessel. Its internality, meaning its coarsest phase, namely phase four in the vessel, receives the inner light. Its externality, meaning its most refined phase, the root phase in the vessel, receives the surrounding light from afar. We should also not ask why phase four is not worthy of receiving because of the power of the restriction and the screen in her, as we are concerned only with the reflected light that rises from phase four (see Inner Observation).

The light of circles is the light of Nefesh, and the light of straightness is the light of Ruach. The circles were emanated first, and the straightness next

4. **The difference between the circles and the straightness relates to the fact that the ten Sefirot of circles (20) are regarded as the light of Nefesh. They have inner light and surrounding light, internal and external. They consist of ten Sefirot of vessels, each consisting of internality and externality. There are also ten Sefirot of lights, where each light consists of inner light and surrounding light.**

However, the ten Sefirot of straightness are regarded as the light called light of Ruach (30), which is a higher degree than the degree of Nefesh. They too consist of inner light and surrounding light, and have ten Sefirot of vessels, in each of which there are internality and externality. Obviously, the Nefesh was emanated first, and the Ruach next.

Inner light

20. All the Sefirot that can only receive lights and have no ability to bestow upon others, the light in them is called light of Nefesh. It has already been explained that all the light in the circles must be received from the light of the line (see Part 2, Chap 1, item 30).

The reason is that the upper light cannot permeate the vessels except by a coupling with the screen that raises reflected light. That is because this reflected light connects the light with the vessels (see Part 2, Chap 1, item 30).

Consequently, the upper light does not connect with the vessels that do not have that screen and they cannot impart unto others from above downward. Instead, they can only receive light from the previous degree, from below upward, for their own sustenance. This light is called the light of Nefesh.

Thus, because there is no screen in the above vessels of circles, the upper light cannot permeate them, and they must receive light from the line, but even that is for their mere sustenance, and not to bestow. For this reason, the light in the circles is called the light of Nefesh.

30. The ten Sefirot of Ruach are regarded as bestowing. For this reason, the light of Ruach is denoted as male light, meaning it bestows. However, the ten Sefirot of Nefesh are called female light, meaning they receive and cannot bestow.

For this reason, the ten Sefirot of the light of the line are regarded as the ten Sefirot of Ruach, indicating that they are regarded as male light, namely bestowing, as we've explained above. The Ruach is regarded as higher than the Nefesh because it bestows upon the Nefesh.

Arich Anpin of the circles shines for Abba and Ima of the circles in the form of windows, from the three lines – right, left and middle in him. The light extends from them to all the circles, and therefore, every detail that is in the straightness also exists in the circles

5. **Even when the ten Sefirot are regarded as circles** (40) **one within the other, they already have all the forms of reception of the abundance that exist in the line of straightness** (50)**. It is so because the circle of Keter (called Arich Anpin after the correction** (60)**) has one foramen and window** (70) **on the right hand side of the circle** (80)**. From there the light of Arich comes to the circle of Abba and shines to it** (90)**.**

There is yet another window on the left hand side of the circle of Arich. The light reaches the left hand side of the circle of Abba, which is inside it, punctures it and makes a window in it (100).

The light extends from there to the circle of Ima inside the circle of Abba and shines in it. Thus, the light that passes in the left of the circle of Abba is not for Abba himself; it only passes there (200), but the illumination is primarily for Ima.

It turns out that Arich Anpin shines for Abba and Ima together, just like their straightness. Even though they are one circle within the other, they still have straight lines, (300) right, left and middle, in the windows in them.

The light extends from there in ten Sefirot of circles, through completely straight lines, in every detail in the ten Sefirot of the straight line of Ruach.

Inner light

40. Meaning the five degrees KHB ZON do not extend in straightness, meaning one below the other, from refined to coarse, but rather the five degrees are equal, and not one below the other, namely with greater coarseness. Of course, there is a differentiation of cause and effect between them, because they do emerge from one another and are drawn from one another.

For example, Hochma came from Keter, Bina from Hochma and Zeir Anpin from Bina, and Malchut from Zeir Anpin (see Inner light, Part 1, Chap 1, item 50). However, that above differentiation of cause and effect is defined by their being one inside the other.

In that state, each reason causes its consequence: Hochma is caused by Keter and Bina is caused by Hochma, etc. Thus, one within the other means that one is the result of the other. However, there is no differentiation of up or down between them whatsoever (see Part 1, Chap 1, item 100)

50. Because that is the impression of the light from the vessel in which it is clothed. Even when it leaves there to go to another, it does not change its conduct from the previous vessel. Thus, while the light in the line was in straightness, it extended and descended, one below the other, meaning gained coarseness in a gradual order because of the screen that is found there (see Part 2, Chap 1, item 6).

Therefore, even after it had left there and came to the ten Sefirot of circles, which do not have a screen, and after it was compelled to become round in them, it still did not change its conduct of expansion from degree to degree. For example, when the light of the line comes to the Sefira of Keter, it becomes round there, meaning it adopts the shape of the vessel, in which case there is no distinction of above and below.

However when the light expands from the circle of Keter to the circle of Hochma, it does not become round, but extends in straightness, distinguishing between above and below. Consequently, the Sefira of the circle of Hochma stands below the circle of Keter and consists of greater coarseness, because their form is not the same.

In much the same way, when light moves from Hochma to Bina, it extends in straightness. It is therefore considered that Bina is below Hochma, meaning it is coarser than Hochma, and this is also the rule for all the Sefirot.

The ten Sefirot of circles are of equal form, without discriminations of above and below in the vessels. However, there is still a discrimination of above and below in them because they do receive the abundance by means of the ten Sefirot of the line of straightness.

60. After the four worlds ABYA were formed, each Sefira became a complete Partzuf with Rosh, Toch, Sof. Because of that they were given different names: the Partzuf that originated from Keter was named Arich Anpin, the Partzuf that originated from Hochma was named Abba, and the Partzuf that originated from Bina was named Ima. The Partzuf that was made from the six Sefirot HGT NHY was named Zeir Anpin and the Partzuf that originated from Malchut was named Nukva [female]. The meaning of these names will be explained in their places.

70. You already know that because of the light of the ten Sefirot of the line that is received in the circles, all the phases of straightness are necessarily imprinted in the circles as well (see item 50). This phase in the line, which is called screen, whose reflected light connects the upper light in the vessels, is imprinted in the circles as well, but without its coarseness.

This is because this coarseness cannot rise from a lower degree to a higher one whatsoever, because of the fact that the upper one does not have the same coarseness as the lower one, and that is what makes it "upper." Only the "gap" that this screen reveals in the lower degree (in the ten Sefirot of straightness) rises from the screen of the line of straightness and is imprinted in the circles.

This "gap" from the screen is called a window. As a window is placed in a room to bring the light into that room, so this screen reveals the ability of the reflected light to connect the light with the emanated being. Thus, if the screen disappeared, the light would also disappear from the emanated being and he would remain in the dark, as if the window had been shut.

Thus, when we refer only to the gap from the screen, excluding its coarseness, we refer to it as a window or a foramen.

80. This means that it was imprinted in the right and left that operated in the ten Sefirot of straightness.

90. The above-mentioned window created a discrimination of extension and descent of light there. It means that it gradually gained coarseness, and thus each lower degree became coarser than its preceding one.

The text "**From there the light of Arich comes to the circle of Abba and shines to it**," means that because of the window the light received coarseness and descended to Abba of circles. In other words, Hochma was lowered and is no longer equal to Keter of circles, as it was before they received the light of straightness through the window. The same principle applies in Bina below Hochma.

100. This window was made in the Sefirot together with the descent of the light to it from the upper circle. It means that then this light imprinted in it the screen that is contained in it. That is why it is considered that the light punctured it and made a window in it.

200. Has already been thoroughly explained above (Part 2, Chap 1, item 4).

300. The light descends from circle to circle by way of extension in straightness, in straight lines. However, this is not regarded as an actual correction of the three lines that descend from the screen and contain the male light with which to bestow upon others. These lines of circles have no power for bestowal because they come down as windows. The windows suffice only for receiving the light for themselves, but not to impart it to others. This is the rule: "Without a screen, there is no male light, only female light, meaning light of Nefesh."

Adam Kadmon extends from Ein Sof to the end of Atzilut, contains all the worlds, and we are not permitted to engage in it

6. This Adam Kadmon (400) extends from one end to the other (1), from the upper end to the lower end throughout the above space of Atzilut. All the worlds are contained in that Adam, but we have no permission whatsoever to delve and speak of this Adam's internality and self (2).

Inner light

400. We should not wonder at the use of the name Adam. It is written (Midrash Raba, Bereshit 27): "Rabbi Yudah said: 'Great is the power of prophets who resemble a form with its Maker, as it is written: 'And I heard the voice of a man between the banks of Ulai etc.' 'and upon the likeness of the throne was a likeness as the appearance of a man upon it above.'" The reason will be explained in its appropriate place.

1. It means that it connects everything from Ein Sof, the most refined of all the worlds down to the middle point, the coarsest phase in all the worlds. Thus, the entire reality before us, upper ones and lower ones, are its branches, which have cascaded from it, hang on it, and clothe it. This is why it connects all of them.

2. The internality, meaning the light of Ein Sof that is clothed in Him, and His self, is considered the GAR in Him. It has already been explained

(Introduction, item 27) that we have no permission to speak of any discernment of GAR in any degree or Partzuf, even in the world of Assiya. However, we are permitted to engage in the ZAT, even the ZAT of GAR of Adam Kadmon.

The circles came out first, and the straightness next. We do not engage in the circles, but only in the straightness

7. **In the beginning, the ten Sefirot came out through the circle (3), one within the other. Afterwards, within the circles, they extended in straightness as an image of one Adam, throughout the length of the above-mentioned circles (4). Still, we have no dealings with the circles (5) but only with the straightness.**

Inner light

3. It has already been explained that the circles appeared immediately after the restriction and the departure of the light. After that the straightness appeared in such a way that the circles were regarded as the cause and the reason for the light of the line. Because of that they are also considered to be preceding it.

4. Meaning, from the top end to the bottom end. Observe, for example, an imaginary corporeal length. Doing that will bring you to know its spiritual root. We understand an imaginary length by three discernments: its top end, its bottom end, and the distance between them.

You can distinguish a spiritual length precisely by the same way: first, you find its bottom end, meaning its last and coarsest phase, such that there is no lower coarseness than that. From knowing the bottom end, you will immediately find the top end too, because the measure of the coarseness at the bottom, is also the measure of the level of the reflected light (see Inner Observation, item 86).

For example, the coarseness of phase four within phase four reaches the level of the Keter of Keter; the coarseness of phase three within phase four reaches only as high as the Keter of Hochma, and phase two within phase four reaches only as high as the Keter of Bina, etc. Thus, by knowing the bottom end, the top end immediately becomes known as well.

Once you know both ends of a degree, you naturally know the distance between them too. That is because a spiritual distance means a disparity of form between two discernments.

The measure of the disparity of form determines the distance between them. For example, if the bottom end is phase one within phase four, then the top end reaches only as high as the Keter of ZA. In that instance, the distance is not so great.

But if the bottom end is phase two, then the top end will be the degree of Keter of Bina. Thus, the distance would be of two levels of coarseness, which are phase one and phase two.

If the bottom end consists of coarseness of phase three within phase four, then the top end would be the Keter of Hochma. In this case, the distance would be that of three levels of coarseness, and so on by the same way.

5. This is because the circles surround the first three Sefirot of straightness (see Part 2, Chap 1, item 90). It is known that their vessels are far superior to GAR of straightness. However, you already know that we are forbidden to study and speak of the GAR. For this reason we have no permission to study the circles.

INNER OBSERVATION

Circles and straightness; containing ten chapters

CHAPTER ONE

Explains the ten Sefirot of circles; contains six issues: 1. Circles are regarded as GAR. 2. In the Sefirot of circles, the more external is the more important. Conversely, in the Sefirot of straightness, the more internal is more important. 3. Two kinds of reception in the vessels: A. Through their internality, B. through their externality. 4. Phase four cannot appear unless the previous three phases cause it to appear. 5. The four phases are like four layers in the walls of a vessel, one on top of the other. The abundance is received in the inner layer. 6. The greater the coarseness of the screen, the higher the level of the reflected light that it raises. There are five levels.

The circles are regarded as GAR.

1. The ARI spoke very little of the ten Sefirot of circles. Even the words he did say seem to be filled with contradictions. However, it is impossible to elaborate on them because they are regarded as the first three Sefirot, which we are forbidden to delve into.

   Nevertheless, the little that the ARI did write should be explained elaborately, enough to accomplish the goal that the ARI had aspired for, meaning as much as it is necessary to understand the interconnections in this wisdom.

In the ten Sefirot of circles, the outer is the more important.

2. We shall begin with a general understanding of the matters. The ARI divides reality into two discernments: circles and straightness. This means that all the Partzufim in the five worlds, Adam Kadmon, ABYA and this world, consists of ten Sefirot of circles and ten Sefirot of straightness.

   We saw that in the Sefirot of circles, more external is better, and more internal is worse. The uppermost circle, the closest to the surrounding Ein Sof that encircles the entire reality, whose name is Keter, is the best among them.

   Inside it there is a second circle, called Hochma, which is worse than Keter through the innermost sphere, which is this world, the worst of all the circles, which is darkness without any light, and full of filth. Thus, the more internal the circle is, the worse it is, and the more external the circle is, the better it is.

In the ten Sefirot of straightness, the inner vessel is more important.

3. It is the opposite with the Sefirot of straightness, in which the more internal is better. That is because the first and innermost ten Sefirot of straightness are the ten Sefirot of the world of Adam Kadmon. They are called the line that expands from Ein Sof and extends almost as low as this world, but without touching it.

Its externality is clothed by the ten Sefirot of straightness of the second world, called the world of Atzilut, whose merit is lower than that of the world of Adam Kadmon. The externality of the world of Atzilut is clothed by the ten Sefirot of straightness of the world of Beria, which is worse than the world of Atzilut. It follows in the same manner until the ten Sefirot of straightness of the world of Assiya, the worst of all the worlds, which clothes the externality of all the worlds.

Thus, in the Sefirot of straightness, more external is worse, and inner is better, the opposite of the ten Sefirot of circles. Indeed, a profound and great concept is presented here in this oppositeness between the Sefirot of circles and the Sefirot of straightness, which should be studied thoroughly.

Two kinds of reception in the vessel: A. through its interior,
B. through its exterior.

4. You already know about the middle point in Ein Sof, where the restriction took place and the light departed from that point and became an empty space (see Part 1, Chap 1, item 50). It explains that it is called the "the middle point" to indicate that it does not receive through its internality and Toch, but only through its externality, from its surroundings. It receives the light without any limitation and measuring because the one that receives from the externality does not limit the light.

As a result, we have two kinds of reception in the vessels: The first kind is receiving through its exterior, and the second kind is receiving through its interior. We must thoroughly understand with which internality and externality we are engaging here, as this certainly does not refer to a place or an area by which you might imagine externality and internality.

The first three phases only cause the appearance of phase four, but they cannot receive; they are like four layers in the wall of the vessel.

5. You already know that the term "spiritual vessel" refers to the desire in the emanated being to receive its abundance from Ein Sof. Also, you already

know that this desire has four phases, one below the other. In other words, this vessel, being the above will to receive, can perform its task only after it gradually passes through the above four phases.

The first phase is a very faint desire; phase two is greater than phase one, etc. Phase four is the full measure of the desire as it should be for the final completion of the vessel.

The reason for it has already been explained (see Part 1, Chap 1, item 50). Since the form of this will to receive is absolutely opposite to the will to bestow in the light of Ein Sof, it cannot appear all at once, but only gradually. It starts from the will to bestow in the root, called Keter, continues to the coarser which is a little different from it, being phase one. From there it continues to the coarser, namely phase two, and so on by the same way until phase four, which is absolutely opposite to the form of the light. She, specifically, is able to serve as a vessel in the emanated being.

However, the will to receive in the previous three phases is not disclosed enough to serve as a vessel for reception. Thus only phase four is regarded as the vessel for reception in the emanated being, and for this reason, it is called the internality and the Toch of the emanated being. Phase three in the desire is considered to be outside phase four; phase two is outside phase three, and phase one is outside phase two. The phase of Keter is the most external.

Like a corporeal vessel that contains four layers one on top of the other, the abundance in that vessel is certainly received in the fourth, innermost layer. The three more external layers that surround it are only there as support for the innermost fourth layer. Here too, the light is received only in phase four, while the three first phases are exterior to it, present only because it is impossible for phase four to appear at once, but only by cascading, as we have explained above.

Internality and coarseness are the same; externality and refinement are the same too.

6. Now you have thoroughly learned about the internality and externality that we must distinguish in every vessel. Because there are four phases in every vessel, the last of them is called the Toch and the internality of that vessel; it is the essence of the reception in the vessel. The phases that precede it are meant to reveal the final phase, and are therefore regarded as the externality of the vessel.

The farther the degree is from the last phase, the more external it is considered to be. You should also know that phase one is more refined than phase two, and phase four is the coarsest. It turns out that internality and coarseness are one and the same thing and the reason that phase four is regarded as the one that receives the abundance is because she is the most coarse.

Similarly, externality and refinement are one and the same, because her desire is faint and refined, and thus closer to the Emanator. For this reason, it is the most external, meaning the farthest from reception, which is internality and Toch.

Closeness to and remoteness from the Emanator are evaluated according to the measure of reception in the emanated being.

7. This is what the ARI wrote about the Sefirot of circles, that the more external is better and closer to the Emanator. That is because the phase of the root, called Keter, is the most refined and closest in form to Ein Sof, meaning closest to the Emanator. It designates her as the most external, meaning farthest from the Toch and the internality, meaning reception.

   After her comes phase one, which is more internal than the Keter, meaning closer to reception. Phase two is more internal than her, meaning closer to phase four, being the phase of reception. Thus, phase four is the actual internality, meaning the abundance is received in her. For this reason, her form is also the farthest from the Emanator.

8. In the ten Sefirot of straightness there is the matter of reflected light that rises from the coupling of the screen with the upper light. The amount of reflected light is measured by the coarseness in the screen that performs the coupling with the upper light. The greatest coarseness in the screen, namely phase four, reveals a full measure of ten Sefirot, as high as Keter. If the amount of coarseness in the screen is less by one phase, consisting only of phase three, it reveals ten Sefirot that have the level of Hochma, and the Keter is missing. If all it has is the coarseness of phase two, it only reveals ten Sefirot, where each has the level of Bina, without the degrees of Keter and Hochma. If the screen has only the coarseness of phase one, it only reveals ten Sefirot where each has only the level of Zeir Anpin. Finally, if the screen is refined and hasn't even the coarseness of phase one, it does not reveal any level, only the discernment of Malchut. The reason for this will be explained below, in part three.

CHAPTER TWO

Explains the five primary discernments in the five worlds of AK and ABYA; contains six issues: 1. The five worlds called AK and ABYA, which are differentiated by the four levels of coarseness in the screen. 2. The upper one bestows upon the lower one only through the coarsest, and the lower one receives only through the most refined. 3. The reason for the departure of the light from the three phases that preceded phase four, though only phase four was restricted. 4. Explanation of coupling by striking. 5. What is the reflected light that rises from below upward through coupling by striking? 6. The reflected light that rises from the coupling by striking becomes a vessel of reception for the upper light instead of phase four.

The differentiation between the five worlds of AK and ABYA is primarily according to the coarseness of their screen. In AK it is phase four.

9. Know that what distinguishes the five worlds of AK and ABYA of straightness from one another is the measure of the coarseness of the screen of their vessels. The screen of the vessels in the world of Adam Kadmon is very coarse, meaning the coarseness of phase four, the greatest coarseness in all the worlds.

   Therefore, its ten Sefirot are complete, meaning all of them are at the degree of Keter, the closest to Ein Sof, which is the first and most important world, extending from end to end: from Ein Sof to this world.

   For this reason, it is also considered to be positioned in the internality of all the worlds, for you already know that internality and coarseness are one and the same. Because the screen in the vessels of Adam Kadmon is of phase four, meaning with the greatest coarseness, it is therefore the most interior.

   The world of Atzilut is from the screen of phase three.
   Therefore, it is external to AK, which is phase four.

10. The screen in the vessels of the world of Atzilut is not as coarse as that of the world of AK because the coarseness in the screen of Atzilut is only of phase three. Consequently, none of the ten Sefirot of straightness of Atzilut reach higher than the degree of Hochma and they lack Keter.

Hence, they are evaluated as low compared to the ten Sefirot at the level of Keter in the world of Adam Kadmon. They are also considered exterior compared to the ten Sefirot in AK. This is because the coarseness of phase three is exterior to phase four, and refinement and externality are one and the same. Consequently the world of Atzilut becomes clothing, meaning externality that clothes the interior world of AK.

The screen of Beria stems from phase two, which makes it external to Atzilut.

11. The screen in the vessels of the ten Sefirot of the world of Beria is even more refined than that of the world of Atzilut, consisting only of the coarseness of phase two. Thus, the level of its ten Sefirot does not reach higher than Bina.

    Therefore the world of Beria is regarded as being exterior to Atzilut, where there is coarseness of phase three, making it interior to the world of Beria, which is only the coarseness of phase two. Thus, the world of Beria is considered to be external, clothing the world of Atzilut.

The screen of Yetzira is from phase one, making it external to Beria.

12. The screen of the world of Yetzira consists only of the coarseness of phase one, the faintest. Therefore, the ten Sefirot of the world of Yetzira reach a low level, only as high as Zeir Anpin- lacking the first three Sefirot: Keter, Hochma and Bina.

    This makes the world of Yetzira more external than the world of Beria, where there is coarseness of phase two, which is internal to the coarseness of phase one in the world of Yetzira. For this reason, the world of Yetzira is regarded as external, clothing the world of Beria.

The screen of Assiya comes from the root coarseness.
This is why it is the most external of all.

13. The screen in the ten Sefirot of straightness in the world of Assiya is completely refined, lacking any coarseness. Consequently, there is no issue of coupling in order to raise reflected light with the upper light in it.

    Because they do not have reflected light, they also do not have upper light, because the upper light cannot be in a Partzuf where there is no reflected light. Therefore, these ten Sefirot have only the degree of Malchut lacking the first nine Sefirot: Keter, Hochma, Bina, and Zeir Anpin (containing the six Sefirot HGT NHY).

Because their screen is more refined than in all the previous worlds, they are naturally regarded as exterior to them as well. That is because you already know that refinement and externality are one and the same.

Thus, the world of Yetzira whose vessels still have the screen of phase one is regarded as an internal world compared to the world of Assiya, and the world of Assiya is regarded as external to and clothing the world of Yetzira and all the other worlds for it is the most refined of them all.

An inverse relation between the bestowal of the light and the clothing of the light.

14. This may be surprising, for it is reasonable to think that the more important light should clothe the more refined vessels because the form of the refined vessel is closer to the light. Thus, why is it said here that the greater the coarseness, the greater the degree?

   Indeed, we should know that the issue of the clothing of the light in the vessels is an issue in and of itself, and the bestowal of the upper light to the Partzuf is a different issue altogether. They are far apart and have an inverse relation between them from one end to the other.

   The rule is that the upper one bestows only with its coarsest part, while the lower one receives only with its most refined part. We must thoroughly understand this, as it is a vital key in the wisdom.

The restriction was only on phase four.

15. In order to understand this, we need a thorough understanding of the issue of restriction and line, for you already know that the restriction was only on phase four, called Malchut of Ein Sof, or the "middle point." There is a simple reason for it: restriction means detainment from wanting to receive. In other words, one stops oneself from receiving the abundance from the light of Ein Sof. Thus, the restriction applies only to the receiving vessel. Since there is no other vessel of reception there but phase four, hence the restriction applies only to phase four.

   It has already been explained above that the three phases that preceded phase four are not regarded as vessels of reception but only as causes. This means that the consequence of their emanation is the appearance of this vessel for reception, being phase four. That is why the restriction does not apply to them but only to the middle point, being phase four.

The light departed entirely because there was no other vessel of reception other than phase four.

16. Therefore, since she diminished her desire from phase four, the light departed from the three former phases as well. That is because they do not have other vessels of reception with which to hold the light.

    Even the lights that do belong to the three previous phases must be received in phase four, because they do not have their own vessels of reception. Thus, because phase four stopped receiving, the entire light instantly vanished.

There were only the first three phases in the light of the line.

17. After the light departed because of the restriction, she drew the light from Ein Sof once more in the form of a line. This means only a small amount of light, containing only the first three phases of the will to receive, without phase four (see Part 1, Chap 2, item 2).

    We've explained that there are no vessels of reception in the first three phases of the desire. We should therefore ask: "How can light be received without vessels of reception? After all, these three phases do not contain any form of reception in them. Moreover, phase four, the only vessel for reception in the Partzuf, is here only as a line."

Explaining coupling by striking.

18. Since the restriction is only from the perspective of the emanated being and not at all from the Emanator, the upper light is not at all meticulous about the restriction that the middle point performed. Because of that, it is considered that the upper light descends to phase four as well; but phase four detains it from appearing within her, due to the prior restriction on phase four before that light came.

    The books call this state coupling by striking. It is like two objects where one wants to break through and pass over the fence and the boundary that the other erected. However, the other stands firmly against it and prevents the first from trespassing. In that state each of them is striking the other's boundary.

    It can also be compared to two solid matters because the nature of the liquid lets other things permeate and mix with it, and soft matters too let other matters permeate them a little and push their upper shell. However with two solid matters, one does not let the other push it from its boundary even a little. As a result, when two hard objects meet, they strike one another since the encounter itself is the cause of this striking.

The same applies to the expansion of the upper light from Ein Sof: its conduct is to fill phase four too in the same way it is in Ein Sof. For this reason, the light does indeed come down to clothe phase four, but the force of the restriction of phase four detains it and does not let it descend to her. Consequently, this encounter of the upper light with the force of the restriction is called coupling by striking. This means that each of them interrupts and detains the passage of the other, because the conduct of the light of Ein Sof is to fulfill phase four, and phase four herself has the conduct of rejecting the upper light and not receiving it.

Explaining reflected light.

19. A new light was born and emerged by the above encounter and striking. Like sunlight on a mirror, meaning on a glass that is painted on the other side, the lines of the sun cannot pass through the mirror because of the paint on the other side. Consequently, the lines of the sun return backwards and produce a glitter of light.

    In much the same way, when the upper light meets the force of the restriction in phase four, called screen, this screen turns it back to its root. However, in this case there is no issue of concealment. On the contrary, the return of the upper light from phase four upwards is regarded as a new and special light. It mounts the upper light, clothes it and holds it within. Because of that, it is regarded as a vessel that receives the upper light.

The reflected light becomes a vessel of reception instead of phase four.

20. You should know that there are no other vessels of reception in the Rosh of every Partzuf, other than the above reflected light. The entire force of reception in this reflected light comes because it is born and stems from the striking in phase four. Because it is a consequence of phase four, it becomes a vessel of reception like it. This matter will be explained in full in Part 3, for it belongs there.

Reflected light was the vessel of reception in the line.

21. Now you can understand what we asked above: "How can the upper light expand only in three phases, while there are no vessels of reception in these phases?" From the preceding explanation you can see that now, the reception of that light also stems only from phase four. However, it is accepted in

112

the vessel of reception of the reflected light that rises from the coupling by striking in phase four.

This reflected light is regarded as a vessel for reception in the line that extends from Ein Sof into the space, being exactly like phase four herself, namely reception from Ein Sof. Thus, now after the restriction that was missing in phase four, the reflected light that is generated by the screen in her takes her place.

The vessels of ten Sefirot of Rosh are but roots for the vessels.

22. It has already been explained that although there are four phases in the will to receive, not all of them are regarded as vessels for reception, but only phase four. We have also learned that the vessel for the reception of this line, which extends from Ein Sof into the space after the restriction, is actually the reflected light that ascends from the screen in phase four. Because it stems from phase four, she renders it capable of being a vessel of reception.

It will be explained that this reflected light does not complete its qualification of becoming a vessel for reception before it expands from its screen downwards. Consequently, the screen expands once more into four degrees, up to phase four, and these are the real vessels of the above line.

However, the first four phases that were emanated by the power of coupling by striking from the screen upward to the root, are regarded only as the roots of the vessels. Because the force of the screen cannot ascend with that reflected light from its place upward, hence there is only light there, without any coarseness of screen. Hence, these are not real vessels, but only roots for them.

Afterwards, when this reflected light expands downwards from the place of the screen, it leads the coarseness of the screen with it, and becomes the real vessels.

CHAPTER THREE

Explains the self and the substance in the vessels; contains two issues: 1. Three fundamental discernments in the vessels: a. The self of the substance in them; b. The force of restriction in them; c. The screen in them. 2. There are two discernments in the substance itself, which is in the vessels: a. Malchut of the upper one that became the first substance in the lower one; b. The light that extends into that first substance is regarded as the lower one itself.

Detailed explanation of the four phases of the desire.

23. Now there opens before us a way to understand our previous question about the order of the Sefirot of straightness, in which the coarser is higher and more important. This is opposite from common sense; according to common sense, the more refined vessel should clothe the higher and more important light, and the coarse vessel should clothe a lesser light.

    You can understand it from the aforementioned, but we should first elaborate on the meaning of the four phases in the desire, which are the vessels of the ten Sefirot called: Hochma, Bina, Zeir Anpin (which consists of six Sefirot HGT NHY), and Malchut, and their root, called Keter, which need an elaborate explanation.

Three discernments: the substance of the vessel: the force of restriction in the vessel; the screen in it.

24. There are three fundamental discernments in these vessels: The first is the self of the substance of the vessel. The second is the force of restriction in her, meaning the retirement from the great will to receive, through its own independent choice, and not because of the authority of the upper one. The third is the screen, meaning the retirement from the great will to receive by the authority of the upper one. This is a compelled retirement, not a mindful one. We will explain them one at a time.

The four degrees of the will to receive are the substance of the vessel.

25. You already know that the substance of every vessel consists of four degrees of the will to receive, one below the other. The upper one is the reason and the cause of the emergence of its lower one. The root is the cause for the

emergence of the desire in phase one; phase one is the cause for the emergence of the desire of phase two; phase two is the cause for the emergence of the desire of phase three; phase three is the cause for the emergence of the desire of phase four.

This compelled sequence of cause and consequence has already been thoroughly clarified in Part One (Inner Light, Chap 1, item 50, study it there well for I wish to avoid the repetition of that long text unnecessarily. However, you should study these things in depth as I rely on them in the continuation of my henceforth explanation).

Two discernments in each phase: what it has from its superior; what it has from its own essence.

26. We should note that there are two discernments in each phase of these four phases: The first is the amount of substance that came to it by its own cause. The second is the amount of substance in its essence, which is activated by the light that is clothed in it. It is known that the desire in a degree is called by the name of the Malchut of that degree. Even where no recognition of a vessel is discerned, meaning in Ein Sof, we still denominate the desire there by the name Malchut of Ein Sof. Concerning "He and His name are one, it is known that "name" is an appellation of Malchut, and "His name" is "desire" in Gematria.

Malchut of Keter descended and became the substance in the Sefira of Hochma.

27. Now we shall explain the two discernments that we should make in each of the four phases: The root of the degree, the discernment of the instilling of the light of Ein Sof on it, is called the Keter of that degree. It is known that in the upper light there is only the will to bestow and to do good to others, meaning to the entire reality that exists in the worlds that He created. However, there is nothing in Him of the will to receive, as is written in Inner Observation Part 1. Malchut of Keter is the cause for phase one. That is because the desire in the upper one becomes a compelling must in the lower one.

Thus, the will to bestow and to do good, which is Malchut of Keter, became the "will to receive" in phase one, called Hochma. It is regarded as though Malchut of Keter herself came down and clothed and became the will to receive of phase one, meaning its actual substance. It is so because the desire in phase one is the substance in that phase, and the upper light, called Haya,

115

is clothed in that substance. Hence it is considered that Malchut of Keter became the substance of the Sefira called Hochma. This is the first discernment that should be made in the substance of phase one.

After the appearance of the light of Hochma, the vessel of Hochma itself emerged.

28. The second discernment is that after the upper light, called Haya, expanded in Malchut of Keter, which is the aforementioned substance of Hochma, Malchut of Keter received the real substance of phase one. It means that although Malchut of Keter, namely the will to bestow that is included in the upper light, became a will to receive and the first substance of phase one, it was sufficient only to be a root for phase one, meaning for this will to receive to draw the upper light into it.

    We can denominate it as the first substance of the Sefira Hochma, for it is still regarded as emanator and Keter. It shifts from being emanator and Keter to being emanated being and Hochma, called phase one, only after the aforementioned will to receive extends the light of Haya that is related to it. Then it stops being regarded as an emanator and is regarded as an emanated being or Hochma. Study it thoroughly and you will not miss the aim.

    Now you have learned the two discernments in the vessel of Hochma: the first is Malchut of the upper one, meaning before she drew her light, and the second is called the vessel of Hochma itself, namely Malchut of Hochma. That is because the vessel is always called Malchut.

Malchut of Hochma became the first substance in Bina. With the emergence of her light, the vessel of Bina herself emerged.

29. The same is observed in the substance of phase two, called Bina. Her cause is the desire in phase one, called Hochma, meaning only Malchut of Hochma. The desire in the degree is always called the vessel or Malchut of the degree. This Malchut of Hochma clothed and became the first substance of the Sefira of Bina, so as to extend the light that is related to her. This is the first discernment in the substance of phase two, called Bina. When she then extended the light that is related to her, called Neshama, her substance emerged from being Malchut of Hochma, which is phase one, and acquired its own form, meaning the actual phase two, called Bina.

Malchut of Bina became the first substance in Zeir Anpin. With the emergence of his light, the vessel of Zeir Anpin himself emerged.

30. In this way you will also learn the substance of phase three, called Zeir Anpin. Malchut of Bina is its cause, and she became the first substance of Zeir Anpin, namely phase three, so as to draw the light that is related to it, called Ruach. The second discernment is that after he extended and received his light, his substance stopped being regarded as Malchut of Bina, and received the form of Malchut of Zeir Anpin.

Malchut of Zeir Anpin became the first substance in Malchut.
With the emergence of her light, the vessel of Malchut herself was revealed.

31. So are the two discernments in the substance of phase four: Malchut of Zeir Anpin is her cause, which clothed and became the first substance of phase four, called Malchut. When she received sufficient light of Nefesh that is related to her, Malchut of Zeir Anpin departed from Zeir Anpin to become phase four, meaning regarded as Malchut of Malchut.

The above vessels of reception are only for extension.

32. Understand that although we have clarified and ascribed a discernment of reception in each and every phase in and of itself, it relates only to the drawing of light, where each phase draws for itself its respective light. However, the true vessel, which merits the name "vessel of reception for the emanated being," is specifically phase four, and not the three preceding phases.

CHAPTER FOUR

Explains the accurate meaning of the four phases of coarseness, as our sages wrote about the four phases (Pesachim 25): 1. Impossible and not intending. 2. Possible and not intending. 3. Impossible and intending. 4. Possible and intending.

Explanation of the four phases in the desire according to the four discernments in possible and intending.

33. In order to provide an accurate and elaborate explanation, I will now clarify it through the words of our sages (Pesachim 25): "It is said: Pleasure that comes to a person against his will, Abaie [name of a sage] said – permitted; Raba [name of another sage] said – "forbidden," "possible and intending," "impossible" and "intending," the whole world does not dispute that it is forbidden. Impossible and not intending, the whole world does not dispute that it is permitted. They disputed over possible and not intending, and RASHI interpreted that it is possible, possible for him to be separated. Intending, he intends to come near in order to enjoy it, like a scent of sin, see there.

First discernment is impossible and not intending.

34. Four discernments of receiving pleasure are found in their words: The first discernment is "impossible" for him to be separated and "not intending" to come near and enjoy. That is because by receiving forbidden pleasure in such a way, the entire world does not dispute that it is permitted. The reception and the desire do not matter when there isn't a way or a choice not to receive, and there is also no desire to draw near to the forbidden in order to enjoy it.

Second discernment is possible and not intending.

35. The second discernment is possible for him to be separated, and not intending to draw near and enjoy. Regarding the reception of forbidden pleasure in this way, Abaie and Raba dispute: Abaie thinks that although it is possible, meaning that there is a choice to draw far and refrain from enjoying the forbidden, it is still permitted to draw near and enjoy it because he is not intending.

In other words, because there is no desire in his heart to draw near the forbidden, it is not regarded as reception, although he does draw near and he enjoys the forbidden. Raba said that because he can also refrain from approaching in order to enjoy the forbidden, he is forbidden to come near and enjoy. It is so even if he has no desire to draw near and enjoy.

Third discernment is impossible and intending.

36. The third discernment is impossible and intending. This means that it is impossible to be separated and to draw far from the forbidden so as to refrain from enjoying it. Intending means having a desire to enjoy the forbidden. There is no dispute in the whole world that reception of a forbidden pleasure in such a way is forbidden. Although he cannot, and has no way to separate himself from the forbidden and refrain from enjoying, because he has a desire in his heart to approach and enjoy, this desire is regarded as reception of pleasure from something that is forbidden to enjoy, and he sins. Yet, some say that even here Abaie thought that it was permitted.

Fourth discernment is possible and intending.

37. The fourth discernment is possible and intending. This means that it is possible for him to be separated and distanced from the forbidden and refrain from enjoying it. It is also intending because he yearns to draw near and enjoy the forbidden.

Here the entire world agrees that it is forbidden since it is receiving pleasure from the forbidden in the most lewd manner, for he craves the pleasure, it is possible for him to separate himself, yet he does not do so. Therefore, it is regarded as the greatest will to receive in its final form, which is forbidden according to everyone. Even according to those who say that following Abaie, they permitted in the third discernment, here they admit it is forbidden.

38. Their above words provide us with the precise terms by which to define each and every phase of the four phases of the will to receive in a way that hits the mark and does not miss the desired aim. They have provided us with four degrees, one below the other, in the sin of forbidden pleasure, which depends on the will to receive of the sinner. In the first three degrees: impossible and not intending, possible and not intending, and impossible and intending, the prohibition on reception is not agreed by all; only in phase four.

39. We see that our sages have put two things together here: the possibility to separate and not receive pleasure and the desire and attraction of the heart to want that pleasure. The combination of the two creates the four phases. Now we will accept these words and examine them regarding our matter in

the upper worlds, which are the roots to every kind of desire in reality, and from the lower one, we shall learn the upper one.

When the will to receive emerged in Malchut of Keter, she left the Keter and became phase one.

40. We should distinguish two discernments in phase one, which is called both Hochma and Haya (see Inner Observation, Part 2, item 27): The first discernment is her first substance. You already know (see Inner Observation, Part 2, item 23) that it is her Malchut of the upper one, meaning Malchut of Keter, that received the form of the will to receive. In this new form, Malchut of Keter received a new name: phase one.

You already know that when a spiritual entity acquires a new form, it is regarded as a new authority in and of itself. So it is with Malchut of Keter, being the will to bestow in the Emanator. When the desire to emanate was seemingly born in Him, He certainly does not need the tool of action. Rather, His desire was instantly carried out. It means that she received the form of the "will to receive" which is the first substance of the emanated being, called phase one.

The exit of Malchut of Keter to phase one is like lighting one candle from another; the first is not diminished.

41. Here you should remember that there is no absence in the spiritual. What is said about Malchut of Keter receiving the form of phase one does not mean that Malchut of Keter is now absent from Keter. Rather, Malchut of Keter retained her first virtue, unchanged. It is like lighting one candle from another without the first diminishing. That Malchut of Keter, which received phase one did not diminish Keter in any way, but only added a new phase. In other words, Malchut of Keter remained in her place, as complete and virtuous as before, but a new phase of Malchut of Keter has been added, namely the Malchut that received phase one and became the first substance in the Sefira of Hochma. Remember this henceforth and you will not be confused.

After the first substance received the light, the vessel of Hochma herself emerged.

42. The second discernment is of the substance of that vessel after it had received its light. The vessel is then completed and is called Hochma. In other words, before she received her light, she was named only after her own phase, meaning phase one, and was not a vessel of Hochma yet, but only Malchut of Keter.

This can be likened to a fetus in its mother's abdomen. Before it is born and given its light and vitality, it does not have a name. So it is with the first substance: it does not bear the name Hochma before it receives its light, but is still included in Malchut of Keter.

Afterwards, when the substance draws its light, called Haya, it then acquires its unique name, meaning Hochma (see item 27). We should distinguish these two discernments in each and every Sefira. They are: the vessel before it receives the light, when it is still named after the upper one; and the vessel after it receives the light, for it is then regarded as its own authority.

From the perspective of the first substance, Hochma is regarded as impossible. From the perspective of her being filled with light, she is regarded as not intending.

43. Now you will understand that phase one, which is Hochma, is regarded as impossible and not intending. From the perspective of the first substance, being Malchut of Keter when she received the new form, phase one, when the Sefira of Hochma still did not have its own name, this appearance of the will to receive is certainly regarded as impossible with regards to the Sefira of Hochma itself.

Also, from the perspective of Malchut of Keter, she is regarded as impossible, because she cannot emanate the Hochma without Hochma having a will to receive. Receiving the abundance without a will to receive it is regarded as coercion and labor, the opposite of the intention of the Emanator, which is to do good and delight.

She is also regarded as not intending, meaning she has no attraction and yearning to receive the light. You already know that a desire is not complete before the yearning and attraction to the light appear in it (see Part 1, Chap 1, item 50).

It has also been thoroughly clarified there that the yearning appears only when there is no light and abundance in the vessel, because then she can yearn for it. However, that cannot come to be when the vessel is filled with her light.

Thus, because the above vessel of Hochma is filled with its light, it still has no yearning for the abundance. This is why Hochma is considered as not intending, meaning that she does not have attraction and yearning for the abundance.

The intensification in the desire in Bina is regarded as possible. Because it comes to her from the first substance, it is regarded as not intending.

44. Phase two, which is Bina, is regarded as possible and not intending. Her first substance (see Inner Observation, Part 2, item 29) is her Malchut of the upper one, meaning Malchut of Hochma, that received the new form of phase two inside her, meaning through her intensification (see Part 1, Chap 1, item 50). From that perspective, the intensification of that desire is regarded as possible. This means that it was possible for her to avoid awakening that desire.

She is also regarded as not intending because she is Malchut of Hochma, and is filled with her light. For this reason, the yearning does not appear in her.

You should understand that any appearance of additional desire that appeared in phase two more than in phase one, is only regarded as possible. In other words, it is the intensification of the desire that she made, by the power of the emanated being himself (see Part 1, Chap 1, item 50).

The light of Hochma is sufficient and she did not have to intensify and draw Hassadim.

45. We might ask: "But Malchut of Keter, when she became phase one in the Sefira of Hochma, also had the same possibility not to take on that new form of the will to receive. Thus, why is phase one regarded as impossible?"

Indeed, there is a big difference here: Malchut of Keter could not emanate the emanated being without it having a will to receive. However, Malchut of Hochma, which is the emanated being itself, could be satisfied with her own will to receive, without an awakening with a desire to bestow, which is phase two, and drawing light of Hassadim. That is because the light of Haya is quite sufficient for the emanated being, and he does not need any addition.

Zeir Anpin is regarded as impossible because he lacked the light of Hochma.

46. Phase three, being Zeir Anpin, is regarded as impossible and intending. It is impossible because after phase two awakened and drew the light of Hassadim, it caused a detainment on the light of Hochma in the emanated being. The will to bestow is opposite to phase one, which is a will to receive, where there is light of Hochma.

That light is given the name Haya [alive/life] because the light of Hochma is the essential vitality of the Partzuf. For this reason, Malchut of Bina necessarily drew illumination of the light of Hochma once again into her light of Hassadim. Thus, when Malchut of Bina drew it and created that new form, she emerged from being phase two and became phase three, called Zeir Anpin (see Inner Observation, Part 2, item 30).

Zeir Anpin is regarded as intending because it had a yearning for Hochma.

47. We should discern two things in this extension, being phase three: The first is Impossible, meaning she has no other choice because the light of Haya was absent in the emanated being. The second is Intending, for here there is a yearning for the illumination of Hochma that she extended, because she extended it when she was empty from it because phase two covered the light of Hochma and she had only light of Hassadim without Hochma. For this reason, her Malchut, which extended the illumination of Hochma, extended it as a yearning, called intending. Hence, the phase of Zeir Anpin is called impossible and intending.

Malchut is regarded as possible because she could have sufficed for the Hochma in Zeir Anpin, and as intending because she had a yearning.

48. Phase four, being Malchut, is regarded as possible and intending. It is possible because there is already illumination of Hochma in Zeir Anpin, meaning in phase three. Thus, Malchut of Zeir Anpin does not have to perform this intensification once more in order to draw a greater light of Hochma than in phase three. It is regarded as intending because this intensification to draw the light of Hochma created a yearning. In other words, it is when she does not have light of Hochma that the yearning appears.

The difference between light of Hochma and illumination of Hochma.

49. We might ask: "Since there is illumination of Hochma in phase three, which is why phase four is regarded as possible, how then does the yearning for light of Hochma appear in phase four?" You must understand that there is a big difference between the illumination of Hochma and the light of Hochma. Illumination of Hochma means that the self of the degree is the light of Hassadim, but it receives illumination from the light of Hochma. The light of Hochma, however, means that the entire self of the light is Hochma, and not Hassadim at all.

Illumination of Hochma is quite sufficient for the vitality of the degree, as it is in phase three, being Zeir Anpin. That is why Malchut of Zeir Anpin, which intensified her desire to draw light of Hochma, did not have to have it. It is only that she yearned for the self of the light of Hochma, which is much higher than the illumination of Hochma in phase three. She is considered to be empty of that light of Hochma with regards to the above light. Hence it is possible that a yearning for it will awaken in her.

Phase four alone is regarded as a vessel for reception because she is possible and intending.

50. Thus we find that not all desires are regarded as vessels of reception, but only phase four. That is because the desire is not regarded as reception, except under the two conditions - possible and intending. This means that there should not be coerced reception, and that a yearning to receive will appear there. However, since there is a yearning to receive in phase three, meaning intending, because the reception is a must, being that it is the necessary vitality, it is not regarded as a vessel of reception.

Conversely, although phase two does not have to receive, since there is no yearning there, she is not regarded as a vessel for reception. It is all the more so with phase one, who has neither, for she must receive her light, for it is her vitality, and at the same time she has no yearning for it. Thus it is certainly a completely faint desire.

CHAPTER FIVE

Explains the restriction and the screen; contains four issues: 1. The restriction was even on all sides. 2. The issue of the screen: because any extension of light is carried out in phase four, there needs to be a detaining force that will prevent the light from expanding into phase four. This force is called the screen. 3. Two discernments in Malchut: a. she is restricted so as not to receive light inside her by her own will. This is the conduct in circles; b. she is restricted because of the force of detainment on her, namely the screen. This is the conduct in the Sefirot of straightness. 4. The upper light is in complete rest and does not stop shining even for a minute. When the emanated being yearns, it extends the light to it.

The difference between the restriction and the screen.

51. Once we learned the four degrees in the will to receive one below the other well, in its accurate measure, we will now explain the matter of the restriction, the screen and the difference between them.

    The restriction has already been thoroughly explained in Part One and in Inner Light, and we need not repeat the words here. The primary issue that we need for our concern is the equivalence that was there (see Inner light, Part 1, Chap 1, item 90).

The four phases received in restriction, the matter of cause and consequence.

52. It has been explained above that since the light of Ein Sof is completely even, it had to restrict itself evenly on all sides. This means that all four phases that were restricted are of equal level, without a discernment of refinement and coarseness that make four degrees be one below the other down to phase four, the lowest and coarsest of them all. Rather, they are all even.

    All that was added in the restriction, to distinguish in it more than in Ein Sof, is the matter of the four phases: how they cause each other and cascade from each other by way of cause and consequence. Phase one is the reason and the cause of the emergence of phase two; phase two is the cause of phase three; and phase three is the cause of phase four. However, in terms of refinement and merit, they are even.

The cause and consequence in the four phases did not exist in Ein Sof.

53. This matter of cause and consequence that nevertheless divides them into four phases could not emerge in Ein Sof prior to the restriction. Even the vessel in general is not apparent there; rather it is completely light, as it is written in Part 1.

   However, after the light of Ein Sof departed from these phases, they became apparent and what we must now discern became disclosed, namely the light of Ein Sof itself, meaning what they had before the restriction. The four phases themselves remained empty of light because after the restriction it became apparent that these phases have nothing in common with the light of Ein Sof as it was prior to the restriction.

This is like a candle that is incorporated in a torch: It is indistinguishable. However, when separated from the torch, it becomes apparent to all.

54. There seems to be a question here: Since the restriction occurred primarily in phase four, it became evident that that phase is unworthy of receiving the light. However, it became evident that the three preceding phases that were not restricted are worthy of receiving the light. Thus, we have a distinction of above and below and the importance of one over the other. In other words, phase four is lower than the first three phases.

The restriction was not because of the inferiority of phase four, but solely for the purpose of adornment.

55. The thing is that the restriction of the light in phase four did not occur because of her inferiority, for we are still dealing with Malchut of Ein Sof, where phase four was as the light of Ein Sof itself. Thus, how can we even think that the restriction occurred due to the inferiority of phase four?

   Indeed, the restriction did not occur because of the inferiority of phase four; rather, it occurred only as an adornment. It means that this Malchut wanted to reach adhesion, the highest possible degree, to adhere to the Emanator completely, which is the greatest equivalence of form with the Emanator (see Part 1, Chap 1, item 90). Thus, phase four did not lose her merit after the restriction as well.

The extension of the line began in phase four. That is why there had to be a detaining force on phase four, so that the light would not enter her.

56. Now we will explain about the screen that was placed over phase four, being Malchut, when the world of restriction, meaning Malchut of Ein Sof was

clothed there. It is known that every degree begins with the Malchut of the upper one that becomes her substance (see item 27). When this restricted Malchut drew the upper light over the first three phases once more, this extension was necessarily with the yearning in phase four in her. That is because the first three phases are not vessels of reception and extension whatsoever.

Thus, it was necessary for her to first draw the light into all four phases, even to her phase four. However, in order to prevent the light from reaching phase four, she had to add a new force so as to detain the light from reaching phase four.

The detaining force that was placed on phase four is called a screen.

57. This new force that she added is called a screen. This screen is the fundamental factor in the extension of the light of the line over the three phases. It is so because the restriction she performed, meaning revoking her desire from receiving in phase four, sufficed only for the upper light to depart from her. However, afterwards she drew the light once more, and was forced to reawaken her phase four in order to draw that new extension. Thus, if she had not made that new force toward the expansion of light, the light would reach phase four once again.

Thus, the primary factor in the extension of the light of the line on the three phases is the force of the screen exclusively, which she has made once more with regards to the light. You must understand these two discernments thoroughly, namely the restriction and the screen, for they are the foundations for the rest in this wisdom.

The restriction was of her own volition. The screen pushes the light through an authority not of her own volition.

58. You must understand the difference between the restriction that Malchut of Ein Sof performed, being the departure from the great will to receive due to her desire and choice to equalize her form the most with the Emanator, and the screen, which is the detaining force, through authority and compulsion, that prevents the light from reaching phase four.

59. The reason for it is that although both the restriction and the screen were performed by Malchut of Ein Sof, you already know that when a spiritual entity acquires a new, additional form, it is then regarded as two spiritual entities, and as two discernments that are as far apart from one another as the measure of their disparity of form.

Just as corporeal objects become separated from one another by an ax, and are distanced from each other by place and area, so are the spirituals distinguished from each other by an innovation of form. Their distance from each other is as is the measure of disparity between one form and the other, whether less or more.

The screen is a result of the restricted Malchut. A desire in the upper one is a force in the lower one.

60. Thus, after the above Malchut performed an extension on the light of the line over three phases, this extension is regarded as a new form, added to the form of restriction. Thus, there are now two discernments in the above Malchut: The first is the restricted Malchut, being the first form that was made in Malchut of Ein Sof, which now adopted the new form, called the "restricted Malchut." Later, when this Malchut performed an extension on the light of the three phases, a new form was born and emerged. It was called a screen, preventing the light from appearing in phase four.

It is known that every desire in the upper one becomes an authority in the branch that extends from it. The screen is a branch, a consequence of the restricted Malchut. Hence, Malchut restricted herself voluntarily and knowingly without any control by her upper one. However, the consequence that extends from her, namely the screen, is already completely controlled by the restriction, since it is a second degree in the world of restriction.

The difference between circles and straightness is in the screen that was innovated in the ten Sefirot of straightness

61. It follows that there are two discernments of Malchut: The first is the restricted Malchut, and the second is Malchut that has a screen. Know that this is the entire difference between the Sefirot of circles and the Sefirot of straightness, called line. The Malchut in the ten Sefirot of circles is the restricted Malchut, where there is no screen whatsoever, and the Malchut in the ten Sefirot of straightness is the corrected Malchut with the above screen.

The reason why the light strikes and wants to enter phase four is that the emanated being extended it this way.

62. Now you can thoroughly understand the matter of the reflected light that rises through coupling by striking from the encounter of the upper light with the screen on phase four that we have begun to explain above (see item 18). You should understand what we said above, that the upper light is not

meticulous about the restriction that the emanated being performed, and it comes down to expand in phase four as well.

The reason for it is that the emanated being himself necessarily extends it to begin with. It has already been explained (see Part 1, Chap 1, item 2) that the upper light is always in a state of complete rest and does not stop shining to the lower ones even for a minute. That is because it does not come under the definition of an incident and innovation. Rather, all the issues of the expansion of upper light that were discussed refer to the drawing on the part of the emanated being, who receives from the upper light as much as the will to receive is prepared, meaning the yearning in it (see Inner Observation, Part 2, item 50).

We refer to the extension of the emanated being as expansion of upper light.

63. At the very moment when the emanated being yearns to receive from the upper light, he immediately sucks the upper light. It is like one who lights a candle from another and the first is not lessoned by it. By the same manner, when the emanated being extends the upper light to itself, the upper light is not lessened in any way because of that part that the emanated being extended.

Also, it is not affected or impressed in any way by the extension of the emanated being. However, in order to simplify matters, we refer to the extension of the emanated being as expansion of upper light.

Remember this in every place, for we always speak of expansion of the upper light, and mean the extension of the emanated being by his yearning alone.

The part of the light that should have entered phase four and was rejected from her became reflected light.

64. Therefore, after the restriction, when Malchut of Ein Sof extended the light once more, because she extended it through the yearning in her phase four, the upper light was also drawn to phase four. However, by the power of the screen that she had erected to detain the light from expanding to phase four, that part of the light returned backwards.

By this she fulfilled her initial desire that the light would reach her only in three phases. However, that part of the light that the screen pushed back to its root, meaning that part that was intended for phase four, did not vanish from her.

Instead, it became a great light, clothing the three phases of the upper light, from the place of the screen up to the root. This reflected light became a vessel for reception of the three phases of upper light instead of phase four (see Inner Observation, item 21).

CHAPTER SIX

Explains why the screen of phase four raises reflected light up to Keter, and phase three up to Hochma, etc. The reason is that the measure of reflected light is as the measure of light that could have clothed phase four, had the screen not pushed it back. It also explains that the ten Sefirot of direct light expand from above downward, meaning the more refined among them is better, and the ten Sefirot of reflected light expand from below upward, meaning that the more coarse among them is better.

The reflected light is divided into Sefirot according to its clothing of the Sefirot of direct light.

65. From the aforementioned you can thoroughly understand the measure and size of that reflected light. It is no more and no less than the measure of the light that the screen pushes backwards. In other words, it is that part that was worthy of expanding in phase four had it not pushed it back. It ascended and clothed the phases of the upper light, meaning phase three, called Zeir Anpin, phase two, called Bina, phase one, called Hochma and also the root phase, called Keter.

For this reason, it is considered that phase four herself was divided into those four degrees that her reflected light clothed, which became four degrees one above the other in the vessel of phase four herself. That is because the light that had belonged to her ascended and clothed these four degrees. It is for this reason that phase four is regarded as their root, called the Keter of this reflected light.

The ten Sefirot of direct light expand from above downward and the ten Sefirot of reflected light from below upward.

66. Now there are two kinds of ten Sefirot in the emanated being: ten Sefirot from above downward and ten Sefirot from below upward. It is so because there are ten Sefirot in the upper light, called the Keter of the upper light.

Also, four phases expand from the Keter: phase one is called Hochma; phase two is called Bina; phase three [containing six Sefirot HGT NHY] is called Zeir Anpin; and phase four is Malchut. Their order is from above downward, meaning from the more refined to the more coarse. It means that the more refined is also more important, and the most refined of all, namely the root, is called Keter.

Following it, meaning with a little more coarseness than Keter, it is called Hochma, and continues through the coarsest, who is Malchut, the most inferior of all.

From below upward means that the coarser is more important.

67. There are ten more Sefirot in the emanated being. They have an inverse relation to the ten Sefirot of the aforementioned upper light, namely the ten Sefirot of reflected light that rises from the screen in phase four. They clothe the ten Sefirot of upper light, and their order is from below upward, meaning from coarse to refined. The coarsest one is the first the highest, and the greater the refinement, the lower it is. This is an opposite order to that of the ten Sefirot of upper light.

The Malchut of direct light is the Keter of reflected light.

68. The coarsest of all, namely phase four, is the most important. That is because she is the root of all these ten Sefirot of reflected light. It is so because this reflected light is no more than the part of the light that belongs only to her, and which the screen pushed back. Therefore, phase four is regarded as the Keter, meaning the root.

The Malchut of reflected light is in the Keter of direct light.

69. Phase three, which is less coarse than phase four, is regarded as the Sefira of Hochma of the reflected light, meaning second to Keter in degree. Phase two, which is more refined than phase three, is regarded as the third degree from Keter, meaning Bina. Phase one, which is even more refined than phase two, is regarded as the fourth degree in merit from Keter, meaning the Sefira of Zeir Anpin, consisting of six Sefirot HGT NHY.

The Keter of direct light, the most refined of all, is regarded in relation to the aforementioned reflected light only as Malchut, meaning of the least merit. That is because the greater the coarseness, the greater the importance, and the greater the refinement, the lower the degree, since the degrees expand from coarse to refined. Remember that well.

Malchut consists of all ten Sefirot of reflected light.

70. Phase four herself is also divided into ten Sefirot, meaning four phases and Keter, by the power of her reflected light that expands to ten Sefirot. It is so

because phase four herself is the Keter of reflected light, namely the root, and the nine Sefirot of reflected light that expand and rise from her are her branches.

It is known that all the branches exist in the root. Thus, phase four herself is regarded as five phases, which are Keter and the four phases, expanding from below upward.

The refinement of the screen divides phase four into five phases.

71. Now you can understand what we have said above (see Inner Observation, Part 2, item 8). The extent of reflected light is measured by the amount of coarseness in the screen. The coarsest screen, namely the screen of phase four, manifests the complete degree, meaning reaching up to Keter. The screen of phase three reaches only up to Hochma; the screen of phase two up to Bina; and the screen of phase one only as high as Zeir Anpin.

A screen that has not even the coarseness of phase one, which is like the root, manifests no level of light, but only Malchut. With the above explanation you will understand the aforementioned matter of refinement of the screen over the above five phases. It is the matter of the division of phase four herself into the five aforementioned phases. The conduct of the screen is to ascend and be refined in these partial degrees of coarseness that exist in phase four, for a reason that we will learn henceforth.

Chapter Seven

Explains the matter of the refinement of the screen, and the emergence of the five levels KHB, ZA and Malchut, one below the other, because of the refinement of the screen.

The detaining force in the screen and the measure of the coarseness in Malchut are equal.

72. In order to understand the issue of the refinement of the above screen, we must first present two forewords: the first is the detaining force, being the force of detainment in the screen. It is measured by the level of the coarseness, which is the yearning in phase four, like the two sides of the scales.

There is a simple reason for it: if there is a great yearning to receive, it necessitates great efforts to refrain from receiving; and if there is a small yearning, it does not take a great effort to refrain from receiving. Thus the detaining force in the screen is equal to the measure of coarseness in phase four, whether more or less.

The surrounding light refines the screen.

73. The second foreword is that the surrounding light, which is not clothed in the emanated being, its nature is to refine the coarseness in phase four. It does that slowly, by order of the four phases, until it refines its entire coarseness. First, it refines it from phase four to phase three, then to phase two, phase one, until it makes it completely refined, without any coarseness.

Because it wants to clothe, but the screen detains it.

74. The reason for it is that surrounding light is the upper light that cannot clothe the emanated being because of the screen that detains it from expanding further than its own level, it remains outside the Partzuf and surrounds it. In other words, it shines on it from afar.

Because the surrounding light wants to shine in the internality of the Partzuf as it did in Ein Sof, when it shone in phase four as well, it strikes the screen and refines it. In other words, it revokes the coarseness and the hardness in it so it can clothe.

First the screen intensifies, and then the light intensifies.

75. In the beginning, the screen intensifies and pushes it back. Afterwards, the light intensifies and refines the screen. However, it revokes only the level of coarseness over which there was coupling by striking. If the coupling by striking is on phase four, it revokes the coarseness of phase four that detains it from clothing in the Partzuf, leaving the coarseness of phase three, with which it had no dealings. If the coupling by striking was on the coarseness of phase three, it revokes only the coarseness of phase three, leaving the coarseness of phase two, etc. (see Talmud ten Sefirot, Part 4, Inner light, Chap 1).

Phase four does not become absent although it has been refined into phase three.

76. You already know that with any new form that forms in spirituality, the previous form does not become absent as a consequence. That is because there is no absence in spirituality, but only an additional form. From this you may conclude that this phase four that has now become refined into its phase three, is considered to have emerged from that emanated being and to be regarded as a new emanated being that was added to the first. Its Phase four is not the phase four within phase four, but phase three within phase four. However, that refinement did not cause any change at all in the first emanated being.

Immediately as it refined into phase three, the upper light coupled with her because it never stops shining.

77. It has been explained earlier that the upper light does not stop shining in the lower ones even for a minute. The expansion to the emanated being depends solely on the preparation of the vessel, meaning according to the measure of the will to receive in the emanated being. Any time the emanated being awakens and yearns for the upper light, it immediately receives it, to the extent of its desire (see Inner Observation, Part 2, item 63).

Therefore, after phase four had been refined into phase three, became a new emanated being in and of herself, and extended the upper light to herself, new ten Sefirot of upper light had emerged in her from above downward, as well as new ten Sefirot of reflected light from below upward, just as the first emanated being expanded. However, there is a significant difference between their statures because the new emanated being lacks the level of Keter and has only the level of Hochma.

The reason why phase three lacks the Keter.

78. The reason for the absence of the degree of Keter in the second emanated being is that it does not have the coarseness of phase four, which with respect to the reflected light, is the Keter of phase four. For this reason, the screen did not push back the upper light but only from Hochma downward, meaning that measure that was intended to enter phase three of phase four.

However, there would not be expansion in Keter of phase four even if the screen had not detained it, since the vessel that extended the upper light did not extend more than Hochma downward to begin with. For this reason, the screen did not push the light of Keter back, but only from the light of Hochma downward, and thus, the light of Keter lacks this reflected light.

Because the reflected light lacks the light of Keter, the light of Keter of the upper light is absent there, as well, since no light can clothe in the emanated being without reflected light to clothe it, being its vessel of reception (see Inner Observation, Part 2, item 21). This is why it has only the level of Hochma.

Any drawing is done by phase four. This is why she needs a screen, so the light will not expand into phase four.

79. The rule is that any extension of light must only be in phase four in the emanated being, even though there is no intention to draw the light into there. The reason is that the coarseness, which is above phase four, is unfit for extension (see Inner Observation, Part 2, item 56). Even phase one in phase four is more worthy of extension than the real phase three, which is above, meaning more refined than the entire phase four.

Therefore, if all the coarseness has vanished from phase four, there is no one there to draw light from Ein Sof and the light stops entirely. The extension must be done with phase four, while at the same time she has to guard herself so that the light will not expand into her due to the restriction on phase four. For this reason, she erected the screen that guards precisely that.

Thus, when the light expands and reaches phase four, the screen awakens and pushes that part of the light back to its root. That part that is pushed back does not disappear, but is turned into the reflected light. It is that which constitutes the vessel of reception for the upper light.

With respect to the extension of light, phase four and the screen are as one.

80. Regarding the extension of light from Ein Sof, phase four and the screen that is placed on her are regarded as one because the hardness of the screen lies over the coarseness of phase four. Hence, in most cases, only the screen is mentioned. Regarding the extension of light, it necessarily refers to both. To keep our words brief, we too will name the extension of the light from Ein Sof only after the screen.

Regarding the emergence of the degrees from one another, we will also refer to it with the name refinement of the coarseness, although it really refers to the hardness in the screen. Remember that it really refers to the levels of the coarseness in phase four, which created four levels of hardness in the screen.

The emergence of the degree of Hochma from phase three.

81. The emergence of the degree of Hochma from the degree of Keter has already been explained in detail above. The first ten Sefirot emerged after the restriction by the encounter with the upper light in the screen that consists of the complete coarseness of phase four (see Inner Observation, Part 2, item 64). For this reason, it raised reflected light in the entire level up to the root, called Keter.

Once that degree was completed with Rosh, Toch, and Sof, a part of the coarseness in the screen refined from phase four to phase three (see Inner Observation, Part 2, item 74). Because the screen had acquired a change of form, it is regarded as having left the degree of Keter.

Then, by the encounter of the light of Ein Sof with the screen that was refined to phase three, there came about a second ten Sefirot. Their level reached only as high as Hochma, lacking Keter (see Inner Observation, Part 2, 78).

The emergence of the degree of Bina from phase two.

82. Once that degree of Hochma was complete with Rosh, Toch, and Sof, the surrounding light returned and refined another part of the coarseness in the screen, meaning from phase three in phase four, to phase two in phase four. This new screen of phase two in phase four is considered to have left the degree of Hochma for the same reason mentioned concerning the degree of Keter (see Inner Observation, Part 2, item 76). From the encounter of that upper light with that new screen of phase two emerged new ten Sefirot at only the level of Bina, lacking Keter and Hochma.

The reason for the absence of Hochma in the screen of phase two.

83. The reason for the absence of Hochma from this new degree is the same reason mentioned above (see Inner Observation, Part 2, item 75) regarding the absence of Keter. Because this phase four does not have more than the coarseness of phase two, which is regarded as Bina of phase four, this extension that it performed was not from her beginning, but only from Bina downward. Therefore, even had the screen not detained the upper light, it would not have expanded to phase four herself, but only from Bina downward. Thus, now the screen did not push back the Keter and the Hochma intended for phase four. Consequently there aren't any Keter and Hochma in this reflected light. Because this reflected light is not there, the upper light of Keter and Hochma is not there as well, for the lack of the vessels to receive them.

The emergence of the degree of Zeir Anpin from the screen of phase one.

84. After this new degree of Bina was completed with Rosh, Toch, and Sof, the surrounding light returned and refined yet one another part of the coarseness in the screen, meaning from phase two to phase one. Consequently, it too is considered to have left the degree of Bina. From the encounter of the upper light with the screen of phase one of phase four emerged ten new Sefirot in the degree of Zeir Anpin. The first three Sefirot Keter, Hochma, and Bina, are absent here for the above reason.

The emergence of the degree of Malchut.

85. Once the degree of Zeir Anpin had been completed with Rosh, Toch, and Sof, the last part in the coarseness of phase four was refined, as well. It is also considered that this screen was completely refined, departed from the degree of Zeir Anpin, and it is called "the degree of Malchut." There isn't any new light here, but it receives illumination from Zeir Anpin, for it no longer merits extension. For this reason, all it has is the light of Nefesh. The rest about this matter will be explained in Part 3.

CHAPTER EIGHT

Explains: 1. Why during extension of lights, the greater the coarseness, the better, and when they are clothed in vessels, the greater the refinement, the better. 2. The reason for the inverse relation between vessels and lights: with vessels, the upper ones grow first; with lights, the lower ones enter first. 3. Why are the circles regarded as light of Nefesh?

The measure of the light that is extended depends on the extent of the coarseness of the screen.

86/a. A. It has been thoroughly clarified how the entire measure of imparting upper light in the emanated being depends on the measure of the coarseness of the screen. The greatest coarseness, namely phase four, is imparted in the level of Keter, and the lesser degree is imparted only in Hochma etc. Finally, in the most refined screen, the upper light does not impart anything to it because it has no coarseness.

The measure of the clothed light depends on the refinement of the vessel.

86/b. However, all this refers to the imparting and expansion of the upper light to the emanated being, because the giver always gives into the coarsest thing. It is so because the greater the coarseness of the screen, the higher the light that expands to it (see Inner Observation, Part 2, item 62). However, it is not so with regard to the manners of reception of upper light by the emanated being. There, the most important light is received in the most refined vessel, and the lowest one is received in the coarse vessel.

The upper ones come first in the vessels, and the lower ones come first in the lights.

87. A. We have said above (see Chap 2, item 14) that the giver gives into the coarsest thing, but the receiver receives in the most refined thing. In order to explain these words, I will clarify for you the order of the entrance of the lights into the emanated being after the correction. At that time, it receives the lights slowly, gradually. First, it obtains the light of Nefesh, then it obtains the light of Ruach, etc., up to the light of Yechida. It is the opposite in the vessels; Keter is acquired first, then Hochma etc.

When it obtains the light of Nefesh, it dresses in the vessel of Keter.

87/b. This is the order: First, the emanated being emerges with ten vessels – Keter, Hochma, Bina, ZA (that consists of HGT NHY) and Malchut. In other words, the higher vessels come first. Then, when Nefesh is imparted to it, it is considered that this Nefesh comes to it in the vessel of Keter, the most refined vessel.

The reason why it still does not have the light of Ruach is that the screen in Keter still does not have any coarseness, not even that of phase one, and light of Ruach is only imparted by the encounter of the upper light with the screen of phase one. Because the screen is in the vessel of Keter, meaning it is refined, without any coarseness, it therefore has only the light of Nefesh, attributed to Malchut.

When it obtains the light of Ruach, the light of Nefesh descends to Hochma and Ruach dresses in the vessel of Keter.

88. When it acquires coarseness of phase one, the light of Ruach is imparted to it through the encounter of the upper light with this screen of phase one. However, although the screen in the vessel of Hochma is the one that extended the light of Ruach to the Partzuf, the light of Ruach dresses in the vessel of Keter and the light of Nefesh that it previously had in Keter descends to Hochma. The reason is that the order of the reception of the lights is that the more important light dresses in the more refined vessel, and the lower one in the coarser vessel. In other words, it is the opposite of the order of imparting. Hence, Ruach, which is more important than Nefesh, ascends and dresses in Keter, and Nefesh descends and dresses in Hochma.

When it obtains Neshama, it dresses in the vessel of Keter, Ruach descends to Hochma, and Nefesh to Bina.

89. Afterwards, when its screen acquires the coarseness of phase two, it is regarded that the screen is in the vessel of Bina. By the encounter of the upper light with this screen, the light of Neshama is imparted into it, which is more important than the lights of Ruach and Nefesh.

Here too, it receives the light of Neshama in the most refined thing, meaning in the vessel of Keter. That is, because the light of Nefesh, the lowest of them all, which is in the vessel of Hochma, descends to the vessel of Bina, where there is a screen of phase two, which is now the coarsest vessel. The light of Ruach descends from Keter to the vessel of Hochma, and the light of

Neshama, the most important of them, clothes the vessel of Keter, the most refined of them.

When it obtains the light of Haya, she dresses in Keter; Neshama descends to Hochma, Ruach to Bina and Nefesh to ZA.

90. When its screen acquires the coarseness of phase three, it is regarded that the screen is now in the vessel of ZA, being phase three. Then, by the encounter of the upper light with this screen of phase three, the light of Haya is imparted to it, which is more important than the light of Neshama. For this reason, it must be received in the more refined vessel.

Consequently, the light of Nefesh, the lowest of all, descends from the vessel of Bina to the vessel that is now the coarsest, being the vessel of ZA, where there is the screen of phase three. Now the light of Ruach, which is in Hochma, descends to Bina, and the light of Neshama that is in Keter descends to Hochma. The light of Haya, the most important one, dresses in the vessel of Keter.

When it obtains Yechida, it dresses in Keter. Then Haya descends to Hochma, Neshama to Bina, Ruach to ZA and Nefesh to Malchut.

91. When the screen acquires the coarseness of phase four, it is considered that now the screen is in the vessel of Malchut, which is phase four. At that point, through the encounter of the upper light with this screen of phase four, the light of Yechida, the most important light, is imparted into it.

For this reason, it is received in the most refined thing, meaning in the vessel of Keter. Consequently, the light of Nefesh, the lowest light, descends from ZA to the vessel of Malchut, where there is the screen of phase four and is the coarsest. The light of Ruach descends from Bina to the vessel of ZA, the light of Neshama descends from Hochma to the vessel of Bina, and the light of Haya descends from Keter to the vessel of Hochma. Then the newly arrived light of Yechida dresses in Keter. Now each light from NRNHY has reached its true vessel, attributed to it.

The difference between the imparting of the light and the order of the clothing of the light.

92. Now you see the great difference between the order of the imparting of the upper light into the Partzuf and the order of the clothing of the light in the vessels. The giver needs the coarsest phase because the light of Yechida can come to the Partzuf only when it has a screen on the vessel of phase four.

Prior to this, when such coarseness was not present there, but rather a fainter coarseness, meaning that of phase three, it was impossible for this important light, called Yechida, to be imparted into the Partzuf. Nevertheless, when this important light is drawn to the Partzuf, it does not dress in the vessel of phase four, but in the most refined of all, namely the vessel of Keter.

Each light that comes to the Partzuf is received only in the vessel of Keter.

93. By the same manner, the light of Haya, which is only imparted in a screen of the vessel of ZA, meaning phase three, when dressing in the emanated being, it does not dress in the vessel of ZA, but in the most refined vessel, namely the vessel of Keter. It is the same with the light of Neshama, which is imparted only with a screen with the coarseness of phase two in the vessel of Bina. Yet when it dresses in it, it dresses only the vessel of Keter. Likewise, the light of Ruach, which is only imparted into a screen of phase one in the vessel of Hochma, still, when it dresses in it, it does not dress in the vessel of Hochma, but in the most refined vessel, namely the vessel of Keter.

Thus, each and every light that comes to the Partzuf, first comes in the vessel of Keter, as we have said that any receiver receives only in the most refined vessel, even though the imparting came to it through the coarsest vessel.

The circles do not receive the upper light because they have no coarseness.

94. From the aforesaid you can also understand why the circles do not receive any imparting from the upper light, but must receive all their lights from the light of the line. It is so although the vessels of the circles precede the vessels of straightness of the line.

It is a simple matter: they do not have any coarseness because all their four phases are equal (see Part 1, Chap 1, item 100). Thus, only the vessels of straightness in the line, which do have a screen and coarseness, are imparted upon by the upper light, and the circles receive from them.

Any degree that receives from another and does not have any form of bestowal in and of itself is regarded as Nefesh.

95. For this reason, the light of the circles is regarded as the light of Nefesh. The rule is that any degree that is not imparted upon by the upper light, but receives its illumination from another degree, that light is called the light of Nefesh, or female light.

Because the circles do not receive from the upper light, but receive their illumination from the line, they are considered as female light, or the light of Nefesh. It has also been explained about the vessels of straightness (see Inner Observation, Part 2, item 85) that if the entire coarseness in the screen had been purified, there is no imparting of upper light there any longer. In that state, there is only the illumination from the previous degree there, which is therefore called the light of Nefesh.

Chapter Nine

Explains why each and every Sefira consists of ten inner Sefirot, and the inner one consist of ten inner of inner Sefirot, and so they continue to expand endlessly and infinitely.

Each inner Sefira in each and every world consists of ten inner of inner Sefirot, etc., endlessly and infinitely.

Concerning the division of the Sefirot to inner and inner of inner ones indefinitely.

96. It is a wonderful law in the upper Worlds that in every Sefira that we choose to examine, we will find ten inner Sefirot. If we take a single Sefira from those ten inner Sefirot, we find another ten inner Sefirot inside the first Sefira. Also, if we take one Sefira from the inner of inner Sefirot, we find in it ten Sefirot once more, which are inside the previous inner of inner ones, and so on indefinitely.

Any light that passes through the degrees leaves its root in each degree it passes through.

97. You will understand the reason for it according to the rule that there is no absence in spirituality (see Inner light, Part 2, Chap 1, item 4). It explains that it is impossible that there will be any kind of light in the lower one that will not exist in all the upper ones above it up to Ein Sof.

The reason is that even a very small illumination that emerges in the lowest degree in the worlds must emerge from Ein Sof and pass through all the worlds and degrees before that low degree, until it comes there. Because this illumination cascades and passes through the degrees, it cannot be absent from the first degree because it has come to the second, and absent from the second degree when it comes to the third, etc., until it reaches the last degree, which receives it, as with corporeal objects that move from place to place. This is not at all possible in the spirituals where there are no absence and replacement. Instead, when an illumination travels through a certain degree, even if only in passing, it necessarily acquires its place there.

A light that appears once in a degree remains there for eternity.

98. Her coming and transitioning to the following degree does not decrease the light that she had left and has acquired its place in the previous degree in any way. Rather, it is like lighting one candle from another without diminishing the first. Here too, when the light leaves the first degree and descends to the next, the light remains complete in both the first and the second. Likewise, when it enters the third, the light does not move from the second at all; the light is complete in both the second and the third. In this way, it passes through all the degrees that precede the last degree, being the actual receiver for which the light came down from Ein Sof, becoming fixed in all of them. The reason for this is that there is no absence in the spiritual. Any light that shone in a spiritual phase once will not move from that phase forever, not even a bit.

When the light of Hochma passes to its place through the Keter, it leaves its root in the Keter.

99. From the aforesaid you can thoroughly understand the matter of the incorporation of the ten Sefirot in one another and in one another endlessly. For example, when the first two Sefirot emerge, namely Keter and Hochma, the light of Hochma must emerge from Ein Sof and must therefore pass through the Keter before it comes to the Sefira of Hochma.

Because the light of Hochma shone in the Keter once, namely as it passed through it, it is therefore impossible for it to ever be absent from there. Consequently, it necessarily implies that even after the light of Hochma has reached the Sefira of Hochma, the light of Hochma still remains complete in Keter. Thus, the Sefira of Keter now has two lights, being the light of Keter and the light of Hochma.

When the light of Bina passes through Keter and Hochma it leaves its root in them, and so on in the same manner.

100. It is the same with the light of Bina. Because it must travel through the two preceding Sefirot before it comes to Bina, it necessarily acquires its place in Keter and Hochma as well. Thus there are now three lights in Keter: the light of Keter, the light of Hochma and the light of Bina. Likewise, there are two lights in Hochma: the light of Hochma and the light of Bina, and one light in Bina, namely her own light.

It continues in the same manner until the light of Malchut emerges. At that time Keter has all the ten Sefirot because the lower nine lights have necessarily traveled through Keter, thus acquiring their place there. There are also nine Sefirot in Hochma, because all the eight lower Sefirot below her traveled through her and remained there.

Likewise, there are eight Sefirot in Bina, seven in Hesed, six in Gevura, etc., through Malchut, who has but her own light because there is no other Sefira below it to pass through it.

There is no direct light in the vessel of Malchut, but only reflected light.

101.   Regarding the above-mentioned light of Malchut, both the light inside her and the light that is incorporated from her in the first nine Sefirot, is only reflected light. You already know that since the restriction onwards, a screen was erected on the Sefira of Malchut and the light of Ein Sof is not received there.

Instead, a coupling occurs there because of the encounter of the light of Ein Sof with that screen, at which time a new light emerges and rises from the screen of Malchut, called reflected light, that shines up to the Sefira of Keter. It thus clothes all the ten Sefirot from below upward, which is the only way by which it is contained in each Sefira of the upper nine Sefirot (see Inner Observation, Part 2, item 19).

Malchut is regarded as the Keter of the ten Sefirot of reflected light.

102/a. The Sefira of Malchut is the source of the new light, and every source is regarded as Keter. Hence, Malchut is regarded as the Sefira of Keter of that new light. The Sefira before her, namely Yesod, is regarded as the Hochma of the new light, and the one before her, meaning Hod, is regarded as Bina. Finally, the upper Keter is now regarded as Malchut, meaning the one that receives from this new light.

Ten Sefirot of direct light expand from above downward.

102/b. We have learned that in each degree of the ten Sefirot, we should distinguish two courses of ten Sefirot that extend from Ein Sof. The first is of the ten Sefirot that extend from Ein Sof, from above downward, from Keter to Malchut. These are called the ten Sefirot of the direct light, for they descend in straightness from above downward by a gradual order from the refined vessel to the coarser and from there to the coarser still, through Malchut, the coarsest of all.

Ten Sefirot of reflected light expand from below upward.

103. We have another course of ten Sefirot there. These extend from the Sefira of Malchut, from below upward, meaning from Malchut to Keter. In that case, Malchut becomes the origin of the new light, called the ten Sefirot of the reflected light.

They are called by that name for they are imparted and emerge in an opposite order of degree. That is, it does not extend and travel from the refined vessel to the coarse one, so the last receiver is the coarsest. On the contrary, it extends and travels from the coarsest vessel to the one that is less coarse. Finally, the last receiver is the most refined, which is why it is regarded as illuminating from below upward.

All the Sefirot of the reflected light that come in the Sefirot of the direct light travel through Malchut.

104. We have explained above about the incorporation of the Sefirot in the order of the ten Sefirot of direct light. Because there is no absence in spirituality, any illumination that passes anywhere remains there in completeness even after it moves to a different location.

With regards to the ten Sefirot of direct light, all the ten Sefirot are present in Keter, nine in Hochma, eight in Bina etc. (see item 99). For that reason it also appears by the same way in the ten Sefirot of reflected light. That is because here the Sefira of Malchut becomes the origin of that reflected light.

Thus, it is considered that every phase of reflected light that reaches its upper Sefirot must travel through Malchut, since that Malchut emanates that light by the power of her screen, which makes a coupling with the light of Ein Sof that meets that screen.

When the reflected light of Yesod travels through Malchut, it leaves its root in Malchut and so on by the same manner.

105. Therefore, when the Sefira of Yesod receives her light from Malchut, it necessarily means that Malchut received that light first, via a coupling with the light of Ein Sof that passed through Malchut and came to the Sefira Yesod. It follows that the light of Yesod is present both in Malchut and in Yesod.

It is the same with the reflected light that Hod receives, which necessarily acquired its place by passing through Malchut and Yesod. In that state we find that there are three lights in Malchut, two in Yesod and one in Hod.

Similarly, when Keter receives the last reflected light, there are already ten lights of the ten Sefirot of reflected light in Malchut, nine in Yesod, eight in Hod etc. as was explained regarding the ten Sefirot of direct light.

By the incorporation of the reflected light through passing, ten Sefirot were established in each and every Sefira. Keter has nine Sefirot of direct light and one of reflected light.

106. It turns out that we have ten Sefirot in each and every Sefira of the above ten Sefirot, meaning together with the reflected light. In other words, the light of Malchut that is received in each and every Sefira completes to ten Sefirot. In Keter there are nine Sefirot of direct light – KHB HGT NHY – and one of reflected light, namely Malchut, for she receives last from the ten Sefirot of reflected light. Consequently, he has only one light of the reflected light.

Hochma has eight of direct light and two of reflected light; Bina has seven of direct light and three of reflected light.

107. Hochma has eight Sefirot of direct light – Hochma, Bina and HGT NHY – and two of reflected light. These are her own part, which she received from the reflected light of Malchut, being Yesod of reflected light, and the second one is the part of Keter that passed through her and does not move from there, namely Malchut of the reflected light.

Bina has seven lights of direct light, which are Bina, HGT NHY, and three Sefirot of reflected light: Hod, Yesod, Malchut. She has Hod from her own; Yesod from the part of Hochma that traveled through her, and Malchut from the part of Keter that traveled through her, meaning from Bina upwards.

Hesed has six of direct light and four of reflected light; Gevura has five of direct light and five of reflected light; Tifferet has four of direct light and six of reflected light.

108. Hesed has six Sefirot of direct light, which are HGT NHY, and four Sefirot of reflected light, which extend from Hesed upwards. In other words, she has her own part, namely Netzah, and the parts of Bina, Hochma and Keter, which are Hod, Yesod and Malchut that traveled through her and were established there.

Likewise Gevura has five Sefirot of direct light: Gevura, Tifferet, Netzah, Hod and Yesod. She also has five Sefirot of reflected light from Gevura upwards, meaning the four parts of Keter, Hochma, Bina, Hesed, being

Netzah, Hod, Yesod, Malchut, which passed through her, and her own part, which is Tifferet of reflected light.

Tifferet has four Sefirot of direct light from Tifferet downwards, and six of reflected light from Tifferet upwards. In other words, it has five parts KHB HG, which are TNHYM that passed through him, and his own part, being Gevura of the reflected light.

Netzah has three of direct light and seven of reflected light; Hod has two of direct light and eight of reflected light; Yesod has nine of reflected light and one of direct light, and Malchut has ten Sefirot of reflected light.

109. Netzah has three Sefirot of direct light from Netzah downwards, which are – Netzah, Hod and Yesod of direct light. It also has seven Sefirot of reflected light from Netzah upwards, which are the six parts KHB HGT that passed through her. Those are GTNHYM and her own part, which is Hesed of the reflected light.

Hod has two Sefirot of direct light – Hod and Yesod, and eight Sefirot of reflected light from Hod upwards. Those are the seven parts, KHB HGT and Netzah that passed through him, which are HGT NHYM of the reflected light, and his own part, which is Bina of the reflected light.

Yesod has one Sefira of direct light and nine Sefirot of reflected light, from Yesod upwards. Those are the eight parts KHB HGT Netzah and Hod that passed through him, which are Bina, HGT NHYM of reflected light, and his own part, being Hochma of reflected light.

With her reflected light, Malchut completes every single Sefira to ten Sefirot.

110. It has been thoroughly explained that every manifestation of ten Sefirot, wherever they might be, must be incorporated in one another. However, when the ten Sefirot of direct light first emerge, they still do not have ten Sefirot in each of them until the light of Malchut is incorporated in them, too, namely the ten Sefirot of reflected light. Malchut has no other light, and that light of Malchut completes what is missing from this number - ten Sefirot – for each and every one of the ten Sefirot. Thus there are ten Sefirot in each and every one of them.

It is likewise in the inner of the inner. When you take the Keter of the ten Sefirot in Keter, it, too, necessarily has nine Sefirot of direct light and one of reflected light.

111. If, for example, you take the general Sefira of Keter from the general ten Sefirot, it already consists of ten inner Sefirot, meaning after the light of Malchut appears there, we can immediately see that in the first Sefira of that general Keter, which is now called Keter of Keter, meaning the inner Keter, there are necessarily nine Sefirot of direct light, which are in it, below it. These are Hochma and Bina and HGT NHY of direct light in the Keter.

Keter of Keter is its own phase, and the nine lower Sefirot are passing lights.

112. Although it is only the Keter in them that is considered its own phase, the other nine Sefirot in it are but passing lights there. In other words, they are lower lights that have acquired their place there through passing from Ein Sof, through Keter to the lower Sefirot.

Still, since they are in Keter, the highest Sefira, namely their inner Keter, it necessarily, in and of itself, contain the nine inner Sefirot below it, too. Because these nine Sefirot are below it, they must have passed through it. Because they passed through it, they must have acquired their place in it, for there is no absence in spirituality, just as we have said about the general ten Sefirot.

It turns out that now this inner Keter itself also has ten inner of inner Sefirot that are nine of direct light, KHB HGT NHY, and one of reflected light, the light of Malchut, as mentioned regarding the Keter of the general ten Sefirot.

Hochma in Keter, too, necessarily consists of eight Sefirot of direct light and two of reflected light.

113. Likewise, when you examine the inner Sefira of Hochma from the ten inner Sefirot of the general Keter, called Hochma of Keter, by necessity, it now contains ten inner of inner Sefirot by the same manner we mentioned regarding the inner Keter. Because all eight inner Sefirot of the general Keter of direct light below her must have passed through that inner Hochma from above downward, having passed through her, they have necessarily acquired their place in her in addition to the two Sefirot of reflected light, meaning from the light of the inner Malchut, which also passed through that inner Hochma from below upward. These parts are her own part of the reflected light and the part of the reflected light that relates to the inner Keter. Thus, there are ten inner of inner Sefirot in the inner Hochma in the inner ten Sefirot of the general Keter, as well, as it is in the general Hochma of the general ten Sefirot.

Bina in Keter also has seven Sefirot of direct light and three Sefirot of reflected light.

114. Also, when you examine the inner Bina in the ten inner Sefirot of the general Keter, called Bina of Keter, you will also find that it necessarily contains ten inner of inner Sefirot, as we have seen in the above-mentioned inner Hochma. This is because all six iner Sefirot HGT NHY of direct light of the general Keter below her necessarily passed from above downward through that inner Bina and acquired their place in her. Now, together with Bina herself, they are seven Sefirot of direct light. Also, the three inner Sefirot of reflected light passed through that Bina from the inner Malchut of the general Keter from below upward, meaning her own part of the reflected light, the part of the reflected light of the inner Hochma, and the part of the reflected light of the inner Keter. Thus, there are ten inner of inner Sefirot in the inner Bina in the ten Sefirot of the general Keter, as is written concerning the general Bina in the general ten Sefirot.

Hesed in Keter also has six Sefirot of direct light and four of reflected light, and so on by the same manner.

115. By the exact same manner, you find ten inner of inner Sefirot in the inner Hesed in the ten inner Sefirot in the general Keter. They are six of direct light, HGT NHY from above downward, and four of reflected light from Hesed and above through Keter. By the exact same manner, you will find ten inner of inner Sefirot in Gevura, etc., through the inner Malchut in those ten Sefirot, called Malchut of Keter.

116. You might ask: In the ten inner Sefirot of the above-mentioned general Keter, there is no reflected light that rose from the general Malchut, but only Nefesh, meaning the last part of the reflected light, the smallest of the entire ten Sefirot of reflected light (see item 112), so how can we say that that small part of reflected light has now expanded by itself into ten new Sefirot of reflected light, to the point of completing in each inner Sefira, all the inner of inner Sefirot that they need in order to complete their number to ten Sefirot?

The Nefesh of reflected light in the general Keter is necessarily divided into the clothing of the ten inner Sefirot in Keter.

117. Indeed, the answer is that it is ultimately necessary for that part of Nefesh of the inner reflected light that rose from Malchut to the general Keter to have clothed all nine inner Sefirot in the general Keter. Otherwise, these nine Sefirot of direct light would not have been captured in the Partzuf and

illuminate there at all, for it is known that direct light cannot connect with a Partzuf except through the vessels of reception of the reflected light.

Since this light of Nefesh clothed the nine inner Sefirot of Keter, we necessarily find that in passing from below upward, it completed each and every one of those inner Sefirot to the number ten inner of inner Sefirot that it lacked. It gave Hochma the two lights that she is missing: one light for her own clothing, and another light in passing, to clothe the Keter. It gave three to Bina and four to Hesed, as explained above.

It is likewise in the ten inner of inner Sefirot in the general Hochma. Keter of the inner of inner in Hochma has nine Sefirot of direct light and one of reflected light.

118. Just as we have explained the ten inner of inner Sefirot in the ten inner Sefirot in the general Keter, so we will explain the ten inner of inner Sefirot in each and every one of the ten inner Sefirot of the general Sefira of Hochma. In Keter of the ten inner Sefirot of the general Hochma, called Keter of Hochma, you necessarily find ten inner of inner Sefirot, which are its own light, and the inner eight Sefirot Bina, HGT NHY, which passed through it from above downward, thus nine, and one reflected light that rose from the inner Malchut of the general Hochma. Thus you have ten inner of inner Sefirot in the Keter of the general Hochma.

Hochma of the inner of inner in Hochma has eight of direct light and two of reflected light.

119. Likewise, the inner Hochma in the ten inner Sefirot of the general Hochma, called Hochma of Hochma, has eight of direct light from above downward, and two of reflected light from below upward. Similarly, the inner Bina in the ten inner Sefirot of the general Hochma has seven of direct light from above downward and three of reflected light from below upward. So it is in Hesed, and so it is in Gevura, etc., through the inner Malchut in those ten Sefirot of the general Hochma, called Malchut of Hochma. She, too, has ten inner of inner Sefirot of reflected light, meaning because she necessarily clothes all the ten inner Sefirot of the general Hochma and sends them her illuminations. Thus, you find that they all necessarily passed through her and acquired their place within her.

120. Just so, the ten inner of inner Sefirot of Bina are discerned in the inner Bina, and likewise in the inner Hesed, inner Gevura, through inner Malchut, and there is no need to elaborate further on this.

Instead, we will explain one more Sefira from the inner of inner ones so as to show how it, too, in and of itself, is discerned by the same necessity as ten Sefirot in itself, which are now ten inner Sefirot of the inner of inner.

121. When we examine Bina of the inner of inner, which is, for instance, one Sefira of the ten inner of inner Sefirot in the inner Hochma in the ten Sefirot of the general Hochma, called Bina in Hochma of Hochma. Here, too, we find that she has ten Sefirot of her own, according to the same principle, meaning seven of direct light that passed through her from above downward, and three of reflected light that passed through her from below upward.

122. We can elaborate and make such discernments indefinitely, for whenever you take any Sefira, even after it has been divided a thousand times, that Sefira still comes from an arrangement of ten Sefirot. Thus, some of those ten Sefirot have necessarily passed through that Sefira from above downward and some of them passed from below upward. Thus, these ten Sefirot have necessarily acquired their place in that Sefira for all eternity, as we've explained above. Thus, in that Sefira you necessarily have all ten Sefirot.

123. However, know that even when you divide the ten to ten, and the second ten to a third one and so on, do not think that all the Sefirot remain equal. Rather, they change significantly as they divide, and one is not equal to the other since the lights of direct light never come in their place, as the Sefirot divide, except in Keter. Thus, in Hochma there are only eight of direct light, meaning from Hochma downward, and two of reflected light, Yesod and Malchut.

Therefore, the eight lights of direct light come in the more refined vessels, from Keter to Hod, and the two of reflected light in Yesod and Malchut. It follows that the light of Hochma comes in the vessel of Keter, and the light of Bina in the vessel of Hochma, etc., through the light of Yesod in the vessel of Hod. Thus, all the lights of direct light do not come in their place, and only the reflected light always comes in its place: The reflected light of Yesod comes in the vessel of Yesod and the reflected light of Malchut in the vessel of Malchut of Malchut.

124. Similarly, Bina has no more than seven lights of direct light, which clothe the more refined vessels, since any receiver receives in the more refined thing, meaning from Keter to Netzah. It follows that the light of Bina is in the vessel of Keter and the light Hesed is in Hochma. Finally, the light of Yesod in the vessel of Netzah. Only the three lights of reflected light come in their place: the lights of Hod, Yesod, Malchut, in the vessels of Hod, Yesod, Malchut.

125. According to the above, there is a big difference between the inner Bina of Keter, the inner Bina of Hochma, and the inner Bina of Bina, etc. Only in Bina of Keter is the light of Bina in her own vessel. However, in Bina of Hochma there is only the light of Hesed in the vessel of Bina, and in Bina of Bina there is only the light of Gevura in the vessel of Bina. That is the case with all of them, for one is not like the other.

126. We can discern changes in the manner of division even in the lights of reflected light, which do not change their places. This is so because wherever the reflected light is, illumination from direct light spreads to it. Therefore, in Yesod of Hochma, for example, illumination from the direct light of Hod of Hochma spreads to it. However, in Yesod of Bina, illumination from Netzah of Bina spreads to it since there is no direct light in Hod of Bina.

127. The exception to the aforementioned rule is if you divide only the general Sefira. That is, if, for example, you take the general Sefira of Bina and divide it to ten, and to another ten, meaning divide the inner of inner Bina from the ten Sefirot of the inner Bina of the ten Sefirot of the general Bina, called Bina of Bina of Bina, they will all be equal, without any difference, for you will find in all of them the seven of direct light in the seven upper vessels KHB HGT Netzah, and three of reflected light in the three bottom vessels, Hod, Yesod, Malchut. It likewise even after a thousand divisions, and likewise in the rest of the Sefirot.

Chapter Ten

Explains the topic of coupling by striking, which consists of two forces: a pulling force and a repelling force. They operate simultaneously, one in the coarseness, and the other in the hardness of the screen.

A detailed explanation about the meaning of the words coupling by striking

128. The topic of coupling by striking requires an elaborate explanation. There is an apparent positive and negative together here, for coupling and striking mean rejection and separation, and great hatred. Thus, how can you say "a coupling of striking," which implies love of hatred, or adhesion of separation, or extension of rejection? It is indeed perplexing.

129. Indeed, they are two opposites under one governance. However, this governance consists of two unique carriers, meaning two forces: a pulling force and a repelling force. The pulling force is in the coarseness of the vessel, and the repelling force is in the screen of the vessel. They have been assembled together and both govern simultaneously, at one time in two places.

130. I will elaborate in order to examine it thoroughly and make it acceptable to the mind without arousing any confusion or bafflement. I will give you an allegory from the corporeal reality that is depicted and appears to our eyes: When you see a rock or a person falling off a high place to the ground, you see that that person is being pulled from above downward with great force and speed. Still, when he reaches the ground and touches it, the ground strikes him and pushes him a bit upward.

131. There are two conjectures here: One conjecture is that the earth has a great force that pulls everything that is placed in the air, if there is nothing solid to protect it. Thus, when one disconnects from the roof of the house into the air, that pulling force of the earth immediately operates on him. This explains the matter of the speedy fall to the ground.

    However, there is a question here, for accordingly, the earth should have lovingly embraced him, without letting him move even a bit. Still, we see the opposite: The minute that person touches the ground, it pushes him back quickly and he returns slightly upwards.

132. Conversely, there is another conjecture, that there is another force, which repels from above, from the air, a repelling force operates on anything airborne and pushes it to the ground.

At the same time, our earth has only the repelling force, and none of the pulling force. Thus, when that person disconnects from the roof of the house and becomes airborne, the repelling force from above instantly operates on him and lowers him to the ground. Hence, when he touches the ground, it pushes him back, upwards.

133. If we deduce from the branch about its root in the upper worlds, for things are mostly very similar, we will find that both conjectures are incorrect. We might also say that each and every planet has a pulling force and repelling force that are combined in one another. In other words, there is a force of coarseness, which the pulling force that wants to draw inwards everything that is outside of it, and opposite it there is a force of hardness, which repels any external body from entering into it.

Thus, any extension must certainly come from the central point in its internality, for that is where its pulling force lies. It is so because the central point is coarser than the entire planet, and therefore pulling into it anything within that peripheral space under its force of operation and control.

134. However, it does not pull it to the point of swallowing it, as it should have, had it only the pulling force. Instead, at the very moment when the pulled object touches the outer crust, the repelling force in the crust, which is the hardness, promptly awakens and repels it back up.

135. It turns out that what it pulled to it was received not by pulling, but in another way, since it was stopped midway by the force of hardness that repels it and detained it in its way.

Thus, both coupling and striking operate here together; the coupling pulls and the hardness repels. As a result, it receives it on it, and does not swallow it alive into its belly.

We can therefore say that the vessel for reception is primarily the repelling force in it, which receives it and sustains it as it should be, for without the repelling force, it would be swallowed alive within it.

136. You can also see that the pulling and the repelling are as even as two drops of water in the measure of their strength. Had the pulling force been a little stronger than the repelling force, it would have been impossible to move on it, for anything moving would be glued to it like iron to a magnet. Alternately,

had the repelling force been somewhat stronger, the whole world would be dancing on it and would not be able to touch it. Thus, they are evidently even.

137. In the same manner, you can thoroughly understand the matter of coupling by striking conducted in the upper ones. Even though the coupling and the striking are two opposites, they still partake in one governance, simultaneously, at one time, but in two places, which are the coarseness and the hardness, and remember this for the rest of this wisdom.

TABLE OF QUESTIONS FOR THE MEANING OF THE WORDS

1. What is Adam Kadmon
2. What is reflected light
3. What is direct light
4. What is surrounding light
5. What is inner light
6. What is length
7. What is Bina
8. What is not adhered
9. What is a boundary
10. What is top
11. What is Guf
12. What is wheel
13. What are GAR
14. What is corporeality
15. What is by passing
16. What is illumination from afar
17. What is refinement of the screen
18. What is "utterly distant"
19. What is lowering of the Rosh
20. What is incorporation of the Sefirot
21. What is attachment
22. What is one inside the other
23. What is coupling by striking
24. What is Zeir Anpin [ZA]
25. What are ZAT
26. What is matter
27. What is Haya
28. What is externality

62. What is a ration
63. What is bottom
64. What is a Rosh
65. What is Ruach
66. What is "spirituality"
67. What is "far"
68. What is the beginning of the expansion
69. What is "at once" [immediately]
70. What is "The last of them"

TABLE OF QUESTIONS FOR TOPICS

1. Adam Kadmon (Part 2, Chap 1, Inner light, 400)

   Adam Kadmon is the first world that receives from Ein Sof. It is also called "one line" because it is extended immediately after the restriction, from Ein Sof almost as far as this world. The name Adam relates only to the Sefirot of straightness in the first world, namely to the light of Ruach, meaning a light of bestowal. It does not relate to its Sefirot of circles, which only have the light of Nefesh, meaning a light of reception for themselves, without the ability to bestow upon others. It is the root of the quality of man in this world.

2. Reflected light (Part 2, Inner Observation, 79)

   Reflected light is the light that is not received in phase four. It is the light that is designated to fill phase four, and which she does not receive because of the screen that detains it and pushes it back. This operation is called coupling by striking. All the vessels of reception in the Partzufim, from the restriction onward, extend from this reflected light, which serves them instead of phase four in Ein Sof.

3. Direct light (Part 2, Inner Observation, 94)

   Direct light is the upper light that extends from Ein Sof, which is imparted to the Partzufim, from the restriction onward. It is called by that name to indicate that it is not imparted into the vessels of circles, or to any degree that does not have any coarseness of phase four in it. It is imparted only in the Sefirot of straightness, according to the rule that the giver only gives in the coarser thing, which is the coarseness in phase four.

4. Surrounding light (Part 2, Chap 1, Inner light, 40)

   Surrounding light is the light that is designated to clothe the degree, but is detained because of some boundary in it. That name has two meanings: 1) Distant illumination, 2) Certain illumination, meaning an illumination that is certain to finally clothe there, since the light "surrounds" it from all sides without giving her any room to escape from it until she is fit to receive it in full.

5. Inner light (Part 2, Chap 1, Inner light, 40)

   Inner light is the light that is clothed in the vessel.

6. Length (Part 2, Chap 2, Inner light, 4)

   The distance between the two ends of a degree, from the most refined to the coarsest, is called length, since so is the imaginary corporeal length, implying the distance between the upper end and the lower end.

7. Bina (Part 2, Chap 1, Inner light, 200)

   Contemplating the manners of cause and consequence in order to scrutinize all the consequences that are born and emerge from something is called Bina.

8. Not adhered (Part 2, Chap 1, item 3)

   Equivalence of form between two spiritual entities is adhesion, and disparity of form between them makes them not adhered to one another.

9. Boundary (Part 2, Inner observation, 79)

   In each degree, the screen measures and makes a "boundary" over the degree of reflected light that the screen raises according to its coarseness (see item 2 above), since the screen of phase three limits (places a boundary on) the level of the degree so that it does not acquire the light of Keter. The screen of phase two limits it from light of Hochma, too, etc.

10. Top (Part 2, Chap 1, Inner light, 1)

    The Top is the Keter in each degree, as well as in the Sefirot and in the worlds.

11. Guf (Part 2, Chap 1, Inner light, 90)

    The real vessels of reception in each degree, which expand by the power of the reflected light in the screen, from it and below, are called the Guf [body] of the degree, since they precede the lights. It is unlike the lights that expand for a coupling by striking on the screen, which precede the vessels.

12. Wheel (Part 2, Chap 1, item, 2)

    The Sefirot of circles are called wheels because the lights become round in them. This means that it is impossible to distinguish refinement and coarseness in them.

13. GAR (Part 2, Chap 1, Inner light, 90)

    GAR are the lights that preceded the vessels that are clothed in the reflected light that rises to them from the screen and above, meaning the first three Sefirot—Keter, Hochma, and Bina. They are also called the Rosh [head] of the Partzuf.

14. Corporeality

    Anything that is depicted and perceived by the five senses or occupies place and time is called "corporeality."

15. In passing (Part 2, Chap 1, Inner light, 4)

    The lights that extend from Ein Sof to the lower Sefirot necessarily pass through the upper Sefirot. Since the spiritual does not become absent from one place as it moves to another place but remains in both place A and place B, we distinguish two kinds of light in each Sefira: lights of their own quality, and the lights that remained in them "in passing."

16. Illumination from afar (Part 2, Chap 1, Inner light, 40)

    The illumination that operates in a Partzuf when it has no vessels of reception for that light is called "illumination from afar." It means that when there is a great distance and difference between the light and the vessels of the Partzuf related to that light, the vessels cannot receive and clothe that light. Instead, they receive from it an illumination from afar.

17. The refinement of the screen (Part 2, Inner observation, 74)

    The refinement of the screen is the refinement of the coarseness in phase four. The level of reflected light that the screen raises and clothes on the direct light depends on the measure of the coarseness in phase four, meaning the measure of the desire in her. Therefore, once the degree is filled with the light that it extended, the surrounding light intensifies and refines the screen to a certain measure of the level of the yearning. This is considered that she has been refined from the coarseness that was in her, and it is also called "the refinement of the screen."

18. Completely distant (Part 2, Chap 1, item, 8)

    When the disparity of form is so great that it reaches oppositeness of form, from one end to the other, it is called "completely distant."

19. Lowering of the Rosh (Part 2, Chap 2, Inner light, 3)

    When the lights of ZAT also operate in the Rosh, which is also called GAR since the lights of GAR that should be in the Rosh are missing there, it is called "lowering of the Rosh [head]," meaning that the Rosh is lowered to the same level as the ZAT, which are called Guf [body].

20. The incorporation of the Sefirot (Part 2, Inner Observation, 97)

    The Sefirot incorporate with one another "in passing" (see answer 15). Since the ten Sefirot of direct light extend from Keter to Malchut, it is impossible for them to appear in the degree, except by clothing in the ten Sefirot of reflected light that extend and rise from Malchut to Keter.

    Thus, there is not a single Sefira among them that does not have two Sefirot within it, one of direct light and one of reflected light, as well as eight other Sefirot that were incorporated in it in passing. Some of them passed through it in passing from above downward, and some of them passed through it in passing from below upward.

21. Attachment (Part 2, Chap 1, Inner light, 20)

    The clothing of the ten Sefirot of the Rosh of a degree in the ten Sefirot of reflected light that rise from Malchut from below upward, is called "attachment" since here, it is discerned that the lights precede the vessels and coarseness does not ascend with this reflected light above its place, which is Malchut, even a bit. Therefore, these ten Sefirot of reflected light are not regarded as complete vessels, fit for clothing the self in them. For this reason, this clothing is only called "attachment." In other words, the direct light attaches to and is present on the Partzuf through these ten Sefirot of reflected light, although it does not actually clothe in them.

The clothing of direct light in the vessels refers only to the reflected light that expands below the screen, where the coarseness of the Malchut of Rosh can spread and descend, and clothe the ten Sefirot of direct light that enter it.

22. One inside the other (Part 2, Chap 2, Inner light, 40)

It means that one is caused by the other. The outer circle is the reason and the cause of the circle within it, which is caused and extended from the outer one. Thus, "one inside the other" indicates a relation of cause and consequence, or cause and effect, between them.

23. Coupling by striking (Part 2, Inner Observation, 18)

The act of the screen, which detains and conceals the light from phase four and rejects the light that belongs to her back to its root, is called coupling by striking. The name indicates that this act contains within it two opposite matters: On the one hand, it "strikes" the light, meaning rejects and conceals it from illuminating. On the other hand, it "couples" with the light, meaning causes it to multiply and expand extensively, since this measure of light that is concealed and rejected from phase four becomes a great revealed light that clothes the direct light, and it is called "reflected light." Without it, it is utterly impossible for the light of Ein Sof to clothe the Partzuf.

24. Zeir Anpin (ZA) (Part 2, Inner observation, 13)

Zeir Anpin means "a small face." The light of Hochma is called the light of the face, as it says, "A man's wisdom illuminates his face." That is why the general Partzuf of Keter in the world of Atzilut is called Arich Anpin, meaning "a long face," for its essence is the light of Hochma.

Therefore, phase three, whose essence is only the light of Hassadim that extends from Bina, but which also has illumination of Hochma, though its essence is not of Hochma, is called "a diminished face", meaning Zeir Anpin, because the light of its face is diminished and reduced compared to phase one.

25. ZAT - Seven lower Sefirot (Part 2, Chap 1, Inner light, 90)

The ten Sefirot that expand from the screen downward are called Guf, or ZAT (see answer 11). While the entire Partzuf is sometimes regarded as having only ten Sefirot, the first three Sefirot (KHB) are in the Rosh of the Partzuf, and the ZAT, which are HGT NHYM are in the Guf of the Partzuf.

26. Matter (Part 2, Inner Observation, 40)

The coarseness in the Partzuf that comes from phase four in the desire is called the matter of the Partzuf. This name is borrowed from the imaginary corporeal substance that consists of the three dimensions: length, width and depth, and six directions: up and down, east, west, north and south.

27. Haya (Part 2, Chap 2, Inner light, 6)

Haya [living] is the light of Hochma, as it says, "Wisdom gives life to its owner."

28. Externality (Part 2, Inner observation, 6)

The more refined part of each vessel is regarded as its externality. It is regarded as the vessel for the surrounding light that shines in it from afar.

29. Hochma (Part 2, Chap 1, Inner light, 200)

Knowing the final purpose of every element in the entire reality is called Hochma [wisdom].

30. Window (Part 2, Chap 2, Inner light, 70)

The force of the coarseness in the screen, either in the ten Sefirot of the Rosh of the degree, or in the ten Sefirot of circles. That force of coarseness, which operates in them along with the reflected light that rises to them from the screen, is called a "window".

Interpretation: The reflected light rejected from phase four because of its coarseness became a vessel of reception for the upper light instead of phase four, which was the vessel of reception in Ein Sof. This is so because the reflected light really does consist of the coarseness of phase four, because she extended it to her from Ein Sof.

However, this coarseness is apparent only in the vessels of the Guf, for they expand below the screen, meaning below phase four of the ten Sefirot of Rosh, which is why the coarseness of phase four in the screen controls them. Therefore, they are considered complete vessels for clothing of upper light in them.

However, the ten Sefirot of Rosh are necessarily above their phase four. Thus, reflected light rises to them from below and the coarseness of phase four in the screen cannot incorporate there and rise along with the reflected light, above its place, to its first nine Sefirot. Therefore, this reflected light does not become complete vessels there, but only roots to the vessels. Because of this, the clothing of the nine Sefirot in this reflected light is regarded only as attachment.

Nevertheless, with regard to the nine Sefirot of the Rosh, this reflected light is also regarded as a force of coarseness, as it nevertheless becomes a force of attachment, attaching them to the emanated being.

This force is called a window, because when the reflected light and direct light enter in order to illuminate the refined vessels of the circles, which do not have even a trace of coarseness, the force of coarseness in the reflected light is much lower than them and therefore inferior, and lowers the walls of the vessels of circles as it enters them.

It is like a foramen and a hole in a room, which is a cavity and deficiency in the wall of the room. However, it is also an entrance for the sunlight. Similarly, the cavity and deficiency in the walls of the vessels of the circles, which happened because of the coarseness in the reflected light, is not at all regarded as a deficiency in them, but as a window. Without it, they would not have had any light, for they can receive light only through the line, through the force of the screen in it.

31. Yechida (Part 2, Chap 2, Inner light, 6)

The light clothed in the Sefira of Keter is called Yechida.

32. Going Outside (Part 2, Inner observation, 59)

A disparity of form that is attained in the spiritual is called "going outside" of it, since the disparity of form that forms in a part of the Partzuf is considered that that part went outside the Partzuf. This is akin to lighting one candle from another without the first diminishing, as there is no absence in the spiritual.

It follows that when the part begins to change its form, along with this changing, it begins to separate from the Partzuf and exit the Partzuf into a new authority of its own. Thus, disparity of form and "going outside" are one and the same.

33. Descent (Part 2, Chap 1, Inner light, 5)

Growing coarser is considered a "descent," meaning a decline from its degree. Refinement means an "ascent," since it ascended in equivalence of form with Ein Sof. The rule is that the greater the refinement, the higher it is, and the greater the coarseness, the lower it is.

34. Straight (Part 2, Chap 1, Inner light, 5)

When the upper light descends to vessels that have coarseness of phase four, namely yearning, for she extends it through her yearning, it is considered that the light descends in straightness, meaning in absolute proportion to the measure of coarseness and yearning in her. This is similar to a heavy object that falls to the ground from above. It falls in a completely straight line from above downward, and at a great speed because of the earth's gravitational force affecting it. Conversely, when a light object falls to the ground, and the gravitational force does not affect it, it sways slowly in the air until it rests on the ground.

So it is here: In vessels that have no coarseness, such as the vessels of the circles, it is considered that the light that comes there by the power of the Sefirot of straightness becomes round because there is no coarseness there, meaning yearning that would draw it with a pulling force.

Conversely, in the vessels of straightness, where there is coarseness that draws the light very strongly, the light comes down fast and with accurate straightness, like a straight line.

35. Keter (Part 2, Chap 1, Inner light, 200)

The impact of the root on a degree is called Keter (crown). It comes from the word Machtir [crowning], meaning encircling. Because it is more refined than the entire degree, it encircles the entire Partzuf above it.

36. Slowly (Part 2, Chap 1, Inner light, 200)

A gradual extension of lights by way of cause and effect is called "slowly."

37. Connecting (Part 2, Chap 1, Inner light, 30)

Malchut of the upper one becomes the Keter for the lower one. It follows that Malchut connects every upper one with its lower one, meaning that an equivalence of form has occurred between them. By this, a connection is made among all the degrees, from the world of Adam Kadmon through the end of Assiya. This matter applies to the vessels of straightness, called a "line," but not to the vessels of circles. Therefore, the whole connection of the circles in one another is done by the line.

38. The water of light (Part 2, Chap 1, Inner light, 90)

A light that descends from its degree is called water, or the water of light.

39. Malchut (Part 2, Chap 1, Inner light, 200)

The last phase is called Malchut because the authority that extends from it is firm and in absolute control, as is the fear of the Kingship.

40. From above downward (Part 2, Inner Observation, 102)

A light that expands in the vessels gradually, from a more refined to coarser, is called "from above downward." This light is called "direct light."

41. From below upward

A light that extends gradually, from coarser to more refined, and up to the most refined, is called "from below upward." This light is called "reflected light."

42. Effect

That which causes the appearance of a degree is regarded as effecting it. This comes from the term "cause and consequence." The cause is the reason for something, and the consequence is extended and born out of that cause and reason.

43. Screen (Part 3, item 2)

A screen is the force of restriction that awakens in the emanated being toward the upper light to stop it from descending to phase four. This means that as soon as it reaches and touches phase four, that force promptly awakens, strikes it, and pushes it back. This force is called a "screen."

You must understand the difference between the screen and the restriction in the emanated being: They are two completely separate matters. The force of restriction that was performed on phase four is aimed toward the vessel in the emanated being, which is a yearning to receive. This means that because of the desire to equalize the form with the Emanator, he detained himself from receiving while yearning to receive, since the yearning in him, called "phase four," is an upper force that the emanated being cannot revoke or diminish even a little. Rather, he can detain himself from wanting to receive despite the great yearning.

This force of detainment is always placed on phase four in the emanated being, except when he extends a new light. In that event, he must necessarily revoke the force of detainment, meaning the restriction in him, and a yearning for the upper light appears in him. That gives him the power to draw the light to himself.

Here begins the operation of a screen in the emanated being, since any yearning draws the upper light in completeness, as it was in Ein Sof, since it is an upper force, which the lower one cannot diminish. Hence, the light comes down in order to fill phase four.

However, the moment the light touches phase four, the screen awakens, strikes the light, and pushes it back. As a result, he receives only the light of the three phases, and phase four does not receive it.

You see that the screen operates only when the light comes, after the restriction is temporarily revoked in order to extend a new light, as was explained.

However, the act of the restriction is permanent, restraining himself from extending light. Thus, the restriction and the screen are two completely separate discernments, and know that the screen is a result of the restriction.

44. Surrounding (Part 2, Chap 1, Inner light, 40)

See answer No. 4.

45. Annulled (Part 2, Chap 1, Inner light, 10)

When two spiritual entities become completely equal in their form, without any disparity, they literally become one. In that state, the smaller one becomes annulled in the greater one.

46. Extending (Part 2, Chap 1, Inner light, 90)

A descent of light by the power of the coarseness, meaning the power of yearning that there is in the emanated being, is called "extending" or "extension."

47. Nefesh (Part 2, Inner observation, 95)

A light that does not come to a Partzuf as bestowal from the light of Ein Sof, but is rather received from a higher adjacent degree, is called the light of Nefesh, or female light.

48. NRNHY (Part 2, Inner Observation, 87)

The vessels in the ten Sefirot are called KHB ZON. The lights in the ten Sefirot are called Nefesh, Ruach, Neshama, Haya, Yechida. The reason the lights are named from below upward, meaning NRNHY, and not from above downwards, meaning YHNRN, is that this is the order by which the lights enter the Partzuf. Nefesh enters first, then Ruach, and so on. This order is opposite to the order of the vessels, where Keter is revealed first, then Hochma, etc., through Malchut, which is the last.

49. Neshama (Part 2, Chap 2, Inner light, 6)

The light that clothes the vessel of Bina is called Neshama. It comes from the Hebrew word Neshima [breathing], since the Neshama is the origin of Zeir Anpin, which is considered as the light of Ruach and it breathes its sustenance from there. It does that by way of ascent and descent, as it is written, "And the animals ran back and forth," and also, "and breathed into his nostrils the breath of life."

50. Cause

That which makes a degree appear is considered its cause.

51. Sium (Part 2, Chap 1, Inner light, 7)

Phase four is called Sof [end], or Sium [conclusion] because it stops the upper light from expanding to it, and therefore ending the degree.

52. Near (Part 2, item 2)

Similarity of form with another is called nearness.

53. Coarseness (Part 2, Inner observation, 5)

A great will to receive, with a great yearning, is called regarded as great coarseness. Little yearning is considered a lesser coarseness. It is the vessel for drawing the abundance in every Partzuf, and is therefore called the "internality" of the vessel.

54. Passing (Part 2, Chap 2, Inner light, 4)

An illumination from a lower degree must pass through the one above it. That is, because the lower one is caused by and emerges from the upper one, it is regarded as passing through the upper one. And because it passes through the upper one, it is set there, and is called there "passing light." It does not move from there, but an extension of it exits and comes to its place, meaning to the lower one. It is akin to lighting a candle from another candle without the first diminishing. In this manner you can understand any shifting of lights from degree to degree, since the light does not leave its first place when it moves to another place, as with corporeal objects.

55. Upper one and lower one (Part 2, Inner observation, 86)

We should make two primary distinctions in each Partzuf: The vessel for drawing the abundance, and the vessel for receiving the abundance in it. These distinctions are completely opposite to each other, because the amount of abundance depends on the measure of the coarseness of the vessel extension.

The greatest light in the Partzuf is called Yechida. That light needs the vessel with the greatest coarseness to extend it, meaning from phase four of phase four. It is the opposite from the vessel of reception because the greatest light, meaning Yechida, clothes only the most refined vessel.

Hence, when discerning a vessel for extension of abundance, we discern them under the names internality and externality. The more interior the vessel, the coarser it is and it extends a greater level. Conversely, the more exterior is more refined, extending a smaller level.

When discerning the vessels for reception of the lights in the Partzuf, we refer to them as upper and lower. The upper is more refined, and a greater level is clothed in it. Conversely, the lower is coarser and a smaller level clothes it.

56. Self (Part 2, Chap 2, Inner light, 2)

The light of Hochma is called the "self," as it is the essence and the sustenance of the emanated being.

57. Internality (Part 2, Inner observation, 86)

The coarseness in the Partzuf is regarded as its internality, because it is the place of the extension of the abundance.

58. Internality and externality

See answer No. 55

59. Pipeline (Part 2, Chap 1, Inner light, 2)

The vessels of straightness are called pipelines, because they extend and limit the light within them like a pipeline that bounds the water that travels through it.

60. Line (Part 2, Chap 1, Inner light, 2)

From the perspective of their vessels, the ten Sefirot of the vessels of straightness are called a pipeline, and from the perspective of the light inside them, they are called a line. The ten Sefirot of the world of Adam Kadmon are called "one line," but in the ten Sefirot of the world of Atzilut there are three lines.

61. Upright (Part 2, Chap 2, Inner light, 3)

When the lights of Rosh cloth the vessels of Rosh, it is considered that the Partzuf is standing upright.

62. Ration (Part 2, Chap 1, Inner light, 70)

The reflected light measures itself and "rations" the upper light. That is because the only way for the light to be in the emanated being is if it is clothed in reflected light.

63. Ground (Part 2, Chap 2, Inner light, 1)

The Malchut of every degree of every world is regarded as its bottom.

64. Rosh (Part 2, Chap 6)

The nine Sefirot of the upper light that expand to coupling by striking on the screen in Malchut so as to raise reflected light are regarded as the Rosh of the degree. That is because these lights come before the screen and the reflected light, and the coarseness of the screen cannot rise to them.

65. Ruach (Part 2, item 4)

The light clothing the vessel of Zeir Anpin is called Ruach. It is called by that name because it rises to Bina, sucks abundance and descends to Malchut, to pour it onto her. In that, it is like the wind that goes back and forth (see answer 49).

66. Spirituality

The term "Spirituality" as it is expressed in books of Kabbalah, means that it is devoid of any corporeal contingency, meaning time, space, imagination, and so on. Sometimes, this term indicates only the upper light in the vessel, although a vessel is also completely spiritual in every way.

67. Far (Part 2, Chap 1, Inner light, 40)

The term "far" indicates a great measure of disparity of form.

68. Beginning of the expansion (Part 2, Chap 1, Inner light, 7)

The root of every expansion of light is called the "beginning of the expansion," or Keter.

69. At Once (Part 2, Chap 1, Inner light, 6)

A light that comes down, but not by the gradual order of the four phases, because it has only one of them, is regarded as descending "at once." If it comes down in a gradual order, it is regarded as descending "slowly."

70. The last of them (Part 2, Chap 1, Inner light, 7)

The last phase in all the degrees, meaning phase four of phase four, is called "the last of them." It is so because it has the greatest coarseness, called Sof, and all the degrees appear only in order to correct that phase.

TABLE OF ANSWERS FOR TOPICS

71. **What is the origin of the vessels of circles**

    Ein Sof is the origin of the vessels of circles, since these vessels were already included in Ein Sof but they were not apparent there because "He is one and His name, One."

    (Inner Observation, Part 2, item 52)

72. **What are the records that remained in the circles after the restriction**

    After the restriction, when the light of Ein Sof departed from all four phases, there still remained a record in each and every phase; a kind of the light of Ein Sof that was in it prior to the restriction.

    (Inner light, Part 2, Chap 2, item 80)

73. **Why are the circles located one inside the other**

    It indicates that there is no other distinction there besides that of cause and consequence (see answer 22).

    (Inner Observation, Part 2, item 53)

74. **Why is there no discernment of one being inside the other in Ein Sof**

    Because there is no recognition whatsoever of a vessel in Ein Sof.

    (Inner Observation, Part 2, item 53)

75. **What is the root of all the lights**

    Ein Sof is the root to all the lights in the worlds.

    (Inner light, Part 2, Chap 1, item 4)

76. **What is the root of all the vessels**

    The circles are the roots to all the vessels in the worlds.

    (Inner light, Part 2, Chap 1, item 80)

77. **What is the origin of the reflected light**

    Phase four, called Malchut, is the origin of the reflected light.

    (Inner Observation, Part 2, item 66)

78. **Why do the lights precede the vessels**

    In the beginning, the lights emerged in three phases one below the other. These three phases are not regarded as vessels before phase four appears, which is the only phase regarded as a vessel. Thus, the vessels are a consequence of the lights.

    (Inner Observation, Part 2, item 5)

79. **Why does Bina not precede Hochma**

In the order of the emanation of the worlds from above downward, completeness always precedes and causes the appearance of incompleteness. This is how the degrees cascade from one another: Each lower degree is inferior to the higher one until the appearance of this world, the most corrupted of them all.

(Inner light, Part 2, Chap 1, item 200)

80. **From where comes the source for the controlling force in the worlds**

The screen is the first source of a controlling force in the worlds.

(Inner light, Part 2, Chap 1, item 2)

81. **Where does the screen come from**

It is a consequence of the first restriction.

(Inner light, Part 2, Chap 1, item 2)

82. **How many causes preceded the screen**

Two causes preceded the screen: the restriction and the arrival of the light, since the screen appears only when the upper light comes and touches phase four (see answer 43).

83. **What is the origin of the vessels of straightness**

The circles are the origin of the vessels of straightness because Malchut of the circles extended the light of the line, and her power created the screen.

(Inner Observation, Part 2, item 56)

84. **From where do the circles get their light**

From the vessels of straightness, and they, themselves, cannot draw light from Ein Sof since there are no screen and coarseness in them.

(Inner light, Part 2, Chap 1 item 30)

85. **How do the circles receive light from one another**

Through the force of the screen impressed in them without carrying its coarseness with it. This above-mentioned impression of the screen is called the windows of the circles.

(Inner light, Part 2, Chap 2, item 70)

86. **Why must the circles receive from the straightness**

Because there is no screen in the circles.

(Inner light, Part 2, Chap 1, item 30)

87. **What are the windows at the top and at the bottom of each circle**

(See answer 85)

88. **What caused the circles be one below the other**

The light of the line that the circles received caused in them a recognition of degrees, one below the other. These became windows from the impression of the screen, and all the degrees of the line also emerged in circles.

(Inner light, Part 2, Chap 2, item 90)

89. **Why the circles need the line to connect them**

The vessels of the circles are on the same level as the Rosh of every Sefira in the vessels of straightness above the screen. Because of that, they are considered to be in the place of the Rosh of the Sefira, and do not expand at all below the Rosh of the straightness.

The vessels below the Rosh are below the screen of the Malchut of Rosh, and are controlled by the coarseness. For this reason, they are below the circles, because lower implies having greater coarseness.

There are no screen and coarseness in the circles. Thus, the Guf of every Sefira is devoid of circles. In that state, all ten Sefirot of Keter of circles clothe the ten Sefirot of the Rosh of Keter of straightness, and the ten Sefirot of the Guf of Keter are vacant of the circles. Also, the ten Sefirot of Hochma of circles clothe the ten Sefirot of the Rosh of Hochma of straightness and so on by the same way.

It turns out that the Guf of straightness separates each two Sefirot of circles, so that there is no connection between the Sefirot of the circles. That is why they need to be connected by the line.

(Inner light, Part 2, Chap 1, item 3)

90. **What is the difference between the Sefirot of straightness and the Sefirot of circles**

The difference between them is only in the screen: it exists in the straightness and does not exist in circles.

(Inner light, Part 2, Chap 1, item 2)

91. **Why is the restriction not enough and there is a need for a screen, as well**

(See answer 43)

92. **What are the lights of straightness?**

They are considered as the light of Ruach.

(Inner light, Part 2, Chap 2, item 30)

93. **What is the difference between straight illumination and circular illumination**

(See answer 34)

94. **In what are the circles finer than the straightness**

From the perspective of the vessels, the circles are finer than the straightness because there are no screen and coarseness in the vessels of the circles, and there are a screen and coarseness in the vessels of straightness.

Also, the vessels of the circles precede the vessels of straightness.

(Inner light, Part 2, Chap 1, item 2)

95. **What makes the Sefirot of straightness better than the Sefirot of circles**

From the perspective of the lights, the straightness is finer than the circles, because the Sefirot of straightness draw upper light and bestow upon the circles. The lights of straightness are called the lights of Ruach and the lights of circles are called the lights of Nefesh.

(Inner light, Part 2, Chap 2, item 30)

96. **Why is it that in the circles, the more external the circle, the better it is.**

External means refined, and you find that the more it is external, the better it is and the more it is in equivalence of form with Ein Sof.

(Inner Observation, Part 2, item 7)

97. **In vessels of straightness, the more internal the vessel, the better it is. Why?**

Inner means coarser, meaning having greater yearning. For this reason, it also draws a greater measure of light, and the level of reflected light that it pushes back is also greater.

(Inner Observation, Part 2, item 5)

98. **Why the world of Assiya the most external of all the worlds**

Because its phase four hasn't any coarseness that is fit to draw the upper light, in that sense, it is regarded as the most refined of all the worlds (See answer 55).

(Inner Observation, Part 2, item 13)

99. **Who caused the appearance of the screen**

When the upper light reached and touched phase four in order to expand in it, it caused the force of the screen to appear immediately, block it, and push that light back.

(Inner Observation, Part 2, item 18)

100. **When was the screen formed?**

When the upper light reached phase four and touched it in order to expand in it, the force of the restriction was awakened, which is a screen to stop it and push it back.

(Inner Observation, Part 2, item 56)

101. **Why does the quality of the screen depend on the coarseness of phase four**

Because the reflected light that the screen raises is only the same measure of light that wanted to expand according to the measure of coarseness in phase four, meaning the measure of its yearning and drawing of the upper light. If there is great coarseness, meaning phase four in phase four, the light that wants to expand in phase four is also great. If the coarseness is small, meaning only phase one in phase four, the light that wants to expand in phase four is also very small. You find that the measure of the level of reflected light in the screen and the measure of coarseness in phase four are one and the same.

(Inner Observation, Part 2, item 60)

102. **What are the vessels of reception in the light of the line**

Even though the light of the line has but three phases, still, its vessels of reception are only due to phase four. However, phase four itself does not receive light.

(Inner Observation, Part 2, item 16)

103. **What are the two kinds of ten Sefirot in each emanated being**

There are two movements of ten Sefirot in each degree: The first move is from above downward, beginning in Keter and ending in Malchut. They are called ten Sefirot of direct light. The second move is from below upward, beginning in Malchut and ending in Keter. They are called ten Sefirot of reflected light.

(Inner Observation, Part 2, item 104)

104. **Why is the reflected light considered a vessel of reception**

Because this entire light belonged specifically to phase four. It would have qualified to clothe in phase four, if the screen did not push it back. For this reason, it became a vessel of reception instead of phase four.

(Inner Observation, Part 2, item 21)

105. **How is the amount of reflected light measured?**

By the measure of light that was fit to come into phase four had the screen not pushed it back.

(Inner Observation, Part 2, item 60)

106. **Why is Malchut regarded as the Keter of the reflected light?**

Because reflected light is nothing more than a light that was fit for phase four, which is Malchut. Because Malchut did not receive this light within her, this light became a garment and a receptacle for all nine Sefirot above her. Thus,

Malchut is the origin for all ten Sefirot of the reflected light and is therefore regarded as the Keter of the reflected light.

(Inner Observation, Part 2, item 102)

107. **Why do the screen and the coarseness function as one**

(See answer 101)

108. **Why are the coarseness and the reflected light interdependent**

(See answer 101)

109. **What refines the screen**

The coarseness in a screen is the measure of the yearning in it. Therefore, acquiring and clothing the inner light in a Partzuf intensifies the surrounding light and refines the coarseness in the screen.

(Inner Observation, Part 2, item 74)

110. **Why are the Sefirot of the circles regarded as Nefesh**

Since there is no screen and coarseness in the Sefirot of the circles, they do not have a vessel that draws the upper light. Instead, they receive their lights through the vessels of straightness. Therefore, their lights are regarded as "light of Nefesh." This means that there is no bestowal in this light, but only for their own needs.

(Inner Observation, Part 2, item 95)

111. **Why are the Sefirot of straightness regarded as Ruach**

Because the vessels of straightness have a screen and coarseness, they are fit to draw the upper light and impart upon others. A light that has bestowal in it is called "a light of Ruach" or "male light."

(Inner light, Part 2, Chap 2, item 30)

112. **What is the merit of the first three Sefirot of straightness**

GAR are clean with respect to the coarseness of the screen, since the screen and Malchut are their last phase and no coarseness ever ascends to them because coarseness can never rise beyond its own place, not even a bit. Know that the first three, namely KHB, are the Rosh of a degree that has complete ten Sefirot (See answer 13).

(Inner light, Part 2, Chap 1, item 90)

113. **How are the Sefirot of straightness positioned inside the circles**

Each and every Sefira is considered to have a Rosh, called GAR, and a Guf, called ZAT (See answer 64). The Sefira of Keter has GAR and ZAT; so does Hochma, and so does Bina, and so on.

The position of every ten Sefirot GAR and ZAT of circles is only in the place of the Rosh and GAR of straightness since the ten Sefirot of circles of the Sefira of Keter revolve only around the GAR of Keter of straightness, and ZAT of Keter of straightness are vacanct of circles (see item 89).

Also, every ten Sefirot of Hochma of circles revolve solely around the GAR of Hochma of straightness, and ZAT of Hochma of straightness are vacant of circles, and so are the rest of them.

(Inner light, Part 2, Chap 1, item 90)

114. **Why are the circles positioned in the place of GAR of straightness**

Because both haven't any of the coarseness of the screen.

(Inner light, Part 2, Chap 1, item 90)

115. **What is the distance between each two circles**

It is as the measure of ZAT of the Sefira of straightness that separates between each two circles. ZAT of Keter of straightness separate between the ten Sefirot of the circle of Keter and the circle of Hochma; ZAT of the Sefira of Hochma of straightness separate between the ten Sefirot of the circle of Hochma and the circle of Bina, and so on.

(Inner light, Part 2, Chap 1, item 90)

116. **Why the circles don't surround the ZAT of straightness**

(See answer 89)

117. **Why is it forbidden to engage in the GAR of each degree**

Because the lights preceded the vessels (See answer 13), and the reflected light that ascends from below upward and clothes them is not regarded as actual vessels, but only as roots of vessels. We do not have attainment in the light without a vessel.

(See answer 21)

118. **Why is it forbidden to engage in the ten inner Sefirot of the GAR?**

There are inner GAR and ZAT even in the GAR of the degree, and engaging in the ZAT of the GAR is also permitted.

(Inner light, Part 2, Chap 2, item 5)

119. **Why do we not engage in the Sefirot of the circles**

Because they are GAR, as for this reason, all ten Sefirot of the circles are positioned in the place of GAR of straightness.

(See answer 13)

120. How are the ten Sefirot divided among the five phases of the desire

The root of the four phases is called Keter. Phase one is called Hochma and phase two, Bina. Phase three is called Tifferet, or Zeir Anpin, and consists of six Sefirot of its own: Hesed, Gevura, Tifferet, Netzah, Hod, Yesod. Phase four is called Malchut.

121. What exactly does "Ten and not nine, ten and not eleven" mean

It means that phase four, meaning Malchut, does not receive anything from the upper light after the restriction. However, because of the virtue of the reflected light in her, she is considered just as important as the rest of the Sefirot. That is why it says, "ten and not nine." It says "ten and not eleven," to indicate that you should not think that there is any form of reception of upper light in phase four. If there were, Malchut would be regarded as two Sefirot: Malchut of direct light and Malchut of reflected light. That would bring the number of Sefirot to eleven. For this reason, the text warns us, "ten and not eleven," because Malchut receives none of the direct light.

122. Why doesn't the will to receive appear all at once

Because it is opposite from the root. The only form of the root is that of bestowal, and that of phase four is only of reception.

Two opposites cannot stem from one another by way of cause and consequence, but rather through a gradual, slow cascading of the degree, since the root is only the cause of phase one, the closest to it, phase one of phase two, and phase two of phase three. After phase three, it is possible for phase four to appear.

(Inner Observation, Part 2, item 5)

123. Why is coarseness **regarded as** internality

Because coarseness is the vessel of drawing and the primary vessel of reception, through the reflected light that ascends from it. For this reason, the coarseness in the vessel is regarded as its internality. The lesser the coarseness, the more external it is considered, and that which is completely refined in it is regarded as completely external (See answer 55).

(Inner Observation, Part 2, item 5)

124. Why is specifically internality regarded as a vessel of reception

It can be likened to the thickness of the wall of a vessel that is made of four layers one around the other, so the abundance in the vessel touches only its internality, meaning the innermost layer in the vessel.

(Inner Observation, Part 2, item 5)

125. **How is the greatness or smallness of the worlds measured?**

By the measure of reflected light that the screen in that degree or world raises.

(Inner Observation, Part 2, item 55)

126. **Why did the light also depart from the first three phases during the restriction**

The vessels of reception of all four phases are actually only phase four. The other three phases do not have any form of drawing or reception in them. Consequently, when phase four restricted herself from receiving, the first three phases also remained without vessels of reception; therefore, their lights departed, too.

(Inner Observation, Part 3, items 24, 27)

127. **What are the three discernments in the vessels**

The first is the substance itself of the vessel, meaning the measure of its coarseness. The second is the force of restriction that is placed on phase four in the coarseness in her. The third is the screen in it (See answer 43).

There are two inner discernments we must make in the first discernment: The first is the first substance in her, regarded as the Malchut of the previous degree, which is considered her cause and emanator. This is discerned primarily before the light reached the emanated degree. The second is the substance of the emanated degree itself, after all the light intended to reach that degree has come to it.

(Inner Observation, Part 2, item 24)

128. **What are the two discernments in a spiritual substance**

The first is what is regarded as the Malchut of the upper one. The second is what is regarded as the substance of the emanated degree itself (See answer 127).

129. **To which point is the emanated being named after its upper one**

As long as the emanated degree does not receive the light that is intended for it, it is named after the Malchut of the degree above it (See answer 127).

130. **When is the emanated being regarded as emerging from the upper one into its own authority**

When the emanated degree acquires its own light, from that moment it is regarded as having left the Malchut of the upper one, called Emanator, and to have come into its own authority.

(See answer 127)

131. **What does not possible mean**

Coerced reception is called "not possible." It relates primarily to the light of Hochma or the illumination of Hochma, considered the self and vitality of the Partzuf, from which it is "not possible for the Partzuf to part," like a person who must maintain his existence and sustenance.

(Inner Observation, Part 2, item 46)

132. What does not intending mean

A great desire is regarded as intending. When one wants to receive something very much, we say that one's heart is greatly intending to draw it, for the yearning is felt in the heart, and the intention is also felt in the heart.

This is so only when he lacks the light. When he has light, it is called "not intending."

(Inner Observation, Part 2, item 43)

133. Why phase one is regarded as not possible and not intending

Only the light of Hochma is intended for phase one. It is the vitality and self of the Partzuf, which is why it is regarded as not possible, since it is must receive its sustenance and self, and compelled reception is not regarded as reception.

It is also discerned that no yearning for light of Hochma is revealed in her because yearning appears only when he does not have that light, and he yearns to obtain it, and not when he is filled with this light.

(Inner Observation, Part 2, item 43)

134. Why phase two is regarded as possible and not as intending

Phase two is an intensification of the desire to bestow, by which she draws the light of Hassadim. She does not have to make this intensification whatsoever, and it was possible for her to completely separate herself from it. This is why she is regarded as possible.

However, she is still regarded as not intending because this above mentioned yearning must only be for the light of Hochma, not for the light of Hassadim, since the desire for the light of Hassadim is not considered coarseness as the restriction was only on the light of Hochma, and not at all on the light of Hassadim. Hence, the yearning for the light of Hassadim is not considered an intention.

(Inner Observation, Part 2, item 43)

135. Why is phase three regarded as not possible and intending

Phase three is the extension of illumination of Hochma into the light of Hassadim that Bina extended. This extension is called not possible because the illumination of Hochma is a mandatory reception for the Partzuf.

It is considered intending because this extension was done when the illumination of Hochma was absent, which is why there was yearning there.

136. Why is phase four regarded as possible and intending

Because there was already illumination of Hochma in phase three, she did not have to perform a new intensification for the light of Hochma itself because the illumination of Hochma alone is quite sufficient for her sustenance. This is why this extension is regarded as possible, meaning it was possible to become separated from it.

She is regarded as intending because she lacked that light of Hochma itself that she extended, and she had a great yearning when she extended it.

137. Why are not all the phases of the desire fit of being vessels of reception, but only phase four

Because a vessel is not complete unless it has a yearning to receive. This is revealed only under two conditions: possible and intending (See answer 136).

138. Why does every disparity of form in phase four become a new emanated being

The rule is that the upper light does not stop shining for the emanated beings even for a moment. Wherever a proper vessel of extension is revealed, the upper light immediately shines there.

Therefore, after the extension of phase four within phase four was filled, she engendered a form of a new vessel of extension, in which there is the coarseness of phase three in phase four, and it, too, was instantly filled with the upper light.

Afterwards, when a new form of coarseness, of phase two within phase four, was emanated and emerged from it, it too was instantly filled with the upper light, and this is always so.

139. Why is the upper light incessant in the emanated beings

Because the upper light is always in a state of complete rest, without any novelty of form. In spirituality, innovation is regarded as movement, and any innovation of form that is done as an expansion of the upper light is through the force of extension that is revealed only in the emanated being (See Part 1, answer 64).

Even this expansion of upper light is like lighting one candle from another, while the first is not diminished whatsoever. Thus, only that part of the expansion of the upper light that the emanated being received is regarded as receiving a new form, a common relation between the vessel and the light that is clothed in it. However, the upper light itself is not diminished at all because of this expansion that has reached the emanated being.

140. **What is the difference between bestowal and reception in the vessels**

The difference is truly as from one end to the other since bestowal of the upper light requires that there be a great measure of coarseness in the Partzuf, the greatest measure in reality, for then it draws the greatest and most complete light.

Its complete opposite is the clothing of the upper light in the vessels, since the greatest and most complete light clothes only the most refined vessel that can exist in reality.

Hence, we must always discern the above two matters in every Partzuf: The bestowal measured in the additional coarseness is regarded as internal and external, and reception and clothing in the vessels are regarded as upper one and lower one.

Thus, the greatest Partzuf in reality should also be the most internal, meaning the coarsest of all the Partzufim in reality. At the same time, it should be the highest of all the Partzufim in reality, meaning the most refined of all the Partzufim in reality since they are two separate vessels: one to extend the light, and the other to receive it (See answers 55 and 141).

141. **Why the giver gives to the coarsest while the receiver receives in the most refined**

The upper light is captured in the Partzuf only to the extent of the reflected light that rises from the screen in the *Partzuf*, and its measure depends on the measure of the coarseness in phase four (See answers 101 and 2). For this reason, the giver needs the excessive coarseness in the lower one. Conversely, the receiver needs the most refined vessel, so that the light may clothe in it, meaning to have equivalence of form between the light and the vessel as the disparity of form removes the light from the vessels (See answers 16 and 140).

142. **How should we understand the innovation of form in the expansion of the upper light**

See answer 139

143. **How does the emanated being emerge from the upper light**

The upper light necessarily contains a desire to bestow. This desire is regarded as the last phase incorporated in the upper light. This part, meaning the above-said desire to bestow, is inverted and becomes an extension of the light of phase one. This extension of light is certainly an innovation of form in the above desire to bestow. This is why it is considered to have split in itself, exited from the desire to bestow and became phase one of the will to receive.

That is, it emerged from the quality of Emanator into the quality of emanated being, since disparity of form separates and distances the spiritual from one another. However, the abovementioned distinction of "part" does not diminish anything the "whole" whatsoever. Instead, it is as lighting one candle from another candle without the first diminishing in any way.

144. **What is the difference between the names of the four phases and the names KHB ZON**

When we discern only the substance in the vessels, we define them as "four phases." When we want to include the records in each and every vessel, too, we define them as KHB ZON.

145. **What is the order of the entry of the lights into the emanated being after the correction**

First, the smaller ones enter, then the greater ones, beginning with Nefesh, then Ruach, and so on through Yechida.

(See answer 48)

146. **What is the order of the growth of the vessels in each Partzuf after the correction**

The more important vessels grow first, then the smaller vessels, beginning with Keter, then Hochma, and so on through the vessel of Malchut, which comes last.

147. **What is the first substance of every emanated being**

Malchut of the upper one becomes the Keter of the lower one. In other words, the will to bestow in the upper one becomes the first substance of the lower one (See answer 143).

148. **What are the two Ketarim (pl. of Keter) in each degree**

The root of the four phases is called the Keter of the ten Sefirot of direct light in the degree. Malchut of the degree is regarded as the Keter of the ten Sefirot of reflected light in the degree.

149. **Why does the light not become absent in the first place when it moves to another**

Had it been transient and exchangeable, it would not have been eternal. This is simple.

150. **How is every upper one incorporated with its lower ones**

In the ten Sefirot of [direct light], since any light is extended only from Ein Sof. Therefore, the lower one must pass through all its upper ones in a manner of cause and consequence until it reaches the bottom consequence, for which the light is intended.

And since the light does not become absent in place A when it passes to place B, all the lights that pass through the upper one become fixed in it.

151. How is every lower one incorporated with its upper ones

In the ten Sefirot of reflected light, in which Malchut is regarded as the root and the Keter (See answer 148). All the parts of reflected light that clothe her upper ones pass through her from below upwards. For this reason, every lower one is regarded as containing all of the parts of reflected light that belong to the Sefirot above it.

152. What is the key to finding the distinctions between the Sefirot that are incorporated in each other

The incorporation of the Sefirot in one another until each one consists of ten, and ten from ten indefinitely, is by the two directions of the ten Sefirot of direct light and ten Sefirot of the reflected light in each degree (See answer 20). We must find the key to easily identify the changes in the order of the inner ten Sefirot in a Sefira only through incorporation and are not from its self.

Hence, remember three facts that you may always use. For example, if you want to know the ten Sefirot incorporated in Bina, the first fact is that there are two Sefirot in her self, which are Bina of direct light and Hod of reflected light. Second, count the Sefirot from her down to Yesod. These are the direct light in her, meaning HGT NHY that pass through her from above downward. Third, count the Sefirot from her up to Keter, which are two, Yesod and Malchut, and know her Sefirot of [reflected light] that pass through her from below upward.

Now think: Two Sefirot of her self, six of [direct light], and two of reflected light are ten. Think of every Sefira in this way and you will know all the phases incorporated in her with a single scan.

153. Which are the phases of direct light and reflected light in Keter

Nine of direct light, from Keter to Yesod, and one of reflected light, meaning only Malchut.

154. Which are the phases of direct light and reflected light in Hochma

Eight of direct light, from Hochma to Yesod. They clothe the more refined vessels, meaning the light of Hochma in the vessel of *Keter*, etc., and two of reflected light, Yesod and Malchut, which clothe the vessels Yesod and Malchut.

155. **Which are the phases of direct light and reflected light in Bina**

Seven of direct light, from Bina downward. Here too, the light of Bina is in the vessel of Keter, etc., through the light of Yesod in the vessel of Netzah, and three of reflected light, Hod, Yesod and Malchut, in the vessels of Hod, Yesod and Malchut.

156. **Which are the phases of direct light and reflected light in Hesed**

Six of direct light, from Hesed to Yesod, and four of reflected light, from Netzah to Malchut. The reflected light of Netzah is in the vessel of Netzah, etc.

157. **Which are the phases of direct light and reflected light in Gevura**

Five of direct light, from Gevura to Yesod, and five of reflected light, from Tifferet to Malchut. They clothe as above, meaning direct light in the more refined vessels, and the reflected light, each in its appropriate vessel.

158. **Which are the phases of direct light and reflected light in Tifferet**

Four of direct light, from Tifferet to Yesod, and six of reflected light, from Gevura to Malchut.

159. **Which are the phases of direct light and reflected light in Netzah**

Three of direct light, from Netzah to Yesod, and seven of reflected light, from Hesed to Malchut.

160. **Which are the phases of direct light and reflected light in Hod**

Two of direct light, from Hod to Yesod, and eight of reflected light, from Bina to Malchut.

161. **Which are the phases of direct light and reflected light in Yesod**

One of direct light, from Yesod, and nine of reflected light, from Hochma to Malchut.

162. **Which are the phases of direct light and reflected light in Malchut**

Only ten Sefirot of reflected light, without any direct light.

163. **Which are the phases of direct light and reflected light in Keter of Keter**

Nine of direct light, from Keter to Yesod, and one of reflected light, in Malchut.

164. **Which are the phases of direct light and reflected light in Hochma of Keter**

Eight of direct light, from Hochma to Malchut, and two of reflected light, from Yesod to Malchut.

165. **Which are the phases of direct light and reflected light in Bina of Keter**

Seven of direct light, from Bina to Malchut, and three of reflected light, from Hod to Malchut.

166. Which are the phases of direct light and reflected light in Hesed of Keter of Keter

Six of direct light, from Hesed to Yesod, and four of reflected light, from Netzah to Malchut.

167. Which are the phases of direct light and reflected light in Gevura of Hochma of Netzah

First, we must understand the inner ten Sefirot contained in the general Netzah. They are three of direct light—the light of Netzah, clothing the vessel of Keter of the general Netzah, the light of Hod, in the vessel of Hochma of the general Netzah, and the light of Yesod in the vessel of Bina.

Now, take the inner Hochma of the general Netzah. The inner Hochma, too, necessarily contains ten Sefirot, by the eight Sefirot of direct light that pass through her from above downward, even in those that have only reflected light, since when the Sefirot were incorporated, the Sefirot of direct light always shone into the Sefirot that had reflected light.

However, the eight Sefirot of direct light that passed from Hochma downward are not regarded as light of Hochma, but as light of Hod, since the light of Hod is clothed in the vessel of Hochma in the general Netzah.

Thus, in the ten Sefirot of Hochma of Netzah, there are now only passing lights of direct light from Hochma of Hod downward. Hochma of Hod is in the vessel of Keter, Bina of Hod in Hochma, and Hesed of Hod in Bina. Gevura of Hod is in Hesed, and Tifferet of Hod in Gevura. Thus, we find that there is direct light from the light of Tifferet of Hod in Gevura of Hochma of Netzah.

Now let us take that Gevura of Hochma of Netzah, which necessarily contains ten inner Sefirot, as well, direct light that passes through her from above downward, and reflected light that passes through her from below upward. In that Gevura, there are five Sefirot of direct light from Gevura downward. However, this is not at all the light of Gevura, but the five lower phases of the light of Tifferet of Hod, which clothe the more refined vessels.

It follows that the light Gevura of Tifferet of Hod clothes the vessel of Keter of Gevura of Hochma of Netzah. Also, the light of Tifferet of Tifferet of Hod clothes the vessel of Hochma of Gevura of Hochma of Netzah. The light of Netzah of Tifferet of Hod is in the vessel of Bina of Gevura of Hochma of Netzah, and the light of Hod of Tifferet of Hod clothes the vessel of Hesed of Gevura of Hochma of Netzah, and the light of Yesod of Tifferet of Hod clothes the vessel of Gevura of Gevura of Hochma of Netzah.

There are five additional Sefirot of reflected light that clothe according to the vessels, as they always do.

168. **Which are the phases of direct light and reflected light in Tifferet of Bina of Hod**

Initially, when you take Bina of Hod, it has only reflected light and no direct light. However, the direct light of the adjacent degree, namely the light of Yesod, shines in it. Consequently, this Bina is incorporated with the lights that pass through it, which are seven lights of direct light from Bina downward.

Because its light is only the light of Yesod of direct light, the direct light in it begins from Bina of Yesod downward. The light of Bina of Yesod clothes the vessel of Keter, and the light of Hod of Yesod clothes the vessel of Tifferet of Bina of the general Hod.

Afterwards, when you take the inner Tifferet of Bina of Hod, which also contains ten Sefirot, there are four of direct light there, from Tifferet downward. These clothe in the higher vessels, meaning Tifferet of Yesod of Yesod in the vessel of Keter, Netzah of Yesod of Yesod in the vessel of Hochma, Hod of Yesod of Yesod in the vessel of Bina, and Yesod of Yesod of Yesod in the vessel of Hesed.

In addition, there are six phases of reflected light that pass through it from below upward, from Gevura to Malchut, clothing according to the vessels as they always do.

169. **Which are the phases of direct light and reflected light in Netzah of Yesod of Keter**

Initially, when you take Yesod of Keter, its ten Sefirot have only the light of Yesod in the vessel of Keter, and the rest are reflected light. Also if you take Netzah of Yesod of Keter, there is only reflected light there.

However, the light of Yesod of direct light that stands in Keter shines there, and Netzah of Yesod of Keter is regarded as the direct light of Yesod. When it consists of ten Sefirot, it has three lights NHY of direct light from it and below through Yesod. They pass from above downward from Yesod of direct light. Netzah of Yesod clothes in the vessel of Keter, Hod of Yesod clothes in the vessel of Hochma, and Yesod of Yesod clothes in the vessel of Bina. Also, the seven lights of reflected light clothe in the Sefirot HGT NHYM according to the vessels.

170. **Which are the phases of direct light and reflected light in Hod of Tifferet of Malchut**

There is only reflected light there, since anything that extends from Malchut has only reflected light.

171. **How are the lights of direct light and reflected light clothed in the vessels?**

This is the rule: The more important lights clothe in the more refined vessels, and the less important clothe the lesser vessels. Thus, in the Sefira of Keter, Malchut of reflected light clothes in Malchut of Keter.

In the Sefira of Hochma, the eight Sefirot of direct light, which are HB-HGT-NHY, clothe in the vessels of KHB HGT, Netzah and Hod, while Yesod and Malchut of reflected light clothe in Yesod and Malchut there.

In the Sefira of Bina, the seven Sefirot or direct light, Bina and HGT NHY, clothe in the vessels KHB HGT, Netzah, and Hod, Yesod and Malchut of reflected light clothe in Hod, Yesod and Malchut there. This is also how it continues.

172. **What is the order of cause and consequence from Ein Sof to Malchut of Adam Kadmon**

There are ten causes here, which are as follows:

The cause of all the causes is Ein Sof. It is the cause for the four phases, in a way that they will become apparent once the light is restricted. However, in Ein Sof itself, no vessel is discerned. Rather, it is all light. Indeed, only from the lower one, meaning from the world of restriction, will the upper one be studied.

Second cause: The first three phases are caused by one another. They are regarded as the cause for revealing the possibility of the greatest craving for equivalence of form, in phase four, called Malchut of Ein Sof.

Third cause: Malchut of Ein Sof is the cause for the Keter of the world of restriction, because that craving to yearn for the greatest equivalence of form that Malchut of Ein Sof acquired is regarded as disparity of form in Malchut of Ein Sof. By this, it is distinguished from Malchut of Ein Sof and emerges with its own name outside of that Malchut, and it is called Keter of the world of restriction (See answer 32).

Fourth cause: This Keter is the cause for the first restriction because it expanded once more down to phase four in it (See answer 38), and then restricted that will to receive and the light departed.

Fifth cause: The departure of the light that is done after the restriction is the cause of the appearance of the vessels of the ten Sefirot of circles (See answer 72).

Sixth cause: The vessel of Malchut of circles, meaning phase four in them, is the cause for the drawing of the upper light once more from Ein Sof (See answers 83 and 138).

Seventh cause: The upper light that was drawn once more is the cause of the appearance of the force of the screen in the vessel of Malchut (See answer 43).

Eighth cause: The screen is the cause of the ten Sefirot of reflected light that rise from it and above to the Keter of direct light. They are called the Rosh of AK (See answer 101).

Ninth cause: The reflected light that rises from the screen is the cause of the appearance of the vessels of straightness. In other words, it renders the force of expansion in phase four so she may expand by herself to ten Sefirot from her and within her down to Malchut of Malchut.

Tenth cause: The above-mentioned phase four, which received the force of expansion through the reflected light, is the cause for the ten Sefirot of the vessels of Adam Kadmon, which are called the Guf of Adam Kadmon down to his Malchut (See answer 11).

PART THREE

Ohr Yashar and *Ohr Hozer*; containing fifteen chapters

CHAPTER ONE

Explains the four phases in the coarseness, which are the four vessels and their root; containing eight issues:

1. The Sefirot of all the worlds have self and vessels. 2. The light of Ein Sof first expanded as vessels, and then the lights clothed them. 3. The expansion of the light implies a greater coarseness than before, meaning the light grew coarser and became ten vessels. 4. A screen is made in the vessel of Malchut. 5. This screen separates the world of Atzilut and the world of Beria. 6. The coupling by striking of the light of Ein Sof in the screen that raises reflected light from below upward. 7. To the place that the light Ein Sof reaches, regarded as the world of Atzilut. 8. Four phases in the coarseness of the upper light: a) In its expansion from Keter to Hochma; b) In its expansion to Bina, where distancing is added to it; c) In its expansion to ZA, where a window and a narrow foramen were made in it; d) In its expansion to Malchut, where a narrow foramen and a distancing were made in it.

There is self and vessels. The light of Ein Sof expanded first as vessels. Afterward, the lights clothed them, which are the self.

1. All the worlds (1) have self (2) and vessels (3). First (4) expanded (5) Ein Sof (6) as ten Sefirot of Atzilut, as vessels. That is because expansion (7) indicates a greater coarseness of light than before (8).

It turns out that these ten Sefirot are ten vessels that were created by the expansion of Ein Sof itself, except now the light became coarser, and vessels were made through the expansion (9). After this expansion, by which ten vessels were made, the self of Ein Sof clothed inside of them (10). This is the meaning of self and vessels.

Inner Light

1. There are five worlds, called: Adam Kadmon, Atzilut, Beria, Yetzira, Assiya. The word Olam [world] comes from the word He'elem [concealment] because each time, the light of Ein Sof becomes more concealed in them, as the ARI will explain henceforth.

2. See Table of Questions, Part 2, item 56.

3. See Table of Questions, Part 1, item 25.

4. Meaning the very beginning of every single world.

5. See Table of Questions, Part 2, item 14.

6. Meaning it is unattainable. It is called Ein Sof to indicate that the Sefira of Malchut that ends and stops all the degrees does not make an end and a stop here on the upper light (See Table of Questions, Part 1, item 40). Quite the contrary, the bestowal of the light begins in it.

7. Expansion indicates the light growing coarser than it was in the Emanator. Otherwise, in would that light exit the Emanator and merit the name "expansion of light" from it outwards? Growing coarser is the disparity of form that the light acquires because it becomes an emanated being (see Inner Observation, Part 2, item 5).

8. See above Inner Observation Part 2, item 5.

9. It teaches us that the vessels are consequences of the light itself. That is because as the light expands to the emanated being, it descends by four phases HB ZON, until it causes the will to receive in the emanated being, and it is this desire that is phase four, which is the essence of the vessel of the emanated being. It is the coarseness that the light acquired during its expansion.

However, the first three phases merely cause phase four to appear. The inevitability and the order of these four phases were explained in the previous parts and it is needless to elaborate on them here, too (see Part 1, chapter 1, item 50).

10. Clothing is like concealment. That is because the clothes hide the one who wears them, yet it is done because of his desire to be seen. Without the correction of this concealment, it is impossible for him to become revealed. For this reason, he hides himself in it and is revealed by it.

Such a correction is always called clothing or garment. Thus, the garment is used for two things: concealment and revelation.

It is the same with our matter because it is impossible to attain the light in the lower ones without a vessel. Hence, the light clothes and becomes concealed in a vessel, so the lower one may attain it by that vessel it is clothed in, and examine it closely.

———

The correction of the screen to detain the upper light from expanding in the vessel of Malchut separates the world of Atzilut from the rest of the worlds.

2. When the above expansion reached the Malchut of Atzilut(20)**, the Upper Emanator saw that the lower ones do not have the strength to receive that light**(30) **should it expand further. Then, when the tenth vessel of Atzilut was completed**(40)**, one screen and curtain was made there**(50)**, separating Atzilut from the rest of the worlds below it**(60)**.**

Inner Light

20. This means that after the light had expanded in the first three phases, called: Hochma, Bina, ZA, and after it completed its expansion in ZA, it came to expand in phase four, called Malchut. The light cannot expand in Malchut before it expands in the three former phases, for they cause one another by way of cause and consequence.

30. Because the force of the restriction rides over phase four, which is the lowest of them all, phase four does not have the strength to receive light (see Table of Topics, Part 1, item 81, and Part 1, chapter 2, item 2).

40. That refers to phase four, called Malchut. By that he tells us that we should note that the vessel of Malchut and the screen in it are two separate matters. The vessel of Malchut is a light that grew coarser into phase four, upon which rides the force of the restriction. The screen and the curtain upon her were erected in her later (see Table of Questions, Part 2, item 43).

50. The screen and curtain are one thing. It means that a detaining force was made there, like a protective partition above Malchut, so that the upper light would not break into her (see Table of Questions, Part 2, item 43).

60. It means that this screen not only protects Malchut, as mentioned above, but also separates the world of Atzilut from the rest of the worlds.

By the power of the striking of the light of Ein Sof in the screen, the light returned upward as reflected light that clothes the upper light. Up to the place where the line of the light of Ein Sof reaches, it is called the world of Atzilut.

3. Then the light of Ein Sof that expands up to there struck that screen (70)**. By the power of the striking of the descent** (80)**, it struck it and returned upward as reflected light to its place** (90)**. Then the world of Atzilut was completed in its vessels** (100) **and the light of Ein Sof clothed them once more as self** (200)**. Thus,** (300) **up to the place where the light of Ein Sof reaches by this**

manner, it is called the world of Atzilut, (400) because it is the light itself, but after it became coarse.

Inner Light

70. The encounter of the upper light with the screen is likened to two hard objects where one of them is trying to break the other's boundary. The other stands firmly against the first and prevents the first from trespassing. Such an encounter is called striking.

In contrast, when two liquids meet, they do not prevent each other from trespassing and mixing; hence there is no striking between them. The same applies to two supple objects; their striking is not really felt because they let each other permeate the other's boundary and push their outer shell to some extent.

However, with hard objects, one does not let the other move it from its boundary even a little. Consequently, their encounter is perceived as striking.

Since the restriction was primarily done by the emanated being and not at all by the Emanator, the light of Ein Sof is not at all meticulous about that restriction in Malchut. Instead, it extends and descends to expand in Malchut, too. Moreover, it does so forcefully, because Ein Sof filled phase four, too, before the restriction (see Part 1, chapter 1, item 20 and item 50). For that reason it has no reason to change its way and it always descends to fill the vessel of Malchut with its light.

However, the screen and curtain erected in Malchut detain it and stop the light, not letting it expand within even a bit, which is why we find that "the light of Ein Sof that expands to there struck that screen (see Table of Questions, Part 2, item 43)."

80. Has been explained in the above item.

90. That measure of light that should have been received in Malchut, which she did not receive due to the detainment of the screen, that entire measure rose back up and clothed all three phases of the upper light up to Hochma. This is regarded as the "place" of that reflected light. This is the meaning of the words of the ARI **"returned upward as reflected light to its place"** (see Inner Observation, Part 2, item 62).

100. That is because the ascent of the reflected light and its clothing of the upper light from above downward make the vessels for the upper light.

200. After the reflected light rose back up, the light of Ein Sof clothed this reflected light as self that is clothed in the vessels.

300. Meaning up to the screen in the vessel of Malchut, because the screen pushed it back up and did not let it expand further.

400. He wishes to say that the force of detainment in the screen did not act on the Sefirot of Atzilut above Malchut at all, but only from Malchut downward. This is why the light of Ein Sof expands down to the screen in Malchut as Atzilut, without any detainment. However, the light of Ein Sof that sparkles and passes through the screen downward is greatly diminished because of this and is no longer regarded as the actual light of Ein Sof.

There are four phases in the coarseness of the upper light: 1) Reception from the upper one, which is Hochma. 2) Distancing from Hochma, which is Bina. 3) Window and narrow foramen, which is ZA. 4) Distancing from Hochma and a narrow foramen, which is Malchut.

4. The matter of the light becoming coarser (1) is because he who sees a very great light cannot tolerate it, unless through distancing or a screen, or both. However, the Ein Sof shines in the Keter of Atzilut (2) without any screen and distancing at all. This is why Keter is called Ein Sof.

Hochma receives through Keter (3) but Bina receives the light of Ein Sof through distancing (4), since now the Ein Sof is far from her and she can receive it (5). ZA receives the light only through a window and a narrow foramen (6). The self of the light passes through that window without any screen, but there is no broad passage, only a very narrow one.

However, he is near (7) because there isn't a great distance between Bina and ZA (8). Nevertheless, Nukva of Zeir Anpin receives her light through the foramen and window as does ZA, but it is in distancing (9).

Inner Light

1. This coarseness has already been explained. It does not appear in the light at once, since it is opposite from the light. Instead, it cascades down from the refined to the slightly coarser and from there to the coarser still, until it completes its coarseness, called phase four, or Malchut.

These four phases are called: Hochma, Bina, ZA and Malchut and must be present in every emanated being. The reason for the necessity and the definition of these four phases has been explained thoroughly above (Part 1, chapter 1, item 50). Study there, for I rely on it, and I do not bring it here due to its length, though every word of it is very needed here.

2. Every world and every Partzuf, wherever it is, must receive its abundance from Ein Sof. Hence, the induction of Ein Sof that is ascribed to a certain world or Partzuf is called the Keter of the world and the Keter of the Partzuf. It is also called the Emanator of that world.

It is written, "**the Ein Sof shines in Keter of Atzilut.**" It means that there is an induction of Ein Sof there, with respect to the world of Atzilut. This is why Keter is called Ein Sof or Emanator.

3. The expansion of the light of Ein Sof that extends first from the Keter to the world is called light of Hochma. It is necessary that the desire to receive the light will be immediately incorporated in that light of Hochma, for otherwise the light of Ein Sof would not be regarded as expanding.

However, this will to receive is not really regarded as disparity of form and coarseness because this will to receive came to her from the upper force, meaning from Keter. This is because the will to bestow in the Keter necessitates the will to receive in Hochma.

That is the meaning of the words of the ARI "**Hochma receives through Keter.**" It means that the reception in Hochma came to her from Keter and by its power. Thus, the coarseness due to that will to receive is very faint, and it is called phase one.

4. Hochma becomes coarser as it expands because when she completes her expansion, the desire in her intensifies and she draws light of Hassadim from Ein Sof and distances herself from the light of Hochma (see Part 1, chapter 1, item 50). Because this intensification was made by her own awakening and not by an upper force, that desire is regarded as little coarseness, but more than the coarseness in Hochma.

It is therefore necessary that due to this change, she became a separate phase from Hochma, called Bina or phase two. This is the meaning of the ARI's words "**Bina received the light of Ein Sof through distancing,**" since this coarseness of phase two is called distancing, for she distanced herself from receiving the light of Hochma, in order to receive the light of Hassadim.

This intensification of the desire is still not regarded as complete coarseness because it comes from a desire to bestow and equivalence of form with the Emanator (see Part 1, chapter 1, item 50). However, it is coarser than phase one because the entire desire in phase one is not hers but comes from Keter. Phase two already acts out of her own intensification of desire, and that is why phase two is regarded as the root of the complete will to receive, for by that she is regarded as coarser than phase one.

5. After Bina awakened to draw light of Hassadim from the Emanator, she grows far from the light of Hochma. Otherwise she would not have been able to receive the light of Hassadim, because light of Hochma is drawn by the will to receive, and light of Hassadim is drawn by the will to bestow (see Part 1, chapter 1, item 50).

Thus, phase one and phase two are opposite to one another from the beginning of their emanation. That is why the ARI writes, "**now the Ein Sof is far from her and she can receive it.**" It means that she grew far and became a third degree from Ein Sof, which is the medium between Bina and Ein Sof.

She left it because now that she distanced the light of Hochma and became a third degree, Hochma being phase one, second to Ein Sof, and Bina being phase two and third from Ein Sof, she could now receive the light of Hassadim that she drew. Had she not distanced herself to a third degree, she would not have been able to receive.

We must know that the word "far" is a term that indicates diminution of obtainment of Hochma, as it is written, "I said: 'I will get wisdom'; but it was far from me." It is also the meaning of the verse, "And his sister stood afar," and there is no reason to discuss it any further.

6. Bina also becomes coarser at the end of her expansion because she distances the light of Hochma from her. It is known that light of Hochma is the primary vitality and essence of the emanated being. Thus, at the end of her expansion, the desire to receive illumination of Hochma into the light of Hassadim intensified in her.

Because all the difference between spirituals is due to the disparity of form, this new illumination emerged, meaning the light of Hassadim within which there is an illumination of Hochma, and acquired a separate name, being Zeir Anpin. It is called by that name because light of Hochma is called light of the face, as it is written, "A man's wisdom makes his face shine." Because it has no more than illumination of Hochma, but its essence is only the light of Hassadim of Bina, it is called Zeir Anpin, meaning "Small Face," indicating a small amount of light of Hochma.

It is also called phase three. Its coarseness is called "a window and a narrow foramen" because it has explained above (Part 1, chapter 2, item 70) that a screen that appears in the upper one because of the incorporation of the lower one in it is called window. That is because it has no judgments, but only a reason for the illumination, like a window.

Because any coarseness and screens in Atzilut come from the incorporation of BYA in it, the coarseness of ZA is called a window for the illumination of the light of Gadlut, and the name "narrow foramen" is given to the illumination of Katnut. However, phase two is not even called a window, but a distancing.

7. Meaning, it does not have the same distancing of Hochma that exists in Bina, because the only difference between him and Bina is that he has an illumination from the light of Hochma. That is why the ARI writes, **"However, he is near,"** meaning there is no distancing in him.

8. The expansion of light of Bina to phase three, which is ZA, does not cause distancing. On the contrary, it causes nearing of Hochma. It has already been explained that "near" and "far" are definitions of Hochma.

9. Meaning, after the three phases of coarseness expanded fully to the point that ZA expanded fully, the complete will to receive that is fit for reception had awakened. It is called phase four, or Malchut, or Nukva of ZA (see Part 1, chapter 1, item 30), and in it was the restriction.

Thus, from the restriction onward this phase four no longer receives the light of Ein Sof. Hence, her phase of coarseness is called distancing. She too has two degrees called window and narrow foramen as in ZA. The bestowal of Gadlut is called a window, and the bestowal of Katnut is called a narrow foramen.

There is a big difference between the distancing in phase two and the distancing in phase four: The distancing of phase two is a voluntary distancing, as it says, "because He delights in mercy," meaning she wants Hassadim and not Hochma. The distancing of phase four, however, is a forced distancing, due to the screen that was erected in phase four.

CHAPTER TWO

Explains the four worlds ABYA and the differences among them; containing six issues:

1. All the elements in the world of Atzilut are evaluated by the above four phases of coarseness. 2. The light of Ein Sof expands in the world of Atzilut without any screen. 3. The light of Ein Sof does not spread below Atzilut, except in an illumination that extends from it through a screen. 4. The ten Sefirot of the world of Beria emerge from the coupling by striking of the upper light with the screen between Atzilut and Beria, and the ten Sefirot of the world of Yetzira emerge from the coupling by striking between Beria and Yetzira, and so it is from Yetzira to Assiya. 5. The differences among the four worlds are that in Atzilut there is no screen at all; in Beria there is one screen, in Yetzira two screens and in Assiya three screens. 6. There is no difference of coarseness whatsoever between the worlds; as it is in Atzilut, so it is in BYA.

There is no screen in the world of Atzilut.

1. They are four phases in which all the elements of Atzilut are distinguished from it and from within it, but they are all without a screen whatsoever (1). It is called the world of Atzilut because the light of Ein Sof itself expanded throughout it without a screen.

Inner Light

1. It is a rule that coarseness and screen cannot diminish or blemish above the place where they appear, not even a bit. Although the reflected light ascends because of the screen in the vessel of Malchut and clothes all nine Sefirot from itself upward, the force of coarseness in the screen does not rise upward whatsoever.

For this reason, the nine Sefirot of Atzilut are considered to be without any screen at all. Although we discern many screens in the world of Atzilut, as well, such as the screen of Peh and of Chazeh, etc., which is the conduct in every singe Partzuf in Atzilut, these are not actual screens; they come from the incorporation of the lower one in the upper one. Only the screen of Sium Raglaim of Atzilut is an actual screen that stops the upper light (see Inner Observation, chapter 14).

Ein Sof does not expand below Atzilut except through a coupling by striking in the screen at the Sium of the world of Atzilut. Then the ten Sefirot pass through the screen to the world of Beria. Also, ten Sefirot pass to the world of Yetzira by the coupling by striking at the Sium of Beria. The same occurs between Yetzira and Assiya.

2. Indeed, Ein Sof itself does not expand from there downward, but only in an illumination that extends from it through a screen (2). There is a screen and curtain that separates between Atzilut and Beria. Because of that striking of the upper light that reaches there (3), it struck that curtain, and by the power of the ten Sefirot of Atzilut that reached there, it struck their light there and lights glittered (4) and went through that screen and became the ten Sefirot of Beria below from the glittering of the ten Sefirot of Atzilut atop them by the power of the screen.

By the power of the ten Sefirot of vessels, ten Sefirot of other vessels were made, and by the power of the ten Sefirot of the self, another ten Sefirot of the self of Beria were made. Also, another screen was erected at the end of Beria (5), and the ten Sefirot of Yetzira were made because of the striking of the ten Sefirot of Beria (6) in the self and vessels in the screen. The same happened through that screen from Yetzira to Assiya.

Now you can see why one is called Atzilut, one is Beria, one is Yetzira, and one is Assiya. It is because there is a screen that separates between them, and one is not at all like the other (7).

Inner Light

2. The light that is in the world of Beria necessarily extends from Ein Sof, for there is no illumination in the worlds that does not extend from Ein Sof. Yet, because the light Ein Sof that expands to Beria passes through the screen, its illumination is greatly diminished. In fact, the light of Ein Sof is regarded to have been stopped above the screen. The ARI will explain in the following how light passes through a screen.

3. It means that there is a law in the upper worlds, that each lower degree causes additions of light to a higher degree, that entire measure of additional light is imparted back to the lower one that caused it. It is the same with our matter: the screen on Malchut of Atzilut caused that reflected light to rise and clothe all nine Sefirot of Atzilut and become vessels for them.

Without it, the light of Ein Sof would not be grasped and clothed in Atzilut, for a light cannot be attained without a vessel. But since the screen caused all that additions, meaning the above-mentioned reflected light and ten Sefirot, the screen and vessel in Malchut expanded because of the descending reflected light that came back to it from the screen downward, and it drew to itself all those ten Sefirot of Atzilut above in their exact likeness.

Thus, Malchut of Atzilut alone descends and expands into ten Sefirot from her and within her, like the ten Sefirot of Atzilut, meaning from Keter to Malchut. They are called the ten Sefirot of the world of Beria.

This is the meaning of the words of the ARI, that "**Because of that striking of the upper light that reaches there (3), it struck that curtain, and by the power of the ten Sefirot of Atzilut that reached there, it struck their light there and lights sparkled (4) and went through that screen and became the ten Sefirot of Beria.**"

There are two things we should understand here: the first discernment caused the reflected light that rises by the striking of the upper light in the screen. That reflected light descends back to the degree that caused its appearance. The second discernment caused the clothing of the light of Ein Sof itself in the ten vessels of the reflected light that rose and became the ten Sefirot of Atzilut. They, too, descend back to the degree that caused their appearance.

The ARI states about the first discernment: "**because of the striking of the upper light in the curtain.**" It means that this reflected light returns and descends from above downward to the world of Beria. The ARI states about the second discernment: "**by the power of the ten Sefirot of Atzilut**" etc. From these two forces the ten Sefirot of the world of Beria were formed.

4. Any place where reflected light appears is called sparkling.

5. All ten Sefirot of Atzilut were copied and sealed in the world of Beria. Hence, the screen and Malchut were also sealed in the world of Beria, and the same coupling by striking of upper light in the screen applies there, and the ascents of reflected light that rises and clothes from the screen upwards all nine Sefirot of the world of Beria. This reflected light became the ten vessels of the world of Beria where the self of the light of the world of Beria is clothed.

6. The reflected light of the screen of Atzilut expanded once more from the screen downward and imprinted the ten Sefirot of Beria as was explained in item 3 above. By the same manner, the reflected light that rose from the screen of Malchut of

Beria, also returned, expanded downward and imprinted the ten Sefirot of the world of Yetzira. The same also applies from Yetzira to Assiya.

7. As we have written, phase four, which is called Malchut in which the screen was made, she herself divides into four phases of a screen, where all the changes and differences between the worlds appear. The screen of phase three operates in Atzilut, the screen of phase two operates in Beria and the screen of phase one in Yetzira.

———

The difference between Atzilut and BYA is that in Atzilut there is no screen at all. In Beria the light is diminished by a single screen, in Yetzira by two screens, and in Assiya by three screens. Still, in the four phases of coarseness of the upper light there is no difference between the worlds.

3. The difference between Atzilut and the three worlds is that in Atzilut, the light of Ein Sof punctures it and passes it to the end of Atzilut without any screen. However, from there downward there is a screen.

The difference between Beria and Yetzira is that Beria has one separating screen, Yetzira has two screens, and Assiya three screens. However, within each world, just as there are four phases in Atzilut (8), so there are four phases Beria itself and in Yetzira itself (9).

Inner Light

8. It refers to the four phases of coarseness, namely HB TM, previously referred to as the expansion of the light of Ein Sof to make vessels. They are also called the ten Sefirot of direct light because Tifferet contains six Sefirot HGT NHY. Through the coupling by striking in the screen in the Sefira of Malchut of direct light, the light rises once more as reflected light, clothes all ten inner Sefirot of direct light, and turns them into one general degree, according to the level of the reflected light.

9. He thus tells us that these four phases of direct light exist in every world and in every Partzuf. There is no difference between a high degree and a low degree. All the differences in the Partzufim and in the worlds are because of the screens and the reflected light in them. In that, the screen in one is not like the screen in another.

CHAPTER THREE

Explains the four couplings by striking in the four phases of the screen that elicit four levels HB TM one below the other in the four worlds ABYA; containing five issues:

1. Ein Sof shines in the world of Atzilut by clothing the level of Hochma. 2. The level of Hochma disappears in the world of Beria and clothes the level of Bina. 3. The level of Bina also disappears in the world of Yetzira and clothes the level of Tifferet. 4. The level of ZA also disappears in the world of Assiya and clothes the level of Malchut. 5. The level of Hochma that emerged in Atzilut was extended from the coupling by striking above the world of Atzilut. Also, the level of Bina that emerged in Beria was extended from a coupling by striking above Beria, meaning from the screen between Atzilut and Beria. The level of ZA in Yetzira is extended from the coupling by striking on the screen at the end of Beria, and the level of Malchut in Assiya emerged from the screen at the end of Yetzira.

Ein Sof shines in the world of Atzilut by clothing the level of Hochma.

1. You should also know that in order for the light of Ein Sof to shine in the entire Atzilut, its self must be clothed inside Hochma (1). After it is clothed in Hochma it expands in the entire Atzilut. Only by that clothing can the entire Atzilut receive from Ein Sof. This is the meaning of the verse, "You have made them all in wisdom [Hochma]. (2)"

Inner Light

1. In order to understand the ARI's words from here on, we must repeat the explanation about the five discernments in the screen: They emerge from the gradual refinement of the screen from the great coarseness of phase four, to the great refinement in the phase of Keter, and the root of the screen. By that they create five Partzufim.

You will find the explanation to these matters in Part Two (Inner Observation), for all these things pertain here, but it is impossible to present them here due to their length. For this reason, I must rely on what I have written there, and I can only present an abbreviation and summary of everything, as much as is needed for the ARI's words here.

It has been explained there that the light Ein Sof, which contains four phases, called the ten Sefirot of direct light, does not stop shining for the lower ones, not even for a moment. However, since there is no perception of the light without a vessel, it is only the vessel for reception that we need. Any Partzuf or degree that acquires a vessel, simultaneously acquires the light as well, according to the measure of the vessel that has been acquired.

It has also been explained there that the root of all the vessels in all the worlds is the reflected light that ascends from the coupling by striking on the screen in the vessel of Malchut. Thus, the very moment when a new screen is formed in some Partzuf, the light of Ein Sof, which contains ten Sefirot of direct light, immediately expands to it and strikes that screen. Then reflected light rises and clothes the light of Ein Sof according to the measure of that reflected light.

This is called the clothing Ein Sof in the vessels, or in some Sefira. That is because the name of a Sefira indicates the measure of the light of Ein Sof that clothes it. For example, when referring to the clothing of Ein Sof in the Keter, it implies that the reflected light clothes the entire ten Sefirot of direct light up to the Keter. When referring to the clothing of Ein Sof in Hochma, it indicates that the reflected light clothes only up to Hochma.

We might ask, how does such clothing apply only to nine Sefirot, while there are ten and not nine? Indeed, there is Keter there too, but this Keter is clothed in the internality of Hochma and thus does not merit a name, but only the Sefira Hochma, and in this way you can understand all the levels of the other Partzufim.

The measure by which the extent of the reflected light is measured has also been explained there; it is the discernment of the measure of the coarseness incorporated in the screen in the vessel Malchut.

They are five discernments: the coarsest screen, being phase four, reflects the greatest measure of the reflected light. It clothes the level of Keter in the light of Ein Sof, meaning in the ten Sefirot of direct light. A screen with coarseness of phase three clothes the level of Hochma of the ten Sefirot of direct light; a screen, whose coarseness is only phase two clothes the level of Bina of the ten Sefirot of direct light. A screen with only coarseness of phase one clothes the level of ZA of the ten Sefirot of [direct light], and a screen whose coarseness is only of the root phase of the screen, called the Keter of the screen, there is no coupling by striking in that screen and no level at all, but only at the level of Malchut. However, we should remember all the reasons and arguments regarding the matters as they were explained there in the above-mentioned Inner Observation and in the previous parts. Study it there, for without understanding the reasons and the necessity in these matters it is impossible to understand even a single word here in its true meaning, for here I must be brief, of course.

2. It means that the world of Atzilut is regarded as the Rosh of all the worlds. Even though there are many worlds above Atzilut, meaning all the many worlds contained in Adam Kadmon, are indeed all concealed within the world of Atzilut. They are not at all roots to the worlds, but are merely regarded as the root of the world of Atzilut. This is why they are concealed inside it and shine only in it and in concealment.

It has been explained in previous parts that the screen of phase four operates only in the world of AK. Hence, the measure of reflected light there is indeed great, clothing up to the level of Keter in the light of Ein Sof. Consequently, all the worlds contained in the world of Adam Kadmon are called the world of Keter.

The world of Atzilut uses only the screen of phase three (see Inner Observation, Part 2, chapter 2, item 10). The measure of its reflected light that ascends from the coupling by striking on that screen reaches only up to Hochma, and does not reach the Keter of the light of Ein Sof. Rather, Keter is hidden and concealed inside Hochma.

For that reason, the world of Atzilut is called the world of Hochma. This is the meaning of the verse, "You have made them all in wisdom [Hochma]." It means that everything is rooted only in Atzilut and not in AK, which is the world of Keter. It is so because the world of AK is not regarded as the root of the lower worlds at all, and it will appear in the worlds only after the end of correction, as it says, "And His feet shall stand upon the Mount of Olives."

We must know that the entire ten Sefirot are named after the highest Sefira: if it is Keter, all the Sefirot are regarded as Keter; if it is Hochma, they are all Hochma etc. By the same manner, every world is named after its first Partzuf.

The world of Beria shines by clothing the level of Bina and Hochma is hidden there.

210

2. But in order to shine in Beria, Hochma must be clothed in Bina. Through those two, when the light of Ein Sof clothes within them, it shines in Beria. This is the meaning of the screen between Atzilut and Beria, for this screen extends from Bina, where Hochma is clothed so as to shine in Beria.

———

The world of Yetzira shines by clothing in the level of Tifferet and Bina is also hidden there. In the world of Assiya it shines by clothing in the level of Malchut and Tifferet becomes hidden there too.

3. In order to shine in Yetzira, it adds one more screen and clothing, by Bina also clothing in Tifferet. After that Ein Sof shines in Yetzira through Tifferet.

In order to shine in Assiya, it adds another screen and clothing. It means that Tifferet also clothes in Malchut and Ein Sof shines to the entire Assiya through Malchut.

This is the meaning of "upper Ima nesting in the chair, and the middle pillar nesting in Yetzira, and Malchut nesting in Assiya."

———

The coupling by striking to elicit the ten Sefirot of Atzilut was made in the world of AK above Atzilut, in the screen of phase three, which is the level of Hochma.

4. Indeed, to improve your understanding, know that the verse says, "you have made them all in wisdom." It means that in Atzilut, the light of Ein Sof is clothed in Hochma$_{(3)}$, and through it, it shines in all of Atzilut. This wisdom shall be clarified to you from what I had let you know, that "for one higher than the high watches," etc., and there are several worlds above Atzilut$_{(4)}$, and in that Hochma that there is above Atzilut $_{(5)}$, Ein Sof clothes within it and shines in Atzilut.

Inner Light

3. This has already been explained. However, that does not mean that when the world of Atzilut was emanated, it received the level of Hochma immediately. That is because the smaller levels were emanated there first, called conception and suckling. Rather, it refers to the highest level that finally emerged there, in AA, which is in fact the level of Hochma, lacking the Keter.

4. It has been explained above that all the innumerous worlds that exist prior to Atzilut, are all included in the name Adam Kadmon, or the world of Keter, for the above reason.

5. You already know about the diminution of the reflected light that comes because of the refinement of the level of the coarseness in the screen (see Inner Observation, Part 2, chapter 7, item 72). You can therefore see that after the world of AK has been completed, over the clothing in reflected light of its screen of phase four, that screen was refined to phase three for the above reason in Inner Observation.

This does not mean that there was a change in the screen of phase four in the world of AK itself, because there is no absence in spirituality. Instead, any change denotes an addition, for by the refinement to phase three, a new screen of phase three was added and born, and the upper light promptly spreads to it for a coupling by striking, raising reflected light from the screen upward to the level of Hochma (see chapter 3, item 1).

This is called "a new clothing in the world of AK," meaning clothing the light of Ein Sof in Hochma. However, this new clothing is not required for itself, but only for the world of Atzilut.

The above screen of phase three, whose reflected light rose from the place of the screen upward, clothed the light of Ein Sof up to the level of Hochma. Consequently, all ten Sefirot above the screen return and descend from the place of the screen downward (see Chap 3). This is regarded as the screen and Malchut expanding from her downward, to the ten Sefirot, because of the reflected light that is drawn to it once more from above.

Thus, Malchut expands to ten Sefirot of reflected light that rose from the screen of phase three from above, meaning in the level of Hochma, and they are the ones called "ten Sefirot of Atzilut."

The ARI writes "and in that Hochma above Atzilut there inside the Ein Sof clothes and it shines in Atzilut." He wishes to say that this coupling by striking on the screen of phase three had to be in the world of AK above Atzilut, because the screen of phase three is but a refinement from phase four, and phase four is in the world of AK.

Thus, the refinement and the coupling by striking had to be in the world of AK above Atzilut. After Ein Sof clothed there, in the reflected light that rose up from the screen, the ten Sefirot of Atzilut descended and extended from the place of the screen downward.

The coupling by striking to elicit the ten Sefirot of Beria was done in the world of Atzilut in the screen of phase two, which is the level of Bina. The coupling by striking to elicit the ten Sefirot of Yetzira was done in the world of Beria in screen of phase one, which is the level of Tifferet. Also, the coupling by striking to elicit the ten Sefirot of Assiya was done in Yetzira in the screen of the root, which is the level of Malchut. The coupling by striking was done above Atzilut in the screen of phase three, which is the level of Hochma, for the ten Sefirot of Atzilut.

5. Thus, when he wanted to shine in Beria (6), he also clothed Bina in Atzilut, which is above Beria, and by that Bina, he shines in Beria (7). Also, in order to shine in Yetzira (8), he clothes in Tifferet of Beria. Likewise, from Yetzira to Assiya, he clothes in Malchut of Yetzira. So is the matter in Atzilut, as in order to shine in Atzilut, he clothes in the above-mentioned Hochma above Atzilut, and through it, he shines in Atzilut. Thus, you should not think that it is the Hochma of Atzilut itself.

Inner Light

6. Here too, as in Atzilut, it does not mean that the level of Bina emerged in the world of Beria right at the beginning. Instead, he wishes to say that the highest level that finally emerged there is not more than the level of Bina, and the coupling by striking was above in phase two of Atzilut.

It also means that for the above-mentioned reason, the refinement of the screen from phase three to phase two, called Bina, had to have been in the world of Atzilut, the place of the screen of phase three, called Hochma. In the four Partzufim AB SAG MA BON of AK, the coupling of every Partzuf occurred in the Peh of Rosh of its upper Partzuf. The coupling of AB, which is phase three, was made in the Peh of Rosh of Partzuf Galgalta. The coupling of SAG was made in the Peh of Rosh of AB etc. (as is explained clearly in Inner Observation, Chapter 9).

It is the same in the worlds of ABYA, where the coupling for every world was done in its upper world. After the screen of phase three is refined there to phase two, it is considered that a new screen of phase two was born and added there. The light of Ein Sof promptly expands to it for a coupling by striking, and the reflected light rises and clothes the degree of Bina of the ten Sefirot of direct light. Then Keter and Hochma of direct light clothe the internality of Bina.

When the clothing of Ein Sof in Bina is completed from the screen upward, the reflected light descends once more from the place of the screen downward, and expands that Malchut into ten Sefirot from her and within her, meaning from Keter to her Malchut. It is like the ten Sefirot from the screen upward in Atzilut, meaning only at the level of Bina, in which Keter and Hochma are concealed.

However, these ten Sefirot are the ten Sefirot of the world of Beria, so the ten Sefirot in the level of Bina that emerged above the screen are in the world of Atzilut. The ARI says about them, **"when he wanted to shine in Beria, he also clothed Bina in Atzilut,"** and the second ten Sefirot that extended and emerged downward from the screen are called the ten Sefirot in the world of Beria.

7. It means that everything that exists in the ten Sefirot of the world of Beria extends in the ten Sefirot of the level of Bina above Beria, for the reason explained above (see also chapter 2, item 3).

8. Meaning also for the reason explained above in Atzilut and in Beria, namely that the world of Yetzira extends from the screen of phase one and the refinement from phase two to phase one must be in the world of Beria. It is so because that is where that screen is, and after the refinement is done there, ten Sefirot emerge there from the screen upward on the level of ZA, called Tifferet.

The first three Sefirot Keter, Hochma, Bina of direct light are concealed and clothed in the internality of Tifferet. After this clothing is completed, a second ten Sefirot descend once more from the place of the screen downward in the level of ZA, and they are called the "ten Sefirot of the world of Yetzira."

Chapter Four

Explains that if the clothing of upper light is in the reflected light of
the level of Hochma, all ten Sefirot will be in the light of Hochma.
If on the level of Bina, all ten Sefirot will be in the light of Bina.
If on the level of ZA, all ten Sefirot will be in the light of ZA. If on
the level of Malchut, all ten Sefirot will be in the light of Malchut.
Contains four issues:

1. When Ein Sof shines in Bina of Atzilut, it does not shine through clothing in
the reflected light of the screen of Bina. Rather, the light of the level of Hochma
shines in Bina, too. Consequently, even ZA that receives from Bina has the light
of Hochma as well. 2. But in order to shine in the world of Beria, it clothes in the
reflected light of the screen of Bina. Hence, all ten Sefirot are the light of Bina, even
the Keter and Hochma there. 3. In the world of Yetzira it clothes the reflected light
of the screen of ZA, and all ten Sefirot are from the light of ZA. It is the same in
the world of Assiya: it clothes the screen at the level of Malchut, and all ten Sefirot
are in the light of Malchut, even KHB ZA there. 4. The four letters Yod, Hey, Vav,
Hey, imply the four worlds ABYA.

When AK clothed to shine in Atzilut, it only clothed in the reflected light
at the level of Hochma, not in the reflected light of phase two, which
is the level of Bina. Thus, only Keter disappeared from that level, and
Keter clothed within Hochma.

**1. You should indeed know that when the Emanator wanted to shine in Atzilut,
He clothed in Hochma above Atzilut, and through the Hochma He clothes in,
He enters and shines in Keter and Hochma of Atzilut and did not have to clothe
in Bina above Atzilut, as well (1). He only clothed in Hochma above Atzilut, and
through her, He shines in the Keter and Hochma of Atzilut (2).**

Inner Light

1. Here the ARI labored to explain the difference between the four phases of direct
light, called Hochma, Bina, ZA and Malchut, and the four phases of reflected light,
which are also called by the same names Hochma, Bina, ZA and Malchut. The ARI

has already explained (Chap 1, item 3 and in Inner Light, item 70) that the vessels of Atzilut are made by the reflected light that rises to its place, where the the light of Ein Sof itself is clothed, which are the four phases of direct light. You can see how the four phases HB ZA and Malchut of direct light clothe the reflected light that rises through a coupling by striking in the screen in Malchut of direct light.

You can therefore see that where it specifies the word clothing, it means that direct light clothes reflected light. When he says that Ein Sof clothed Hochma it means that the four phases HB TM of direct light that expand from Ein Sof, clothed the Hochma of reflected light.

It means that according to the measure of reflected light that has the level of Hochma of direct light, the reflected light of that level of Hochma clothes all four phases of direct light, Hochma, Bina, ZA and Malchut, besides Keter of direct light, which is concealed in the Hochma of direct light.

It is certain that the four phases of direct light that expand from Ein Sof also come gradually by way of cause and consequence. That is because they emerge and extend from one another, Hochma extends from Keter, Bina extends from Hochma, ZA extends from Bina, and Malchut extends from ZA (see Inner Light, Part 1, Chap 1, item 50).

However, this is still not considered clothing. That is because the four phases of direct light do not clothe one another, as it says, for example, that the upper light clothes in Bina in order to shine for ZA. That is because clothing refers to the clothing of reflected light that rises through coupling by striking from the screen that is erected in phase four, which is Malchut (see chapter 1, item 3 and Inner Light, there, item 100).

Here in Bina, there was no restriction and of course there is no screen there that is ready for the striking of upper light into reflected light, so that you say that the light clothed in Bina of direct light in order to shine in ZA of direct light. Rather, this is called "in passing." It means that the light of Ein Sof that belongs to ZA of direct light necessarily passes through the Sefirot of Bina of direct light, since she is the cause and the reason for ZA of direct light. That ZA of direct light cannot acquire any light if not through its cause, namely Bina.

However, this is not regarded as clothing in the screen of Bina, since there is no screen there, as it says that there is a screen only in phase four, meaning in Malchut.

Remember the difference between the four phases of direct light and the four phases of reflected light well, so that you will not be confused by the similarity in their names. When we say Hochma of direct light, we mean the second Sefira following the Keter of direct light, called Hochma. But when we say Hochma of reflected light, it means that there is a coupling by striking involved, and ten Sefirot of reflected light that clothe the ten Sefirot of direct light, meaning twenty complete Sefirot.

When they are all incorporated in one another, they are one hundred Sefirot. We call all of them by the name Hochma of reflected light, because it designates the level of the reflected light, and because it rises and clothes up to Hochma. That is why we call all one hundred Sefirot by the name Hochma. Remember that, for it is the most important key in this wisdom.

Much the same applies to Bina of reflected light, which is also twenty Sefirot, except Keter and Hochma are concealed inside Bina. ZA of reflected light also has twenty Sefirot, but Keter, Hochma and Bina are concealed inside ZA (see chapter 3, item 1).

The ARI wrote, "and did not have to clothe in Bina above Atzilut as well. He therefore clothed only Hochma above Atzilut." He wishes to say that for the purpose of the ten Sefirot of Atzilut, He clothed the Hochma above Atzilut, meaning the Hochma of reflected light (Inner Light, chapter 3, item 10), through a coupling by striking in the screen of phase three in Malchut.

However, it did not have to clothe Bina of reflected light, meaning through a coupling by striking in the screen of phase two in the vessel of Malchut. That is because the level of Bina of reflected light belongs to the ten Sefirot of Beria and not to the ten Sefirot of the world of Atzilut, where it clothes the level of Hochma of reflected light (see Inner Light, chapter 3, item 1).

2. It means that it shines in the ten Sefirot of Atzilut at the level of Hochma. Since Keter is concealed here inside Hochma, as written above, he includes Keter and Hochma as one in this level.

Bina passes the light at the level of Hochma through a window to ZA and Malchut, without a second clothing in the reflected light of the screen of phase two.

2. Indeed, when He wanted to shine from Bina of Atzilut through the end of Atzilut (3), He certainly had to clothe Bina of Atzilut as well (4). That is because ZA and Nukva receive light only through Bina (5).

However, the thing is that Bina was helpful only as a passageway for the light of Ein Sof that is clothed in the upper Hochma and passed through Bina to Atzilut

(6). Bina did not become a second screen and garment to shine for ZA (7), but rather the light itself came through a window, without any screen (8).

Thus, even though it extended through Bina, it is not regarded as clothing, because there is no screen there whatsoever. For that reason, what ZON of Atzilut receive is the light of Ein Sof itself that is clothed only in Hochma.

Inner Light

3. Meaning from the Sefira of Bina of direct light to Malchut of direct light.

4. He did not use the term clothing here, as the ARI deduces immediately afterwards, when he says, "even though it extended through Bina, it is not regarded as clothing, because there is no screen there." It has already been explained in elaboration above, that the word clothing means that ten Sefirot of direct light clothe the reflected light that rises through a coupling by striking in the screen. This is what the ARI meant when he said that because there is no screen in Bina, it is not regarded as clothing.

5. Bina is the cause and the reason for ZON, even in the four phases of direct light. Consequently, every consequence must receive everything it has from its cause, as explained above.

6. This has been thoroughly explained above.

7. It means that there is no screen there for the light of Ein Sof to expand upon for a coupling by striking and raise reflected light in the level of Bina. This reflected light at the level of Bina will become a second garment on the light of Ein Sof, in addition to the first garment from the reflected light in the level of Hochma.

8. Look up the word window in the Table of Questions, item 30. In any place where the screen acts to raise reflected light from below upward, the coarseness is called window (see also Part 2, Inner Light, chapter 2, item 70). Here too the coarseness operates from below upward, as the ARI says above (Part 3, chapter 1, item 3).

For that reason the ARI calls the coarseness of the ZA and Malchut phases by the names window and narrow foramen (chapter 1, item 4). That is because the screens below the level of Hochma operate only from below upward.

We should not compare this with what is explained in a different place, that there are five Partzufim in the ten Sefirot of Atzilut as well. Indeed, there is a great difference between them, as all these five Partzufim of Atzilut are five parts of the ten Sefirot at the level of Hochma. This will be explained in its place and there is nothing more to add here.

In order to shine in the world of Beria, the upper light clothes the level of phase two, which is Bina. Thus, Hochma disappeared too, and Keter and Hochma became incorporated inside Bina.

3. However, in Beria, Ein Sof wears a different garment in Bina of Atzilut (9). This Bina becomes a "blocked screen" and a "complete garment," by which all ten Sefirot of Beria receive, even Keter and Hochma of Beria (10).

Inner Light

9. It means that the screen and Malchut refine to phase two, called Bina, and the light of Ein Sof expands to coupling by striking on that screen and raises reflected light in the level of Bina (see Inner Light, chapter 3, item 6). That reflected light is a different and new garment over that light of Ein Sof, which greatly differs from the garment of reflected light of Atzilut itself.

It is so because the garment of Atzilut comes from the striking in the screen of phase three that extends the light of Hochma in the entire ten Sefirot. That new garment is from the striking in the screen of phase two, whose level does not reach clothing the Hochma of direct light, but only the Bina of direct light. For that reason, it has none of the light of Hochma.

This coupling is necessarily done in Atzilut (see Inner Light, chapter 3, item 6), but the entire ten Sefirot that clothe the garment at the level of Bina extend from the screen downward and come to the world of Beria.

10. The reflected light first rises from the screen in Bina upward, meaning in the world of Atzilut, and the Sefirot of Atzilut necessarily clothe this garment at the level of Bina. Nevertheless, the coarseness and the blocking of that screen do not rise there even a bit, since the coarseness and the blemish cannot affect the ones above them in any way. Such a reception is called window and foramen (see Inner Light, Part 2, chapter 2, item 70), meaning without any coarseness.

However, in the descending reflected light below the screen between Atzilut and Beria, meaning in the ten Sefirot in the world of Beria, the force and the coarseness of the screen is the entire root of the expansion of the light of Ein Sof in them. Hence, the screen becomes a blockage and complete clothing that limits the light of Ein Sof from shining any of the light of Hochma there, since it is the screen of phase two where reflected light does not reach Hochma, but only Bina of direct light.

That is why the ARI writes that it became a "blocked screen," that is, it blocks the light of Atzilut, meaning the light of Hochma, from appearing in the world of Beria, even a bit. It is so because this screen imparts to Beria from above downward, as we have said above.

The highest Sefira in any level of ten Sefirot shines in any ten Sefirot of that level, in such a way that all ten Sefirot of the world of Atzilut receive the light of Hochma, and all ten Sefirot of the world of Beria receive the light of Bina.

4. It turns out that Atzilut receives the light of the upper Hochma because Ein Sof is clothed within her, and is therefore regarded as receiving only from Hochma (20).

Beria receives the light of Bina because Ein Sof and Hochma are clothed within her (30). For this reason, Beria receives only from Bina. This is the meaning of "upper Ima nests in the chair" (40), because the chair receives light from the above Bina of Atzilut, as it became a screen that separates Ein Sof and Hochma from Beria.

Inner Light

20. Meaning only from the level of Hochma. However, Atzilut cannot receive from the Keter because the screen of phase three operates there from above downward, as it clothed phase three above Atzilut. Hence it became a blocked screen on the light of Keter and is considered to be receiving only from Hochma.

30. It means that Keter and Hochma are concealed within the level of Bina since that reflected light does not reach them, but only the level of Bina. Hence Beria receives only from Bina and cannot receive from Keter and Hochma, because the screen blocks them, as it is above Beria.

This is the meaning of the words of the ARI, that a separating screen was erected between Keter and Hochma and Beria. You should remember that Keter is called Ein Sof.

40. An intermittent illumination is called "nesting." It is like a bird that does not always sit over its chicks, but only sometimes. Because the above coupling of phase two is not a perpetual illumination in the world of Beria, he calls it "nesting." He says, "upper Ima nests in the chair." Read my book Panim Meirot uMasbirot (p. 61) for the reason why Bina is called upper Ima.

Bina of Atzilut passes the light of Hochma to ZON, and Bina of Beria passes the light of Bina to ZON.

5. If you say: It follows that ZA and Nukva of Atzilut and Beria are all equal because they all receive from Bina of Atzilut, we should say that we have already explained that Zeir and Nukva receive the light of Hochma itself, for "you have made them all in wisdom," and Bina is used only as a passageway.

After Atzilut, Bina becomes a screen and a complete clothing from the externality of the vessel of Bina of Atzilut, and through that screen, all ten Sefirot of Beria receive the light of Ein Sof.

ZA of Beria passes the light of Bina to Malchut.

6. Know that Beria too, although the light returned to clothe ZA of Beria, nevertheless Malchut of Beria receives the light of Bina of Atzilut herself. ZA does not stop her; it is only a passageway (50), such as in Atzilut. So it is in the inner Yetzira from her and within her (60), and also in the inner Assiya from her and within her.

Inner Light

50. As was explained above regarding Bina of Atzilut, the coupling was made in the screen of phase two for Beria, and reflected light rose and clothed Bina. However, it did not stop the light of Hochma with respect to ZA of Atzilut, which stands past that Bina. It is so because the screen that operates from below upward does not carry with the reflected light that rises by it any new boundary and coarseness to those who receive from it.

ZA of Atzilut, too, receives from this reflected light, but it is not diminished because of it to become unable to draw the light of Hochma. That is because reception by the power of a screen from below the degree is called only a window and foramen, but it does not block or limit anything.

It is so also in any screen in all the places, that the boundaries that are always made because of the screens, these boundaries are apparent only to the receivers below the screen, but not at all to the receivers above the screen.

This is the meaning of the ARI's words, that "although the light returned to clothe ZA of Beria" and made a coupling by striking in the screen of phase one, this reflected light has the degree of ZA. Although Malchut of Beria receives from this reflected light, still, because this screen operates from below upward, it does not limit Malchut of Beria so as not to draw the light of Bina for herself.

It is so because "ZA does not stop her," Malchut of Beria, through his screen from below upward, for "it is only a passageway," meaning as a window and not as a screen (see Part 3, item 4 in Inner Light item 6). So it is in all other places too.

60. Regarding the reflected light that descends from above downward, whose conduct is to broaden the screen and the vessel of Malchut until they expand to ten Sefirot from above downward on their own, from Keter to Malchut (see chapter 3, item 5). This expansion of Malchut is always referred to as expansion "from her and within her."

It means that the one vessel called Malchut expands to ten Sefirot from her and within her, and you already know that the limited ten Sefirot in all the worlds are made solely by the reflected light that expands to them from above downward. Thus, these ten Sefirot are called "the inner ten Sefirot from her and within her," in Atzilut, in Yetzira and in Assiya.

In the world of Yetzira, the upper light clothes the reflected light of phase one, which is the level of Zeir Anpin. In the world of Assiya, the upper light clothes the reflected light at the root level of the coarseness, which is the level of Nukva of ZA.

7. In order to shine in Yetzira, the Ein Sof becomes clothed in a complete garment in ZA of Beria as well (70), and becomes a screen and clothing to Yetzira, by which the entire Yetzira receives. In order to shine in Assiya, the Ein Sof becomes clothed in a complete garment and screen in Nukva of Zeir Anpin of Yetzira as well, and Assiya receives through it. This is the meaning of "six Sefirot nest in Yetzira (80), and lower Ima nests in the wheel (90)."

Inner Light

70. The reflected light that expands from the screen downward is called a "complete garment", since it limits the lights that it clothes with its unique coarseness, so that they will not be able to draw any light outside its boundary. However, the reflected light that rises from below upward, even though it, too, is a garment over the ten Sefirot of direct light, that garment does not limit the light it clothes in any way.

Hence it is regarded as an incomplete garment, and only as a root for the garment. The issue of the expansion of ten Sefirot of Yetzira and Assiya has already been explained above thoroughly.

80. ZA is called "six Sefirot" because of the absence of GAR KHB, and the absence of Malchut. It only has the Sefirot HGT NHY, and the word "nesting" has already been explained above.

90. Malchut of Atzilut is sometimes called "lower Ima" because Malchut of Atzilut is the primary root for all those who are in BYA. The ARI names Malchut of Yetzira the "lower Ima" after Malchut of Atzilut, since they are one root.

ABYA are the four letters Yod, Hey, Vav, Hey. Yod is Atzilut, which is Hochma; Hey is Beria, which is Bina; Vav is Yetzira, which is ZA; the last Hey is Assiya, which is Malchut.

8. Now you can understand why the four worlds Atzilut, Beria, Yetzira, Assiya are implied in the four letters HaVaYaH (100). Yod is Atzilut, Hey is Beria, Vav is Yetzira, and Hey is Assiya.

The light of Atzilut is by the upper Hochma and is therefore called Yod (200). Beria is by Bina of Atzilut, hence the name Hey. It is likewise with Vav in Yetzira and the lower Hey in Assiya.

Inner Light

100. As he explains in the following, the name HaVaYaH consists of ten Sefirot. The four worlds ABYA are ten Sefirot that include all of reality. However, even though each and every world in and of itself contains inner ABYA and inner of inner, we must still know that they are all arranged in ten Sefirot, implied by the four letters HaVaYaH.

This is a very important piece of knowledge that should always be kept before the eyes of the reader, since we must always deduce from the particular ten Sefirot to the general ten Sefirot. They always have parallel properties and one is learned from the other.

200. Although Atzilut has only ten Sefirot, implied in the four letters HaVaYaH, because the level of these ten Sefirot is up to Hochma, it is regarded as the light of Hochma entirely. The Yod of the name HaVaYaH insinuates her, for the lights that

are smaller than Hochma do not bear their own name with respect to the important light of Hochma, which greatly surpasses them. For that reason Beria is called only light of Bina, and so do all of them, meaning after the names of the most important lights in them.

———

Consequential rule: The main difference between each two worlds in ABYA is according to the screens in the four phases of the coarseness, HB TM.

9. We find that there is a consequential rule: Atzilut receives light only from Hochma. That is because Hochma became a blocked screen between Ein Sof and Atzilut.

Beria receives from Bina of Atzilut after the light of Ein Sof and upper Hochma clothed inside her. It is called the light of Bina because she becomes a screen that completely separates.

Likewise, Yetzira receives from ZA of Beria herself, and Assiya from Nukva of ZA of Yetzira herself. Were it not for these screens and garments, they would not be able to receive the upper light, except that each world is at a lower degree than the other, as explained above (300).

Inner Light

300. It means that each world cannot not receive any light except for what the screen above it gives it, as explained above.

Chapter Five

Explains how every emanated being and created being consists of the four above phases of coarseness called HB TM. The upper light spreads within them to a coupling by striking on the screen in Malchut, and their root is the Emanator, called Keter. Because every phase is different from the other, there must be a median phase between them that contains both phases. Contains seven issues:

1. Every created being contains four elements, fire, wind, water, and dust, corresponding to the four letters HaVaYaH, which are HB TM, namely tastes, points, tags, letters, and ABYA. 2. These are the four phases in the lower Adam: a) the spirituality (Ruach) in him; b) the body; c) the garments; d) the house one dwells in. Each of them consists of four. The spirituality in him contains Nefesh, Ruach, Neshama, Haya. The body in him contains bones, tendons, flesh, skin. In the clothes there are shirt, trousers, bonnet, belt. In the house there are house, yard, field, desert. 3. In the four phases of Adam, there is one that contains all of them. There is also an intermediate phase between each and every phase that contains both. 4. The phase that contains all of them is called light of Yechida, containing two phases: a) a spark of the Creator; b) a spark of the created being. 5. The median phase between the spiritual phases in a person, which are NRNHY, and the discernment of the body, is called a quarter blood, which clothes the Nefesh of Nefesh. It contains the spirituality and the body. 6. The median phase between the body and the clothes is the hair and nails of a human. 7. The median between the clothes and the house is tents, which are made of wool and flax.

There is Emanator and emanated being. Each emanated being is divided by the four phases of coarseness, by which the light expands from the Emanator to become the vessels of the emanated being. Those are HB TM and they are the four letters HaVaYaH, and they are tastes, points, tags, letters, and they are the four phases in Adam: NRNH, body, garments, and the house one dwells in. It is so because there is no emanated being with less than four parts.

1. There are Emanator and emanated being (1)**. The emanated being has four elements: fire, wind, water, dust** (2)**, which are the four letters HaVaYaH and**

are Hochma, Bina, Tifferet, and Malchut. They are also tastes, points, tags, letters, and they are Atzilut, Beria, Yetzira, Assiya. These are also the four phases in Adam: A. The inner Adam, which is the spirituality, called Nefesh, Ruach, Neshama, Haya, Yechida. B. The body. C. The clothes over the body. D. The house one dwells in, his body and his clothes.

Inner Light

1. Any upper Partzuf is regarded as an Emanator toward its lower Partzuf. That is because the Partzufim emerge from one another by way of cause and effect from the beginning of the line to the end of Assiya; every Partzuf is emanated by the one above it.

2. These are the four phases, mentioned above in the words of the ARI (Part 3, chapter 1, item 4). Ein Sof first expanded to make vessels over the four phases, until it encountered the screen in the vessel of Malchut. There are many names to these four phases, because there is not a single, tiny detail in reality that is not arranged by the above four phases, and reality in general is also arranged by them.

They are the four worlds: Atzilut, Beria, Yetzira, Assiya, which contain the entire reality. You must understand that although the order of the four phases is imprinted in every element of reality, it does not mean that all elements are the same. In fact, each element has a distinct value according to the measure of its vessel of reception.

Each phase of the four phases in Adam consists of four: Spirituality is Haya, Neshama, Ruach, Nefesh; The body is bones, tendons, flesh, skin; The garments are shirt, trousers, bonnet, and belt; The house is house, yard, field, desert.

2. All these phases consist of four phases (3), as follows: Phase one of spirituality is: Neshama to Neshama, Neshama, Ruach, Nefesh (4). Phase two, which is the body, is the bones, the marrow inside them, the tendons, the flesh and the skin, as it says, "you have clothed me with skin and flesh, and knit me together with bones and tendons." Phase three is the garments. It is known that these are the mandatory garments for a Laic Cohen (Priest): shirt, trousers, bonnet, and belt. These four of the Great Cohen are higher garments than these, as it is written in the Zohar, that these are the garments of the name ADNI, and these are the garments of the name HaVaYaH, but in principle they are only four phases. Phase four is the house. There are house, yard, field, and desert.

Inner Light

3. This incorporation is because of the refinement of the screen, which necessarily occurs in the emanation of each and every degree (see Inner Observation, Part 2, chapter 7, item 72).

4. It is the light of Hochma, also known as the light of Haya. The light of Yechida is opposite Keter, which is considered the Emanator. Also, the marrow in the bones corresponds to Keter.

———

Between each two phases there is a median phase that contains both.

3. Indeed, in all these four inner phases there is one phase that contains all of them (5). It is the median between each two phases and contains both of them (6). For example, biologists write that between the still and the vegetative there is the coral; between the vegetative and the animate there is the ledges of the field, mentioned in *Masechet Kilaim*. It is like a dog that grows on the ground with its navel rooted in the soil, from which it sucks its sustenance. When you cut off its navel, it dies. Between the animate and the speaking there is the monkey [ape].

Inner Light

5. It means that it contains all four phases, namely the second phase of Keter (see chapter 6, item 2), being the root of the expansion of the four phases. The light of Keter is called Yechida.

6. It means that a second phase in Keter is regarded as the median between the upper degree and the lower degree, meaning between the Emanator and the emanated being. Any upper one is always regarded as the Emanator of the lower one (see chapter 5, item 1).

———

Between Creator and created being, which is the spirituality in a person, there is a median phase. It is said about it, "You are the sons etc.," "You are Gods." The patriarchs are the chariot [structure].

4. In much the same way, there is a median phase between the Creator and the created being (7), which is the general spiritual phase. It is said about it, "You are the sons of the Lord your God," "I said: You are God," and it is said "and God

went up from Abraham," and our sages said, "The patriarchs are indeed the chariot (8)."

Inner Light

7. This relates to the two worlds—Atzilut and Beria. Atzilut is called Creator, and the four phases in the world of Beria are generally called created being. Also, every element in the world of Beria has the above four phases, and the souls of the righteous are imparted from Atzilut to Beria.

This is what the ARI means when he says, "**there is a median phase between the Creator and the created being, which is the general spiritual phase.**" It means that there is a median phase between the Creator and Keter, which is the general spiritual light of Yechida of Adam. In other words, it is the aforementioned (item 1) spirituality of Adam, called Nefesh, Ruach, Neshama, Haya. Yechida, which is their Keter, contains all of them.

8. It means that the Yechida of the patriarchs is the chariot to that median phase between the Creator and the Yechida in them. "Chariot" means placement, like a rider placed on his designated chariot. Likewise, Godliness is placed over the patriarchs.

———

The median phase consists of two sparks: a spark of the Creator, which clothes the spark of the created being, in which there are the roots of NRNH in man.

5. It means that there is a very small spark (9), which is Godliness that extends from the last phase in the Creator (10). That spark clothes by the power of another spark, a created being, which is a very fine *Neshama,* called Yechida (20). That spark contains the roots of the four phases of spirituality (30), which are Nefesh, Ruach, Neshama, Haya (40).

Inner Light

9. Know that this does not refer to an imaginary Gadlut [adulthood/greatness] or Katnut [infancy/smallness] whatsoever, but only to the absence of attainment, for the unattainable is called very small. You should also not be mistaken in the name spark, and interpret it literally, as an imaginary spark of fire. Rather, spark means reflected light (Table of Questions Part 2, item 2), as direct light is called lights, and reflected light is called sparks.

10. It is phase four, namely Malchut.

20. Meaning in Keter, which is Yechida. The spark of the Creator is called Ein Sof, and the spark of the created being is called the Keter of the degree. It is also called GAR, the Rosh of the degree, containing within it the four phases of direct light, in which Ein Sof expands for coupling by striking, raising reflected light and clothing the direct light from below upward.

That, in turn, created the roots of the vessels (see Inner Observation Part 2, item 202). All this is called a spark of a created being, or Yechida. It is called a spark after the reflected light that rises, where the spark of the Creator clothes this reflected light. That is why the ARI wrote: **"That spark clothes by the power of another spark, a created being."**

30. Because the clothing of Ein Sof in reflected light that rises from below upward does not create complete vessels but only roots of vessels, hence the words of the ARI, **"the roots of the four phases."**

40. You already know that Nefesh is clothed in Malchut, Ruach in ZA, Neshama in Bina, and Haya in Hochma. These vessels are the above four phases in the words of the ARI (Part 3, chapter 1, item 4).

Between the spirituality of man and man's body, there is the discernment of the quarter blood in the Nefesh, which consists of both. The Nefesh is spiritual, and the quarter blood, where the Nefesh clothes, is the body.

6. **Between the phase of spirituality and the phase of the body there is also one phase that consists of both. It is the phase of a quarter blood of the Nefesh, for it has the last spark of the Nefesh, being the quarter of the Nefesh, meaning Nefesh of Nefesh, and hence the name quarter** (50).

That spark clothes the above-mentioned quarter blood and it is all one, as it says, "for the blood is the Nefseh," said about this quarter blood. This quarter blood is the finest part of all the aforementioned four phases of the body, where each part is divided into four.

It is the first and the top quarter from the perspective of the self of the Mochin [the internality of the light of Hochma], which is the vitality inside it, being the blood that expands in them to revive them. All the roots of the above four phases are in that quarter in the upper blood because it is the median between spirituality and the body and consists of both.

50. Nefesh, too, has four phases HB TM of its own, which expand from Malchut herself, and Nefesh in Nefesh is clothed in Malchut of Malchut.

———

Between the body and the garments there are the discernments of hairs and nails of man, which contain both. Between the garments and the discernment of a house there is a median, which is tents.

7. Also, there is a median between the second phase and the third, which are the hairs and nails of men, as it is known that this was the initial garment of Adam HaRishon. They are attached to the skin of Adam and are like the body of man [T1] itself, but when they depart from there, these hairs become a garment like the ones made from goat and sheep wool.

Moreover, even when they are attached to the body of man, they are like a garment, like animals and beasts whose hair is their garment. The example for that is Adam HaRishon, regarding the nails.

We also find in Nebuchadnezzar, whose garment was this, as it says, "Till his hair was grown like eagles' feathers, and his nails like birds' claws." Also, between the garments and the house, there are tents, made of wool and flax, which are garments that are used in houses too. This phase of the tents requires further scrutiny, if it is so or there is something else there.

CHAPTER SIX

Explains how the Sefira of Keter contains two phases: 1. The last phase of Ein Sof, for example, Malchut of Malchut of Ein Sof, called Atik; 2. The root of the emanated beings, called Arich Anpin. Together they are called Keter. Containing four issues:

1. In the ten Sefirot, there are no more than four phases HB TM, and Hochma is the first. 2. Keter is sometimes counted in the Sefirot, and it is sometimes not counted in the Sefirot, and Daat is counted instead. 3. Keter is the median between the Emanator and the emanated being, containing two phases: A. The Emanator, for example, Malchut of Malchut of Ein Sof, called Tohu and Atik; B. The emanated being, which is the root of the emanated beings, called Bohu, or AA. 4. Similarly, Malchut of Malchut of the world of Atzilut is Atik in the world of Beria.

There are no more than four phases HB TM in every emanated being, and Hochma is the first Sefira in the emanated being.

1. We will now speak once more of the upper worlds. After we have explained the allegory, we will now explain the lesson. The lesson is made of four rudiments only (1), being the four letters HaVaYaH, namely Hochma, Bina, Tifferet and Malchut, and that is why Hochma is first.

Inner Light

1. He wishes to say that the allegory he introduced, that there is a median phase between each two phases, you should not take from it to the lesson—that this is why there are five phases in the upper ones, meaning four phases and a median phase. He warns and says that the upper ones have no more than four rudiments: fire, wind, water, dust, which are the four letters HaVaYaH.

It is so because the median phase is not counted among the four phases. And the ARI concludes, **"and that is why Hochma is first."** It indicates that no phase is counted prior to that, for the median phase, namely the spark of the Creator, is Ein Sof, which is not counted in the degree.

Also, the spark of the created being, called Yechida or Keter, it has been clarified that its essence is only the root of the four phases HB TM (see chapter 5, item 20). Hence, the beginning of Yechida is phase one too, called Hochma, which is why there are only four letters in the name HaVaYaH, and there is no letter there that designates the Sefirot of Keter.

Keter is sometimes counted among the ten Sefirot and is sometimes not, and Daat is counted instead.

2. You should also understand what is written, that Keter is always the highest phase (2), which is not included in that world. It is like the crown of a king, which is above his head and not a part of him. Hence it is not regarded as a part of the Sefira, and Daat, mentioned in Sefer Yetzira (Book of Creation), is counted instead. However, sometimes we do count it in the ten Sefirot. It will be explained by our earlier words that there is a median phase between each and every two phases. It is similar to what nature scientists have written and the Rambam wrote in the beginning of the verse, "Now the earth was Tohu [unformed] and Bohu [void]." He also wrote in *Sefer HaBahir* [*The Book of the Bright One*], that before He created the four rudiments, He created one substance, called primordial. This is something that is prepared for acquiring the form of the four rudiments later on, but it does not clothe in any form whatsoever. Because it precedes the Tohu, it is called "nothing," as in "They are regarded by Him as less than nothing and meaningless."

Inner Light

2. It refers to the spark of the Creator that is clothed in the Keter, being Ein Sof, which is not at all the Partzuf itself.

Ein Sof is called nothing. Following it, Keter is called Tohu, and following it Bohu, which consists of four rudiments.

3. The thing is that Ein Sof is called "nothing" because there is no perception of it. It has no substance (3) and no form (4). After that comes Tohu, which is the Keter (5), and after that Bohu, which consists of four rudiments HB TM.

Inner Light

3. (See Table of Questions, Part 2, item 26). The will to receive in the emanated being is light that became coarse and it is the entire substance of the emanated being, from which his vessels of reception were formed. It is certain that there is nothing whatsoever of that will to receive in Ein Sof (see Inner Light, Part 1, chapter 1, item 50).

The ARI wrote, "**Ein Sof is called 'nothing' because there is no perception of it. It has no substance,**" meaning the will to receive, and it is known that there is no attainment in the light without a vessel.

4. The four phases HB TM are called "four forms" because they are degrees one below the other, which form in the substance of the emanated being (see Inner Light, Part 1, chapter 1, item 50), but all this is not in Ein Sof.

5. Meaning in the median between the Emanator and the emanated being because it contains the roots of the four forms of the emanated being in potential, but not in actual fact.

Tohu contains the four rudiments of the emanated being, potentially, not actually.

4. Explanation: It is necessary to have a median degree between the Emanator and the emanated being, for the distance between them is as between heaven and earth. How can one shine in the other and how can create one create the other when they are two ends, if there is no median between them that connects them, and be a phase that is close to the Emanator and close to the emanated being? This phase is Keter, called Tohu (6), for it contains no rudiment and is therefore not implied in the name HaVaYaH at all, only in the tip of the Yod. However, it is a median, since Keter is like the prior substance, called primordial, containing the roots of all four rudiments in potential, but not in practice. It is called Tohu because it perplexes humans' thoughts, and they say: "We see that it is formless, yet we see that it is an emanated being (7) and has the potential of all four forms (8)."

Inner Light

6. It means that the four phases HB TM are also called "four rudiments," for there is no phase of them in Tohu.

7. It means that it has already left the Emanator, which is Ein Sof, called "nothing."

8. Meaning the four phases HB TM, also called "four forms." However, they are there only in potential, but not in actual fact. Bohu is the spark of the created being, containing the roots of the actual phases, which is the expansion of Ein Sof to make vessels by striking on the screen (see Part 3, chapter 1, item 1).

The four phases of direct light that expanded from Ein Sof are clothed with reflected light that rises from below upward, and the self of Ein Sof is clothed in this reflected light as the Rosh of a degree. However, these vessels are called "Roots of Vessels" that are not completed until after their expansion below the screen.

———

Keter might be called an emanated being in relation to Ein Sof, and in relation to the emanated beings, he is the Emanator.

5. It turns out that we can call it Ein Sof and Emanator, as is the opinion of some Kabbalists, that Ein Sof is the Keter, but we can also call it emanated being, because Ein Sof is certainly greater than it. This is why the sages warned regarding it, "Do not ask about that which is beyond you." However, it is all we can speak of, for the Keter is the median between the Emanator and the emanated being. The reason for it is that it is the last phase in Ein Sof. It emanated one phase (9) that contains the root of the entire ten Sefirot in concealment and great subtlety. In fact, the emanated being cannot be subtler than that, for Tohu, which is above it, there is nothing more but the absolute zero (10).

Inner Light

9. Called Bohu, for it is already called the Rosh of the degree.

10. Relates to the beginning of matters, meaning that the very last phase in Ein Sof is called Tohu.

———

Keter contains two phases: the last phase of Ein Sof, which emanated a second phase, which is the root of the emanated beings.

6. Thus, this phase has two degrees: The first is the lowest and the most inferior among all the phases of Ein Sof. It is as though we say, as an allegory, that it is the phase of Malchut in Malchut, although it is not so, since there is no image or a Sefira there whatsoever; we only say so for the purpose of clarity. That lowest

degree in Ein Sof contains all that is above it and receives from everyone, as it is known that Malchut receives from everyone. This low degree emanated the second phase, which is the highest degree in the emanated beings. It contains the root of all the emanated beings and bestows upon all of them. Thus, the smallest in all of the Emanator emanated the finest of all the emanated beings, and there is no other degree between them whatsoever because beyond that Emanator, there is no emanated being closer and more similar to Him than this one.

The phase of the Emanator in Keter is called Atik and the phase of the root of the emanated beings in Keter is called Arich Anpin.

7. These two phases are actually one phase called Keter. With respect to phase one in her, some Kabbalists called it Ein Sof, and with respect to phase two in her, some Kabbalists called it Keter, counted as one of the ten Sefirot. However, our opinion is like neither, but rather that it is a median phase between Ein Sof and the emanated beings and has a phase of Ein Sof and a phase of the emanated beings. These two phases are called Atik and Arich Anpin, and they are both called Keter.

The last phase of Atzilut, being Malchut of Malchut of Atzilut, became Atik in the world of Beria and clothed in AA in Beria.

8. It is written elsewhere that Malchut in Malchut in the world of Atzilut that clothes the Rosh of Beria, which is Keter, called Arich Anpin, is Atik of the world of Beria.

CHAPTER SEVEN

Explains how Malchut of Atzilut descended and became the Keter of the world of Beria. Contains ten issues:

1. In the world of Beria, Rosh of AA has only HGT, and KHB is missing. 2. The Rosh of every Partzuf does not clothe the lower one. 3. Two phases descend from the screen in the upper world to the lower world: A – ten Sefirot of direct light and reflected light that extend from the screen by a coupling by striking; B – light of Malchut of Malchut in the upper world breaches the screen and descends to become Keter in the lower world. 4. In the beginning, Malchut was as great as ZA, but she complained, for she wanted to rule alone. She was told to go and diminish herself, descend to the world of Beria and rule there. In other words, the point of Malchut became the Keter of the world of Beria. 5. During the diminution, the lower nine Sefirot departed from Malchut and ascended to their root in ZA. 6. If the nine Sefirot of Malchut depart due to the blemish in the lower ones, they do not rise to ZA, but fall to the shells. 7. Just like the point of Malchut of Atzilut descended and became the Keter to Beria, so it is in each and every world. 8. Because Malchut of the upper one becomes Keter of the lower one, the worlds connect with one another. Hence GAR of Beria can ascend to the world of Atzilut on Shabbat. 9. When we count the actual emanated beings, they are only four, meaning HB TM; and when we count the root with them, they are five, namely KHB TM. 10. Similarly, in each and every Partzuf and in each and every Sefira, the upper one is called Emanator and the lower one emanated being. There is a median phase between them, called Keter. It is all as it is written in the worlds, as it says, "I am the first, and I am the last." Keter is the last in the upper one and the first in the lower one.

Two phases descend from the upper world to the lower world: A) Ten Sefirot of direct light clothed in reflected light, which expand by the screen in coupling by striking; B) The last phase of the upper world, which is Malchut of Malchut, which descends and becomes Atik in the lower world, does not expand by the reflected light in the screen, but breaches the screen and descends.

1. I have found that Rabbi Gedaliah wrote that the upper three of the six edges of AA of Beria, which are HGT (1), remained bare without clothing (2). These three are regarded as a screen. It means this: We have explained that each of these three

worlds has one screen. However, when the image of all the lights of Atzilut passed through the screen between Atzilut and Beria to create the corresponding ten Sefirot of Beria, they did not breach that screen and pass through it (3), but only their light passed through that screen and all ten Sefirot of Beria were engraved.

These upper three of AA of Beria, which are HGT, also pass through the screen and do not breach the screen. They are only diminishing light that some of which passes through the screen. However, that point of Malchut of Atzilut that descended to clothe these GAR of AA is the light of Malchut of Atzilut itself. Hence, she breaks and breaches the screen itself and descends and clothes GAR of AA [of Beria] (4).

Inner Light

1. All ten Sefirot of Beria are indeed on the level of the light of Bina, even Keter and Hochma (see chapter 4, item 2). Since the level of Bina of Atzilut clothes HGT of AA, Beria can never be extended from it, but only its HGT NHYM, which are its VAK. Hence, HGT of AA of Beria are regarded as GAR of AA in that place.

2. The Rosh of every Partzuf does not clothe its lower Partzuf because the clothing of the lower one begins from the Peh of Rosh of the upper one downward. Since HGT of AA are Rosh, they are revealed, without clothing.

3. Breaching implies that the light overpowers the boundary in the screen, disregarding the force of detainment in it. It breaks, passes and shines below the screen as well.

You should remember well what we have explained above regarding the striking of the upper light on the screen (Inner Light, Part 2, item 3): The screen stops the expanding upper light from reaching below its boundary and brings it back to its place, as the ARI says (Part 3, chapter 1, item 3). However, a certain part of the upper light broke through and did not return backward. Instead, it descended below the screen and shone there, which is like breaching, breaking, and making a hole in the Guf of the screen, passing through it and below.

However, it is nothing like making a corporeal, physical and tangible hole; it is only about trespassing. It is so because the screen limits the light. Some of the upper light, which the screen did not limit and detain, is considered to have breached the screen, meaning its boundary and detainment, and passed from the screen downward too.

That part, which breached the boundary of the screen and went below, is called Malchut of Malchut of the upper degree, or the point of Malchut of the upper one.

Hence, we should make two discernments in the coupling by striking before us: The first is that the screen overpowered the light and pushed it back to its place. By this, the reflected light became a clothing over the four phases in the upper light from below upward.

In that manner, Malchut expanded to ten Sefirot from her and within her from the screen downward. As a result, the entire ten Sefirot that came from the screen upward sparkled with the illumination from the screen downward too, and thus imprinted their model there from above downward (see Inner Light, Part 2, item 3). This is the first discernment in the coupling by striking.

The second discernment is that part of the upper light that breached and broke the screen and went below the screen without the help of reflected light, but in the form of His Self. This part is called "the point of Malchut of the upper one" or "Malchut of Malchut of the upper one," which canceled the boundary and did not notice the detaining force in the screen.

You should thoroughly understand that with respect to that point, the screen is regarded as nonexistent. That is why the ARI made the precision of saying that she **"breaks and breaches the screen itself."** You will understand the rest of the ARI's words according to the above two discernments.

4. Meaning in HGT of AA, which are His GAR, because this AA of Beria has only VAK, meaning HGT NHY, and thus His HGT are His GAR. You should see here that that point of Malchut of Atzilut that breached and passed from the screen downward as in the second discernment is Ein Sof. It was referred to earlier as Tohu.

It has Ein Sof, but not a single phase of the four phases HB TM. Instead, the four phases are incorporated in it in potential, not in practice. These GAR of AA that the point of the upper one clothed in come from the first discernment, called Bohu, and contain four roots of four phases HB TM in actual fact, meaning by clothing reflected light, which are actual vessels, and remember that.

In the beginning, Malchut was as great as ZA, and she complained, meaning she wanted to rule alone. She was then told to diminish herself of the nine Sefirot of Atzilut and descend to Beria to rule there. These nine Sefirot that departed from her connected to ZA in their root, and then she descended and became Atik in Beria.

2. The meaning of this point is that it is known how the two lights were emanated on an equal level (5). When the moon complained and was diminished (6),

it means that after she was a complete Partzuf, she was diminished and stood as a small dot comprised of ten Sefirot.

The other nine points departed from her (7), as it is known that to begin with, her root is but one point, and nine other points were added by ZA later on. That is why it is called a mirror that has nothing of its own (8), and hence ZA took them once more and she remained as a small dot. She could not stand in him because of her Katnut, and she descended to the Rosh of Beria instead.

Inner Light

5. ZA and Malchut are called two lights since they bestow upon the lower worlds. It is so because the lower ones cannot receive from GAR, Keter, Hochma and Bina. Consequently, only ZA and Malchut shine upon the lower ones and are therefore called "lights."

When emanated, they were on the same level. It means that Malchut received her abundance from Bina, not through ZA. Thus, they were both equal; just as ZA was emanated from Bina and received his abundance from Bina, so Nukva received her abundance from Bina. However, when Malchut is not fit to receive from Bina, but through ZA, then she is considered to be lower than ZA, for the receiver is naturally below his giver. The reason for this will be explained in its place.

6. It has already been explained that the moon, which is Malchut, was equal to ZA, which is the sun. At that time they were both at the level of VAK, HGT NHY. Both lacked the Rosh, they lacked the first three, and suckled from Bina, called Keter.

Our sages said (Hulin, 60; 72), that she said: "No two kings use a single crown," meaning Ima. Malchut wanted to rule alone, and was then told, "Go diminish yourself," meaning exit from Atzilut to Beria, and rule there.

Malchut's being a complete Partzuf of ten Sefirot in Atzilut, and diminishing by her descent to Beria, and standing there as a small dot, consisting of "potential" ten Sefirot, not actual, shall be explained below.

7. Meaning they remained in ZA in Atzilut and did not descend to Beria, but only the phase of Malchut of Malchut.

8. A mirror means light, because Malchut is called "light." It says that she has nothing of her own because her root is merely a point, as the ARI says earlier. The nine Sefirot that she had while in Atzilut are not her own phase, meaning the phase of direct light of Malchut. It is only the reflected light that she raised by the screen, from her upward to ZA.

This reflected light returns from ZA to Malchut from above downward and builds Malchut with ten Sefirot (see Inner Light, Part 2, item 3). This is what the ARI means when he says that nine other Sefirot came as an addition by ZA.

Thus, when Malchut was diminished and descended to Beria, only the self of Malchut descended, while all nine upper Sefirot, which are the reflected light, remained in Atzilut, in their root, namely ZA. This is why the ARI says, "**Hence ZA took them once more**," and this is why she is called "**a mirror that has nothing of her own.**"

Malchut remained as Atik in Beria even after the diminution of Malchut was corrected.

3. Indeed, that was during the diminution of the moon during the creation of the world. However, after she had been corrected and returned to her place back-to-back, Adam HaRishon was created and had brought her back to face-to-face as in the beginning (9).

Afterwards, by the sin of the lower one, she was diminished once more and descended , for that is the entire meaning of our prayer, to correct her when we pray. Then she returns as in the beginning for we have no strength for more. Thus, every holy thing leaves an impression in its place, even though it departed from it (10), and this phase of the point always remains in the Rosh of Beria.

Inner Light

9. This is a long issue, and this is not the place to elaborate on it.

10. It is so because there is no absence in spirituality, and any change or diminution and so on does not mean that the first phase becomes absent and another one replaces it. It means only that the first phase remains as it was, and the change that we distinguish in it is an additional phase to the first.

Thus, wherever it is said that some phase has changed, it means that a new phase has been added to the first phase. We should remember that, for it is impossible to always remind it.

This is the meaning of the ARI's words, "Every holy thing leaves an impression in its place, even though it departed from it, and this phase of a point always remains in the Rosh of Beria." This point always remains at the Rosh of Beria, meaning the ascent and return of the point back to its place in Atzilut does not cause any absence in the point that descended to Beria, as there is no absence in spirituality.

Therefore, we should understand the return of the point to Atzilut as a new, additional issue, like lighting a candle from another without the first being lessened. Thus, the point remains at the Rosh of Beria and also rises to Atzilut as well, and now there are two points.

When the departure of the nine Sefirot of Malchut is due to the sin of the lower ones, her nine Sefirot do not ascend to ZA but fall to the shells.

4. During her diminution (because of the flaw of the lower ones) the other nine points that depart from her do not return to ZA, from which they came. Due to our sins, they descend to the shell, called the Shechina in exile, and there is no need to elaborate on that.

Just as the point of Malchut of Atzilut descended and became Atik in Keter of Beria, so it was in each and every world, where Malchut of the upper world clothed the Keter of its lower world.

5. Let us return to the issue that this point was first a tail for the lions at the end of Atzilut [20]. This is because Eve was the tail of Adam, and then descended and diminished herself into her point, and became a head for the foxes, an actual Rosh to Beria [30].

So it was in every world, for the point of Malchut of Yetzira descended in the Rosh of Assiya, and also Beria in Rosh of Yetzira. It was the same in Rosh of Atzilut as well, as it says, "You have made them all in wisdom [Hochma]."

It is so because the light of Ein Sof clothed the upper Hochma above Atzilut and that Hochma herself descended [40], broke the screen over Atzilut and descended and clothed Atzilut. Also, it is through her that Atzilut receives the light of Ein Sof. That is the meaning of "you have made them all in wisdom," mentioned in the world of Atzilut.

Inner Light

20. Meaning the end of all the Sefirot of Atzilut, which with respect to the Sefirot of Beria, are presented in the parable as lions toward foxes. Then, Malchut descended from the Sium of the Sefirot of Atzilut and became the Rosh of the Sefirot of Beria.

30. ZA and Malchut are called Adam and Eve. Malchut is the Sium of all the Sefirot of ZA. That is why our sages said about Adam HaRishon, prior to the creation of Eve, that Eve was the tail of Adam, meaning his Sium.

40. It means that Malchut of AK, in which the screen of phase three is erected, being the level of Hochma, that Malchut descended and became Atik in Atzilut.

Because Malchut of the upper one became Keter to the lower one, the worlds connect with one another to receive illumination from each other.

6. Indeed, this phase that was in all the worlds was beneficial to the worlds, in order to connect them one with the other so as to receive illumination from one another. It is done by the Sium of Atzilut being the Rosh of Beria, as it is also in the other worlds.

Because Malchut of Atzilut is clothed in Keter of Beria in the hall of the holy of holies, that hall can ascend to Atzilut on the day of Shabbat.

7. This is the meaning of the day of Shabbat. On that day, Kedusha is added to the worlds, and the upper hall, the holy of holies (50) of Beria ascends once more to Atzilut and becomes complete Atzilut, for the above reason. It is the same in all the other worlds as well.

Inner Light

50. The Rosh of Beria, where the point of Malchut of Atzilut is clothed, is called the hall of the holy of holies. This entire hall rises to Atzilut on Shabbat along with the point, by the power of the point of Atzilut that is clothed there.

The emanated being has no more than four degrees HB TM, and a middle phase between the Emanator and the emanated being, which is Keter, in which there is a phase of Emanator and a phase of emanated being.

8. It leads to the rule that in fact, the emanated being has only four degrees, being the four letters HaVaYaH. They are Atzilut, Beria, Yetzira, Assiya, and they are Hochma, Bina, Tifferet, and Malchut.

This is why the Torah begins with Beresheet (lit. in the beginning), and there is no beginning but Hochma. Our sages presented it in the form of negation so as to exclude the Keter (60). Indeed, there is a middle phase that consists of two phases: Emanator and emanated being. It is called Keter, and this Keter incorporates everything that is above it. Although it is smaller than all of them, it suckles from all of them, and it has the root of all ten Sefirot that were emanated, and bestows in all of them.

60. They should have said that Hochma is the beginning; why did they say that there is no beginning but Hochma? It means "and not something else", meanng to exclude the Keter. This teaches you that Keter is not the beginning of the world, but rather Hochma is the beginning of the world.

It is so because the world in general has four phases HB TM. Hochma is the first phase in them, but Keter is not included in the world, but regarded as a median, and contains its own four phases.

When counting four, it is the actual number of the emanated beings. When counting five, we include the Keter with them, where there are Emanator and emanated being.

9. **Do not be surprised that we sometimes say that the ten Sefirot are divided into four letters HaVaYaH (70), and sometimes we say that they are divided to five Partzufim. When we say that it is four, it is the actual number of the emanated beings, and when we count five Partzufim, we include the root of the Emanator along with the emanated beings.**

Inner Light

70. Indeed, the ten Sefirot are not divided into ten Partzufim. The reason for it is that six Sefirot HGT NHY do not create six Partzufim as they are all regarded as one phase in the coarseness of the screen and the level, meaning phase three. Hence, they all emerge from a single coupling by striking and are therefore regarded as one Partzuf. The differentiation among the six Sefirot HGT NHY will be explained in the following lessons.

In every degree in the worlds, the upper one is regarded as the Emanator, and the lower one as the emanated being, in which there are four phases. There is a median phase between them called Keter, in which there is an Emanator and an emanated being. Because Keter is Malchut of the upper one, it is called Ani [I], and because it is Keter of the lower one, it is called Ein [absence]. This is the meaning of "I am the first, and I am the last."

10. **Know that it is the same in every ten Sefirot in each and every world, as well as within each and every Partzuf. This is because in each and every phase, the upper one is always regarded as the Emanator, and the lower one is regarded as the emanated being.**

The emanated being is not less than four letters HaVaYaH $_{(80)}$, even in the particular and the inner ten Sefirot, and there is also a median phase between them, called Keter. Understand that thoroughly for by that all the issues will become clear.

This is the meaning of "I am the first, and I am the last." Keter is the first and He is the last; He is the Ein and He is the Ani $_{(90)}$. It is so because He is last in the phase of Malchut of the Emanator in Him, and it is called Ani, which is Malchut. In the root phase, the emanated beings in Him, which is the phase of Keter, is the first, and it is called Ein, having the letters of Ani [in Hebrew].

Inner Light

80. The four letters HaVaYaH are HB TM. Tifferet alone contains six Sefirot and the median between the Emanator and the emanated being is called Keter. Together, they make up ten Sefirot, where each inner Sefira of the ten must contain ten inner Sefirot as well. Each inner Sefira must also contain ten inner Sefirot and so on as has been explained in Inner Observation Part 2 (item 96).

90. There is a most notable hint here: The word Ein implies absence of attainment, while the word Ani refers to the absolute and total attainment. Even though there are no two opposite matters that deny each other more than these two words, "Ein, Ani", still their letters are the same (in Hebrew) and alike. This is indeed surprising.

It is written: "I am the first and I am the last." This means that in fact, they are not two matters, but are one and the same, as the ARI has written, "It is so because He is last in the phase of Malchut of the Emanator in Him, and it is called Ani, meaning Malchut. He is first in the phase of root of the emanated beings in Him, which is the phase of Keter, called Ein, having the letters of Ani [in Hebrew]." These words are deeper than deep and higher than high, and that is why the ARI says, "Understand that thoroughly for by that all the issues will become clear."

We must thoroughly understand the meaning of the two opposites here, which are not even two unique phases, but must be perceived as one phase. From the perspective of it being Malchut of the upper one and the self of the upper one, which breached and broke the screen, the act of boundary in the screen does not influence the point of Malchut of the upper one at all. For that reason Keter is called "I am the last," meaning utter wholeness.

This is because Malchut of the upper one receives from all ten Sefirot in the upper one, and these ten Sefirot necessarily contain all the degrees and the Partzufim that are worthy of clothing in the worlds below them. For this reason, that point is incorporated in the final wholeness, hence, "I am the last." This is the meaning of Keter, called Atik, which is also called Tohu, and the spark of the Creator, and Ein Sof.

From its perspective of being a root to the emanated beings in it, it is the phase of Keter to the emanated lower one. This is the meaning of "I am the first," called Ein, with the same letters as Ani. This means that with respect to the emanated beings, these letters of Ani themselves form the combination of Ein.

It has the opposite meaning of the combination Ani, for it is Malchut of the upper one, as well, but as "light that diminishes and passes through the screen," as it is written above, for which it contains the four phases HB TM in actual fact. This is why it is called the Rosh of the emanated being, as all that there is in the Guf is extended from the Rosh.

It is called Ein because all the degrees and the worlds below it reveal what is in the Rosh. Until they finish what is upon them, the Rosh is considered to be Ein, as it says, "I am the first," meaning only the beginning and the root of the disclosure.

It is called Arich Anpin, and Bohu, and a spark of the created being, and it is called Keter. Study these words and perhaps you will be rewarded and find an inlet to the wisdom. However, when it says that the phase of Atik is called, "I am the last," it pertains only to His ascent to Atzilut on the day of Shabbat, where it becomes Malchut of the upper one once more, as the ARI says.

Chapter Eight

Explains that the four phases HB TM are like a person with a soul clothed in his body, and the body is clothed in a garment, sitting in his hall. Hochma is the entirety of the lights in the world of Atzilut, and it is the soul of the entire Atzilut, called "the upper Adam." He is clothed in Bina, which is the entirety of the vessels, called the body of Atzilut. The body is clothed by ZA, which is a garment, and Malchut is the hall of them all. Containing four issues:

1. The four phases HB TM are called soul, body, garment, hall. The world of Atzilut, where the upper Adam resides, is a soul clothed in a body, garment and the hall of the King. 2. Keter is their root. It is divided into four: the root of Neshama is Hochma in Keter; Bina in Keter is the root to the body; ZA in Keter is a root to the garment and Malchut in Keter is a root to the hall. 3. All that was explained in the world of Atzilut applies to the world of Beria, as well, being that it is a light of consequence. It is so because Beria was imprinted from the world of Atzilut. Thus, Keter of Keter of Atzilut imprinted Keter of Keter of Beria; Hochma of Keter imprinted Hochma of Keter of Beria etc. and so it is in all the Sefirot. 4. The lights do not extend directly from Keter of Atzilut to Keter of Beria, for the world of Beria does not receive but only through Malchut of Atzilut. Malchut of Atzilut imprinted everything that exists in the world of Atzilut in the world of Beria, and similarly in the world of Yetzira and Assiya.

1. We've already explained how all the emanated beings are one phase, containing all four elements, which are the four letters HaVaYaH, being the four worlds ABYA, having a fifth, upper phase, between them and Ein Sof. Now we will elaborate on each and every world, in general, and afterwards we will return to explain all of them as one whole.

Everything that exists in the worlds ABYA is not more than the four phases HB TM, which are the letters Yod, Hey, Vav, Hey, and are soul, body, garments, house.

2. Everything that was created in all the worlds is only four phases, which are HaVaYaH. They are: the spiritual (1), called soul, the organs of the body, the clothes, and the house.

Inner Light

1. This refers to the time when BYA are in completeness, when they rise to Atzilut, such as on Shabbat. At that time they clothe each other like the upper Adam who is soul and body and garment, residing in the King's hall.

> The light in Atzilut is the spirituality called soul, which is Hochma. The soul is clothed in the vessels of Atzilut called body.

3. We will speak of the world of Atzilut and from that the rest will be understood. The internality of the entire Atzilut is the spirituality, called soul. It is clothed inside the organs of the body, called vessels, which are the ten Sefirot called Rosh, arms and Guf (2).

Inner Light

2. They are names for the ten Sefirot of the Partzuf: Rosh is the Sefira of Keter in it; the arms are HG: the Sefira of Hesed is the right arm, and the Sefira of Gevura is the left arm. The Guf is the Sefira of Tifferet, and from Tabur downward they are four Sefirot NHY and Malchut.

> There are ten vessels in the Guf, which are ten Sefirot in the boundary and measure that exist in Atzilut, which is Bina.

4. Let us return to the issue of the Guf (3): This phase is ten Sefirot, ten measures, because they contain a boundary and a measure, as it is written in Pirkey Heichalot, of the degree of 236 thousands of tens of thousands parasangs [a measurement unit] etc.

Inner Light

3. Relates to his above words (Chap 5, item 1), that Hochma is a soul, Bina is a body, ZA is a garment, and Malchut is a hall. It has already been explained that there is no boundary from the perspective of the light. Moreover, it is not meticulous with the boundary in the vessels, which is why it performs striking (see Chap 1, item 70 in Inner Light).

The vessels that limit begin only from Bina downward. They are: body, garment, hall, which are phase two, phase three and phase four. Although phase one is Hochma, called soul, it is not regarded as a vessel, as the ARI writes, that the ten Sefirot of the body are called ten measures. It is so because the vessels that place a boundary and a measure begin in phase two.

However, in the ten Sefirot of the soul, meaning phase one, called Hochma, there is no measure whatsoever. It is so because phase one is not regarded as coarseness, and therefore has no vessel and measure.

And the body of Atzilut is clothed in garments, and it is ZA, which clothes Bina.

5. This body is clothed inside the garments of Atzilut, as our sages said: "The Creator was clothed with ten garments: a garment of pride, as it says, 'the Lord reigns; He is clothed in majesty.'" It is written in Pirkey Heichalot that the robe (4) of the Creator is called Zahariel there, but the soul inside has no measure at all. However, when compared to Ein Sof (5), we can call them by the names "measures" and "Sefirot" in relation to the soul, as well.

Inner Light

4. It is a garment.

5. It means that compared to Keter, called Ein Sof, Hochma is also regarded as having coarseness, for Ein Sof does not have any will to receive, hence the name phase one (see Inner Light, Part 1, Chap 1, item 50).

The garments are inside the houses, which are the seven halls of Atzilut, being Malchut. Altogether, it is considered that the upper Adam, which is a soul that is clothed in a body, and the body in garments is placed in the King's hall.

6. These clothes are inside the discernment of the houses, which are the seven halls of Atzilut, which are the discernment of the world itself, being the heaven and earth and the air between them. All this is the discernment of the houses and they are called the world of Atzilut, where the upper Adam resides, who is a soul, body, and garment of Malchut placed in the upper hall of the King, which is the world of Atzilut in general.

The four phases, soul, body, garment, hall, are HB TM. Keter is their fifth, containing the roots of these four phases NGLH.

7. These four phases are the ten Sefirot that begin at the above Hochma and have four phases. Then there is also the discernment of Keter, which is the fifth phase, the root of them all, which contains the root of the above four phases as well.

Each of the four phases NGLH (Neshama, Guf, Levush, Heichal, lit. soul, body, garment, hall) in Atzilut contains ten Sefirot HB TM. The soul in Keter is the root of the ten Sefirot HB TM of the soul in Atzilut, and the body of Keter is the root to the ten Sefirot HB TM of the bodies. The garments of Keter are the root to the ten Sefirot HB TM of the garments, and hall in Keter is the root to the ten Sefirot HB TM of the halls.

8. It turns out that the light and the soul in Keter are the root of the ten Sefirot of the souls of Atzilut, which begin from Hochma. The body in Keter (6) is the root of the ten Sefirot of the bodies in the ten Sefirot of Atzilut, which begin in Hochma. The garments in Keter is the root of the ten Sefirot of garments in the ten Sefirot of Atzilut, which begin in Hochma. The hall in the Keter is the root of the ten Sefirot of Atzilut that begin in Hochma.

Inner Light

6. It has been written above that in Keter too there are the four phases, called: soul, body, garment, hall, which are HB TM, but as mere roots.

All that exists in the world of Atzilut is imprinted in the world of Beria.

9. Then the world of Beria was created the very same way. That is because through the screen (7), which is the bottom of the hall of Atzilut, it illuminated downward and there imprinted everything that was in the world of Atzilut (8). It is called the world of Beria because it is a light of consequence (9), and is not the upper light itself. However, because it is a seal of Atzilut, it should have all the phases that are in Atzilut.

Inner Light

7. The Sium of the degrees in any place is only because of the screen in their vessel of Malchut. Thus, the expansion of the degrees from Ein Sof to the emanated being stops and remains "standing" from expanding when it touches the screen. It is like standing on the ground above it, where the bottom does not let it expand inside and within it. By the same manner, the screen stops the light from expanding inside and within it, hence the screen is called "ground".

It has already been explained (Part 3, Chap 3, item 6) that the ten Sefirot of the world of Beria were created by the refinement of the screen of phase three in the world of Atzilut into phase two (see also Inner Observation, Part 2, item 72). It is written there that it illuminated downward through the screen, which is the bottom of the hall of Atzilut, meaning because of its refinement, as it explains there.

8. It means that just as the imprint does not lack any of the forms that exist in the seal, so all the forms in the world of Atzilut emerge in the world of Beria, hence the names seal and imprint. There is yet another most original reason: the entire upper light that comes to Beria comes because of that reflected light that rises by the power of the coupling by striking on the screen of phase two in the bottom from her and above in Atzilut itself.

That very same reflected light sparkled once more and passed through the screen, broadening the vessel of Malchut into ten Sefirot from her and within her. It expanded in her from above downward (as thoroughly explained in Inner Light Part 3, Chapter 2, item 3).

By this, all the phases that the reflected light clothed in Atzilut from the gound up returned, extended, and went from the gound downward as well. Thus, this reflected light is completely similar to a seal: everything imprinted in it is copied to its imprint.

Similarly, regarding that reflected light, all the phases and the level that it clothed from below upward, it once again brought them to Beria from above downward and copied them there in Beria without any absence and change. For that reason this act is called seal and imprint.

9. This is the rule: In any place where this reflected light rises from below upward, the upper light itself is clothed in that reflected light. This indicates the expansion of the light of Ein Sof to make vessels, which the ARI speaks of above (Part 1, Chap 1, item 1).

However, in a place where reflected light is considered to be expanding from above downward as it is in the ten Sefirot of Beria, this upper light that is clothed here in this reflected light is no longer the upper light itself. Instead, it is regarded as a light of consequence, extending from the upper light, but "it is not the upper light itself".

The reason is that it extends by the power of the screen that raises reflected light because of the detainment in it. For that reason, the force of the lower one is already involved in it, and it too is limited in the measure of the vessels and the level of the screen, for the screen precedes the expansion of these ten Sefirot.

It turns out that the screen is the reason that causes the appearance of these ten Sefirot. As a result, the light is limited by it, and is no longer the upper light itself, but is regarded as a light of consequence. However, reflected light that rises from the screen upward cannot raise any of its coarseness (see Part 3, Chap 4, Inner Light, item 50). Indeed, this applies from the world of Beria downward, but in Atzilut there is no screen whatsoever. Consequently, any light there, until Sium Raglin, is regarded as the light itself.

Keter of Atzilut imprinted the four roots of NGLH in Keter of Beria. From the soul in Keter of Atzilut, the soul in Keter of Beria was imprinted. From the body in Keter of Atzilut, the body of Keter of Beria was imprinted, from the garment, the garment, and from the hall, the hall.

10. It is because the phase of Keter, which is the fifth phase, comprising the above four phases, imprinted Keter in the Rosh of Beria as itself. From the light of Keter of Atzilut the light of Keter of Beria was imprinted, and from the body of Keter of Atzilut, the body of Keter of Beria was imprinted. The garment of Keter of Beria was imprinted from the garment of Keter of Atzilut, and the hall of Keter of Beria was imprinted from the hall of Keter of Atzilut.

NGLH of Keter of Atzilut, which are extended to NGLH of Keter of Beria, are extended through Malchut of Atzilut that was clothed in Keter of Beria. Likewise, the rest of the Sefirot of Atzilut that were imprinted in Beria were extended through Malchut of Atzilut by the coupling by striking on the screen in her.

11. However, these lights did not extend from the actual Keter of Atzilut to Keter of Beria but through Malchut in Malchut of Atzilut, which is Atik of Beria, clothing Keter of Beria. She extended these four phases in Keter of Atzilut (10) and created them in Keter of Beria.

The ten Sefirot of Atzilut did similarly and extended their light through the above Malchut in the above Keter. They imprinted a seal of Atzilut in Beria: soul from soul, body from body, garment from garment and hall from hall.

Inner Light

10. Because of that, Malchut of the upper one is called the spark of the Creator, since it extends and emanates its inferior degree. It is written above that all the degrees and the Partzufim and the worlds from the beginning of the line to the end of Assiya emerge and are emanated from one another by way of cause and effect.

It means that Malchut of Malchut of every upper one descends below her degree and extends to all four phases of the lower one, as is explained in detail in Part 2, Inner Observation, Chapter 5, item 59. (All these things should have been written here as well, had I not spared the costs of print).

Malchut of Beria descended and clothed Keter of Yetzira. She extended the seal of the five Partzufim KHB TM of Beria, which are NGLH, to the world of Yetzira, souls from souls, body from body, garment from garment, hall from hall, as it is in Yetzira and Assiya as well.

12. Similarly in Yetzira, Malchut of Beria was Atik, connected with AA of Yetzira. There it was named Keter of Yetzira, and the five Partzufim of Beria extended and imprinted their seal in Yetzira by the same way as in Beria: souls from souls, bodies from bodies, garments from garments and halls from halls.

Similarly, the five Partzufim of Yetzira imprinted their phases in Assiya: souls from souls, bodies from bodies, garments from garments and halls from halls and so on by the same way, all the worlds together as one whole.

CHAPTER NINE

Chapter nine explains that the desired perfection is that all the Sefirot in the five worlds AK and ABYA will connect together to the phase of the upper Adam. The root and the soul are clothed in his body, and he is clothed in the garment and dwells in his hall. Containing four issues:

*(The suffix ot is female plural form and the suffix im is male plural form)

1. The entire reality is divided into five worlds called AK and ABYA. They represent five phases KHB TM, called root, soul, body, garment, hall. Each world contains five inner phases SNGLH (Shoresh, Neshama, Guf, Levush, Heichal, lit. root, soul, body, garment, hall). Each of those phases is divided once more into five phases SNGLH, meaning twenty-five sub-phases in each and every world from AK and ABYA. All twenty-five phases SNGLH in AK are regarded as the roots, meaning Keterim. Also, all twenty-five phases SNGLH in the world of Atzilut are regarded as souls, meaning Hochmot. All twenty-five phases SNGLH in the world of Beria are regarded as bodies, meaning Binot, and all twenty-five phases SNGLH in the world of Yetzira are regarded as garments, meaning Tifferet. All twenty-five phases in the world of Assiya are regarded as halls, meaning Malchuyot. 2. The interior twenty-five phases SNGLH in the five worlds AK and ABYA connect with each other in the following manner: The five Ketarim in AK and ABYA, called "five roots," connect with each other so as to connect the SNGLH in the roots. Keter of AK is the root and Keter of Atzilut is the soul in them. Keter of Beria is the body in them, Keter of Yetzira is the garment in them, and Keter of Assiya is the hall in them. Similarly, the five Hochmot in AK and ABYA, called "five souls," connect with each other so as to connect SNGLH of souls. Hochma of AK is the root in them, Hochma of Atzilut is the soul in them, and Hochma of Beria is the body in them. Hochma of Yetzira is the garment in them and Hochma of Assiya is the hall in them. Similarly, the five Binot in AK and ABYA, called "five bodies," connect with each other so as to connect SNGLH of the bodies. Bina of AK is the root in them, etc. The same applies to the five Tifferets in AK and ABYA and with the five Malchuyot of AK and ABYA. It is this way in the inner SNGLH in AK and ABYA too. 3. The five phases SNGLH are also called: Yechida, Haya, Neshama, Ruach, Nefesh. 4. They are also implied in the four letters HaVaYaH: the tip of the Yod is

the root, the Yod is the soul, and the first Hey is the body, the Vav is the garment and the last Hey is the hall.

Adam Kadmon is the world of Keter to the four worlds ABYA. He has five phases KHB TM, each containing four roots NGLH.

1. Adam Kadmon is as Keter to the ten Sefirot in each and every world, and in this manner, AK is the Keter to the four worlds ABYA (1). It turns out that AK contains the root of all the above five phases in each and every world. The Keter in Him is the four roots of the four phases of the ten Sefirot in Him, being: souls, bodies, garments and halls. This is the particular, but the general will be explained henceforth (2).

Inner Light

1. It has already been explained that in the four phases of direct light there is no difference between each world or between each Partzuf from the Rosh of the line to the end of Assiya. It is so because there is not a single degree that does not have the four phases of direct light, which are: Hochma, Bina, Tifferet and Malchut. The only difference between the degrees is the level of the reflected light (Inner Light, Part 3, Chap 3, item 5).

That level depends on the coarseness of the screen in Malchut of the degree: the screen of phase four raises reflected light and clothes up to Keter; phase three raises up to Hochma, lacking Keter. Consequently, Keter of direct light must clothe the internality of Hochma and is not apparent there.

The screen of phase two raises reflected light only as high as Bina, lacking the level of Hochma, too. Hence, Keter and Hochma of direct light clothe the internality of Bina here. The screen of phase one raises reflected light only as high as the level of Tifferet, called ZA. It lacks the level of Bina, too, and therefore GAR KHB are clothed in him in the internality of Tifferet, and are therefore not apparent (see Inner Observation, Part 2, item 72 to understand the reasons for these things).

Now you can see that the five worlds, called Adam Kadmon, Atzilut, Beria, Yetzira, and Assiya, which contain the entire reality from the restriction downward, are also regarded as ten Sefirot that contain the entire reality, and are measured by the values of the levels in the five phases of the screen.

It is so because phase four, over which there was the first restriction and the first coupling by striking, these first ten Sefirot are called ten Sefirot or four phases of

Adam Kadmon. Their level is up to Keter of direct light, and that is why Adam Kadmon is called the world of Keter.

After the four phases of AK had been completed, the screen of phase four was refined to phase three and the light of Ein Sof, which never stops, returned and expanded in four phases of direct light over this screen of phase three in coupling by striking. However, here their level reaches only Hochma, and they are called ten Sefirot or four phases of the world of Atzilut.

Once the world of Atzilut had been completed, the screen was refined once more to phase two, and ten Sefirot on the level of Bina emerged, called the world of Beria. Afterwards it was refined into phase one and ten Sefirot in the level of Tifferet emerged, called ten Sefirot or four phases of the world of Yetzira.

After that, when it was refined entirely and no coarseness was left in the screen, but only a root to the coarseness, there was no striking in it at all. All it had were ten Sefirot on the level of Malchut, called ten Sefirot or four phases of the world of Assiya. The reason for this refinement was explained in Inner Observation, Part 2, item 72.

Now the ten Sefirot that contain the entire reality have been thoroughly explained: the world of AK is the general Keter, the world of Atzilut is the general Hochma, the world of Beria is the general Bina, the world of Yetzira is the general ZA, which in turn consists of six Sefirot HGT NHY, and the world of Assiya is the general Malchut.

However, in each and every world of these five worlds there are also ten particular Sefirot. In each world there are levels one below the other, even in the world of Adam Kadmon. However, as in the particular levels of the ten Sefirot, we consider the level of the light according to the highest Sefira. If the highest Sefira is Keter, all the Sefirot have light of Keter; if the highest Sefira is Hochma, all the Sefirot contain Hochma.

Similarly, we consider the level of the light in each world according to the first Partzuf in it. In AK it is the level of Keter; in Atzilut, the level of Hochma and in Beria, the level of Bina, etc.

2. We must speak at great length in order to explain these matters well. It will be explained here in Inner Observation, but I will explain it somewhat here, enough to arrange the issues so that we do not muddle with the multitude of similar names, the general, the particular, and the particular of the particular, brought before us.

We shall first examine the Sefira of Keter: We find five phases of Keter here in the words of the ARI. Each of them is given a special name: 1. Keter of the four phases of direct light. 2. Keter that contains four potential phases. 3. Keter that contains the four actual phases. 4. Keter that contains an entire world, called AK. 5. Keter of each particular degree in all the worlds, that take from the world of AK.

You should know that all the above phases of Keter are always presented by the single name Keter, without interpretation. However, they are immeasurably far from one another and it is impossible to tell them apart, except by the relevant issue. For that reason we must first know the exact discernment for each of them accurately.

Keter of direct light was called expansion of Ein Sof as vessels and as coupling by striking (Part 3, Chap 1, item 1) by the ARI. Thus, Ein Sof is the root to the four phases of direct light, called Keter of direct light.

Know that this is Ein Sof before the restriction, for there is no new light in the worlds that is not extended from the light of Ein Sof before the restriction. You already know that these four phases of direct light are equal without any difference from the beginning of the line to the end of Assiya, and so is their Keter.

Indeed, Keter, called Atik, contains four potential phases, as the ARI says (Part 3, Chap 6, item 4). Also, Keter, called AA, contains roots for the actual four phases, meaning it is the complete root for the emanated beings, as the ARI says above (Part 3, Chap 6, item 6).

These are completely separate matters from Keter of direct light, because they are regarded as the Rosh of the world, or of a Partzuf, containing ten Sefirot of direct light and ten Sefirot of reflected light, as has been explained above in Inner Light. These ten Sefirot are called Rosh or Keter wherever reflected light rises from below upward.

However, the ARI distinguishes between two phases of Keter in this Rosh: He calls the first Atik or "I am the last," containing the four potential phases, and the second AA or "I am the first," (see Part 3, Inner Light, Chap 7, item 90), containing the four actual phases. The difference between these two Ketarim has already been explained above, and here in Inner Observation they will be explained elaborately.

The Keter that contains all the worlds is called Adam Kadmon. It is a different and separate matter from all the other three phases of Ketarim because the Keter of direct light is regarded as Ein Sof before the restriction.

The two Ketarim called Atik and AA are discerned according to their refinement, since the screen operates in them from below upward, and this reflected light cannot raise the coarseness in the screen with it. There is no consideration of the level of these ten Sefirot here, because these two Ketarim, Atik and AA, are discerned even in Yetzira and Assiya, as the ARI says (Part 3, Chap 6, item 7, and Chap 7, item 5).

However, the world of Adam Kadmon, called Keter, is only because of the level that is dependent on and measured by the coarseness of the screen. Reflected light rises and clothes up to Keter of direct light from the screen of phase four, but the reflected light of the screen of phase three is too short to clothe the Keter, and it reaches only up to Hochma (see Inner Observation Part 2, item 65).

Because the screen of phase four operates only in the first world, called AK, the level of ten Sefirot that reaches Keter is found only in that world, but nowhere else. Consequently, all the degrees in that world are regarded as Keter, even the degrees of the Guf and the degrees below the Tabur down to the Sium; they are all regarded as Keter.

However, we should still know that the above three kinds of Ketarim are found in AK itself as well, even though it is Keter from its Rosh to its Sof, for the Keter of direct light in it is necessarily the phase of Ein Sof from before the restriction.

There are also two phases of Keter, called Rosh, whose reflected light is from below upward. There are always two Ketarim in this Rosh: Atik and AA. However, they are called "the inner Keter of AK itself," for it has Rosh and Guf too, and the Rosh is its particular Keter. The Rosh itself has a Keter of direct light, which is the instilling of the light of Ein Sof from before the restriction, namely the particular Keter of Rosh itself.

The ARI wrote, "The Keter in it is the four roots of the four phases of the ten Sefirot in it, being: souls, bodies, garments and halls. This is in particular." It means that here he speaks from the perspective of the Rosh, called Keter, because the screen operates in it from below upward, at which time the reflected light does not clothe any coarseness.

Because of that it is only regarded as the roots of the vessels, meaning four roots to four phases of the vessels HB TM that will later appear in the body of AK. They are called soul, body, garment, hall, and because they are merely roots, they are named Keter, for any root is called Keter.

However, the four phases that are subsequently extended from above downward are actually complete vessels, and are called Guf of Adam Kadmon (see Inner Observation Part 2, item 22). For that reason the ARI names this Rosh of AK "Keter in particular," meaning a particular Keter, which is four roots to the four phases from above downward in it.

That is why the ARI wrote, "**the collective of the souls in AK shall be called the root of the souls.**" The collective of the phases of the souls of AK shall be called the root of the souls, and the collective phases of the garments of AK shall be called the root of the garments. The collective of the phases of the halls of AK shall be called root of the halls.

He speaks here from the perspective of the Keter, from which all the phases in AK, its Rosh to its Sium are called Keter. Hence, the four phases below the Rosh in it are also called Keter, meaning complete vessels, where reflected light descends from the screen downward.

They are not regarded as Keter with respect to the inner AK itself because only the Rosh in it is called Keter; they are only regarded as soul, body, garment, hall, namely the four Sefirot HB TM. However, relating to the differentiation of the degrees, they are also regarded as Ketarim to all the worlds.

The level of Keter is found only in the world of AK. For that reason the ARI says that its Hochma is called soul. Even though it is below the Rosh of AK, it is still regarded as Keter to all the Hochmot in the worlds. The Bina in it, called body, is the Keter to all the Binot in all the worlds, and the ZA in it, called garment, is Keter to all the ZA in the worlds. Malchut in it, called hall, is the Keter to all the Malchuyot in all the worlds. It is so because they all have one reason: the screen of phase four operates only in them and not in any other world.

The souls in AK are roots of souls; the souls in Atzilut are the self of the souls; the souls in Beria are the bodies in the souls; the souls of Yetzira are the garments in the souls; the souls in Assiya are halls of souls. Thus, the souls that are Hochma in the five worlds AK and ABYA connect with each other like the upper Adam, in whose body the root and soul are clothed, and he is clothed in a garment and dwells in his hall.

2. The collective of the souls in AK shall be called the root of the souls (3). The collective of the phases of the soul of Atzilut shall be called actual souls of souls; the collective of souls of Beria shall be called bodies with respect to the souls of Atzilut, and the collective of the souls of Yetzira shall be called garments of souls. The collective of the souls of Assiya shall be called halls of the soul.

Inner Light

3. Here too the ARI speaks only from the perspective of the degree, as we have explained regarding the four phases HB TM of AK. It has already been explained

above (Inner Light, Chap 3, item 2) that the four phases of Atzilut come from the reflected light that rises from the screen of phase three. For that reason their degree of ten Sefirot of Atzilut begins only from Hochma, called Neshama.

Hence, all the phases in them are regarded as Hochma and Neshama from Rosh to Sium in the world of Atzilut as well. That is why the ARI writes that all the phases of the souls of Atzilut, meaning Hochma, are phases of souls of souls to all the worlds, meaning the phases of Hochma with respect to the Sefirot of Hochma in all the worlds.

Also, the bodies of Atzilut shall be called souls of the bodies of all the worlds. It is the same with the garments of Atzilut and the halls of Atzilut, as they all emerged by the clothing in reflected light of phase three, clothing up to the level of Hochma.

The bodies of AK are roots of the bodies; the bodies of Atzilut are souls of the bodies, and of Beria are the bodies themselves; bodies of Yetzira are garments of the bodies; bodies of Assiya are halls of the bodies. All the bodies of AK and ABYA connect with each other in the Upper Adam, in whose body the root and soul are clothed.

3. Also, all the phases of the bodies of AK shall be called the root of the bodies (4). The collective of the bodies of Atzilut shall be called souls of the bodies, and the collective of the phases of the bodies of Beria shall be called bodies of the bodies. The collective of the phases of the bodies of Yetzira shall be called garments of the bodies, and the collective of the bodies of Assiya shall be called halls of the bodies.

Inner Light

4. This is also because of the degree, as the entire ten Sefirot of Beria have no more than the degree of Bina, meaning from reflected light of the screen of phase two (Inner Light, Chap 3, item 4). Thus, all the degrees in it are regarded as phases that are called bodies. Even Malchut of Beria is the phase of Bina to the Malchuyot in all the worlds for the above reason.

Similarly, you can see that all the phases of the world of Yetzira are regarded as garments, meaning ZA in all the worlds. It is so because they come from reflected light of phase one, whose degree is up to ZA, called garment. Similarly, all the phases of the world of Assiya are halls, meaning only Malchut without a degree. You will understand the words of the ARI by the same manner and we need not elaborate further here (we shall elaborate in Inner Observation here).

Also, the garments in every world from AK and ABYA connect with each other and become as the upper Adam, in whose body the soul and root are clothed, and he is clothed in garments and dwells in his hall.

4. Also, the collective of the phases of garments of AK shall be called the root of the garments. The collective of the garments of Atzilut shall be called the souls of garments, and the collective of the phases of garments of Beria shall be called the bodies of garments. The collective of the phases of garments of Yetzira shall be called the garments of garments and the collective of the garments of Assiya shall be called the halls of garments.

Also, the halls in every world from AK and ABYA connect with each other like the Upper Adam, in whose body it is clothed etc.

5. The collective of the phases of halls of AK shall be called the root souls of halls. The collective discernments of the halls of Atzilut shall be called the souls of halls and the collective of halls of Beria shall be called the bodies of halls. The collective discernments of the halls of Yetzira shall be called the garments of halls and the collective halls of Assiya shall be called the halls of halls.

SNGLH of AK are roots for NGLH in ABYA; SNGLH of Atzilut are souls inside SNGLH in AK and BYA; SNGLH of Beria are bodies inside SNGLH in AK and AYA; SNGLH of Yetzira are garments inside SNGLH in AK and ABA; SNGLH of Assiya are halls inside SNGLH in AK and ABY.

6. It is so when we speak of it in general because the five phases of AK are roots: for the souls, for the bodies, for the garments or for the halls. The five phases of Atzilut are souls: for the roots, for the souls, for the bodies, for the garments or for the halls.

The five phases of Beria are bodies for the roots, for the souls, for the bodies, for the garments or for the halls. The five phases of Yetzira are garments: for the roots, for the souls, for the bodies, for the garments or for halls. The five phases of Assiya are halls: for the roots, for the souls, for the bodies, for the garments or for the halls.

Beria is called body because she receives from Atzilut as a body from a soul.

7. Now you can understand the words of our sages: "His wife is like his own body." Beria is the wife of Atzilut, for they are Hochma and Bina. Even though there are souls in Beria as well, it is called bodies from the perspective of the souls of Atzilut.

It is so because as the wife receives from her husband, so the body receives from the soul. Our sages also said: "A house (home) is but a wife." This is in Assiya, because Assiya is the house and the hall to all five phases.

Assiya is the wife of Yetzira. This is the meaning of "A house is but a wife," referring to Assiya. It is so in the phase of Assiya in each and every world; it is called the house of that world. The phase of Beria in every world is called the body of that world.

Another way: the lights in AK, meaning the souls in it, are called Yechida. The souls of Atzilut are called Haya, and the souls of Beria are called Neshamot. The souls of Yetzira are called Ruach and the souls of Assiya are called Nefesh.

8. If we want, we can take a different way: All the lights of AK are called Yechida, and lights of Atzilut, Haya. Lights of Beria are Neshama and lights of Yetzira are Ruach, and lights of Assiya are Nefesh.

It is similar in the bodies and garments and halls in AK and ABYA: the bodies in AK are Yechida of the bodies of ABYA, and in Atzilut, Haya etc. It is similar in the garments: the garments of AK are Yechida of garments of ABYA, and the garments of Atzilut are Haya of garments of AK and BYA etc.

9. It is similar in the garments in all the worlds and the bodies and the halls. All the garments of AK are the first and highest garment among all five garments, and all the garments of Atzilut are the second garment etc.

SNGLH are YHNRN, meaning lights of KHB TM.

10. This way is the first way because the Nefesh is called hall, Ruach—garment, soul—body, Haya—soul, and *Yechida*—the root of the soul. Thus, all the above is in each and every world in particular.

How so? The light of Keter of Atzilut is called the root of the soul, and it is called Yechida. The light of Hochma of Atzilut is called the soul to the soul, and it is called Haya. The light of Bina of Atzilut is called body, and it is called Neshama. The light of Tifferet of Atzilut is called garment, and it is called Ruach. The light of Malchut of Atzilut is called Nefesh, and it is called hall. It is the same in the inner of the inner, too.

Each Sefira of the KHB TM in AK and ABYA is divided into five phases SNGLH.

11. Indeed, the median rule, the shortest of them all is this: Every ten Sefirot of Atzilut, and Keter too, contain root, soul to soul, body, garment, hall. It is the same in BYA, as well as in AK , which is the root of the entire ABYA.

AK and ABYA are five phases in the name HaVaYaH, incorporated in one another. In each of them there are AK and ABYA, which are the five phases in HaVaYaH, and are SNGLH, which are twenty five phases.

12. You find that all that was emanated is but one HaVaYaH, which consists of five phases. They are: the tip of the Yod in AK, Yod in Atzilut, Hey in Beria, Vav in Yetzira and Hey in Assiya. Each of these phases consists of all five, because the tip of the Yod in AK contains one HaVaYaH of the other five phases. These are the above five phases in AK Himself, which are AK and ABYA in Him, being the five phases. Those are: root, soul, body, garment and hall.

The Yod of Atzilut also has one HaVaYaH, containing all the above five phases, and it is likewise in the rest of the letters, in BYA. Thus, they are five letters where each one consists of all the others, which are twenty five phases.

Each of the above twenty five phases is divided into five other phases SNGLH, and each of those contains ten Sefirot. Each Sefira is then divided into five Partzufim, which are SNGLH.

13. Afterwards, in this above manner, there is another incorporation. Each of them consists of all twenty five phases. It is so because the Yod of Atzilut has one HaVaYaH, comprising all five phases, and each phase of the five consists of five. These are: ten Sefirot of the root, ten Sefirot of the soul, ten Sefirot of the body, ten Sefirot of the garment, and ten Sefirot of the hall.

It is likewise in the tip of the Yod in AK, in the Yod in Atzilut, and likewise in the letter Hey in Beria, in the letter Vav in Yetzira, etc. Thus, in short, AK is the tip of the Yod, and has one HaVaYaH, which contains five phases: root, soul, body, garment, hall.

Each of these phases consists of five, which are: ten Sefirot of the root, ten Sefirot of the soul, ten Sefirot of the body, ten Sefirot of the garment and ten Sefirot of the hall. Each Sefira of these ten Sefirot comprises five Partzufim, namely the root and ABYA.

CHAPTER TEN

Explains that the garment and the hall were separated from the root, soul and body, and became surrounding lights, and also the explanations of AK, ABYA, NRNH and ASMB (AB, SAG, MA, BON). Contains eight issues:

1. The root, soul, and bodies are in adhesion with each other. The garment and hall were separated from them. 2. The root, soul, and body are inner vessels where the more external is worse. The garment and hall are surrounding vessels where the more external is more important. Hence the shells are between the body and the garments, which is the place of the darkness and the worst. 3. When the Partzufim of AK and ABYA clothe each other, they only clothe three phases: the root, soul, and body in it are in adhesion together, and the ten Sefirot of the bodies do not clothe the ten Sefirot of the garments. 4. The root, soul and body of AK are clothed inside the root, soul and body of Atik of Atzilut. The root, soul, and body of Atzilut are clothed in the root, soul, and body of AA of Atzilut, and root, soul, and body of AA are clothed in Abba, and so on similarly. 5. AK and ABYA are incorporated in one another. There are AK and ABYA in AK, AK and ABYA in Atzilut and AK and ABYA in Beria, in Yetzira and in Assiya. AA is the Part of AK that is unattainable. Abba is Atzilut, Ima is Beria, ZA-Yetzira, and Nukva-Assiya. The souls are extended from Atzilut, the spirits from Beria, the angels from Yetzira and the wheels from Assiya. 6. Adam consists of Nefesh, Ruach, Neshama, Haya from the four worlds ABYA. Each of their phases contains Nefesh, Ruach, Neshama, Haya. Neshama of Nefesh is more important than the light of Nefesh of Ruach. 7. It is possible to be rewarded with Nefesh of Atzilut and even higher. The one who is rewarded with Ruach of Yesod of Atzilut will be the husband of the Shechina. 8. HaVaYaH with the filling of AB is the Yod of HaVaYaH, namely Atzilut. With the filling of SAG, it is the first Hey of HaVaYaH, namely Beria. With the filling of MA, it is Vav of HaVaYaH, namely Yetzira. With the filling of BON, it is the lower Hey of HaVaYaH, namely Assiya.

The root, soul, and bodies are in adhesion with each other. The garment and hall departed from them.

1. Now we shall discuss each of these worlds, and what they are about. Know that the root and the souls and the bodies are one phase (1), and there is no separation

between them. But the garments and the halls are two separated phases from the above three phases. Between these two, meaning between the bodies and the garments, there is the section of the shells, which actually adhere to the posterior of the light of the body.

Inner Light

1. There is a profound and notable matter in these words of the ARI. This is the meaning of the second restriction that occurred in NHY of AK, brought in the words of the ARI. That second restriction is about the association of the quality of mercy with the quality of judgment that our sages wrote of. You can understand that matter thoroughly in my book (Panim Masbirot), but here we shall be brief.

The thing is that only phase four of the four above phases is called the quality of judgment, because the first restriction was on her alone. I have shown in previous lessons that there was no restriction in the first three phases, for which they were called the qualities of mercy.

However, in the second restriction of AK, there was an association and connection of phase four with phase two, as it is written, "So they two went," because Malchut and ZA rose to Bina. Thus, the quality of judgment, which is phase four, is sweetened by the quality of mercy, which is phase two.

In that way, in the first restriction only phase four was restricted, and in the second restriction, Bina was restricted too, due to her bonding with Malchut. This occurred in NHY of AK from its Tabur downward. Consequently, these ten Sefirot that emerged by the association with the quality of judgment are called the world of Nekudim [Heb: dots/points], after the ascent of Malchut, which is called a dot.

For this reason, it is considered that in the above world of Nekudim ZA and Malchut were separated from the four phases HB TM. It is so because phase four rose to the place of Bina and became a screen there. As a result, the upper light stopped at Malchut in Bina and did not expand to ZA, called garment, and to Malchut, called hall, as they are below Bina.

That is why the ARI writes, "**Know, that the root and the souls and the bodies are one phase. and there is no separation between them. But the garments and the halls are as two separated phases from the above three phases.**" It means that because of the screen that was erected at the margins of Bina the light stopped there.

From there onward the upper light does not reach the internality of ZA and the Malchuyot in all the worlds. As a result, they all went out and became surrounding vessels, meaning that they receive the light from afar, as the upper light cannot clothe inside them anymore. The garment is the vessel for the surrounding light of Haya and the hall is the vessel for the surrounding light of Yechida.

Now you may see that these ZA and Malchut in the four phases in all the worlds from the world of Nekudim downward are regarded as ZA and Malchut of the inner Bina. The upper light clothes their internality as well. However, the general ZA and Malchut below Bina were separated from the inner vessels, where the Neshama, Ruach, and Nefesh of the inner light clothe and became surrounding vessels of Haya and Yechida.

The root, soul, and body are inner vessels where the more external is worse. The garment and hall are surrounding vessels where the more external is more important. Hence the shells are between the body and the garments, which is the place of the darkness, the worst.

2. The reason for it is that the three inner phases have inner light inside them. The worst of the inner light emerges inside the skin and ends there. The surrounding light is the opposite: it is known that the more external light is greater (2).

It turns out that the surrounding light in the innermost garment, which is attached to the body, is the smaller surrounding light among all of them. Hence the section of the shells is there in the middle, in a place where there is neither inner light nor surrounding light. It is the middle between the internal light and the surrounding light, and it is called the place of darkness. That thing in each and every world is the phase of the shell in that world.

Inner Light

2. This has been explained in detail in Inner Observation (Part 2, Chap 1, item 7), with which you can understand the rest of the ARI's words by yourself, and there is no reason to elaborate.

When the Partzufim of AK and ABYA clothe each other, each one clothes only three phases: the root, soul, and body in it are adhered together, and the ten Sefirot of the bodies do not clothe the ten Sefirot of garments.

3. Indeed, once we have clarified the matter in particular, we shall speak in general: It is known that the internality of AK is the Ein Sof. It clothes the root of the souls of ten Sefirot in it, while these clothe the phase of the souls of the entire ten Sefirot in it, which then clothe the ten Sefirot of the phase of the body of AK.

It would have been appropriate for the ten Sefirot of the bodies to clothe the ten Sefirot of garments. However, it is not so for the above reason. Rather, the three phases Atik of Atzilut surround these three phases of AK.

The root, soul and body of AK are clothed inside the root, soul and body of Atik of Atzilut. The root, soul, and body of Atik of Atzilut are clothed in the root, soul, and body of AA of Atzilut, and the root, soul, body of AA are clothed in Abba etc. similarly.

4. How so? The ten Sefirot of the bodies of AK clothe inside the ten Sefirot of the roots of the souls of the ten Sefirot of Atik of Atzilut. These, in turn, clothe the ten Sefirot of the phases of the souls of Atik of Atzilut, and these clothe the ten Sefirot of the bodies of Atik of Atzilut.

Similarly, the phases of the roots and souls and bodies of AA clothe the bodies of Atik. Similarly, the three phases of Abba clothe AA and the three phases of Ima to Abba. The three phases of ZA to Ima and the three phases of Nukva to ZA. This completes all the phases of the bodies until Nukva of ZA.

AK and ABYA are incorporated in one another. There are AK and ABYA in AK, AK and ABYA in Atzilut and AK and ABYA in Beria, in Yetzira and in Assiya. AA is the part of AK that is unattainable. Abba is Atzilut, Ima is Beria, ZA is Yetzira, and Nukva is Assiya. Souls are extended from Atzilut, spirits from Beria, angels from Yetzira and wheels from Assiya.

5. Know that the world of Atzilut consists of the four worlds of ABYA; Beria comprises the entire ABYA, and so do Yetzira and Assiya. In this manner, Abba is Atzilut, Ima is Beria, ZA is Yetzira, and Nukva is Assiya. The phase of AA is not apparent in any world since it is very concealed. Thus, from the world of Atzilut – souls, from Beria – holy spirits, from Yetzira – angels, and from Assiya – wheels (3).

Inner Light

3. Souls are the phase of the world of Beria; Spirits are the phase of the world of Yetzira; Souls are the phase of the world of Assiya. That is the meaning of the ARI's words, "**from the world of Atzilut – souls,**" meaning souls in Beria are imparted from the world of Atzilut to Beria. "**From Beria – holy spirits,**" meaning the spirits, in Yetzira, are imparted there from the world of Beria.

It is so because from the coupling of ZON of Atzilut, souls are imparted to the righteous who stand in Beria. From the coupling of ZON of Beria, spirits are imparted to those who stand in Yetzira.

Man incorporates Nefesh, Ruach, Neshama, and Haya from the four worlds ABYA. Each of their phases has Nefesh, Ruach, Neshama, and Haya. Neshama of Nefesh is more important than the light of Nefesh of Ruach

6. Man consists of four worlds. If he is rewarded only with Nefesh of Assiya, and then he sins, blemishes it, and puts it into the shells, he is told, "The gnat came before you," because the gnat did not do anything to enter the shell.

If he did not sin, he is regarded as being in the wheels. Sometimes, he will have only the phase of Nefesh, and he is more important than one who has Ruach (4), such as one who has Neshama in the Nefesh. It is known that each and every world contains all four.

This is man, because when he begins to shine, and correct bit-by-bit, the phase of Neshama in Ruach of Yetzira shines in him immediately, though it has still not clothed him entirely. It is so because it is impossible to clothe in him entirely before he completely corrects his Nefesh. Indeed, this man, who has Ruach inside, who is the phase of Nefesh in Ruach of Yetzira, is certainly worse than this above phase.

Inner Light

4. This is the rule: the Nefesh of the degree is regarded as Ruach of its lower degree. Likewise, Ruach of the upper degree is regarded as Neshama of its lower degree, and Neshama of the upper degree is Haya to the lower, and Haya of the upper is regarded as Yechida to its lower one.

You can therefore understand that Nefesh of Ruach is regarded as Ruach of the degree of Nefesh. Similarly, Ruach of Ruach is regarded as Neshama to the degree of Nefesh, etc. The ARI writes, **"Sometimes, he will have only the phase of Nefesh, and he is more important than one who has Ruach."** He wishes to say that one who has Neshama of Nefesh is more important than one who has Nefesh of Ruach. It is so because Neshama of Nefesh is equal to Ruach of Ruach, but more important than Nefesh of Ruach.

It is possible to be rewarded with Nefesh of Atzilut and even higher. The one who is rewarded with Ruach of Yesod of Atzilut will be the husband of the Shechina.

7. A man may also have Nefesh of Atzilut and even higher. If he has Ruach from Yesod of Atzilut he will be the husband of the queen and he is called "A Man of God."

HaVaYaH with the filling of AB is the Yod of HaVaYaH, namely Atzilut. With the filling of SAG it is the first Hey of HaVaYaH, namely Beria. With the filling of MA it is Vav of HaVaYaH, namely Yetzira and with the filling of BON it is the lower Hey of HaVaYaH, namely Assiya.

8. Four letters HaVaYaH in the four worlds Atzilut, Beria, Yetzira, Assiya: Yod in Atzilut is the name AB of Yodim, for "you have made them all with wisdom [Hochma]" (5). Hey in Beria, the name SAG, for Ima nests in the chair. Vav in Yetzira, the name MA, for six Sefirot nest in Yetzira; The lower Hey in Assiya, the name BON, for Malchut nests in the wheel.

Inner Light

5. There are four fillings in Yod, Hey, Vav, Hey: 1. With a filling of Yodin: Yod Hey Vav Hey, in Gematria AB (72). 2. With a filling of Yodin and Aleph: Yod Hey Vav Hey, in Gematria SAG (63). 3. With a filling of Alephin: Yod He Vav He, in Gematria MA (45). 4. With a filling of Heyin, in Gematria BON (52). The filling of AB implies Hochma, which is Yod of HaVaYaH; The filling of SAG implies Bina, which is Hey of HaVaYaH; The filling of MA implies ZA, which is Vav of HaVaYaH, and the filling of BON implies Malchut, which is the lower Hey of HaVaYaH.

CHAPTER ELEVEN

Explains the expansion of the light of Ein Sof to make vessels in
four phases of coarseness by describing the organs of man, which
are: Eynaim [eyes], Ozen [ear], Hotem [nose], Peh [mouth]. The more
refined is more important. Eynaim are phase one, Ozen – phase two,
Hotem – phase three, Peh – phase four. Contains eight issues:

1. There is no form of description and attainment in Ein Sof whatsoever, and in
order to create the world, he drew many expansions to be roots and origins for
the world of Atzilut. 2. There are four elements in all things, which are the four
letters Yod, Hey, Vav, Hey, which are sight, sound, smell, and speech, which are:
Haya, Neshama, Ruach, Nefesh. They are: Eynaim, Ozen, Hotem, Peh. 3. There is
vapor and Ruach in AHP, where each one is greater than the other: in the Ozen
there is little vapor; it is stronger in the Hotem, and it is the greatest in the Peh. 4.
The Oznayim [pl. for Ozen] are Bina, which is phase two. She has little coarseness,
and she is Neshama. The Hotem is ZA, which is the coarser phase three, and he is
Ruach. Peh is Malchut, with coarseness of phase four, the coarsest. She is the light
of Nefesh. 5. Sight is the light of Haya. There is no actual vapor in the Eynaim as
there is in AHP. It is the very fine coarseness of phase one. 6. Vapor in the Eynaim
is the vessel for surrounding light of Haya. However the direct light in it is extended
downward as a look, which is coupling by striking. 7. The expansion of the light to
make vessels, which is a look, comes from the Eynaim, being light of Hochma, and
not from AHP. 8. The three vapors became vessels to Nefesh, Ruach, Neshama.

There is no form of description and attainment in Ein Sof whatsoever, and in
order to create the world, he drew many expansions to be roots and origins for
the world of Atzilut

**1. It is known that the Ein Sof is completely formless. When He came to think
of the creation of the world by the order of the emanation, He began to extend
from it the expansion of many lights to become roots and origins to the Atzilut
(1) that would be emanated afterwards.**

Inner Light

1. Expansion of lights, as the ARI said (part3, Chap 1, item 3), that Ein Sof expanded
to make vessels through coupling by striking and raising reflected light. He says

here that right in the world of AK, he began to extend from it the expansion of many lights through the above coupling by striking, enough to emanate twenty-five Partzufim in that world. These twenty-five Partzufim of AK would be the roots and the origins of Atzilut that would later be emanated, meaning the twenty-five Partzufim that would be emanated in the world of Atzilut. That is why the ARI writes **"the expansion of many lights to become roots and origins to the Atzilut,"** as he will explain henceforth.

There are four elements in all things, which are the four letters Yod, Hey, Vav, Hey, which are sight, sound, smell, and speech, which are: Haya, Neshama, Ruach, Nefesh. They are: Eynaim, Ozen, Hotem, Peh

2. We shall speak of it by way of parable and allegory: you already know that there are four elements in all things. They are: sight, sound, smell and speech. They are the four letters HaVaYaH, and they are: Neshama to Neshama, Neshama, Ruach, Nefesh. We shall begin to explain from the degree of Neshama, and then return to what precedes it.

There is vapor and Ruach in AHP, where each one is greater than the other: in Ozen there is little vapor; it is stronger in the Hotem, and it is the greatest in Peh

3. The organs of Oznayim [pl. for Ozen) certainly have a fine Ruach inside them (2). The proof of it is that when one thoroughly blocks one's ear with one's finger, one feels as though there is a great sound inside them. This is because of the Ruach accumulated in it, which seeks to come out but cannot.

The next organ in degree is the Hotem. The Ruach that comes out of it is sensed more than what comes out of the Ozen. The next organ in degree is the Peh, for the strongest vapor and Ruach of all come out of it.

Inner Light

2. Know, that this reflected light that is returned to its place through a coupling by striking, as the ARI says (Part 3, chap1, item 3), is called, "vapor that comes out of the Partzuf," or "Ruach that comes out of the Partzuf." It means that it cannot clothe it because of the power of detainment in the screen there. For that reason it must return to its place (see Table of Topics, Part 2, item 2).

You should also know that there are five phases that contain the entire reality after the restriction, namely AK, Atzilut, Beria, Yetzira, Assiya. They are five levels one below the other from Keter to Malchut, caused by the refinement of the screen (see Table of Topics, Part 2, item 17).

Because the screen of phase four that operated in AK had been refined, and remained in coarseness of phase three, ten new Sefirot were emanated on the level of Hochma, called Atzilut. Because the screen of phase three was then refined as well, and remained in coarseness of phase two, ten new Sefirot emerged and were born on the level of Bina, called Beria (see ARI's words in Part 3, Chap 4, item 3, and Inner Light, item 9).

Finally, the entire coarseness was refined from the screen and only its root remained, where there is no striking and no level of reflected light. Consequently, the ten Sefirot emerge here only in the phase of Malchut and they are called the world of Assiya.

For the very same reason and cause that was explained regarding the four general levels, which are AK and ABYA, the five levels of the ten Sefirot must therefore emerge in each and every world, as well. They are called five Partzufim: AA, Abba, Ima, ZA and Nukva.

Moreover, in each and every Partzuf there must also emerge five levels of ten Sefirot one below the other down to Malchut, called Galgalta, Eynaim, Ozen, Hotem, Peh, or KHB ZA and Malchut, or NRNHY. This matter will be explained sufficiently in Inner Observation here, and we should not elaborate it here because of its length.

The ARI wrote here: "**As the value of the organ, so is its fineness.**" It means that the vessel in which the designated light clothes is called an organ. The fineness or the coarseness of the organ is measured by the coarseness of the screen that operates there.

Thus, the place where the screen of phase two operates is called "a fine organ" and the Ruach that comes out of it is very fine. It means that the reflected light that rises and returns from that vessel is very fine, reaching neither Keter, nor Hochma, but rather Bina. For this reason, the level of these ten Sefirot is up to Bina, as explained above.

It is said: "**The next organ in degree is the Hotem. The Ruach that comes out of it is sensed more than what comes out of the Ozen.**" It is so because the place where the screen of phase three operates is called Hotem, where the "Ruach that comes out of it", meaning the reflected light that is turned back and comes out of that vessel is of a greater measure, thus reaching Hochma. This is why the level of the ten Sefirot of Hotem is up to Hochma.

It is said, "**The next organ in degree is the Peh, for the strongest vapor and Ruach of all come out of it.**" It is so because the place where the screen of phase four operates is called Peh. The vapor that comes out of it, being the reflected light that leaves it and rises upward, is stronger than all of them, for its measure is full, reaching up to Keter. For that reason these ten Sefirot have the level of Keter.

The Oznayim [pl. for Ozen] are Bina, which is phase two, which has little coarseness and is Neshama. Hotem is ZA, which is coarseness of phase three. It is coarser and is Ruach. Peh is Malchut, with coarseness of phase four, the coarsest. She is light of Nefesh.

4. As the value of the organ, so is its fineness. The Oznayim are Bina, being finer. Thus, the Ruach that comes out of them is very fine. The organ of the Hotem is also finer than the organ of the Peh, as we have mentioned. Thus, by way of allegory, we can say that the Ruach that comes out of the Ozen is called Neshama (3)**, from the Hotem – Ruach, and from the Peh – Nefesh.**

Inner Light

3. The ten Sefirot from coupling by striking in the screen of the Peh are at the degree of Keter, which is light of Yechida, and from the Hotem – the degree of Hochma, which is light of Haya etc. However, the order of the clothing of the lights in her is not so, but the opposite, for the more important light clothes the more refined vessel.

Thus, light of Yechida clothes only the most refined of all, called Keter or Galgalta. Light of Haya clothes only the vessel of Hochma, which is phase one, called Eynaim. Light of Neshama clothes only the vessel of Bina, namely phase two, called Ozen, and light of Ruach clothes the vessel of ZA, meaning phase three, called Hotem. Finally, light of Nefesh clothes the vessel of Malchut, which is phase four, called Peh.

The rule is that "Any giver needs the coarser phase, and any receiver must receive in the more refined thing." This means that in order to draw upper light to bestow in the lower one, the lower one must have a coarser vessel and screen, as we have said, that the greater the coarseness of the screen, the greater the reflected light that departs from it.

It turns out that it reaches higher too, for if the lower one has no more than a screen of phase three, it lacks the degree of Yechida, and it has only the degree of Haya. However, the reception of the lower one is always in the more refined thing, meaning the light that is imparted to it clothes only the most refined phase, and the more important light needs the more refined vessel. I have already explained that issue elaborately in Inner Observation Part 2, item 87.

Sight is light of Haya. There is no actual vapor in the Eynaim as there is in AHP. It is the very fine coarseness of phase one

5. It has been explained that from the phase of sight itself comes the Neshama to Neshama. However, know that the phase of sight is not the actual vapor that comes out of the Ayin [eye), as is in the Ozen, Hotem, Peh, where Neshama, Ruach and Nefesh are actual vapors expanding from them downward (4).

Inner Light

4. It tells us that the force of the coarseness of the screen is only apparent as it expands from above downward (see Inner Light, Part 3, Chap 4, item 50). It is so because after every coupling by striking, reflected light rises and clothes the ten Sefirot of direct light from Malchut upward to the ten Sefirot of Rosh and the roots of the four phases. After that, it descends once more and expands from Malchut downward by the same measure it has in the ten Sefirot of Rosh from below upward.

Thus, the reflected light that rises from below upward does not carry any coarseness there with it. Rather, the same ten Sefirot that expand from above downward are completely limited in the measure and boundary of the level of the screen, since the screen is their entire root.

Vapor in the Eynaim is the vessel for surrounding light of Haya. However, the direct light in it extends downward as a look, which is coupling by striking

6. The Eynaim are not so, (5) because their vapor itself remains in its place as surrounding light called Neshama to Neshama (6). However, there is something that is drawn from it, being only the sight and the look, not the actual vapor drawn downwards. Thus, the vessels that are called Guf were made from the phase of that sight, but the vapor of the Ayin itself is very internal and cannot extend and expand downward.

Inner Light

5. It means that coarseness of phase one, called Eynaim, is very faint for the reason stated in Inner Light, that the above coarseness refers to the will to receive in every emanated being, which differentiates it from the upper light, in which there is no

273

will to receive. Thus, phase one, whose coarseness is faint since it is extended from the upper force, as the will to bestow in the upper one is a compelling law in the lower one, to have a desire to receive its bestowal. For this reason, it is not regarded as disparity of form and coarseness in the lower one until the desire awakens in it by the power of its own awakening, namely phase two.

Thus, there is no coupling by striking in the light of Eynaim, namely phase one, because the reflected light, which is the vapor that comes out of phase one, remains in its place. In other words, it does not depart from it as reflected light. This is the meaning of the ARI's words, "**The Eynaim are not so because their vapor itself remains in its place.**"

6. It means that light of Hochma does not have a vessel to clothe in, for lack of any reflected light, which is a vessel in the Eynaim. Hence the light of Hochma remains outside and shines from afar without clothing. This light is called light of Haya, or Neshama to Neshama.

The expansion of the light to make vessels, which is a look, comes from the Eynaim, being light of Hochma, and not from AHP

7. **Since this sight was extended from the Eynaim (7), which are higher than the Ozen, Hotem, Peh, that sight alone had sufficient power to create and make the vessels, and their vapor itself was not needed. It is not so in the Ozen, Hotem, Peh, which are lower. That is because their very vapor itself had to expand to make and emanate the above-mentioned phases, and nothing real came out of them except by the power of the vapor itself (8).**

Inner Light

7. You should know that the restriction and the screen relate only to light of Hochma, not to light of Hassadim (see Table of Topics, Part 1, item 6). Thus, relating to the expansion of Ein Sof to make vessels (mentioned in the words of the ARI Part 3, Chap 1, item 3) by coupling by striking in the screen, this coupling by striking relates only to light of Hochma, called sight and look.

It is so because only that light is not received in phase four due to the screen and the restriction. However, phase two and Bina, which is light of Hassadim, is not detained by the screen.

That is the meaning of the ARI's words, "**Sight alone had sufficient power to create and make the vessels and their vapor itself was not needed. It is not so in the**

274

AHP." It means that only the light of Eynaim, called sight, which was restricted, has striking and reflected light, which are the vessels.

The AHP, whose primary light is the light of Hassadim, do not perform any striking. Also, any coupling by striking in the AHP comes only by the power of the light of Hochma that shines in them. This is called the look of the Eynaim in AHP. It means that because of the illumination of light of Hochma in them, the screen detains the lights in the AHP as well.

8. Meaning from vapors that expand from them downward (as written in Inner Light, this chapter, item 4), which is reflected light that descends from above downward. It is similar to what is written about the Sefira of Malchut in Inner Observation (Part 2, item 109).

This is because phase four, called Peh here, does not receive anything from the direct light, because of the screen in her. Instead, after she raises reflected light from her upward, this reflected light descends once more from the screen downward, and expands Malchut into ten Sefirot from her and within her (see Part 3, Chap 2, item 3). She receives the entire level of the ten Sefirot that the reflected light clothed from Malchut upward within them.

By the very same way, the vessels of the Ozen and Hotem do not receive anything from the vapor, namely the reflected light that rises from them upward. It is so because since the screen had been refined from phase four to phase three, it is considered that Malchut rose to the place of ZA, meaning the Hotem.

Because of that, the screen detains vessel of Hotem from receiving any direct light and pushes that light back up, which is called "coupling by striking in phase three". Thus, the vessel of Hotem does not receive any direct light because it departs from it, but only afterwards when the reflected light expands from the Hotem downwards, in Malchut, in the place of phase four, namely the Peh. Similarly, the vessel named Ozen does not receive any direct light for the above reason, but through the reflected light that descends from Ozen downward.

The ARI writes, "**It is not so in the Ozen, Hotem, Peh, which are lower. That is because their very vapor itself had to expand.**" It means that after the vapor itself, meaning the reflected light, descends and expands from above downward, they expand into ten Sefirot and become vessels to receive the light.

It is said, "**nothing real came out of them except by the power of the vapor itself.**" In other words, by the power of their reflected light, called vapor, which turns over and descends from above downward, as has been explained.

The three vapors became the vessels to Nefesh, Ruach, Neshama

8. However, since the phase of the Ayin was not actual vapor [9], but only sight, only vessels were made of it [10]. However, in the Ozen, Hotem, Peh, which could not even make vessels without the actual vapor, but since it is actual vapor, they became Nefesh, Ruach, Neshama [20].

Inner Light

9. It is written above that phase one does not raise vapor, which is reflected light, because her coarseness is very faint, and she does not perform coupling by striking. The ARI writes, "**was not actual vapor, but only sight.**" It means that there is no reflected light there, only direct light, which is light of Hochma, called sight.

10. It means that no vessel was made of the phase of the Ayin itself. That is because there is no vapor there, but her phase of striking makes the vessels in the Ozen, Hotem, Peh. Had it not been for the light of Hochma, called sight, there wouldn't have been any coupling by striking there, and there wouldn't have been a vessel in the AHP as well.

20. It is so because the vapor of phase four that expands from Peh downward became a vessel to Nefesh, vapor of phase three to Ruach and vapor of phase two to Neshama. Remember the inverse relation between bestowal of the light and the reception of the light, as written in Inner Light (this chapter, item 3).

CHAPTER TWELVE

Explains the coupling of the first look of Eynaim in AHP, from which the vessels of the Rosh were made, and also the coupling of the second look, from which vessels of the Guf were made. Contains eight issues:

1. The vessels were made from the light of the look in the vapors of Nefesh, Ruach, Neshama, which are phase four, and phase three, and phase two. 2. "And God saw": this is a look; "Et" [the], is the Nefesh; the "light" is Ruach and Neshama; "divided": made the vessels, which are separation and boundary. 3. In the look there is direct light and reflected light because when the direct light expanded unto the screen on Malchut, the screen reflected the light upward and the light that returned clothed the direct light from below upward. 4. In the beginning of the expansion of the direct light for coupling by striking on the screen in Malchut, it created only the roots of the vessels for the Rosh. 5. Making vessels of the Guf requires a second look on the screen in the Peh, namely Malchut. 6. The root, which is the Keter that is close to the Ayin, emerged in the ten Sefirot of the look. HB and TM expand from the Ayin downward to the Yesod, which is close to the Peh. 7. The root, which is the Keter, emerged in the reflected light close to the Peh, which is Malchut, the root of the reflected light. HB and TM expand and rise from the Peh upward to Malchut of reflected light that reaches near the Ain and clothe the ten Sefirot of direct light. 8. When the ten Sefirot of reflected light are incorporated in the ten Sefirot of direct light, they make the level of all the vessels equal.

The vessels were made from the light of the look in the vapors of Nefesh Ruach Neshama, which are phase four, and phase three, and phase two

1. We must understand the matter of sight and look of the Eynaim. Know that the sight of the Eynaim extended from it a look in the above-mentioned Nefesh, Ruach, Neshama (1), and the vessels were made because of her look upon them.

This is the meaning of "And God saw the light, that it was good; and God divided," etc. The Ruach and the Neshama are called light (2), and the Nefesh is called "Et" [the], because Nefesh is Malchut and it is called "Et".

Inner Light

1. It is called expansion of the light of Ein Sof in coupling by striking to make vessels, because the light of Ein Sof is the light of Hochma, the only one where there is coupling by striking.

2. Meaning the phase of Ruach and Neshama of direct light in and of themselves before the ascents of the screen and its refinement from phase four to their phases. It is so because then they have no phase of vessel, for there is a vessel only in phase four.

However, the first three phases of direct light are regarded merely as causing the appearance of the vessel, meaning phase four (see Inner Observation Part 2, item 15).

The ARI wrote, "**The Ruach and the Neshama,**" meaning phase two and phase three, "**are called light**," because they are not regarded as vessels.

"And God saw": this is a look; "Et" [the]), is the Nefesh; The "light" is Ruach and Neshama; "divided": made the vessels, which are separation and boundary

2. It turns out that upon the look of His sight in the "Et", the light, which is Nefesh, called Et (3), and the Ruach and the Neshama, called light, the vessels emerged, which distinguish and make a separation, a boundary, and a measure in the lights. This is "and God divided."

Inner Light

3. "Et" indicates the collective of the twenty-two letters from Aleph to Tav. Only Malchut raises reflected light and all the changes and the letters and the combinations of the letters in the worlds are formed only because of the reflected light. This is the reason she is called "Et", indicating that she is the source of every separation and measure and boundary.

In the look there is direct light and reflected light because when the direct light expanded unto the screen on Malchut, the screen returned the light upward, and the light that returned clothed the direct light from below upward

3. Know that there are two phases in this look, which are direct light from above downward, and reflected light from below upward (4). First, the sight extended from above to the end of the tenth, lowest phase of the Nefesh.

Then, when the light returned from below upward, the separating vessels were made and formed and clothed all the parts of the Nefesh from below upward.

This matter of the look and how the vessels were made from below upward has been explained above thoroughly in the previous study (brought here in item 6), and study it there carefully.

Inner Light

4. It means that that part of the light that is received in the Partzuf, meaning until Malchut, is called direct light from above downward. The part of the light that is not received in the Partzuf, meaning all the measure of the upper light that belongs to Malchut and the screen in it rejects it and returns it to its place, is called reflected light from below upward.

Thus, the direct light and reflected light are both truly equally regarded as upper light, but the difference is that this direct light is received in the Partzuf, and the reflected light is only the light of departure from the vessel of Malchut.

In the beginning of the expansion of the direct light for coupling by striking on the screen in Malchut, it created only the roots of the vessels for the Rosh

4. Know that this direct light had the power to make vessels for the Rosh (5), yet it would not be apparent before this look strikes the light of Nefesh of the Peh, making the vessels of the Rosh apparent (6).

Inner Light

5. It is written above that there is no perception in the direct light without it clothing the reflected light. For this reason, the Sefirot of direct light above the reflected light are not apparent in the Partzuf although they are there. For example, in the reflected light that reaches the level of Bina, Keter and Hochma in that Partzuf are not apparent, although they are clothed in the internality of Bina (see Inner Light, Chap 3, item 6).

6. It means that by clothing the ten Sefirot of direct light in the reflected light that rises from the screen from below upward, they are sufficient for vessels of the Rosh, meaning only roots for vessels, but not complete vessels.

Making vessels of the Guf requires a second look on the screen in the Peh, namely Malchut

5. However, the vessels of the Guf (7), which are the lower seven, there was no ability to make them in the light of straightness of the abovementioned look by itself, but rather until the look strikes the light of Nefesh of the Peh, and through

both of them (8), the light returns from below upward, makes vessels, and clothes the lower seven, called Guf.

Inner Light

7. Meaning after the light is overturned and descends from the screen downward, at which time Malchut, which is the Peh, expands and spreads into ten Sefirot from her and within her to the Malchut in her (Inner Light, Chap 2, item 3), called "Nefesh of the Peh." At that time, they become complete vessels called "Guf," or "ten Sefirot of the Guf."

8. It means that by the light of the look, which is the expansion of the light of Ein Sof, and by Malchut, which is the screen that strikes and returns the light backwards, these two participate in the making of the vessels.

You must know the meaning of the second look that is mentioned here: it is the ascent of the lights to the Emanator, meaning the refinement of the screen from phase four to phase three, until it is refined to the phase of the root, called Emanator. As it departs, it creates all five levels, called five vessels: KHB, ZA and Malchut of the Guf.

The first expansion to Nefesh of the Peh creates the vessel of Keter of the Guf. When Malchut ascends to ZA, meaning when phase four is refined to phase three, there is a second coupling by striking, and it produces the level of Hochma. By this the vessel of Hochma of the Guf is made.

When Malchut ascends to phase two, the vessel of Bina of the Guf is made in the above manner, and when Malchut rises to phase one, the vessel of ZA of the Guf is made in the above manner. When Malchut rises to her root phase, meaning when she is refined from her entire coarseness, the vessel of Malchut of the Guf is made.

The ARI wrote that by the second look of coupling by striking in the screen of Malchut of the expansion of the Peh, the reflected light rises once more from below upward, until it departs entirely. That creates the ten Sefirot KHB ZA and Malchut of the Guf.

The root, which is the Keter that is close to the Ayin, emerged in the ten Sefirot of the look. HB and TM expand from the Ayin downward to the Yesod, which is close to the Peh

6. Indeed, in the ten Sefirot of the look, the more adhered to its root is higher because Keter is closer and more adjacent to the Ayin then the rest, and similarly the others.

The root, which is the Keter, emerged in the reflected light close to the Peh, which is Malchut, the root of the reflected light. HB and TM expand and rise from the Peh upward to the Malchut of reflected light that reaches near the Ayin, and clothe the ten Sefirot of direct light. When the ten Sefirot of reflected light are incorporated in the ten Sefirot of direct light, they make the degree of all the vessels equal

7. Indeed, the phase of Malchut emerged first [9]. When the light strikes and returns, all the vessels were equal[10]. That is because if Yesod had expanded before it more than Malchut [20], it would have been equal with Malchut, although it is Yesod [because it expanded more].

It would have been so because Yesod would have the strength to expand more [30] because of the multitude of the light of Malchut. It has no merit over Malchut [40], but because of this expansion, it is regarded as reflected light, which returns and comes closer to its origin.

However, in terms of the vessels themselves, they are equal. When the light returns and clothes the vapor [50] you find that when it is close to the Peh, the light of the Peh there is greater than the light of the Ozen, since when the vapor of the Peh [60] is here, it is regarded as Rosh. However, when the vapor of the Ozen is here, it is still regarded as the rest of the Guf [70].

Inner Light

9. It means that in the phase of the ten Sefirot of reflected light, Malchut emerged first. It is so because she is the source and the root of any ten Sefirot of reflected light, for all that reflected light is her own part, which she should have received had it not been for the detaining screen on her.

Therefore, Malchut is regarded as the phase of root and Keter to the entire ten Sefirot of reflected light, and as incorporating all of them. He writes, "**The phase of Malchut emerged first**," meaning the phase of the reflected light.

10. The direct light is arranged from above downward, meaning from refined to coarse. The greater the refinement, the greater the importance. Conversely, the reflected light is arranged from below upward, meaning from coarse to refined. The greater the coarseness, the greater the importance.

Thus, when clothing each other, they are all equal. It is so because the lower in the direct light, such as Malchut, is higher in the reflected light, as Malchut is the Keter of reflected light, and vice versa. It turns out that Keter and Malchut are of equal level, as are the rest of the Sefirot.

A shortcoming in direct light is always a merit and advantage in reflected light, and vice versa. Thus, the entire ten Sefirot are of equal level (see Inner Observation here, Chap 3).

20. Meaning, even though Yesod has direct light above, called "**before it**", whereas Malchut does not take anything of the upper light before her, since the screen detains it and returns all of it upward, nevertheless they are equal, as he explains further.

30. Meaning the abundance of reflected light of Malchut that Yesod received gives it strength to expand more than its measure, for by the power of that reflected light, it reached the level of Keter.

40. It means that its entire merit over Malchut is that because Malchut is reflected light without direct light, meaning light of departure from Malchut, which returns and draws near to its root. However, Yesod, which receives its part in direct light, is certainly a great merit, although from the perspective of the vessels themselves, meaning the reflected light, they are equal.

It means that after this departing reflected light rose and clothed all the Sefirot and became a vessel for them, from that perspective, they are both equal, since all the direct light captured in the Partzuf is only because of the reflected light. No other Sefira of direct light can shine to the Partzuf. Thus, the direct light and reflected light join equally in the illumination of the Partzuf.

You must remember here what the ARI wrote earlier (this chapter, item 3), that direct light and reflected light are both one and the same light, meaning the light of the look. The reflected light is inferior only in that it is the light of departure from Malchut.

However, now it is the opposite. Any expansion of light in general is dependent on and connected to the reflected light. That makes it completely equal to the direct light, for now it has become the light of expansion, since it became vessels. That is why the ARI writes, "**However, the vessels themselves are equal.**"

50. There is a scribe's error here. It should have said "**When the vapor clothes the light once more,**" because vapor is reflected light that clothes the direct light.

60. Because the Peh is the root of the reflected light and that is why it is a Rosh, meaning Keter.

70. Because reflected light that reaches the Ozen, which is Bina, is the Sefira Hod of reflected light, which is the phase of Guf (see here in Inner Observation, Chap 3).

CHAPTER THIRTEEN

Chapter thirteen explains the matter of coupling by striking of the looking of the Eynaim in AHP, from which the vessels were formed, with an added explanation.

1. A Drush [homily] that I wrote regarding the roots of the emanation of the self and vessels that were made of AHP and Eynaim as sight, sound, smell, and speech. I have found this in the words of Rav Gedaliah Halevi. When the lights expanded from Ozen and Hotem up to opposite the Peh, where all the vapors join, in the place they join they all have the phase of Nefesh.

The vapor of the Ozen cannot connect to the vapor of the Peh, but only at a distance. The same applies for the vapor of the Hotem, but it does not need as great a distance as the vapor of the Ozen to connect to the vapor of the Peh.

For that comes the look of the Eynaim, and the vessels were made in the striking that it struck in this vapor. There is internal and external in this look, as there is internality and externality in all the organs, and thus all their vessels were made. Since no vapor comes out in the sight of the Eynaim, but only a look, only the vessels are made.

2. That look is greater than all the above three vapors because the sight is Yod, the sound is Hey, the smell is Vav and the speech is Hey. Thus we have the four letters HaVaYaH, which are HBTM and are NRNH.

The sight is Haya, Yod of the Name, called Hochma. The upper Hochma shines through the Eynaim, but if actual vapor were to emerge through the Eynaim, it would be impossible to receive it below. For this reason, only a look was extended from it, and it had the strength to make vessels for these three phases: Yod of Neshama in the vapor of Ozen, Yod of Ruach in the vapor of Hotem and Yod of Nefesh in the vapor of Peh. This is the meaning of "From afar the Lord appeared unto me."

Regarding the other vapors, had there been a look from them alone through a screen like the Eynaim, they wouldn't have had the strength to make vessels. All this is judgment, whether in the phase of the expansion of the vapor, or in the look of sight. This Reiah [sight] is Gevura in *Gematria*, and Dibur [speech] with four letters is 216 in *Gematria*.

3. This look comes and strikes at the place where the three vapors join together, which is the phase of Nefesh. This is, "And God saw the Light." The light is the phase of the vapor of Ozen and Hotem, which is the phase of Neshama and Ruach. Et [the] is the phase of Peh, which is Nefesh. And when He saw the Nefesh, then "God divided," which is the making of the roots of the vessels.

4. This look in the direct way made an impression in each and every phase (another version—Roshim, pl. for *Rosh*). It is because it struck every single phase of the look: for the phase of vapor, Keter in Keter. Every impression (another version—beginning) of the vessels was made in this manner, the external ones in the external organs, and the internal ones in the internal organs.

It did not end before the look struck the place where the vapors join, which is the place of the expansion of the vapors, namely their externality. From the striking of the light of vapor with the light of the look, the light of the look returned as reflected light and became a vessel in every phase for the rest of the Guf, the external one for the external organs, and the internal one for the internal organs

5. Since in the look, the more adhesive with the root is higher (1), for Keter (another version—the Keter), which is adjacent to the Ayin, emerged last, and Malchut emerged first (2), when it strikes and returns, all the vessels are equal (3). If Yesod had previously expanded more than Malchut (Yod is equal to Malchut), it would have been because of Malchut (although it is Yesod, for it expanded more) (4).

Because of the light of (over) Malchut, Yesod had the strength to expand further, and it has no merit over Malchut (5). However, because this expansion is as reflected light, it returns and draws near to its origin, but in the vessels themselves they are equal.

Inner Light

1. It means that in the ten Sefirot of reflected light that emerge from the coupling by striking called a look, the Malchut, which is the Peh, called Et, is the root for the ten Sefirot of reflected light. Thus, the more it is adhesive with the root, meaning with the phase of Malchut in the Peh, the higher and more important it is. That is because the reflected light was extended from her and emerged from below upward.

2. Meaning, in the ten Sefirot of direct light, Keter, which is adjacent to the Ayin, emerged first and is the root of every ten Sefirot of direct light, and its level is regarded as higher than all.

However, it is the opposite in the ten Sefirot of reflected light that emerge by the look in Malchut. Malchut in the Peh becomes the root for the ten Sefirot of reflected light and gives the light to all ten Sefirot. Thus, Yesod is second in merit, Hod is third etc., up to the Keter, which is adjacent to the Ayin, which is the last recipient.

He said, "**Keter, which is adjacent to the Ayin, emerged last.**" It means that it is the last to receive the expansion of the reflected light from Malchut.

3. It means that since Keter is first in merit from the perspective of the direct light, Malchut is last in merit, for she receives last, and is the farthest from the root. It is the opposite from the perspective of the expansion of [reflected light]: The Sefira of Malchut became the root and is the first in merit, and Keter is the last.

It turns out that by the clothing of reflected light over direct light, all the vessels become equal, on the exact same level. It is so because all that is better in the ten Sefirot of direct light is regarded as worse in the ten Sefirot of reflected light, and vise-versa, all that is better in ten Sefirot of reflected light, is regarded as worse in the ten Sefirot of direct light. Thus, all the vessels become equal.

4. It means that by the reflected light that emerged from Malchut from below upward, all the Sefirot expanded and ascended on an equal level up to Keter which is adjacent to the Ayin. However, it is all because of the Malchut in the Peh.

It is written that the more Yesod expands inwardly, meaning although it is more internal than Malchut, Malchut clothes it from without. However, this is not regarded as merit because its entire expansion up to Keter is by the strength of Malchut. Thus, Malchut is its root in this expansion of its level and its merit.

It is written, "**Because of the light of [over] Malchut, Yesod had the strength to expand further.**" It means that the reflected light of Malchut made it expand its level more than its measure in the ten Sefirot of direct light. It is therefore not better than its root, which is Malchut.

5. It means that in any case, there is merit in Yesod over Malchut, for her entire merit is only in reflected light. Yesod is superior to her in that he is first in the ten Sefirot of direct light, which is known to be far superior to the reflected light.

However, this is only with respect to the lights. From the perspective of the vessels, their essence is primarily of reflected light, as it is said, "**in the vessels themselves they are equal.**" It is so because the level and the merit of the vessels are extended solely from reflected light. See Part 1, *Panim Masbirot*, Branch 3, where it is explained elaborately.

6. When the light returns and clothes the vapor, meaning when it is adjacent to the Peh, the vapor of the Peh is greater than the vapor of the Ozen, since the vapor of the Peh is now adjacent to the Peh as the phase of Rosh, while the vapor of the Ozen is still regarded as the phase of the rest of the Guf, until it ascends opposite the Ozen.

CHAPTER FOURTEEN

Explains the internality and externality of the five worlds Adam Kadmon and ABYA, and how in every twenty-five degrees of each and every world there are internality and externality. It also divides the level of each and every world. Contains ten issues:

1. The internality and externality of the world of Assiya are souls and wheels. 2. The NRNHY of the general Nefesh are extended from the five Partzufim AA, AVI and ZON of Assiya. 3. Each Partzuf of the five Partzufim of Assiya consists of NRNHY. However, in NRNHY of AA they are all Yechida, in NRNHY of Abba they are all Haya and in NRNHY of Ima they are all Neshama. In ZA they are all Ruach and in Nukva they are all Nefesh, and the level of Malchut in the worlds. 4. In general, the entire light in the world of Assiya is regarded as light of Nefesh, and in particular, it has NRNHY of Nefesh. Each of them contains NRNHY, which are twenty-five degrees. 5. The internality and externality of Yetzira are spirits and angels. Each of them contains five Partzufim AA, AVI and ZON. Each Partzuf contains five phases NRNHY, meaning twenty-five phases, and they are all only light of Ruach, the level of ZA in the worlds. 6. The internality and externality of Beria are souls and a throne, in which there are holy spirits. Each of them contains twenty-five phases, and they are all only light of Neshama, and the level of Bina in the worlds. 7. The internality and externality of Atzilut are the self of the light and the vessels. Each one of them contains twenty-five phases, and they are all light of Haya and the level of Hochma in the worlds. 8. The internality and externality of AK are the self of the light and the vessels. Each one of them contains twenty-five phases and they are all light of Yechida and the level of Keter in the worlds. 9. The NRNHY in each world are internality and the vessels that clothe them are externality. 10. All the worlds are one Partzuf made of ten Sefirot: AK is the Keter in them, the world of Atzilut is Hochma, and Beria is Bina. Yetzira is ZA and Assiya is Malchut. The light in all of them is internality and the vessels in all of them are externality. The internality of all of them is the light of Ein Sof, opposite which everything is externality.

Internality and externality of the world of Assiya are souls and wheels.

1. There is internality and externality (1) in all the worlds. In Assiya, their externality is the wheels (2), and the internality is the souls. However, these souls are in general (3).

Inner Light

1. The light is referred to as internality here, and the vessel as externality. Regarding internality and externality, they should always be understood according to the relevant context.

2. The vessels of the world of Assiya are called wheels, and the lights of the world of Assiya are called Nefesh.

3. Meaning relating to the "general" ten Sefirot, which are the five worlds AK and ABYA, corresponding to KHB, ZA and Malchut, in which Yechida, Haya, Neshama, Ruach and Nefesh are clothed. Accordingly, all the lights of Assiya are regarded as only Malchut and Nefesh. However, in the world of Assiya itself, there are all the NRNHY, as he will explain henceforth.

The NRNHY of the general Nefesh are extended from the five Partzufim AA, AVI and ZON of Assiya.

2. However, this Nefesh is divided into five phases NRNHY. These five phases are in the five Partzufim of Assiya, and they are all Nefesh of the worlds in general.

Each Partzuf of the five Partzufim of Assiya consists of NRNHY. However, in NRNHY of AA they are all Yechida, in NRNHY of Abba they are all Haya and in NRNHY of Ima they are all Neshama. In ZA they are all Ruach and in Nukva they are all Nefesh, and the level of Malchut in the worlds.

3. Also, each Partzuf among them has the above five phases NRNHY. However, being that these five phases are in AA, they are all called Yechida in Assiya. These five phases in Abba are called Haya of Assiya, and these five phases of Ima are all called Neshama. These five phases of ZA are called Ruach and these five phases in Nukva are called Nefesh.

In general, the entire light in the world of Assiya is regarded as light of Nefesh, and in particular, it has NRNHY of Nefesh. Each of them contains NRNHY, which are twenty-five degrees.

4. It turns out that they are twenty-five particular phases (4), but in general they are not more than five phases, which are five Partzufim. However, when evaluated in

relation to the four worlds ABYA, they are all only the phase of Nefesh in their general value.

Inner Light

4. Meaning five Partzufim. Each and every Partzuf has NRNHY. Know that these twenty-five phases are mandatory in each and every world because of the emanation of that one degree, by which that world is discerned, as it is written in Inner Observation here. Thus, it is necessary to discern five Partzufim in the world of Adam Kadmon as well, in which there are ten Sefirot KHB, ZA, Nukva, one below the other, in which the NRNHY of that particular Partzuf clothe.

You should also discern here that there are two kinds of ten Sefirot: the first is the ten Sefirot KHB ZA and Malchut, whose level is equal. It means that they emerge from a single coupling by striking, meaning from a single phase. The second is ten Sefirot KHB ZON one below the other, meaning that they emerge by five couplings by striking because of the refinement of the screen, as it is written above regarding the order of the emanation of the five worlds AK and ABYA.

Know that the mandatory twenty-five phases in each world that are mentioned above in the words of the ARI, relate only to the ten Sefirot one below the other. The ten Sefirot of equal level are regarded only as a single Sefira, named after the highest light in that level (see Chap 9, item 3).

> The internality and externality of Yetzira are spirits and angels. Each of them contains five Partzufim AA, AVI and ZON. Each Partzuf contains five phases NRNHY, meaning twenty-five phases, and they are all only light of Ruach, the level of ZA in the worlds.

5. Similarly, there are two phases in the world of Yetzira, internality and externality. The internality are the spirits, and the externality are the angels.

Each of them has five Partzufim: AA, Abba, Ima, ZA and Nukva. Each Partzuf is divided similarly into five, which are the five phases NRNHY found in Yetzira. Those are divided similarly into five inner phases and five general phases. All of them are only the phase of Ruach and the phase of ZA, in relation to totality of all the worlds.

> The internality and externality of Beria are souls and a throne, in which there are holy spirits. Each of them contains twenty-five phases, and they are all only light of Neshama, and the level of Bina in the worlds.

6. Similarly, Beria too has two phases of internality and externality. The internality is the souls and the externality is the throne, where the holy spirits are. Each of them is divided into twenty-five inner phases and five general phases, and they are all called Neshama and Bina, compared to the value of the worlds.

The internality and externality of Atzilut are the self of the light and the vessels. Each one of them contains twenty-five phases, and they are all light of Haya and the level of Hochma in the worlds.

7. Similarly, Atzilut has two phases of internality and externality. The internality is the lights and the self inside it, and the externality is the vessels. Each phase is divided into twenty-five inner phases and together they are Haya and Hochma, in relation to all the worlds.

The internality and externality of AK are the self of the light and the vessels. Each one of them contains twenty-five phases and they are all light of Yechida and the level of Keter in the worlds.

8. Similarly, in Adam Kadmon there are two phases of internality and externality. The internality is the self inside him, and the externality is the vessels. Although in relation to the rest of the worlds they are not yet called vessels, we shall call them vessels only in relation to their own internality.

Each of them contains all the above phases, and they are generally called Yechida and Keter in relation to all the worlds. It is written in the beginning of *Tikkun 70* (*Zohar, Tikkunim*), "AK is the upper Keter" etc.

The NRNHY in each world are internality and the vessels that clothe them are externality.

9. Know that all the inner ones in each and every world of the five worlds are the phases Yechida, Haya, Neshama, Ruach, and Nefesh in that specific world. Its externality is the vessels and the Guf, in which the Yechida, Haya, Neshama, Ruach and Nefesh clothe.

All the worlds are one Partzuf made of ten Sefirot: AK is the Keter in them, the world of Atzilut is Hochma, and Beria is Bina. Yetzira is ZA and Assiya is Malchut. The light in all of them is internality and the vessels in all of them are externality. The internality of all of them is the light of Ein Sof, opposite which everything is externality.

10. It turns out that all the worlds are regarded as a single Partzuf $_{(5)}$, made of only ten Sefirot. Adam Kadmon, in all his phases, is the Keter in them. The Atzilut is Abba in them, Beria is the Ima in them and Yetzira is the ZA in them. Assiya is the Nukva in them, and they are all one Partzuf.

There is the self, which is the internality, and the vessels, which is the externality. Inside all of them there is light of Ein Sof, in relation to which they are all regarded as vessels and externality, and it is the only self and internality inside of them.

Inner Light

5. This is a very important knowledge that is required for the understanding of many issues, and it should always be remembered. The first understanding is that consequently, when any motion and novelty is done in any world, or in the slightest phase there, that particular movement causes a change in all the worlds from the beginning of the line to the end of Assiya, for better or for worse. It is completely similar to a person: It is inconceivable that only a small part of a single organ among all his organs feels pain or pleasure, without the entire body, head to toe, feeling it. So is this matter, and understand this well.

CHAPTER FIFTEEN

Explains the clothing of the lights in the vessels, some inside the vessels, and some surrounding. Contains six issues:

1. There aren't five vessels of the five phases to NRNHY. 2. There are only three vessels to Nefesh, Ruach, Neshama, but there are no vessels to Haya and Yechida and they became surrounding lights. 3. The three vessels of NRN are regarded as external, medial and internal. 4. The direct light expands from above downward and is almost separated from its place in order to descend to the lower ones. For this reason, it is in complete HaVaYot [pl. for *HaVaYaH*] and the letters are all separated. 5. The reflected light that departs from Malchut and rises upward is Elokim in a square. The letters rise and connect with each other until they come to their root. 6. There is anterior and posterior in the vessels, but there is no anterior and posterior in the lights, but only expansion and departure, direct light and reflected light, because they are all internality.

There aren't five vessels of the five phases to NRNHY.

1. After you have learned all that in general, your eyes should be opened so that you do not err in what is written above, and think that just as there are five phases of NRNHY in each and every Partzuf in each and every world, called internality, so there are five corresponding phases of vessels. This is not the case.

There are only three vessels to Nefesh, Ruach, Neshama, but there are no vessels to Haya and Yechida and they became surrounding lights.

2. The thing is that the vessels are externality and coarseness, and could not clothe all five kinds of Neshama, only the bottom three, which are Nefesh, Ruach, Neshama. Only these had corresponding vessels and bodies. However, Haya and Yechida in each Partzuf (1) do not have corresponding vessels in that Partzuf itself to clothe in, so they remain outside without vessels, as surrounding light.

Inner Light

1. This matter was formed in the world of Nekudim by the force of the important correction of the association of the quality of mercy with judgment (see Inner Light, Chap 10, item 1). The point of Malchut, which is phase four, rose with the screen

in her to the edges of Bina, and phase two was established as a screen and the point of Sium.

Because of this new Sium, the general phase four and phase three came out and were separated from the ten Sefirot of the general phase four. It is so because they were under the above new restriction and could not receive the upper light into them.

Thus, they had to receive the upper light from afar, as surrounding lights. Phase three was separated from the Partzuf and became the phase of the vessel for surrounding light, called garment, which is a vessel for the surrounding light of the light of Hochma, called Haya. The phase four that was separated from the Partzuf became the phase of the hall, which is a vessel for the surrounding light of the light of Keter, called Yechida. This is brought above in the ARI's words (Chap 10, item 1).

The ARI writes here, "and could not clothe all five kinds of Neshama, only the lower three, which are Nefesh, Ruach, Neshama. Only these had corresponding vessels and bodies. However, Haya and Yechida in each Partzuf do not have corresponding vessels in that Partzuf itself to clothe in, so they remain outside without vessels, as surrounding light." It means that when he writes that "they remain outside without vessels," he wishes to say, without inner vessels, because they have become vessels for surrounding light, called garment and hall.

We might ask: Since only the lower vessels were separated, which are phase three, namely ZA, and phase four, namely Malchut, the lights of Ruach and Nefesh should have remained without vessels and become surrounding lights. These are the lights that relate to phase three and phase four. Why then did Haya and Yechida remain without vessels? After all, their vessels are Keter and Hochma, which remained in the Partzuf.

You already know the inverse relation between bestowal, which is extension of light to the Partzuf, and the vessel for reception of the light in the Partzuf. As the ARI wrote for us, every giver gives in the coarser thing, and every receiver must receive in the more refined thing, and this has already been explained above (Inner Light, Chap 11, item 3 and Inner Observation, Part 2, Chap 8).

It has been explained there that the expansion of Ein Sof to make vessels is called bestowal upon the Partzuf. For example, it is known that for illumination of Yechida, the expansion of the light of Ein Sof, must encounter the screen of phase four, meaning the coarser thing. By the striking of the light, reflected light rises and clothes up to Keter, which is the light of Yechida.

If the degree does not have the above coarseness of phase four, but only coarseness of phase three, then the expansion of the light of Ein Sof that strikes the screen raises reflected light to a level that reaches and clothes only the level of Haya. Thus, the bestowal of the light must be at the coarsest degree.

However, the reception of the light that is drawn in the above manner is the opposite. Although the light of Yechida is imparted only by the coarsest thing, which is phase four, still that light of Yechida cannot clothe there, but rather in the most refined thing in the degree, meaning only the vessel of Keter. Similarly, the light of Haya, which is imparted by phase three, does not clothe there, but rather in phase one, which is the most refined in that degree, and it is likewise always.

It therefore follows that because of the separation of phase three and phase four from the Partzuf, they drew far apart and became surrounding lights. For this reason, the giver can no longer bestow upon the Partzuf neither the light of Haya nor the light of Yechida, since bestowing the light of Yechida requires phase four, and bestowing the light of Haya requires phase three, which are by now separated and gone from the Partzuf.

Thus, you evidently see that from now on, the light of Yechida and the light of Haya will be absent from the Partzuf, as phase three and phase four have parted and are gone.

We also understand that the garment, which is the surrounding vessel from phase three, is the surrounding light of the phase of Haya, for it is the light that drew far and disappeared because of its disappearance from the Partzuf. Hence, now it only shines from afar as surrounding light.

It is also clear that the hall became the surrounding light of Yechida, for this is the light that disappeared along with phase four when she disappeared from the Partzuf, and must now shine from afar as surrounding light.

The three vessels of NRN are regarded as external, medial and internal.

3. It therefore follows that in externality, there are only three phases, which are three vessels, external, medial, and internal, so that Nefesh, Ruach, Neshama will clothe within them, as they have corresponding vessels. However, Haya and Yechida do not have corresponding vessels to clothe within them and they remain as surrounding light.

The direct light expands from above downward and is almost separated from its place in order to descend to the lower ones. For this reason, it is in complete HaVaYot [pl. for *HaVaYaH*] and the letters are all separated.

4. Know that there is yet another difference: direct light was almost separated from its place in order to (2) descend and bestow upon the lower ones. For this reason, their HaVaYot (pl. for HaVaYaH), simple and full, are all HaVaYot with letters that are separated from one another.

Inner Light

2. Because the direct light has a way of always expanding in phase four, too, were it not for the screen that detains it there. It is said, **"is almost separated,"** because everything that is received in phase four is regarded as separated from the Emanator because of the disparity of form in phase four.

The reflected light that departs from Malchut and rises upward is Elokim in a square. The letters rise and connect with each other until they come to their root.

5. However, the reflected light (3) is a square such as that: Aleph (א׳), Aleph Lamed (אל״), Aleph Lamed Hey (הלא״), Aleph Lamed Hey Yod (יהלא״), Aleph Lamed Hey Yod Mem (םיהלא״). These letters are always connected, indicating that they rise and are connected to each other until they connect with their root and Emanator, as they wish to depart from the lower ones.

Inner Light

3. Square means that the letters of the Name, meaning the five phases in the screen of the vessel of Malchut, come and join and disappear in one another. The letters imply the five phases of the refinement of the screen. The degree of Keter appears first, being the Aleph of Elokim.

When refined from phase four to phase three, only the level of Hochma appears, which is the Lamed, and the Keter disappears, clothes inside the level of Hochma, and they become Aleph Lamed (א״ל).

When refined to phase two, only the degree of Bina appears, which is the Hey. Thus, the Lamed too, which is Hochma, clothes inside Bina, and they become Aleph, Lamed, Hey (הלא). When refined to phase one, and only the level of ZA appears, which is the Yod, Keter, Hochma and Bina clothe ZA. They become Aleph, Lamed, Hey, Yod (י״הלא).

When refined completely to its root, which is the final Mem (ם), Keter, Hochma, Bina and ZA disappear and join in that final Mem and become (ם"יהלא).

> There is anterior and posterior in the vessels, but there is no anterior and posterior in the lights, but only expansion and departure, direct light and reflected light, because they are all internality.

6. We should thoroughly understand the truth of the matter of anterior and posterior. In the lights they are called expansion and departure, and they are called direct and reflected. In the vessels they are called anterior and posterior. Meaning in the light there is no anterior and posterior, for it is all internality.

INNER OBSERVATION

Direct Light and Reflected Light, containing fifteen chapters that explain thirteen kinds of ten Sefirot

CHAPTER ONE

Containing two issues

1. The ten Sefirot of direct light that are four phases of coarseness where the upper light expands for coupling by striking. 2. These four phases are equal in every single illumination from the beginning of the line to the end of the world of Assiya without any changes among them.

We must understand the difference between the thirteen kinds of ten Sefirot that the ARI introduces in this Part.

1. There are thirteen kinds of ten Sefirot KHB TM that we find here in the ARI's words, and we must know the differences between them: 1. The ten Sefirot KHB TM of direct light that are brought here (Chap. 1, item 3). 2. The ten Sefirot KHB TM of reflected light that are brought here (Chap. 2, items 1, 2). 3. The ten Sefirot called Nefesh, Ruach, Neshama, Haya, Yechida that are brought here (Chap. 2, item 3). 4. The ten Sefirot called root, soul, body, garment, hall that are brought here (Chap. 2, item 3). 5. The ten Sefirot KHB TM of equal level that are brought here (Chap. 3, item 4). 6. The ten Sefirot KHB TM that emerge one above the other, brought here (in Chap. 4, item 1). 7. The ten Sefirot KHB TM that emerge one below the other, like the four Partzufim Abba, Ima, ZA and Nukva, brought here (in Chap 5, item 1 and in Chap. 6, item 4). 8. The ten Sefirot KHB TM of the Rosh of Partzuf, brought here (in Chap. 5, item 3). 9. The ten Sefirot KHB TM of the Toch of the Partzuf through the Tabur, called HGT, brought here (in Chap. 5, item 2). 10. The ten Sefirot KHB TM of the Sof of the Partzuf from Tabur downward, brought here in Chap. 7, called NHY. 11. The ten Sefirot KHB TM called four worlds Atzilut, Beria, Yetzira, and Assiya, brought here (in Chap. 14, items 1, 2, 3). 12. The ten Sefirot KHB TM that are four Partzufim Abba, Ima, ZA, and Nukva, called ABYA of the world of Atzilut, brought here in chapter 15. 13. The ten Sefirot KHB TM called "Inner ABYA" inside each and every Partzuf from the Partzufim of ABYA. The Rosh of each Partzuf is Keter, from the Peh to the Chazeh, it is Atzilut; from Chazeh to the Tabur, it is Beria; and from Tabur downward it is Yetzira and Assiya.

2. There are thirteen kinds of ten Sefirot before us. These kinds all bear the same names and coincide. However, there are great differences between them, requiring

prior knowledge to thoroughly grasp the distinction in each and every kind with its own reasoning and validation. Then we can examine in every place which kind of ten Sefirot it refers to.

There is no degree that does not contain ten Sefirot of direct light

3. The ten Sefirot of direct light, which are the four phases HB TM, and their root, called Keter, have already been explained thoroughly (Part 3, Chap 1, Inner Light, item 9). These ten Sefirot are incorporated in the light Ein Sof itself, and there is no new light in all the worlds except from Ein Sof. Consequently, these four phases of direct light exist equally in each and every illumination from the beginning of the line to the end of Assiya, without any differentiations in them (see Chap 2, item 3 and Inner Light there, item 9).

CHAPTER TWO

Explains the ten Sefirot of reflected light, and containing three issues:

1. The measure of the light that would have been suitable for reception in Malchut, had the screen not pushed it backward, is called reflected light. 2. After the restriction, the reflected light became the vessel of reception for the upper light instead of phase four. 3. Since phase four clothed all the phases of Keter, Hochma, Bina, and Zeir Anpin prior to the restriction, there are five phases of light discerned in the reflected light rejected by it, which clothe the five phases KHB TM of direct light. In item three he explains the ten Sefirot called NRNHY and ten Sefirot called SNGLH.

The ten Sefirot of direct light clothe the ten Sefirot of reflected light

1. Regarding the ten Sefirot of reflected light, brought here in the words of the ARI (Chap 1, items 1, 2, 3), they emerge by the expansion of the light of Ein Sof as coupling by striking on the screen in the vessel of Malchut of direct light. The screen detains the direct light that belongs to the vessel of Malchut so it does not expand within her.

Instead, it pushes it back to its place. This reflected light, meaning the entire measure of light that would have been suitable for reception in the vessel of Malchut, but she did not receive it, and it was pushed back from her, is not regarded as having disappeared from there. Rather, it became a vessel of reception that rises and clothes all four phases of direct light. Hence, there are two phases of ten Sefirot here, clothing one another, as the ten Sefirot of direct light are clothed in the ten Sefirot of reflected light.

The light that would have been suitable for reception in phase four had it not been for the screen that detains it is called reflected light. After the restriction the reflected light became the vessel of reception instead of the restricted phase four

2. Even though all the reflected light that rises is only the light of Malchut, we still discern ten Sefirot in this reflected light. The reason is that only Malchut was the vessel of reception for the entire ten Sefirot prior to the restriction, as the nine Sefirot have no vessels of reception whatsoever. Instead, they are regarded as actual light, as the ARI wrote here (Chap 12, item 1 and Inner Light, item 2).

From the restriction onward, Malchut can no longer receive any direct light. Thus, the reflected light that was rejected by Malchut became the vessel of reception instead of her.

Hence, the light of Malchut from before the restriction is discerned as having five phases of vessels, corresponding to each phase of direct light that Malchut clothed there. Now that the reflected light operates instead of Malchut, we also discern ten Sefirot in this light that was rejected from Malchut, clothing the ten Sefirot of direct light. In addition, we discern five empty phases in the vessel of Malchut, from the light that belongs to her, meaning from what she had prior to the restriction.

Explanation of the ten Sefirot called NRNHY and the ones called SNGLH

3. The difference between the ten Sefirot called KHB TM and the ten Sefirot called Nefesh, Ruach, Neshama, Haya, Yechida, is that the vessels of the ten Sefirot are called KHB TM, and the lights in them are called NRNHY.

The ten Sefirot called root, soul, body, garment, hall bear a specific meaning: they lack ZA and Malchut of vessels, and Haya and Yechida of lights. They have only KHB of vessels, called root, soul, body, and NRN of lights. This happened in the second restriction by the ascent of Malchut to Bina (see here in Chapter 10).

CHAPTER THREE

Explains the ten Sefirot of equal level. Containing five issues:

1. A spiritual acquires its place wherever it passes. Thus, all the lower Sefirot remain in the upper ones, because they passed through them. 2. The ten Sefirot of direct light and the ten Sefirot of reflected light stand in opposite order. 3. The ten Sefirot of reflected light complete each and every Sefira into ten Sefirot. 4. Malchut of reflected light that joined with Keter of direct light acquired the level of Keter. Moreover, since it passed through all the Sefirot, they all acquired the level of Keter. 5. Ten Sefirot emerged lengthwise and ten Sefirot thick-wise.

1. We shall now explain the ten Sefirot of equal level: If the level of the coupling reaches up to Keter, then it contains a hundred Sefirot which are Keter through Malchut thick-wise, clothing one over the other. Each of them contains ten Sefirot lengthwise from Keter to Malchut.

If the level of the coupling is up to Hochma, they have nine Sefirot thick-wise, each containing nine Sefirot lengthwise. If the level of the coupling is up to Bina, they have eight Sefirot thick-wise, each having eight Sefirot lengthwise, and so on similarly. This applies to each and every coupling by striking of the upper light on the screen. It is brought here in the words of the ARI in Chapter 1.

2. The reason for it is that wherever it is said that something spiritual moves from one place to another, it does not mean that it left the first place and came to a second place, as in corporeality. It only implies an addition, as it remains entirely in the first place as it was even after it comes to the second place. It turns out that a second place has been added, for there is no absence in the spiritual.

Since the Sefira of Keter is the root of the four phases HB TM of direct light, they necessarily pass through it. It follows that they have left their roots in it, for there is no absence in the spiritual. Thus, the Sefira of Keter alone necessarily contains all nine Sefirot KHB, HGT, NHY of direct light.

It is the same with the Sefira of Hochma. Bina and TM passed through her and thus set their place in her. Thus, there are eight Sefirot in the Sefira of Hochma, from Hochma to Yesod. It is also the same with Bina, where TM passed through her and set their place in her. Thus Bina has seven Sefirot from Bina to Yesod. It is also the same in HGT NHY in Tifferet and in Malchut.

Thus, Keter consists of nine Sefirot KHB HGT NHY of direct light, excluding Malchut, as Malchut has no direct light, but only reflected light. Hochma consists of eight Sefirot; HB HGT NHY of direct light, and Bina consists of seven Sefirot – Bina, HGT NHY of direct light. Hesed consists of six Sefirot HGT NHY of direct light and so on similarly. Each upper Sefira consists of all the lower Sefirot that had passed inside her, as there is no absence in the spiritual (as has already been explained in Part 2, Inner Observation, Chapter 9).

3. This aforementioned incorporation happened by the force of the ten Sefirot KHB TM of direct light themselves even before the coupling by striking was made on the screen that raises reflected light and clothes them. However, after the coupling by striking was done on the screen in Malchut and the reflected light rose from the screen in Malchut and clothed the Sefirot of direct light, the reflected light equalizes the level of all of them.

For example, if the coupling by striking had been on screen of phase four that raises reflected light to Keter, the ten Sefirot of reflected light KHB, HGT, NHYM, emerged here from Malchut and clothed the KHB HGT NHY of direct light. Thus, the ten Sefirot of reflected light are in reverse order from the ten Sefirot of direct light.

It is so because the root of the ten Sefirot of direct light is up in Keter and they stand from above downward, from Keter to Yesod. However, the root of the ten Sefirot of reflected light is in Malchut, as they emerged from her, and it is discerned that they stand from below upward. Keter of reflected light, meaning the root, is in Malchut, and Hochma of reflected light is in Yesod of direct light. Bina of reflected light is in Hod of direct light and Hesed of reflected light is in Netzah of direct light. Gevura of reflected light is in Tifferet of direct light and Tifferet of reflected light is in Gevura of direct light. Netzah of reflected light is in Hesed of direct light and Hod of reflected light is in Bina of direct light. Yesod of reflected light is in Hochma of direct light, and Malchut of reflected light is in Keter of direct light. Thus, they stand from below upward beginning in Malchut and ending in Keter.

4. When the ten Sefirot of reflected light join with the ten Sefirot of direct light, there are ten Sefirot in each of them. Thus, Malchut, which did not have any direct light, gained complete ten Sefirot of reflected light from Keter to Malchut. It is so because they all went through her and remained in her permanently, as there is no absence in the spiritual.

Yesod of direct light, which had only one Sefira of direct light, now has nine Sefirot of reflected light, from Hochma to Malchut, as all of them went through him. Hod of direct light, which had only two Sefirot, now acquired eight Sefirot of reflected light from Bina to Malchut. Netzah of direct light, which had three Sefirot, acquired seven Sefirot from Hesed to Malchut.

It follows similarly until Hochma of direct light, which had eight Sefirot of direct light HB HGT NHY, now acquired Yesod and Malchut of reflected light and was completed in ten Sefirot. Keter of direct light, having nine Sefirot KHB HGT NHY of direct light, has now acquired Malchut of reflected light and was completed in ten Sefirot.

5. It turns out that Malchut of reflected light acquired the level of Keter, for she has joined with Keter of direct light. Yesod of reflected light acquired the level of Hochma, for he has joined with Hochma of direct light, and Hod acquired the level of Bina as it joined with Bina.

It is therefore considered that Hochma of direct light acquired the level of Keter, since the Malchut of reflected light that has joined with Keter, has become the level of Keter, went through Hochma and was set there. Thus, Hochma too acquired the level of Keter.

Similarly, Bina of direct light acquired the level of Keter because Yesod and Malchut of reflected light that became Hochma and Keter went through her and left their roots in her. Similarly, each and every Sefira of direct light acquired the level of Keter, because of Malchut of reflected light that had connected with Keter, necessarily went through them and was set in them. Hence, after the reflected light rose and connected with the direct light, all the Sefirot became equal in their level, up to Keter.

6. It is considered that that incorporation, where each and every Sefira was incorporated with ten Sefirot by the joining of the direct light with the reflected light, is thick-wise, clothing one another. This is because of their equal level.

Thus, in their internality, all ten Sefirot of Keter stand lengthwise from Keter to Malchut. They are clothed thick-wise by ten Sefirot of Hochma that stand lengthwise from Keter to Malchut. Ten Sefirot of Bina clothe them from Keter to Malchut, etc., until the ten Sefirot in Malchut clothe outside all of them from Keter to Malchut.

It turns out that a hundred Sefirot must emerge from every coupling by striking of the upper light on the screen of phase four, namely ten Sefirot lengthwise, each of which expands into ten Sefirot thick-wise, and all of them are on an equal level up to Keter.

Similarly, from the coupling by striking on the screen of phase three, nine Sefirot of phase three emerge lengthwise and nine Sefirot thick-wise, whose level is equal, up to Hochma. Similarly, in the coupling by striking of phase two, eight Sefirot emerge lengthwise and eight Sefirot thick-wise, whose level is equal, up to Bina, and so on similarly.

CHAPTER FOUR

Explains the ten Sefirot that emerge one above the other, and contains two issues:

1. Each one hundred Sefirot that emerge by coupling by striking at an equal level are regarded as merely one Sefira. 2. The ten Sefirot of equal level emerge from a single coupling by striking, and the ten Sefirot that emerge one above the other emerge from five couplings by striking.

Five levels of ten Sefirot emerge from the five phases of coarseness, one above the other, through refinement.

1. We shall now explain the ten Sefirot that emerge one above the other. Know that because of the five phases in the above vessel of Malchut, five levels emerge through the abovementioned coupling by striking, one above the other, due to the refinement of the screen and its appearance in the above five phases of coarseness in the vessel of Malchut.

When the screen is over the complete coarseness in the vessel of Malchut, called the coarseness of phase four, it is considered that there are five phases in the light reflected from her. Therefore, they clothe all five phases of direct light.

However, if the coarseness of phase four is refined, the reflected light repelled from it is too short to clothe the phase of Keter of direct light, for it has only four phases. This matter is already explained sufficiently in Inner Observation (Part 2, item 72), study it there, and there is no need to elaborate on it here.

2. However, we must know that any expansion of upper light for a coupling by striking by the order of degrees of the five phases of coarseness in the above screen, although there are one hundred Sefirot in every expansion, which are ten Sefirot lengthwise and ten Sefirot thick-wise, it is still regarded as only one Sefira, named after the highest Sefira in it. If the highest one is Keter, they are all called Keter; if its level is the Sefira of Hochma, they are all called Hochma, and so on similarly.

3. Thus, these five levels that emerge because of the refinement of the screen, one above the other, from the level of Keter to the level of Malchut, are regarded as merely five Sefirot KHB TM. Although each of the levels has ten Sefirot lengthwise and ten Sefirot thick-wise, still, because all these one hundred Sefirot are on the same level, they are regarded as a single Sefira named after the highest one.

4. You can therefore see the great difference between the ten Sefirot of equal level and the ten Sefirot one above the other. The ten Sefirot of equal level emerge from a single coupling by striking and are all regarded as a single Sefira. However, the ten Sefirot KHB TM emerging one above the other emerge by five couplings of striking because the screen is refined gradually from phase four to phase three, and so on, up to the root.

Each of them contains ten Sefirot lengthwise and ten Sefirot thick-wise at an even level. Hence, these five levels are regarded merely as KHB TM, one above the other, named after the highest Sefirot in these five levels.

Thus we have explained the great differences between the five kinds of ten Sefirot, namely: the ten Sefirot of direct light as they are in and of themselves; the ten Sefirot of direct light and reflected light whose level is equal; the ten Sefirot of NRNHY; the ten Sefirot SNGLH; and the ten Sefirot one above the other.

CHAPTER FIVE

Explains the ten Sefirot of Rosh and Toch emerging one below the other, and containing four issues:

1. A Partzuf means a complete degree that contains three times ten Sefirot of Rosh, Toch, Sof. 2. The ten Sefirot of Rosh are but roots for the vessels, as the coarseness of the screen cannot ascend from below upward. 3. After the reflected light descends and expands to ten Sefirot from above downward to the Tabur, it creates ten Sefirot of complete vessels, called ten Sefirot of Toch. 4. Malchut of the Rosh is called Peh; Malchut of the Guf is called Tabur.

1. Now we shall explain the ten Sefirot that emerge one below the other, which are five Partzufim AA, Abba, Ima, ZA and Nukva. We shall first explain the difference between a Sefira and a Partzuf, which is indeed a great difference. A Sefira is either a single phase of direct light, or ten Sefirot clothed in reflected light at an equal level. A Partzuf, however, is a complete degree, which is complete in and of itself, as complete vessels, and as the Sium of the degree. Thus, each Partzuf must have three specific phases of ten Sefirot: ten Sefirot of Rosh, ten Sefirot of Toch, and ten Sefirot of Sof.

The reflected light that rises from the coupling by striking from below upward is but roots for vessels and not complete vessels. They are ten Sefirot of Rosh

2. The issue of the Partzuf has been explained here in the words of the ARI (Chap 12, items 3, 4, see Inner Light), but in order to understand it thoroughly I must elaborate here. You already know that from the restriction downward Malchut stopped being a vessel for reception of the light of Ein Sof. Instead, the reflected light that rises from her becomes the vessel of reception.

It has also been explained (Inner Light, Chap 12) that the reflected light that rises from Malchut upward is not regarded as complete vessels of reception, but are only regarded as roots for the vessels. It is so because the force of the screen and the coarseness in the vessel of Malchut cannot rise from the place of Malchut upward even a bit. Only afterwards, when the reflected light descends and expands the vessel of Malchut into ten Sefirot from her and within her, from above downward, are the vessels completed (see Inner Light, Chap 2, item 3). Study it there, for here is not the place to elaborate.

The reflected light that expands from Malchut downward makes the vessels for the Toch of the Partzuf

3. According to the above, it is thoroughly understood that the ten Sefirot must first expand for a coupling by striking, in order to raise ten Sefirot of reflected light to clothe the direct light as roots for the vessels. These ten Sefirot, clothed by the reflected light that rises from below upward, are called ten Sefirot of Rosh. It means that they are the beginning for the vessels, meaning only roots.

To complete the vessels, the reflected light must descend and expand from Malchut downward, with the entire level of direct light that clothed the Rosh from Malchut upward. It is by that expansion that the vessels are made and completed. This expansion is called Guf, or the Toch of the Partzuf, as the ARI explained (Chap 12, item 5).

The ten Sefirot of Rosh are called a look and the ten Sefirot of Toch are called an expansion. Malchut of the Rosh is called Peh and Malchut of the Guf is called Tabur

4. Now we have thoroughly clarified the necessity for the ten Sefirot of the Rosh and ten Sefirot of the Guf, which must be in every Partzuf, since we first need a coupling by striking in order to reveal the reflected light as ten Sefirot that are the roots for the vessels.

When they expand from Malchut downward, the ten Sefirot emerge as complete vessels, called Guf or ten Sefirot of Toch. You should also know that the ARI refers to the coupling by striking that raises the reflected light from Malchut upward as ten Sefirot of Rosh, as a "look".

The ARI calls the ten Sefirot of the Guf that descend from Malchut of Rosh downward, as "expansion." You should also know that Malchut of the Rosh is called Peh, and Malchut of the Guf is called Tabur or Malchut of Malchut of the Rosh, and remember this.

CHAPTER SIX

Thoroughly explains the issue of the ten Sefirot of the Toch, which
are KHB TM that emerge one above the other, containing four issues:

1. The first look is in the Peh of the Rosh to create the roots for the vessels. The second look is in the Tabur to make the complete vessels. 2. Although we need the coarsest vessel for the extension of the degree, still the light that is drawn by that coarseness clothes the more refined vessel. 3. Once the vessel of phase four was refined, the vessel of Malchut was completed, since with respect to the clothing, phase four is regarded as Malchut, and when phase three was refined, the vessel of ZA was completed etc. 4. After the five vessels KHB TM were refined and imprinted one above the other, the light returned and clothed them once again.

Elaborate explanation for the ten Sefirot of Toch that emerge one above the other

1. These words are also brought in the ARI's words (*Tree of Life, Heichal AK Shaar AHP*, Chapter 3). He ends it there with these words, "**But the vessels to the Guf, which are ZAT, still do not have this power in the sight to hit the Nefesh of Nefesh herself. By the second look from below upward, which are the light of Akudim and the light of the Ayin [eye], the light returned and clothed the ZAT.**"

Why the second look is needed for the vessels

2. In these words of the ARI you see how he elaborates and makes the precision that a second look is needed in the vessels of the Guf, besides the look in the Rosh. It is so because they need to have two phases of lights, which are the light of Akudim and the light of Ayin. We should seemingly ask: "Why was the expansion of the ten Sefirot of reflected light from Malchut downward, to produce the ten Sefirot of the Guf, not enough, and a second look was needed?"

Only one level of ten Sefirot emerged in the first look. In the second look, five levels from five couplings emerged, one above the other

3. We learn from the aforesaid (Chapter 4, item 4) that the ten Sefirot that emerge at once through a coupling by striking, and whose level is equal, are regarded as only one Sefira. It means that they are named after the uppermost Sefira in that level. Thus, by the first look that raised the reflected light from Malchut upward to the

ten Sefirot of Rosh, whose level is equal, and also by their expansion from Malchut downward, the ten Sefirot of the Guf emerged here, on an equal level.

However, here there is still only one Sefira in the Rosh, and a Sefira in the Guf. Also, you already know that a degree is not completed with less than ten Sefirot. For this reason, a second look is needed. Through the second look, ten complete Sefirot emerge, which are five levels KHB TM one above the other by five couplings by striking that come as a result of the refinement of the screen (see Inner Light, Chapter 12, item 8).

Regarding the clothing of the lights in the vessels, the more refined clothes a greater light

4. Know that these above five levels that emerge in the Guf by the second look emerge from below upward. First, Malchut emerges, then ZA, then Bina, and above them all Keter. The reason is (as written in Inner Light Chapter 11, item 3) that although bestowal of the more important level requires a coarser vessel, still the light that is drawn by that coarseness cannot clothe there.

It is so because the more important light clothes in the more refined vessel. It follows that although phase four of the vessel of Malchut draws the more important light, meaning the level of Keter, nevertheless, the light of Keter cannot clothe in that vessel of Malchut of phase four, but only in the vessel of Malchut that is completely refined from any coarseness, meaning after it has become as refined as the root phase, and likewise all of them.

The vessels emerged one above the other, from Malchut to the vessel of Keter

5. It therefore turns out that after Malchut had been refined from phase four to phase three, the vessel of phase four remained without light. The vessel of Malchut that is suitable for the lower light, meaning that which is called the light of Nefesh, was formed from that.

After that she was refined from phase three to phase two, and the vessel of Malchut of phase three was left without light as well. That formed the vessel of ZA, suitable for the light of Ruach, which is one degree higher than the light of Nefesh.

Then, when she was refined from phase two to phase one, phase two of Malchut was left without light, as well, thus forming the vessel of Bina, suitable for the light of Neshama. Then, when she was refined from phase one to the root phase, and phase one of Malchut was left without light, as well, the vessel of Hochma was formed, suitable for the light of Haya.

The root phase of Malchut is suitable for the light of Keter, called the light of Yechida. After these five vessels KHB ZA and Malchut were formed one above the other, the upper light returned and clothed them.

An inverse relation between the extension of the lights and the clothing of the lights in the vessels. In an extension, the coarser is more important, while in clothing, the more refined is more important

6. The coupling by striking on the screen of phase four produces ten Sefirot on the level of Keter and in the light of Yechida. Also, when a part of the coarseness of phase four is refined from Malchut, the level of Keter disappears from there. However, that part of Malchut of phase four becomes only a vessel for light of Malchut, which is Nefesh.

Also, a part of the coarseness of phase three in the vessel of Malchut produces the level of Hochma in the light of Haya through the coupling by striking. When that part of the coarseness of phase three was refined from Malchut, the level of Hochma disappeared. However, that part of Malchut of phase three became only a vessel for the light of ZA, which is Ruach.

It is likewise with the part of the coarseness of phase two – the vessel for the light of Neshama, the part of the coarseness of phase one – the vessel for the light of Haya, and her part that was refined to the root phase, and became a vessel for the light of Yechida.

The five vessels KHB TM were made in the second look

7. Thus, in the second look performed during the refinement of the screen, five vessels emerge and are made one above the other. Malchut emerges first, then ZA, then Bina and Hochma, and then Keter.

8. The ARI wrote that "**by the second look from below upward, which are the light of Akudim and the light of the Ayin, the light returned and clothed the ZAT**". He wishes to say that by the second look during the refinement of the screen, it performs four couplings by striking from below upward. Thus, it produces the ten Sefirot to clothe the ZAT, meaning for the light of the Guf of the Partzuf, called the lower seven.

The ten Sefirot that expand from the Peh to the Tabur are called Akudim. The light that expands for coupling by striking is called a look

312

9. It is said that "**they are the light of Akudim and the light of Ayin**". It is so because the five parts of the above Malchut, standing from Malchut of the Rosh to Malchut of Malchut, are called Akudim. It is so because all the lights are Akudim [tied] in one vessel, namely Malchut, as they are all parts of Malchut. The light that expands for striking as the above second look is called the light of the Ayin.

CHAPTER SEVEN

Explains the ten Sefirot of the Sof of the Partzuf, and containing three issues:

1. The coarseness of the screen does not control in the ten Sefirot of Toch because Malchut of Malchut that ends the lights is below, in the Tabur, and her coarseness cannot affect above her place. However, in the ten Sefirot of Sof, where the ending Malchut is above them, the coarseness of the screen controls them. 2. Thus, the ten Sefirot of Sof are called female light, since she receives and does not bestow, for she is only suitable for receiving reflected light. 3. Because of this, they end the Partzuf and stop its illumination.

The difference between Peh and Tabur, and from Tabur downward

1. There is great significance to the fact that the ARI always refers to every Guf by the name "seven lower Sefirot." You already know that the coarseness and the boundary in Malchut operate only during the illumination of the reflected light from above downward, meaning from Malchut downward.

Know that here there is a great difference between the illumination of reflected light from above downward, before the clothing of the light in the complete vessels, meaning from Peh to Tabur, and the illumination of the reflected light from above downward, after there is clothing in complete vessels, meaning from Tabur downward.

It is so because from above downward prior to the clothing is called the "Toch of the Partzuf," meaning the essence of the Partzuf, for the entire direct light in the Partzuf is clothed there. That place is called "from the Peh to the Tabur of the Partzuf," where Peh is the Keter of Malchut and Tabur is Malchut of Malchut.

The ten Sefirot of Sof of the Partzuf are reflected light

2. The reflected light that descends from above downward, after the clothing in the vessels is completed, is regarded as the ten Sefirot of the Sium of the Partzuf. That place is called "From Tabur downward," to the Sium of the Partzuf.

The Tabur is Malchut of Malchut. From the restriction onward she can no longer receive any direct light. Hence, the same ten Sefirot from the Peh to the Tabur, though they sparkle below the Tabur as well, since direct light is not extended with the sparkling, but only reflected light, it is thus regarded as female light, meaning receiving and not bestowing. Also, there is no bestowal and expansion in these ten Sefirot, and therefore they end that degree.

Anything that the lower one causes in the upper one is also granted to the lower one. There is still no reception in the Peh

3. We could ask: "Therefore, how does the direct light pass from the Peh downward, since the Peh, too, is the phase of Malchut, who does not receive direct light from the restriction onward?" You already know that the restriction was done on phase four in the sense of her being a vessel of reception, meaning after Malchut had already expanded by herself, and clothed the entire upper light.

However, the Peh, which is Malchut of the Rosh, operating there from below upward, meaning that she does not have any vessels of reception, but only raises reflected light from her upward. Thus, because she caused the expansion of the ten Sefirot of the Rosh, she can also expand from there downward, from her and within her, over the four phases HB TM.

The first three phases: Hochma, Bina, and Tifferet in Malchut, are suitable for receiving direct light. Only Malchut of Malchut, namely Tabur, is considered the vessel of Malchut here. The restriction rides over her and she cannot receive within her any of the direct light.

The Tabur that has come to receive is unfit for expansion with direct light, but only in reflected light

4. From this you can always discern that the Malchut that operates from below upward has the ability to expand from her and within her over four phases, and she receives direct light in the first three phases. However, the Malchut that already operates from above downward, meaning the Malchut within that Malchut that expanded, is no longer fit for receiving any direct light within her, because the force of the restriction is already riding over her. The Malchut that operates from below upward is called Keter of Malchut, or Peh. The Malchut that operates from above downward is called Malchut of Malchut, or Nefesh of Nefesh, or Tabur.

In the Rosh, there are only roots for the vessels, in the Toch, vessels for direct light, in the Sof, only reflected light

5. We have clarified the difference between the Rosh, Toch, and Sof of every Partzuf. The ten Sefirot of Rosh do not have complete vessels of reception, as the reflected

315

light that rises and clothes them from below upward is not regarded as vessels, but are useful only for capturing the direct light in the Partzuf. In this manner, it can afterwards sparkle and pass from above downward, and for this reason they are called roots for the vessels.

The ten Sefirot of the Toch of the Partzuf from Peh to Tabur are the complete vessels where most of the clothing of the direct light in the Partzuf occurs. The ten Sefirot of the Sof of the Partzuf are regarded as female light since they are reflected light without direct light. They receive and do not bestow, and therefore end the Partzuf and stop its lights.

Chapter Eight

Begins to explain the order of the cascading of the ten Sefirot that emerge one below the other, called AA, AVI, and ZON, or Galgalta, AB, SAG, MA and BON that are emanated from one another through cause and effect, and contains three issues:

1. The first ten Sefirot that emerged after the restriction are called Adam Kadmon. 2. Adam Kadmon is called the world of Keter because phase four operates in it for coupling by striking. 3. The coupling for every Partzuf is in its upper Partzuf.

Explaining the reason for the cascading of the five Partzufim GASMB and their emergence from one another

1. We shall now explain the order of the cascading of the Partzufim from one another, and how they are generated by one another by the necessity of cause and effect. To use fewer words and broader meaning, we shall refer to the five phases of the Rosh as: Galgalta, Eynaim, Ozen, Hotem, Peh, and the five phases of the Guf as: Keter, Hochma, Bina, Zeir Anpin, and Malchut.

We shall refer to the refinement of the screen as an ascent, because an ascent means refinement. When we want to say, for instance, that phase four was refined into phase three, we shall say that Malchut ascended to ZA. Make certain you do not forget that.

Four fillings in the four letters HaVaYaH, which are ASMB

2. We shall refer to the names of the five Partzufim AA, Abba, Ima, ZA, Nukva as: Galgalta, AB, SAG, MA, BON, in accordance with the Gematria of the four fillings of the name HaVaYaH. We shall call Partzuf AA, which is the Keter, by the name Galgalta.

Partzuf Abba, which is Hochma, also called AVI, shall be called AB, which is HaVaYaH filled with Yodin (pl. for Yod), like this: Yod (דוי), Hey (יה), Vav (ויו), Hey (יה), which amount to AB (72).

Partzuf Ima, which is Bina, also called YESHSUT, shall be called SAG, which is HaVaYaH filled with Yodin, and with Aleph in the Vav, like that: Yod (דוי), Hey (יה), Vav (ואו), Hey (יה), which amount to SAG (63).

Partzuf ZA shall be called MA, which is HaVaYaH filled with Alephin [pl. for Aleph] like that: Yod (דוי), He (אה), Vav (ואו), He (אה), which amount to MA (45). Partzuf Nukva, which is Malchut, shall be called BON, which is HaVaYaH, filled with Heyin [pl. for Hey] like that: Yod (דוי), Heh (הה), Vav (ואו), Heh (הה).

The reason for these fillings and calculations has been explained in my book "Panim Meirot u Masbirot," regarding the 288 sparks, and there is nothing to add here.

The first ten Sefirot in the line of Ein Sof are called the world of Adam Kadmon. Its level reaches Keter. The coupling for each Partzuf should be in its upper one

3. You already know that the first ten Sefirot that were emanated after the restriction are called Adam Kadmon. It contains five *Partzufim*, Galgalta, AB, SAG, MA, BON, each of which contains its own Rosh, Toch, Sof, as has been explained above. It is generally called the world of Keter, or the world of Adam Kadmon. The reason its entirety is called Keter has been explained in "Inner Light," that it is because the screen of phase four, in its true measure, does not operate in any other world.

You should know that the coupling by striking for the ten Sefirot of Rosh of each Partzuf must be in the Peh of Rosh of its upper Partzuf. It is as the ARI explained here (Part 3, item 12) regarding the four worlds ABYA, that the coupling for ten Sefirot of Atzilut was done in the world above Atzilut, namely AK, and that for Beria it was done in Atzilut etc.

CHAPTER NINE

Explains the order of the emanation of Partzuf Galgalta of AK, and
contains three issues:

1. The first expansion of the light of Ein Sof for a coupling by striking. 2. The
coupling was done on a screen of phase four that raises reflected light up to Keter,
and ten Sefirot of Rosh, ten Sefirot of Toch and ten Sefirot of Sof, emerged. 3. The
reason that Malchut can expand from the Peh downward into ten Sefirot of the
Guf is that all the light that the lower one causes in the upper one, the lower one is
also rewarded with it. Since Malchut with its reflected light caused the ten Sefirot
of Rosh to be captured, she therefore acquired ten Sefirot, as well.

The ten Sefirot of Rosh of Galgalta of AK

1. We shall first explain Partzuf Galgalta of AK, which is the first Partzuf in the
world of AK. First, you already know that Ein Sof expands until the coupling by
striking on the screen in the vessel of Malchut. At that time, the reflected light
rejected from the vessel of Malchut rises and clothes the four phases of direct light
up to the level of Keter.

You also know that this clothing of the ten Sefirot of direct light in the ten Sefirot
of reflected light is called ten Sefirot of Rosh, meaning roots to the vessels. It is
so because the clothing of reflected light from below upward is sufficient only to
capture the light in the Partzuf, but not to actually clothe it.

The reason for the expansion of Malchut of Rosh for ten Sefirot is that each degree that causes light in its upper one, it, too, is rewarded with it

2. It is known that the law in the upper worlds is that any degree that causes an addition of light to its upper one, that entire addition of light returns and is imparted
also to the degree that caused it. Thus, since Malchut did not receive the light that
belongs to her, and returned it back to its place, meaning it is the reflected light that
became a clothing for the upper light, by which it captured the upper light in the
Rosh. Without this reflected light, this upper light would not have been captured
there at all.

It therefore necessitates that the entire level of ten Sefirot of Rosh that she caused
there will return and expand into the vessel of Malchut herself, as well. It is like ZA,

about which it is said: "Three emerge from one; one exists in three." Here, too, in Malchut, since nine Sefirot emerge from one, one exists in nine Sefirot, and both are called Guf.

The ten Sefirot of the Toch of Galgalta of AK

3. Thus, the reflected light will once more shine in the vessel of Malchut, in a way that expands her to the five phases KHB TM. The ten Sefirot of direct light of the Rosh also sparkle and expand in the ten Sefirot of Malchut, meaning to the Malchut in her, called Tabur. These above five phases of the expansion of Malchut become complete vessels for clothing the upper light in the Partzuf, which is why they are called Guf (see Inner Light, Part 3, item 3, and Chapter 3, item 1).

The ten Sefirot of Sof of Galgalta of AK

4. From the Tabur downward, the upper light can no longer expand there due to the restriction and the screen in it. Thus, there is only an illumination of reflected light there, without direct light, which doesn't have the power to expand, and therefore end the Partzuf (Chapter 7, item 2). Thus the Rosh, Toch, Sof of the first Partzuf of AK, called Galgalta, have been explained.

CHAPTER TEN

Explains the second Partzuf of AK, called AB, and contains four issues:

1. The Surrounding light refines the screen of phase four into phase three. The upper light, which doesn't stop shining, struck it, and the screen raised reflected light and clothed the ten Sefirot of direct light up to Hochma. It is called AB of AK. 2. There is no "some" in the spiritual. Thus, prior to receiving the coarseness of phase three, she had been completely refined to the root. 3. The refinement to the root is called an ascent from the Tabur to the Peh. 4. After the screen acquired the coarseness of phase three, while it was in its root in the Peh of Galgalta, it came back down to its place—the place of Chazeh of Galgalta of AK. A coupling by striking was done on it and Rosh, Toch and Sof of the Partzuf AB of AK emerged from the Peh [Chazeh] of Galgalta of AK downward.

Surrounding light refines the screen of phase four to phase three

1. You already know the law of refinement that applies to the coarseness of the vessel of Malchut. It states that even though the coarseness in the vessel of Malchut draws and causes the entire level of the Partzuf, still, after the upper light is drawn there and clothes the Partzuf, it is the nature of the surrounding light to refine the coarseness in Malchut (see Inner Observation, Part 2, item 72). Thus, after the upper light clothed in the above Partzuf Galgalta of AK, it caused a refinement of the coarseness of phase four in the screen in Malchut in it. Because of it, a new screen on Malchut of phase three emerged.

The emergence of ten Sefirot of the Rosh at the level of Hochma on the screen of phase three

2. The upper light does not stop shining for the emanated beings for even a moment. Consequently, at the very moment when a screen on the coarseness of phase three is initiated, the light of Ein Sof promptly expands to it for a coupling by striking, when Malchut raises reflected light and clothes the upper light. However, because the coarseness of phase four has become absent, the measure of reflected light that is rejected and rises from Malchut has been diminished, and no longer reaches clothing the level of Keter as before, but only the level of Hochma.

The level of Hochma has been separated into its own Partzuf, called AB of AK

3. You already know that just as corporeal matters are separated from one another by a distance of location, spiritual matters are separated from one another by the disparity of form that is initiated in them. The measure of the distance is as the measure of the disparity between them.

Therefore, once the screen of phase three has been initiated and emerged inside Partzuf Galgalta of AK, with the new level of light, that disparity of form now separates and detaches that new level into its own distinct phase. We thus distinguish this new level as a second Partzuf of AK, called Partzuf AB of AK, reaching only up to Hochma.

AB of AK emerged from the coupling by striking on the screen of phase three that was done in the Peh of Partzuf Galgalta of AK

4. Thus we find that the reason and the cause for the emanation of the second Partzuf of AK is the law of refinement that always operates in the coarseness of the screen in the vessel of Malchut, because of the clothing of the upper light. Thus, after the completion of the clothing of upper light in the first Partzuf of AK, called Galgalta, the coarseness of phase four in the screen of Malchut had been refined to the measure of the coarseness of phase three. Consequently, this coupling by striking that is done in the screen of phase three that ascended to the Peh of Galgalta of AK, emanated the second Partzuf of AK at the level of Hochma, called Partzuf AB of AK.

The refinement of the coarseness in the screen to the phase of coarseness of the root is regarded as an ascent to the Peh of Rosh

5. However, it does not mean that immediately after Malchut had been refined from phase four and stood at the coarseness of phase three, Partzuf AB was emanated and emerged there. This is so because there is no "some" in the spiritual, and it is utterly impossible that some coarseness will be refined from Malchut and some coarseness will remain in Malchut.

Rather, since Malchut began to be refined, she must continue to be refined from all her coarseness until she is completely refined, when she is like the root phase in her, where the light of Keter is clothed (Chapter 6, item 4). Know that this refinement to the root is called "the ascent of Malchut to Keter", or "the ascent of Tabur to the Peh of Rosh," since the Peh is the Keter of Malchut and Tabur is the Malchut of Malchut (see Chapter 7, item 4).

An ascent means refinement, and a descent means growing coarser

6. You must remember here that an ascent means refinement, and a descent means growing coarser. More refined is regarded as higher. The issue of the standing of the ten Sefirot KHB ZA and Malchut of the Guf of the Partzuf one above the other, from the Peh to the Tabur, does not refer to an imaginary place whatsoever, but only to the matter of refinement and coarseness.

Thus, Keter, being the most refined vessel, is regarded as standing near the Peh of the Rosh of the Partzuf, meaning above them all. Malchut, who is the coarsest, is regarded as standing below, at the place of Tabur of the Guf of the Partzuf, meaning below them all.

Equivalence of form of the lower one with the upper one is regarded as coming to the place of the upper one

7. However, you should understand simply that when we say that Malchut was refined from the coarseness of phase four in her and remained as refined as her root phase, it follows that because of it, she truly came to the place of her root, meaning her Keter, called Peh, since being as refined as he is, she is with him on the same degree.

After the screen rose and became incorporated in the Peh of Galgalta, the coarseness was renewed in it, except for the last phase

8. Thus, when Malchut is completely refined and remains in the root phase, she thus ascends to her emanator, meaning Peh of the Rosh, since the phase of Peh of the Rosh is the root for the entire previous expansion from above downward. There she is incorporated in the coupling by striking that operates in Malchut of the Rosh.

For this reason, Malchut receives once more the coarseness she had had before she was refined, except for the last phase, which is lost and does not return, since the last phase does not leave a record. Thus, by the incorporation in the coupling by striking in the Peh of Rosh of Galgalta, she received only the coarseness of phase three and ten Sefirot in the level of Hochma emerged on her.

The emergence of ten Sefirot of the Rosh of AB and its descent to the place of Chazeh of Galgalta

9. After the screen was incorporated in the coupling by striking in the Peh of the Rosh of Galgalta and the coarseness in it has been renewed once more, it was

recognized that the coarseness in it is the coarseness of the Tabur below the Peh of Galgalta and is not related to the Peh of Galgalta.

This recognition is regarded as the screen being separated from the Peh of the Rosh of Galgalta and exiting it. It descended, meaning became coarser, with the coarseness of phase three in the Guf of Galgalta, called Chazeh.

Since it was already incorporated with a screen of coarseness of the Rosh from the time it was in the Peh of *Galgalta*, the light of Ein Sof expanded to it once more for a coupling by striking, while it was at the place of the Chazeh, as well, and ten Sefirot of Rosh at the level of Hochma emerged on it. It lacks the Keter since a screen with a coarseness of phase three draws only the level of Hochma, and they are called the Rosh of Partzuf AB of AK.

It turns out that the origin of the ten Sefirot of the Rosh of Partzuf AB of AK emerged in the Peh of Partzuf Galgalta of AK, meaning during the incorporation of the screen in the coupling by striking in the Peh of Galgalta. Afterwards, they descended from there to the place of Chazeh, and from the coupling by striking in the place of Chazeh emerged the ten Sefirot on the level of Hochma, and clothed the Galgalta of AK from the Chazeh up to near the Peh of Galgalta, meaning up to Hochma of the Guf of Galgalta, but not actually to the Peh, since the Peh is the Keter of the Guf of Galgalta, and the Rosh of AB lacks the Keter.

Toch, Sof of Partzuf AB of AK

10. Then that reflected light returned and expanded Malchut into ten Sefirot from her and within her: from her downward to the Malchut in her, where ten Sefirot of the Guf emerged, called the ten Sefirot of Toch. Ten Sefirot of reflected light without direct light expanded from there downward, which are female light, ending the degree. Thus we have clarified Rosh, Toch, Sof of Partzuf AB of AK.

CHAPTER ELEVEN

Explains the third Partzuf of AK called SAG of AK at the level of Bina, and contains two issues:

1. After AB of AK had been completed, the surrounding light returned and refined the coarseness of phase three into phase two, and ten Sefirot of Rosh, Toch, Sof at the level of Bina emerged, called SAG of AK. 2. First, the screen in the Tabur ascended to its root in the Peh, as it is written about AB of AK.

The refinement of the screen of phase three into phase two. There is no refinement in the screen of Rosh, but rather in the screen of Tabur.

1. After the above Partzuf AB of AK had been completed, the upper light clothed it, and the surrounding light refined the coarseness in it once more, as in Partzuf Galgalta of AK (see Chapter 10, item 4), namely the coarseness of the screen in its Malchut of Malchut, which is Malchut of the Guf of AB, called Tabur. It is so because there is no refinement in any Partzuf in Malchut of Rosh, called Peh, as it operates from below upward, and the light is not limited at all within her, and because of that it does not refine her.

The emergence of Rosh, Toch, Sof of the Partzuf SAG of AK

2. Malchut of AB, called Tabur, had been refined from her entire coarseness, namely the coarseness of phase three, and became as refined as the root. It is thus considered that Malchut rose to her emanator, namely the Peh of the Rosh of AB of AK. This Peh is the root and the emanator of the ten Sefirot of the Guf of AB of AK.

Because she rose to the Peh, the root bestowed the coarseness upon her as in the beginning, except for the last phase, which has been lost and does not return (see Chapter 10, item 9). As a result, Malchut became coarse again, with a coarseness of phase two. We refer to her growing coarser as a descent to her initial place, meaning in the Chazeh, near the Tabur of AB of AK, from which she came (see Chapter 10, item 10).

There, a coupling by striking was done once more, and ten Sefirot of Rosh emerged on the level of Bina, since the reflected light of phase two does not reach higher than that. Ten Sefirot of Toch and ten Sefirot of Sof expanded from there downward (see Chapter 10, items 9, 10). This Partzuf is called Partzuf SAG of AK because it has only the level of Bina. The remaining Partzufim of AK emerged likewise.

CHAPTER TWELVE

Explains the fourth and fifth Partzufim of AK called MA and BON of AK, contains four issues:

1. The emergence of MA and BON of AK. 2. Coarseness is called vapor and the five phases in it are called: Metzach [forehead], Ayin, Ozen, Hotem, Peh. 3. Phase four connects with the coarseness of phase one and the root of AK. This is why there was a coupling by striking in them. 4. The inner and outer MA and BON of AK.

The emergence of MA and BON of AK

1. Once Partzuf SAG had been completed, the surrounding light returned and refined the coarseness of phase two into phase one. Then the upper light, which never stops shining, struck it and educed ten Sefirot at the level of ZA, called Partzuf MA of AK, and expanded into Rosh, Toch, Sof.

This Partzuf is called the world of Nekudim. A refinement of the screen occurred in it too, as in the previous Partzufim of AK, but here the refinement is regarded as the "breaking of the vessels," as the coarseness of phase four is involved here (see Part 4, item 36), and only root coarseness remained in it.

Thus, the upper light, which never stops shining, struck that coarseness of the root, and ten Sefirot on the level of Malchut emerged, regarded as Partzuf BON of AK, and it is called the world of Atzilut and BYA.

Coarseness is called vapor and the five phases in it are called: Metzach (forehead), Ayin, Ozen, Hotem, Peh

2. We have thus thoroughly clarified the matter of the emanation of the five Partzufim of AK from one another, called Galgalta, AB, SAG, MA, and BON. Know that these five phases of screens are called five vapors because the coarseness in the screen is called vapor.

Thus, Partzuf Galgalta of AK emerged from the vapor of the Peh, which is phase four. Partzuf AB of AK emerged from the vapor of the Hotem, which is phase three. Partzuf MA of AK emerged from the vapor of the Eynaim, which is phase one, and Partzuf BON of AK emerged from the vapor of the Metzach, which is the phase of Keter, meaning the root of the coarseness.

Phase four connects with the coarseness of phase one and the root of AK, which is why there was a coupling by striking in them

3. We might ask: "But the vapor of the Eynaim, being phase one, has faint coarseness, insufficient for a coupling by striking (as the ARI wrote in Part 3, item 80). It is even more so with the vapor that comes from the Metzach, which is root coarseness, and is insufficient for a coupling by striking.

The thing is that before a coupling on the vapor of the Eynaim was done, a new thing was established there, called the second restriction, which is the ascent of phase four to Bina. As a result, phase one and the root phase had gained coarseness, until they were sufficient for a coupling by striking. The reason the world of Nekudim that emerged from the Eynaim is called SAG, and the world of Atzilut is called the new MA that emerged from the Metzach, is that there are two levels there: male and female.

In the world of Nekudim, a record of clothing remained from phase two, which connected with the record of coarseness from phase one, and the level of SAG, called "male", emerged on them. Likewise, in the world of Atzilut, there remained a record of clothing from phase one, which connected with the coarseness of the root phase. The level of MA, called "male," emerged over them from their joining together. However, from the phase of the record of coarseness, which is the female level, there was only the level of BON. This is why this MA is called "The new MA," as opposed to the level of MA in Nekudim, which is the old MA, preceding this MA.

The inner and outer MA and BON of AK

4. These two levels of MA and BON that emerged in Nekudim and in the world of Atzilut are no longer regarded as MA and BON of AK itself, but as the externality of MA and BON of AK, since they were established in the second restriction, while AK is entirely the first restriction.

However, these two levels, MA and BON, were incorporated in the internality of AK because they passed through it and were set in it, as there is no absence in the spiritual. These MA and BON that were incorporated in AK are called MA and BON of AK, or the inner MA and BON of AK, and the world of Nekudim and the world of Atzilut clothe over them.

CHAPTER THIRTEEN

Explains the clothing of the Partzufim in one another, and contains three issues:

1. The necessity for the five Partzufim to emerge one below the other. 2. The Tabur of the upper one became the Peh of the Rosh to its lower Partzuf. Thus, each Partzuf emerges from the Malchut of Malchut of the upper one called Tabur. 3. The order of the clothing of the Partzufim in one another.

The difference between the five levels one below the other, and the five levels one above the other

1. Now you can thoroughly understand the difference between the ten Sefirot KHB, ZA, Malchut that stand one above the other, and the five Partzufim Galgalta, AB, SAG, MA, BON, that stand one below the other. The ten Sefirot KHB, ZA and Malchut emerged and were emanated during the ascent of Malchut to the emanator, occurring in each and every one of the five Partzufim (see Chapter 10, item 5).

It is so because the birth of a Partzuf requires for the screen and the Malchut in the previous Partzuf to ascend to the Peh of the Rosh there to receive the new coarseness in a new form. At that time, a new coupling is done for the new Partzuf.

However, the ten Sefirot KHB ZON that emerge during the refinement of Malchut (see Chapter 6, item 5) do not receive a new coarseness. On the contrary, they ascend and refine more each time. Refinement means an ascent. Thus, phase three is emanated above phase four, and phase two above in phase three etc.

The Peh of Rosh of the lower one must emerge in the place of the Chazeh of the upper one

2. However, during the emanation of the Partzufim, when (for example) Partzuf AB emerges from Partzuf Galgalta, Malchut of the Guf of Galgalta must ascend to the place of the Peh of Rosh in Galgalta. There, she receives the coarseness of phase three once more (Chapter 10, items 8, 9).

Acquiring the coarseness means returning to its place, to the Tabur of Partzuf Galgalta as in the beginning. It is written there that the new coupling by striking in phase three necessarily occurred in the place of the Tabur [now called Chazeh] of Partzuf Galgalta.

Thus you see that Malchut of the Rosh of Partzuf AB is in the place of Tabur of Partzuf Galgalta. Accordingly, you will always find that Malchut of the Guf of the upper Partzuf becomes Malchut of the Rosh of its lower Partzuf. In other words, Tabur of the upper one becomes Peh of the Rosh of the lower one.

Five Partzufim must emerge one below the other

3. In this manner, the Peh of the Tabur of Galgalta became the Peh of the Rosh of AB, the Peh of the Tabur of AB became the Peh of the Rosh of SAG, and the Peh of the Tabur of SAG became the Peh of the Rosh of MA. Peh of the Tabur of MA became the Peh of the Rosh of BON. Thus, the five Partzufim must emerge one below the other, as opposed to the inner ten Sefirot in each Partzuf that emerge one above the other.

Each Partzuf emerges from Malchut of Malchut of the upper one

4. From here comes the rule that each Partzuf is emanated by the power of Malchut of Malchut in the upper one. As has been explained, Malchut of the Guf in the upper Partzuf, called Tabur of the upper one, is the emanator of its subsequent Partzuf.

For instance: Through the ascent of the Tabur of Partzuf of Galgalta to the Peh of the Rosh of Galgalta, it receives coarseness of phase three there, on whose coupling emerges the subsequent Partzuf, called AB. This Tabur of Galgalta is Malchut of Malchut of Galgalta, because the Peh is Malchut, and the Tabur is Malchut of Malchut. Thus, Malchut of Malchut of the upper one is the root and the emanator of its lower one.

The order of the clothing of the five Partzufim of AK one on top of the other

5. However, you should still understand the order of the clothing in the five Partzufim of AK. Peh of the Rosh of Partzuf AB stands at the place of Tabur of Partzuf Galgalta (see item 3) and is extended from below upward to the Peh of the Rosh of Galgalta because there, it is regarded as the complete level of ten Sefirot of the Rosh of AB due to the Tabur of Galgalta that ascended there and received the coarseness for its coupling (see item 2).

This is why we say that ten Sefirot of the Rosh of AB stand and clothe the ten Sefirot of the Toch of Galgalta, meaning from the Peh to the Tabur. Thus, the Rosh of Partzuf Galgalta always remains exposed, without clothing.

The reason there is no clothing in the Rosh

6. Similarly, the ten Sefirot of the Rosh of Partzuf SAG also clothe the ten Sefirot of the Toch of AB, and the ten Sefirot of the Rosh of Partzuf MA clothe the ten Sefirot of the Toch of Partzuf SAG, and so on likewise. In other words, for the above reason, too, regarding the clothing of AB to Partzuf Galgalta, because they all have a single reason: they all emerge by the power of the ascent of the Tabur of the upper one to the Peh of the upper one. Consequently, the ten Sefirot of Rosh of the lower one stand in the place of the ten Sefirot of Toch of the upper one, meaning from the Peh to the Tabur. From the Peh of every upper one and above, it always remains exposed, without any clothing.

CHAPTER FOURTEEN

Explains that there were two restrictions in the worlds.

The first restriction was only on Malchut, and the upper nine were clear of any restriction. In the second restriction, the restriction intervened from Bina downward of every degree, and Bina, Tifferet and Malchut exited every degree.

The Sium that was made in the place of Bina is called Parsa

1. We shall now explain the ten Sefirot called the "five worlds": Adam Kadmon, Atzilut, Beria, Yetzira and Assiya. Here we must know the two restrictions that occurred in the worlds. The first restriction was only on the vessel of Malchut, to not receive the light of Ein Sof inside her. The upper nine Sefirot remained clear of any screen and restriction. From this phase emerged the first three Partzufim in the world of AK, called Galgalta, AB, SAG, as we have explained in chapter 12.

After that, in that Partzuf Nekudot of SAG of AK, there was a second restriction, where the Malchut that ends the line of the light of Ein Sof that stood at the point of this world ascended to the place of the Chazeh of Partzuf Nekudot of SAG of AK. It ended the line of the light of Ein Sof there, and half of Tifferet and NHYM from the Chazeh of the Partzuf downward remained empty, without light.

Just as a new Sium was done on the light of the line in general, in the place of the Chazeh of Partzuf Nekudot of SAG of AK because of the ascent of Malchut to Bina of the Guf, called Tifferet, so it occurred in the inner ten Sefirot of each and every degree. Malchut of that degree ascended to Bina of that degree and ended the degree there. Bina and TM of that degree exited the degree and fell into the degree below it. That new Sium that occurred in the second restriction in the place of Bina, or Tifferet, is called Parsa.

The general Parsa interrupts between Atzilut and BYA

2. We shall now speak from the perspective of the general Parsa. The ending Malchut that stood at the point of this world ascended to the place of the Chazeh of Partzuf Nekudot of SAG of AK and ended the light of the line there. The Sium that was made in the place of the Chazeh is called "the general Parsa".

The world of Atzilut emerged from this Parsa upward. From this Parsa downward, in the place that has been emptied of the light of the line of Ein Sof, emerged the three worlds Beria, Yetzira, Assiya, through the light of consequence. Thus, in the place of the half of Tifferet, emerged the world of Beria; in the place of Netzah, Hod, Yesod, emerged the world of Yetzira, and in the place of Malchut emerged the world of Assiya.

Following special corrections, the world of Beria receives through the screen of phase two from YESHSUT of Atzilut. The world of Yetzira receives from ZA of Atzilut through the screen of phase one, and the world of Assiya receives from Malchut of Atzilut through the screen of the root of coarseness.

ABYA are four levels HB TM

3. Hence there are five worlds named KHB TM. The world of AK has the degree of Keter, meaning the ten Sefirot of Partzuf Galgalta of AK. That is because the level of every world is measured according to the level of its first Partzuf, just like the measure of the level in the Sefirot is according to its highest Sefira.

The world of Atzilut has the level of Hochma, meaning in the ten Sefirot of Partzuf AA of Atzilut, which is regarded as the first Partzuf, because Atik is higher than Atzilut. The world of Beria has the level of Bina, meaning YESHSUT, the world of Yetzira – the level of ZA, and the world of Assiya – the level of Malchut.

The main difference between AK and ABYA is that AK is from the first restriction, while ABYA are from the second restriction. Atzilut is above the general Parsa and BYA are below that Parsa.

4. The differences between these five worlds are primarily a result of the two restrictions. The world of Adam Kadmon is from the first restriction, where the line of Ein Sof shines up to the point of this world. Its nine Sefirot are clear of any screen and restriction.

However, the four worlds ABYA are from the second restriction, where from Bina downward in each of their degrees, the restriction of Malchut is already involved, due to the ascent of Malchut to Bina of every degree. Even though the world of Atzilut is from the second restriction, it is still clear of any screen and restriction because it stands from the general Parsa upward. Thus the light of the line of Ein Sof shines in it to its end, meaning to the Parsa, which is the place of the Chazeh of the Partzuf Nekudot of SAG of AK.

The world of Beria is already under the general Parsa, meaning after the light from the line of Ein Sof stops. It has only the light of consequence from the light of the line. However, since it stands in the place of half of Tifferet of Nekudot of SAG of AK, and Tifferet is regarded as Bina of the Guf, as KHB of the Guf are called HGT, it has therefore been corrected to receive the illumination of Bina, which is YESHSUT.

The world of Yetzira, standing at the place of NHY of the Partzuf Nekudot of SAG of AK, namely the phase of ZA, has been corrected to receive the illumination of ZA of Atzilut. The world of Assiya that stands at the place of Malchut of the Partzuf Nekudot of SAG of AK has been corrected to receive the illumination of Malchut of Atzilut.

5. You can therefore see that in AK, before the second restriction occurred, there was no actual screen except at the point of this world, which is its Sium Raglin. All the above-mentioned screens in AK above the point of this world are but operations of that screen.

It is known that the coarseness of the screen cannot ascend above its place even a bit. Thus, only the effects of the screen rise above its place, but they are devoid of any coarseness. Therefore, there are no coarseness and screens at all in AK, although its screen is the coarsest of all the worlds, being that it is phase four. It is so because this coarseness becomes active only from its Sium Raglin downward, which is only at the point of this world.

6. The second restriction occurred in the world of Atzilut, and the Parsa had been erected between Atzilut and BYA due to the ascent of Malchut of phase four from the point of this world to the place of the Chazeh of Partzuf Nekudot of SAG of AK. It stopped the light of Atzilut there, and this new Sium is called Parsa.

Therefore, the Sium Raglin of all the Partzufim of Atzilut occurred in the place of that Parsa, for the light of Ein Sof does not shine anymore, but only a light of consequence. The screen of phase three is in that Parsa, ending the Raglaim of AA because of the incorporation of phase four in the Parsa, as well as the screens of the other Partzufim. Thus, from the Parsa downward the power of the screen dominates, as it stopped the upper light from Ein Sof.

However, there is no screen at all from the Parsa upward. Instead, all the above-mentioned screens from the screen of Sium Raglin of Atzilut upward, are but operations that rise by the power of the screen of Sium Raglin of the five Partzufim of Atzilut. Those receive all their illumination by the screen of Sium Raglin, though they do not receive any of its coarseness, as the coarseness of the screen cannot ascend above its place. Therefore there is no screen whatsoever in all the Partzufim of Atzilut.

CHAPTER FIFTEEN

Explains the issue of Keter and ABYA in the five Partzufim of Atzilut and all the degrees, and contains two issues:

1. The Parsa in the Chazeh of Atzilut is an incorporation from the general Parsa, by which the world of Atzilut itself is divided into ABYA. 2. Just like the world of Atzilut is divided into ABYA by the power of the general Parsa, so each and every degree is divided into inner ABYA.

1. We shall now explain the phases of Keter and ABYA in the five Partzufim of Atzilut. AA is the Keter, and the upper AVI that clothe AA from the Peh to his Chazeh are Atzilut. YESHSUT, which clothe AA from the Chazeh to the Tabur, are Beria, and ZA and Malchut, which clothe AA from the Tabur downward, are Yetzira and Assiya.

The Parsa in the Chazeh of Atzilut is an incorporation from the general Parsa, by which the world of Atzilut itself is divided into ABYA.

2. The reason for these names is that after Partzuf Nekudot of SAG of AK has been divided at its Chazeh, where from the Chazeh and above stands the world of Atzilut, and from the Chazeh and below stand the three worlds BYA that emerged from the line of the light of Ein Sof, as was written in the previous chapter, it is incorporated also in the world of Atzilut itself, as an incorporation of the upper one from the lower one. AA is the essence of the world of Atzilut, for as the level of every ten Sefirot is measured by its highest Sefira, so each world is measured according to the level of its first Partzuf, divided at the Chazeh. It is regarded as Atzilut from the Chazeh upward, and as BYA in Atzilut from the Chazeh downward. The Parsa in the place of the Chazeh of AA is an incorporation from the general Parsa that stands under the Sium of the entire Atzilut.

Thus, AA itself, whose Rosh is exposed without clothing, is regarded as Keter. AVI, which clothe it up to the Chazeh, are clear of even the incorporation of the Parsa and are regarded as Atzilut. YESHSUT, however, which stands below the Parsa at the Chazeh of AA where the general Parsa is incorporated, is regarded as Beria. ZA clothes only NHY of AA, and is regarded as Yetzira; and Malchut, which clothes Malchut of AA, is regarded as Assiya. Now you can see how the three worlds BYA are connected in YESHSUT and ZON of Atzilut, which clothe from the Chazeh of AA downward.

Just as Atzilut is divided into ABYA by the power of the incorporation of the general Parsa, so each and every degree is divided into inner ABYA

3. This also explains the matter of the ten Sefirot of Keter and ABYA in each and every Partzuf in the Partzufim of ABYA. As has been explained in the general world of Atzilut, which is AA that was divided at the Chazeh, its Rosh is Keter, and from its Peh to its Chazeh it is Atzilut. From its Chazeh to its Tabur, it is Beria, and from its Tabur down, it is Yetzira and Assiya.

This pertains to all the inner Partzufim in ABYA. In each and every Partzuf in them, the Rosh is regarded as Keter, from the Peh to the Chazeh, it is regarded as Atzilut, and from the Chazeh to the Tabur as Beria. Finally, from Tabur down it is regarded as Yetzira and Assiya.

Table of Questions for the Meaning of the Words

1. What is an organ, organs
2. What is a light of departure
3. What is a diminishing light
4. What is the light of the face
5. What is a light of consequence
6. What are separate letters
7. What are connected letters
8. What is an Ozen [ear]
9. What is posterior
10. What is lower Ima
11. What is middle
12. What is a mirror
13. What is Arich Anpin
14. What is AT [pronounced ET]
15. What is Bohu
16. What is a house [hall]
17. What is breaching
18. What is creation
19. What is flesh
20. What is a Guf
21. What is Galgalta
22. What are tendons
23. What are four forms
24. What is speech
25. What is in passing
26. What is a narrow path
27. What is a wide path
28. What is separation

29. What is vapor

30. What is departing vapor

31. What is Filled HaVaYaH

32. What is simple HaVaYaH

33. What is a hall

34. What is an upper hall

35. What is striking

36. What is a look

37. What is a second look

38. What is departure

39. What is distancing

40. What is clothing

41. What is sparkling

42. What is coarseness

43. What is expansion

44. What is the second expansion

45. What is a tail for the lions

46. What is Zeir Anpin

47. What is a Hotem [nose]

48. What is substance

49. What is a seal

50. What is a window

51. What is engraving

52. What are basic elements

53. What is Yetzira

54. What is a chair

55. What is potential

56. What are complete vessels

57. What is a throne

58. What is Keter

59. What is a garment

60. What is marrow

61. What is from her and within her

62. What is complete clothing

63. What is a screen

64. What is a blocked screen

65. What is a place of darkness

66. What is nesting

67. What is a spark of the created being

68. What is a small spark

69. What is Nefesh

70. What is a narrow foramen

71. What is a point

72. What is Neshama

73. What is adjacent

74. What is a Sefira

75. What is a world

76. What are Eynaim [eyes]

77. What is the self of the light

78. What is Assiya

79. What is Atik

80. What is Peh [mouth]

81. What is actual

82. What is separation

83. What is Partzuf

84. What is form

85. What is very narrow

86. What is the holy of holies

87. What is nesting

88. What are Klipot [shells]

89. What is sight

90. What is Rosh

91. What is the head for the foxes

92. What is a quarter blood

1. What is an organ, organs

These are the vessels of the Sefirot of the Guf, meaning the emanated beings from the screen of the Peh of Rosh downwards.

(Part 3, Chapter 8, item 1)

2. What is a light of departure

Reflected light, meaning the upper light that is not received in phase four, is rejected by her and returns to its place.

(Part 3, Chapter 15, item 6)

3. What is a diminishing light

As the ten Sefirot of direct light pass in order to clothe from the screen downward, their value diminishes because of it, and they are regarded as "diminishing light."

(Part 3, 34)

4. What is the light of the face

It is the light of Hochma.

(Part 3, Chapter 8, item 9)

5. What is a light of consequence

This is the ten Sefirot of direct light that sparkle through the screen downwards.

(Part 3, Chapter 15, item 9)

6. What are separate letters

When the self clothes in the vessels, the four phases HB TM are designated by four separate letters, after the clothing of the lights in the coarseness of the vessels, ignoring the disparity of form between them. This disparity of form means separation in spirituality. (See the term "separation").

(Part 3, Chapter 15, item 4)

7. What are connected letters

The refinement of the coarseness in Malchut of Malchut, which occurs in the Guf of every Partzuf, when the reflected light gradually departs until it rises to the Emanator, at that time, these ten Sefirot are called "connected letters," after the refinement that the vessels acquire more and more each time. That refinement connects them and brings them closer to the root, as written in item 6, where the coarseness separates while the refinement connects.

(Part 3, Chapter 15, item 5)

8. What is an Ozen [ear]

It is the level of the ten Sefirot of Rosh in phase two, namely Bina.

(Part 3, Chapter 12, item 7)

9. What is posterior

When direct light, meaning light of Hochma, is not clothed in the vessel, then the vessel is called posterior, or posteriors. It has been written in item 4 that the light of Hochma is called the light of the face. Thus, when the light of Hochma is absent from the vessel, it is called posterior.

(Part 3, Chapter 15, item 6)

10. What is lower Ima

It is the Malchut of Atzilut.

(Part 3, Chapter 4, item 7)

11. What is middle

It is something that decides and connects two far ends. From this you can understand the meaning of the names "middle line" and "middle pillar" in every place, which consist of three Sefirot – Daat, Tifferet, Yesod.

(Part 3, Chapter 5, item 4)

12. What is a mirror

Malchut is called a "a mirror that has nothing of its own," or "a mirror that does not shine." Zeir Anpin is called "a shining mirror." It is called Light because Zeir Anpin and Malchut are called "the two lights," since all the illuminations of the lower ones come only from them and not from above them.

(Part 3, Chapter 7, item 2)

13. What is Arich Anpin

Partzuf Keter is called Arich Anpin because of the self of light of Hochma in it. Tifferet is called Zeir Anpin because it has no more than a minute illumination of Hochma. The names AA and ZA are parallel, for they relate solely to the light of Hochma in the Partzuf, as Hochma is called light of the face.

(Part 3, Chapter 6, item 7)

14. What is AT [pronounced ET]

Malchut is called AT, because she consists of all the letters from Aleph to Tav (all the letters of the Hebrew alphabet). It is so because the letters are the vessels of the Sefirot, and all the vessels come from Malchut.

(Part 3, Chapter 12, item 2)

15. What is Bohu

Bohu is another name for Arich Anpin. It is parallel to Tohu, which is an appellation for Atik, which means negation of attainment, whereas Bohu designates attainment and existence. It is an acronym of Bo Hu [In Him].

(Part 3, Chapter 6, item 3)

16. What is a house [hall]

The Sefira of Malchut that was separated from the inner vessels and became a vessel for the surrounding light is called a house or a hall (see Answers to Topics, item 176).

(Part 3, Chapter 5, item 1)

17. What is breaching

When the light overcomes the limiting screen that stands in its way, it is called breaching. It means that it completely ignores the boundary that stands in its way, breaks a passage, and shines through the boundary downward.

(Part 3, Chapter 7, item 1)

18. What is creation

An initiation existence from absence is called "creation." The coarseness in the vessels could not be revealed in the world of Atzilut, but only from the bottom of the world of Atzilut downwards. Therefore, from that place downward it is called Beria, after the coarseness that appeared.

The coarseness is the will to receive in the created being, existence from absence, for everything in reality is regarded as emerging from Him existence from existence. This is because one cannot give what one does not have, except for the will to receive, which by necessity is not in Him, for from whom would He receive?

(Part 3, Chapter 2, item 3)

19. What is flesh

Phase three, called Zeir Anpin, is called flesh. This appellation pertains in it only to the ten Sefirot whose level is even. These ten phases are called OBGAM [acronym for Or, Bassar, Gidin, Atzamot, Mochin]. Malchut is called Or (skin), ZA is called Bassar (flesh), Bina is called Gidin (Aramaic: tendons), Hochma is called Atzamot (bones), and Keter is called Mochin (marrow).

(Part 3, Chapter 5, item 3)

20. What is a Guf

The ten Sefirot that pass through the screen downward, where Malchut expands into ten Sefirot from and within her are called Guf. This is because they are the primary force in the Partzuf, for there is the primary clothing of the self in the vessels.

However, in the ten Sefirot of the Rosh from the screen upwards there is no complete clothing, but only roots for the clothing.

(Part 3, Chapter 8, item 6)

21. What is Galgalta

Partzuf Keter. The vessel where the light of Yechida is clothed is also called Galgalta.

(Part 3, Inner Observation, Chapter 8, item 2)

22. What are tendons

The vessel of Bina in the ten Sefirot whose level is even.

(Part 3, Chapter 5, item 3)

23. What are four forms

The coarseness in the emanated being, meaning the desire in it, are called the sum total of the substance of the emanated being. These four phases in the coarseness are called "four forms."

(Part 3, Chapter 6, item 4)

24. What is speech

Malchut of Rosh is called Peh, and the ten Sefirot that pass through her downwards by the sparkling of the screen are called speech. This is how the lights are always imparted and pass from Partzuf to Partzuf.

(Part 3, Chapter 11, item 2)

25. What is in passing

The four phases always relate to each other as cause and consequence, even in direct light: phase one of direct light is the reason and the emanator of phase two, phase two of phase three and so on. Each degree is regarded as the emanator of the existence of its adjacent one.

For this reason, it is also regarded as passing to her from Ein Sof, all its abundance for her sustenance. However, when the degree imparts to its lower one only in the sense that it is the cause that precedes her, it is called bestowal "in passing."

But if it indeed imparts to its lower one sparkling with the screen in it from above downward, it is regarded as imparting to her "in clothing."

(Part 3, Chapter 4, item 1)

26. What is a narrow path

Restricted bestowal is regarded as bestowal that passes through a "narrow path."

(Part 3, Chapter 1, item 4)

27. What is a wide path

Abundant bestowal.

(Part 3, Chapter 1, item 4)

28. What is separation

When the ten Sefirot sparkle and pass through the screen downward, they become enslaved to the boundaries in the screen. In that state they cannot suckle anything from the upper one, but only according to the boundaries in the screen. For this reason, it is considered that the screen separates them from the upper one, for it does not let them suckle all they want from there.

(Part 3, Chapter 12, item 4)

29. What is vapor

Reflected light is called vapor.

(Part 3, Chapter 11, item 4)

30. What is departing vapor

Reflected light that descends from the screen downwards.

(There)

31. What is Filled HaVaYaH

As written by the ARI, the root of the lights and their essence are the four simple letters of HaVaYaH, without any fillings. However, their fillings are the expansion of HaVaYaH and the exit of their lights outside.

There are five Partzufim: Keter, AB, SAG, MA, BON. Partzuf Keter is the principal among them and is their root. The ten Sefirot in it are implied in the four simple letters HaVaYaH, called inner HaVaYaH.

A letter emerges from each Partzuf and clothes it. Partzuf Hochma is extended from the Yod of HaVaYaH of the Partzuf Keter. Its four letters are filled with Yodin [pl. for Yod] in the following manner: Yod, Hey, Viv, Hey (יוד, הי, ויו, הי), in Gematria AB.

Partzuf Bina is extended from the first Hey. Its four letters HaVaYaH are filled with Yodin and Aleph in the following way: Yod, Hey, Vav, Hey (יה, יה, ואו, דוי) etc. Thus, the Partzufim of Keter are implied with simple HaVaYaH while the other four Partzufim that clothe it are implied with full HaVaYaH (see Inner Observation).

(Part 3, Chapter 15, item 3)

32. What is simple HaVaYaH

See item full HaVaYaH.

(Part 3, Chapter 15, item 3)

33. What is a hall

See item house.

(Part 3, Chapter 8, item 6)

34. What is an upper hall

There are seven halls; the highest among them is called the upper hall.

35. What is striking

See Inner Light, Chapter 1, item 70, and Chapter 2, item 3.

(Part 3, Chapter 1, item 3)

36. What is a look

The expansion of the light of Ein Sof for coupling by striking in the screen in the vessel of Malchut to raise reflected light is called a look. It is so because light that expands from Ein Sof is always regarded as the light of Hochma, called the light of Eynaim, sight, or look.

(Part 3, Chapter 12, item 1)

37. What is a second look

The expansion of the light of Ein Sof for a coupling by striking in Malchut of the Guf, meaning when it copulates in her during the refinement of the screen from degree to degree until it elicits ten Sefirot one above the other, it is called a "second look."

(Part 3, Chapter 12, item 5 and Inner Light, item 8)

38. What is departure

Wherever there is refinement of coarseness of a degree, there is also an equal departure of the light and the abundance in her. It is so because the measure of the will to receive in the degree is its coarseness. It is therefore obvious that when the will to receive disappears, so does all the abundance that is received in her, as there is no coercion in spirituality.

(Part 3, Chapter 12 and Inner Light, item 8)

39. What is distancing

The coarseness of phase two of the direct light is called distancing, because it chooses the light of Hassadim and detaches itself from receiving the light of Hochma. Also, after the restriction there is distancing from Hochma in phase four, too, because all the restriction and screen in it pertain to the light of Hochma.

(Part 3, Chapter 1, item 4)

40. What is clothing

Any light should clothe a vessel, and there is no light without a vessel (see "In Passing").

(Part 3, Chapter 12, item 3)

41. What is sparkling

The illumination of reflected light is always called the sparkling or sparks.

(Part 3, Chapter 2, item 2)

42. What is coarseness

It is the acquisition of a great measure of the will to receive.

(Part 3, Chapter 1, item 1)

43. What is expansion

It is the upper light that expands to the emanated being. However, we should understand that it is an extension from the perspective of the desire in that emanated being, who draws that expansion of the upper light to itself according to its measure of yearning. The degree is completed only by two phases of expansion of the light of Ein Sof (see the second expansion).

(Part 3, Chapter 1, item 1)

44. What is the second expansion

The expansion of upper light does not complete its clothing in the vessels at one time. That is because in any Guf, meaning in ten Sefirot that come from the screen downward, there is the issue of the refinement of the coarseness.

At that time all the lights of the ten Sefirot of the Guf return to their root and there is a new coupling in Malchut of the Rosh, called the second expansion. This expansion fills the vessels of the Guf once more and completes the clothing of the self in the vessels of the upper one. At that point, she also elicits a new Partzuf outside herself.

(Part 3, Chapter 12 and Inner Light, item 8)

45. What is a tail for the lions

The Sium of a upper degree is called "a tail for the lions." "Tail" implies Sof and Sium. When the point of Sium descends to the lower degree, it becomes the root phase there, and it is called the "head of the foxes," since in relation to the ten Sefirot of the upper degree, the ten Sefirot in the lower one are regarded as "foxes" compared to "lions."

(Part 3, Chapter 7, item 5)

46. What is Zeir Anpin

See Arich Anpin.

(Part 3, Chapter 4, item 5)

47. What is a Hotem [nose]

The Sefira of Zeir Anpin of the Rosh is called Hotem.

(Part 3, Chapter 11, item 4)

48. What is substance

The will to receive in the emanated being is regarded as its general "substance." Its four phases are regarded as the four forms of the desire, called HB TM (see item 84).

(Part 3, Chapter 6, item 3)

49. What is a seal

Reflected light that ascends from the screen in Malchut upwards and clothes the ten Sefirot of Rosh is called a seal. The lights that sparkle from the screen downwards to the ten Sefirot of the Guf are regarded as the imprints of that seal.

(Part 3, Chapter 8, item 9)

50. What is a window

It is phase three of the Rosh, clothed in reflected light.

(Part 3, Chapter 1, item 4)

51. What is engraving

Engraving and protrusion are two parallel relations in the discernment of the abundance. Protrusion means there is great abundance in the Sefirot, evident and protruding toward the observer. Its opposite is the discernment of engraving, which means that the deficiency of abundance in the Sefirot is manifestly evident there.

Thus, the matter of the seal, where the worlds are imprinted from one another (see item 49), is regarded as a seal whose letters are protruding and a seal whose letters are engraved and depressed.

Thus, the seal of Atzilut is protruding and Beria is imprinted by it, meaning that it is a depressed seal. Yetzira is imprinted by the depressed seal of Beria and thus becomes a protruding seal. Assiya is imprinted by the protruding seal of Yetzira and becomes depressed.

It follows that the ten Sefirot of Atzilut and the ten Sefirot of Yetzira are regarded as protruding, and their opposite, the ten Sefirot of Beria and the ten Sefirot of Assiya are regarded as depressed and engraved.

(Part 3, Chapter 7, item 1)

52. What are basic elements

The four phases in the coarseness of the vessel of Malchut are sometimes called the four basic elements.

(Part 3, Chapter 10, item 1)

53. What is Yetzira

The level of the ten Sefirot that comes through a coupling by striking in the screen of phase one is called Yetzira.

(Part 3, Chapter 3, item 3)

54. What is a chair

The world of Beria is called a chair or throne (see item 57).

(Part 3, Chapter 4, item 4)

55. What is potential

There is "potential" and there is "actual." For example, the seed of a fruit is regarded as including the "potential" fruit, but not in "actual" fact. However, through sowing and growing, the fruit emerges and becomes revealed from "potential" to an "actual" fact.

In much the same way, we discern that before the light of Ein Sof expands to the screen for a coupling by striking, it consists of ten Sefirot in "potential." After the upper light strikes it and it raises ten Sefirot of reflected light that clothe the upper light, it is considered that the ten Sefirot of the Rosh become revealed in actual fact as roots for the vessels.

(Part 3, Chapter 6, item 4)

56. What are complete vessels

The ten Sefirot that sparkle, expand, and descend from the screen downward are regarded as having complete vessels; they are called the ten Sefirot of the Guf.

(Part 3, Chapter 8, item 7)

57. What is a throne

The world of Beria is called the world of Kisse [lit. throne], from the word Kisui [cover] and concealment. This is because the light of Hochma is concealed there (see here Chapter 3, item 2).

It also implies that the lights of GAR that are imparted there from the world of Atzilut are only regarded as Bina and shine there only in a "sitting" state. It is as one who sits on a chair; his level is diminished. The illumination of Hochma is called "standing", because in standing the level is complete.

(Part 3, Chapter 4, item 4)

58. What is Keter

It is the first Sefira of the ten Sefirot, but there are many phases of Keter.

(Part 3, Chapter 6, item 7)

59. What is a garment

It is the phase of ZA that was separated from the inner light and became surrounding light. Also, every lower Partzuf is called a garment with respect to its upper Partzuf.

(Part 3, Chapter 6, item 3)

60. What is marrow

It is the Sefira of Keter in the ten Sefirot whose level is even.

(Part 3, Chapter 5, item 3)

61. What is from her and within her

The expansion and broadening of Malchut of the Rosh from herself downward, to the ten Sefirot called ten Sefirot of the Guf, is called "from her and within her," indicating that all these ten Sefirot are phases of Malchut within her, from the Keter of Malchut to the Malchut in Malchut.

(Part 3, Chapter 4, item 6)

62. What is complete clothing

The screen between Atzilut and Beria that passes the ten Sefirot from Atzilut to Beria becomes a "complete clothing" that limits these ten Sefirot.

(Part 3, Chapter 4, item 5)

63. What is a screen

It is a force of restriction and judgment that was established in Malchut, rejecting the upper light from clothing within her.

(Part 3, Chapter 1, item 3)

64. What is a blocked screen

When the screen between Atzilut and Beria passes the ten Sefirot from Atzilut to Beria, it becomes a blocked screen, blocking them from Hochma (see complete clothing).

(Part 3, Chapter 4, item 5)

65. What is a place of darkness

The Sefira of Malchut in the ten Sefirot of even level is called skin. She ends the illumination of the Partzuf because the skin itself, meaning Malchut, does not receive within her any of the lights in that Partzuf because of the force of restriction in her. For this reason, she ends the illumination of the Partzuf, and from her outwards, it is regarded as a "place of darkness."

(Part 3, Chapter 7, item 2)

66. What is nesting

Intermittent illumination is called "nesting." It is like birds that lie in their nests intermittently when they want to have fledglings, and afterwards leave.

(Part 3, Chapter 4, item 4)

67. What is a spark of the created being

In every degree, the upper one is regarded as the emanator and the lower one as the emanated being. In the world of Beria, the upper one is called "Creator" and the lower one "created being."

The Malchut of the upper Malchut that descends and becomes the Rosh of the lower one comprises two phases of the light of Malchut (see item 222). In other words, with respect to her own existence, she is regarded as the emanator, or Creator, and with respect to her belonging to the lower degree, she is regarded as an emanated being or s created being.

Her own existence is called "the spark of the Creator," and her lower phase is called "the spark of the created being." You already know that the light of Malchut, meaning reflected light, is always called sparks.

(Part 3, Chapter 5, item 5)

68. What is a small spark

The smaller part of the light of Malchut, meaning the reflected light which remains in her as her own existence is called "a small spark." In the lights it is called a record.

(Part 3, Chapter 5, item 5)

69. What is Nefesh

The light of Malchut is called the light of Nefesh.

(Part 3, Chapter 5, item 6)

70. What is a narrow foramen

The screen that detains the upper light from clothing is considered to be a partition that blocks the light. When the screen opens through coupling by striking and the upper light passes in it and expands downward, it is regarded as making a hole, a foramen, in the blocked partition for the light to pass through. A broad expansion is regarded as a window, and a small expansion is regarded as a narrow foramen.

(Part 3, Chapter 1, item 4)

71. What is a point

When Malchut with the screen in her is not coupling and raising reflected light, she is called a point. In other words, she is like a black point without any white, and in the same manner, at that time there is no light in her because of the restriction that rides on her. She is also called point because of the restriction that occurred in the middle point.

(Part 3, Chapter 7, item 2)

72. What is Neshama

It is the light of Bina. When the ten Sefirot divide into root, soul, body, garment, and hall, the light of Hochma is called Neshama [soul] and Bina is called body. From this aspect, a Partzuf has only three lights NRN, because Haya and Yechida have become surrounding lights.

(Part 3, Chapter 9, item 10)

73. What is adjacent

Proximity of form from one phase to another is regarded as "adjacent" to the other.

(Part 3, Chapter 12, item 6)

74. What is a Sefira

The ten Sefirot of direct light clothed in the ten Sefirot of reflected light that emerge through a coupling by striking for the first time are called one Sefira. It is named after the highest Sefira in that level, although it contains ten Sefirot lengthwise and ten Sefirot thick-wise.

(Part 3, Inner Observation, Chapter 4, item 3)

75. What is a world

The name "world" [world] begins primarily from Partzuf BON of AK, called the world of Nekudim. It is called by that name because ZA and Malchut of the inner vessels of phase four disappeared and became vessels for surrounding light, called garment and hall.

Olam means He'elem [concealment], though at times the name is borrowed to refer to the Partzufim and Sefirot that preceded the world of Nekudim, but this is only a borrowed name.

(Part 3, Chapter 8, item 1)

76. What are Eynaim [eyes]

They are the vessel of Hochma of the Rosh.

(Part 3, Chapter 11, item 6)

77. What is the self of the light

The ten Sefirot of the Rosh are regarded as the essence and the self of the light. From the Peh of Rosh downward, they are regarded as the light of consequence of the lights of the ten Sefirot of Rosh. However, this applies from the world of Beria downward.

(Part 3, Chapter 8, item 9)

78. What is Assiya

The ten Sefirot of the level of Malchut that receives from ZA are called the world of Assiya.

(Part 3, Chapter 5, item 1)

79. What is Atik

Malchut of Malchut of the upper one becomes the phase of Atik in the lower one, meaning with respect to her own existence, with respect to the spark of the Creator in her. The discernment of the spark of the created being in her becomes the phase of Arich Anpin (see item 67), and the two of them together are the Partzuf of Keter for the lower one.

(Part 3, Chapter 6, item 7)

80. What is Peh [mouth]

Malchut of the Rosh is called Peh.

(Part 3, Chapter 11, item 5)

81. What is actual

There is "potential" and there is "actual". See "potential" (item 55).

(Part 3, Chapter 6, item 4)

82. What is separation

Disparity of form creates separation and distancing between spiritual things. Proximity of form creates in them adhesion.

(Part 3, Chapter 10, item 1)

83. What is Partzuf

The ten Sefirot one below the other that come through the ascent of Malchut to the Emanator are called Partzufim [pl. of Partzuf]. (see Inner Observation, Chapter 13, item 1).

(Part 3, Chapter 8, item 6)

84. What is form

The four phases of coarseness in Malchut, called HB TM, are called four forms.

(Part 3, Chapter 6, item 3)

85. What is very narrow

Very confined bestowal is called "very narrow."

(Part 3, Chapter 1, item 4)

86. What is the holy of holies

The uppermost hall in the seven halls of Beria, which incorporates KHBD of Beria, the innermost in them is called the holy of holies.

(Part 3, Chapter 7, item 7)

87. What is nesting

See item 66.

88. What are Klipot [shells]

(See above item 82.) Disparity of form separates and distinguishes spiritual things. Know that this oppositeness of form from one end to the other separates and drives them to opposite ends until there is no suckling between them whatsoever.

You already know that there is only a will to bestow in the upper light, and not to receive even a bit. The shells are of completely opposite form, meaning wanting only to receive and swallow everything; they have no will to bestow whatsoever. For that reason they are separated from the Life of Lives and are therefore called "dead", and so is anything that cleaves to them.

(Part 3, Chapter 10, item 2)

89. What is sight

The light of the Eynaim, meaning the light of Hochma of the Rosh, is called sight.

(Part 3, Chapter 11, item 6)

90. What is Rosh

It is the ten Sefirot of direct light clothed in the reflected light that rises from the screen upward, meaning a beginning and a root. They are not regarded as complete vessels yet, fit to clothe all the light, but are only regarded as roots.

(Part 3, Chapter 12, item 4)

91. What is the head for the foxes

See item 45.

(Part 3, Chapter 7, item 5)

92. What is a quarter blood

Nefesh of Nefesh is called a quarter [also forth], for she is phase four. She is clothed as the quarter blood of the marrow, meaning the Keter of the ten Sefirot of the body, whose level is even. That is because these ten Sefirot are called skin, flesh, tendons, bones, and marrow.

(Part 3, Chapter 5, item 6)

93. What is Ruach

It is the light of ZA.

(Part 3, Chapter 9, item 10)

94. What is thin Ruach

It is a reflected light that descends from the coarseness of phase two.

(Part 3, Chapter 11, item 4)

95. What is a square

The couplings by striking performed on Malchut as she is gradually refined (see item 7), meaning from phase four to phase three, from phase three to phase two, from phase two to phase one and from phase one to the root, these couplings are called "square" after the four types of refinement that are done there.

(Part 3, Chapter 15, item 5)

96. What is smell

ZA of the Rosh is called Hotem [nose]. The light in it is called "smell," because the ten Sefirot of Rosh are called Galgalta, Eynaim, Ozen, Hotem, and Peh.

(Part 3, Chapter 11, item 2)

97. What is breaking

Revoking the boundary in the screen is called "breaching and breaking". See "breaching" (item 17).

(Part 3, Chapter 7, item 1)

98. What is a root

All the phases in Keter are regarded as the "roots" of the Sefirot.

(Part 3, Chapter 9, item 1)

99. What is sound

It is the light of Bina of the Rosh. Her vessel is called Ozen [ear].

(Part 3, Chapter 11, item 2)

100. What are roots of the vessels

They are the ten Sefirot of Rosh, called Keter.

(Part 3, Chapter 6, item 4)

101. What is Tohu

Keter consists of two phases called "a spark of the Creator" and "a spark of the created being." The discernment of a "spark of the Creator" in it is called Atik, and it is called Tohu, after the complete absence of attainment in it. The discernment of a "spark of the created being" in it is called Arich Anpin, and Bohu, indicating the root and beginning of attainment that is there.

(Part 3, Chapter 6, item 4)

TABLE OF QUESTIONS FOR TOPICS

125. Why are the *Eser Sefirot* that end the *Partzuf, Eser Sefirot de Ohr Hozer* without *Ohr Yashar*?

126. What is the *Hevel* that comes out of a degree?

127. Why doesn't real *Hevel* come out from the eyes?

128. What comes to be in the *Sefirot* as a result of the *Ohr* of *Histaklut*?

129. What comes to be in the *Sefirot* as a result of the *Hevels* of the AHP?

130. Why isn't any reality made of *Orot* AHP?

131. A. What does it mean that there is no *Masach* at all in *Olam Atzilut*?

B. What is the difference between *Ohr* of *Atzmut* and *Ohr* of *Tolada*?

132. Why is every level of *Eser Sefirot* named only after its uppermost *Sefira*?

133. Why are the two *Orot* of ZON on the same level?

134. How is the *Zivug de Hakaa* performed for the purpose of the *Eser Sefirot de Beria* and *de Yetzira*?

135. How does *Ein Sof* shine in *Atzilut*?

136. Why doesn't *Atzilut* receive above *Hochma*?

137. In which clothing does *Olam Atzilut* receive *Ohr Ein Sof*, and *Olam Beria, Olam Yetzira* and *Olam Assiya*?

138. Why is *Hitnotzetzut* from *Elyon* to *Tachton* called Seal and Imprint?

139. Where do the *Kelim* come from?

140. Why did the *Orot* come before the *Kelim*?

141. How are *Kelim de Rosh* made?

142. How are *Kelim de Toch* made?

143. How are *Kelim de Sof* made?

144. Why must every *Partzuf* consist of three degrees - Rosh, Toch, Sof?

145. What is the ascent of *Malchut* to the *Maatzil*?

146. Who causes the ascent of *Malchut* to the *Maatzil*?

147. When does *Ohr Ein Sof* clothe the *Kelim*?

148. Why aren't the *Eser Sefirot de Rosh* regarded as *Kelim*?

149. How were the *Kelim* formed one above the other?

150. Why wasn't a *Kli* generated from the *Eynaim*?

151. Why do the first three *Behinot* of *Ohr Yashar* not have the *Behina* of a *Kli*, but only *Behina Dalet*?

152. Why are *Neshama* and *Ruach* called *Ohr*?

153. Where do the roots of the *Kelim* come from?

154. Where do the complete *Kelim* come from?

155. How and where do the three *Kelim* of the *Guf*, *Bina*, *ZA*, and *Malchut* formulate?

156. What are the names of the four *Behinot* of the *Aviut de Rosh*?

157. What is a *Hamshacha* and reception of *Ohr Yechida*?

158. What is a *Hamshacha* and reception of *Ohr Haya*, *Ohr Neshama* and *Ohr Ruach*?

159. Why do all the *Kelim* equalize in level in the *Zivug de Hakaa*?

160. Where are the five *Behinot* in the *Kli* of *Malchut* from?

161. How can *Malchut de Rosh* expand from and within her to the extent of receiving *Eser Sefirot* from *Rosh*?

162. How far do *Eser Sefirot de Guf* expand?

163. Why are there no *Kelim* opposite *Haya* and *Yechida* of each *Partzuf*?

164. What are these terms: *Shibolet*, *Chazeh*, *Tabur*?

165. When are the *Kelim* of one above the other filled with *Ohr*?

166. Why does *Ohr Yechida* clothe *Galgalta* and not *Peh*?

167. Why doesn't *Ohr Haya* clothe the *Hotem*?

168. How is *AB* emanated from *Partzuf Galgalta*?

169. How is *SAG* emanated from *Partzuf AB*?

170. What causes the *Hizdakchut* of the *Aviut* of *Malchut*?

171. Why did the *Zivug de Hakaa* become the *Eser Sefirot de Rosh de Tachton* in the place of the *Chazeh de Elyon*?

172. Why is the *Shoresh* of every inferior *Partzuf* in the *Peh* of its superior?

173. What does *Rosh de Partzuf AB* clothes from *Peh* to *Chazeh* in *Partzuf Galgalta*?

174. Why can't *Rosh de AB* clothe above *Peh de Galgalta*, and also *SAG* with regards to *AB* and so on?

175. What do the names *Shoresh*, *Neshama*, *Guf*, *Levush*, *Heichal* refer to?

176. Why where *Levush* and *Heichal* separated from the inner *Kelim* and became surrounding?

177. What do the five *Behinot* implied in the names *Shoresh*, *Neshama*, *Guf*, *Levush*, *Heichal* relate to?

178. Why do *NRN*, which are inferior, clothe *Shoresh Neshama* and *Guf*, which are superior?

179. What are the five *Behinot* in the *Neshama* called?

180. What are the five *Behinot* in the *Guf* called?

181. What are the five *Behinot* in the *Levush* called?

182. What are the five *Behinot* in the *Heichal* called?

183. Why is each of the *Behinot* of the *SNGLH* (*Shoresh, Neshama, Guf, Levush, Heichal*), mingled with all other four?

184. What *Behinot* of ZA and *Malchut* are there after *Tzimtzum Bet*?

185. How do *SNGLH* of *Atik de Atzilut* clothe AK?

186. At which *Olam* does the *Shoresh* for the *Tachtonim* begin?

187. Which *Partzuf* in AK is regarded as the *Shoresh* of the inclusive *Eser Sefirot*?

188. Why do we sometimes mention four *Behinot* and other times five?

189. Why do the *Eser Sefirot* not begin with *Keter*?

190. What are the inclusive *Eser Sefirot*?

191. What are the many *Olamot* above *Atzilut*?

192. What is the difference between the inner NRNHY in each *Partzuf* and the five *Partzufim* AB, SAG, MA, BON in each and every *Olam*?

193. What is the difference between the five *Partzufim* and the five *Olamot*?

194. How are the *Eser Sefirot de Ohr Yashar* and *Ohr Hozer* that emerge through a single *Zivug de Hakaa* called?

195. The five levels that emerge one on top of the other are called by whose name?

196. Why are the five *Partzufim* called AB, SAG, MA, BON?

197. Why is the *Guf* called "Seven lower *Sefirot*"?

198. Is there any difference between AK and ABYA from the perspective of the four *Behinot* of *Ohr Yashar*, and why?

199. Why are ABYA denominated by the four *Otiot HaVaYaH*?

200. Why are all the *Behinot* in *Atzilut* called *Neshamot* (pl. for *Neshama*) and in *Beria Gufim* (pl. for *Guf*)?

201. What is the difference between a *Nekuda* and a *Sefira*?

202. What is the difference between a *Sefira* and a *Partzuf*?

203. How many *Behinot* of *Eser Sefirot* must emerge to complete one degree?

204. Why is the *Keter* called *Ein Sof*?

205. Why is *Keter* called "middle" between the *Maatzil* and the *Ne'etzal*?

206. Why are all the *Roshim* (pl. for *Rosh*) of the degrees called *Ein Sof*?

207. What is the meaning of *Hitlabshut Ein Sof* in *Keter*, in *Hochma*, in *Bina*, in *ZA* and in *Malchut*?

208. What is the need for a "middle" *Behina* between Creator and creature?

209. Why is *Keter* not part of the *Eser Sefirot* and is not implied in the *Otiot* of *HaVaYaH*, but only in the tip of the *Yod*?

210. What is the *Shoresh* of the four potential *Behinot*?

211. What is the *Shoresh* of the four actual *Behinot*?

212. Why did *Malchut de Malchut de Atzilut* become *Atik* in *Olam Beria*?

213. From which perspective is *Keter* regarded "I am the last"?

214. From which perspective is *Keter* regarded as "I am the first"?

215. Where does *Keter de Beria* receive from and who is considered to be his *Shoresh*?

216. Why are all the *Behinot* of AK regarded as *Keter* to the *Behinot* of ABYA?

217. Why are HGT *de AA* regarded as *Rosh*?

218. Why isn't the *Behina* of AA recognized in every *Olam*?

219. Why is *Malchut* called "A mirror that has nothing of its own"?

220. What is the meaning of the *Nekuda* that descends from an Upper *Olam* to a lower *Olam*?

221. How did the moon diminish, meaning *Malchut de Atzilut*?

222. What is the *Nekuda* that descends from *Olam* to *Olam* regarded as in and of herself?

223. Why does the *Nekuda* that descends sucks from all the *Elyonim* although she is the smallest of them?

224. Why does the *Ohr Yashar* in all the degrees extend from *Ein Sof*?

225. Why is there no differentiation in the four *Behinot* of *Ohr Yashar* from the *Rosh* of the *Kav* to the end of *Assiya*?

226. Why can't *Ohr Yashar* reach below *Tabur*?

227. Why is the Upper Degree always regarded as the *Maatzil* of its lower degree?

228. What are the two roots of every *Behina*?

229. What is the name given to *Eser Sefirot* of the same level?

230. Why is the *Mador Klipot* (Shell Section) between the *Levush* and the *Or*?

231. Why is the *Ohr Pnimi* in the *Or* worse than in the *Basar, Gidin, Atzamot* and *Mocha* in the *Partzuf*?

232. Why does every thing in *Kedusha* leave an imprint?

233. How high can one reach?

234. Why is *Nefesh de Elyon* regarded as *Ruach* for the *Tachton*?

235. Where do the NRNHY *de Nefesh* come from?

236. What are the differences between *Olam, Partzuf, Sefira, Nekuda*?

237. What are the differences between *Eser Sefirot de Ohr Yashar* and *Eser Sefirot de Ohr Hozer* in the same level, the *Eser Sefirot* where one is above the other, and *Eser Sefirot* where one is below the other, *Eser Sefirot de Rosh, Eser Sefirot de Toch*, and *Eser Sefirot de Sof*, the five *Behinot* of *Kli de Malchut*, the five *Behinot* of potential *Kelim*, and the five *Behinot* of actual *Kelim*?

102. Why does *Ohr Ein Sof* strike the *Masach* in *Kli de Malchut*?

Since before the *Tzimtzum*, its conduct was to fulfill *Behina Dalet*. For that reason, now too it wants to fulfill her, and that is why it strikes the *Masach* that stops it on its way.

(Part 3, Chap 1, item 3 and *Ohr Pnimi*, item 70)

103. What does it mean that the *Ohr* comes in through a *Halon* and a *Nekev* without a *Masach*?

Where the bestowal and the pouring of abundance of *Ohr Hozer* is recognized without any *Aviut*, meaning in the *Ohr Hozer* that ascends from the *Masach* upwards, its *Behinot* are called *Halon* and *Nekev*.

(Part 3, Chap 4, item 2 and *Ohr Pnimi*, item 8)

104. Why is the *Masach* in *Malchut de Elyon* regarded as the giver to its inferior degree?

Because through the *Zivug de Hakaa*, performed in the *Masach de Malchut de Rosh de Elyon* that raises *Ohr Hozer* from the *Masach* upwards, these *Orot* glitter once more to the inferior degree. Consequently, the *Masach* in *Malchut de Elyon* bestows upon the *Tachton*.

(Part 3, Chap 4, item 9 and *Ohr Pnimi*, item 300)

105. What generates the *Hitnotzetzut* of the *Orot* from the *Masach* downward?

Any degree that *Malchut* causes to clothe the *Rosh* through the *Ohr Hozer* that ascends from her is regarded as *Malchut's* own part, for she is the *Shoresh* of its existence. Thus, this entire level expands once more in *Malchut* herself.

In other words, *Malchut* expands to *Eser Sefirot* from her and within her and receives that same level to the three upper *Behinot* in her, down to the *Malchut* in her, where she is unfit to receive because of the *Tzimtzum*. By that, *Malchut* becomes the ending point, called *Tabur*.

(Part 3, Chap 2, item 2 and *Ohr Pnimi*, item 3)

106. What does *He'arah* through the *Masach* mean?

Hitnotzetzut Orot de Rosh from the *Masach* downwards is called *He'arah* through the *Masach* (see item 105).

(Part 3, Chap 2, item 2)

107. What is the difference between In Passing and through *Hitlabshut*?

"In Passing" is what comes by way of cause and consequence in the four *Behinot de Ohr Yashar*. For example: *Behina Bet* is a consequence, cause by *Behina Aleph* and

Behina Gimel by *Behina Bet*. That which comes by way of *Zivug* and *Ohr Hozer* is called "through *Hitlabshut*."

(Part 3, Chap 4, item 1 and *Ohr Pnimi*, item 1)

108. **What does Hitlabshut in Hochma or in Bina etc. mean?**

The *Hitlabshut* of *Eser Sefirot de Ohr Yashar* in *Eser Sefirot de Ohr Hozer* is named after the first *Sefira* in that level. If it is *Keter*, all *Eser Sefirot* will be called *Keter*; if it is *Hochma*, they will be called *Hochma* etc.

(Part 3, Chap 2, item 12 and *Ohr Pnimi*, item 1)

109. **What is the measurement of the Masach?**

See *Ohr Pnimi* Chapter 3, item 1.

110. **What is the Masach between Atzilut and Beria?**

The *Masach* between *Atzilut* and *Beria* is the *Sium Raglin de Atzilut* performed in *Tzimtzum Bet* after the ascent of *Malchut*, being *Behina Dalet*, to *Bina de Nekudot de SAG de AK*. This *Behina Dalet* is interior.

The *Masach de Behina Gimel*, namely *Malchut de Malchut de AA*, is over it. This is *Malchut ha Mesayemet* the *Raglaim* of AA, clothed by *Masach de Behina Bet*, called clothing in *Bina*, for the *Eser Sefirot de Beria*. The two Upper Ones, *Keter* and *Hochma*, are concealed and hidden inside their *Bina*.

(Part 3, Chap 3, item 2)

111. **How does the Masach of Behina Bet impart to Beria and the Masach of Behina Aleph to Yetzira?**

From above downward.

(*Ohr Pnimi*, Chap 3, item 6)

112. **Why did Bina become a Blocked Masach in Beria?**

Because the giver from above downward is regarded as a "blocked *Masach*," meaning its *Gevul* is shut. Consequently the *Eser Sefirot* beneath it cannot suck higher than its *Gevul*.

However, when the *Masach* bestows from below upward it is regarded as an "open *Masach*," because it lacks the power to limit the *Orot* there, although it clothes in its *Ohr Hozer* (see item 103).

(Part 3, Chap 14, item 3)

113. **Why does the point of Malchut de Atzilut breaches and breaks through the Masach?**

Since it is regarded as *Atzilut*. Her *Shoresh* comes from *Masach de Behina Gimel* and *Masach de Behina Bet* does not control her. For that reason she breaches and breaks it, meaning from her perspective it is not regarded as "blocked" (see item 112); it is considered as open. However, even though she descends beneath it, she is not limited by it, but can always go back to *Atzilut*.

(Part 3, Chap 8, item 1)

114. Why do GAR de AA not breach the *Masach*?

Because that *Masach de Behina Bet* is their *Shoresh* and they are below it.

(Part 3, Chap 7, item 1)

115. Why doesn't the *Aviut* appear at once but in an order of four degrees?

Because they are two complete opposites: one wants only to bestow and to not receive at all, and the other wants only to receive. Two opposites cannot stem from one another unless gradually.

Therefore, the *Ohr* does not leave the *Maatzil* and becomes a *Ne'etzal* before it hangs down through the four degrees HB TM of *Ohr Yashar*.

116. What are the two *Behinot* in the *Ohr* of *Histaklut*?

They are *Ohr Yashar* and *Ohr Hozer*. The received *Ohr de Histaklut* in the first three *Behinot* – Hochma, Bina and Tifferet – is the *Ohr Yashar*, and the *Ohr* of *Histaklut* that is not received but is rejected backwards. In other words, the *Ohr* that is fit for *Behina Dalet* is the *Ohr Hozer* in it.

(Part 3, Chap 12, item 3)

117. Are the four degrees of the *Aviut* of *Ohr Yashar* as limited as they are from above downward and why?

In the four *Behinot* of *Ohr Yashar* it is also considered that *Malchut de Elyon* becomes the *Keter de Tachton*. That is because *Malchut de Behina Aleph* became the *Shoresh* and the *Keter* of *Behina Bet*, and *Malchut de Behina Bet* became *Keter de Behina Gimel*.

Thus, *Bina de Ohr Yashar* is limited to *Aviut de Behina Bet* from above her in *Malchut de Hochma*. Also, *Aviut de ZA* comes from *Malchut de Bina* above. For that reason, each of these four *Behinot* is considered to be receiving its *Aviut* from above downward.

118. Who causes the four *Behinot* of *Ohr Yashar* become distinguished and captured in the degree?

The *Ohr Hozer* that ascends from the *Masach* of *Malchut* upwards makes the *Ohr* be caught in the degree.

(Part 3, Chap 12, item 4)

119. Where do the four *Behinot* in the *Ohr Hozer* come from?

They are five *Reshimot* that remained in *Malchut* from her *Orot* in *Ein Sof* after the *Tzimtzum*. There, *Ohr Ein Sof* filled the entire *Behina Dalet*, and she received all the *Ohr* that is destined for her five *Behinot*.

Since the *Masach* now detains all the *Ohr* that should fulfill these *Reshimot*, you find that there are five *Behinot KHB TM* in this *Ohr Hozer* that are rejected from the five *Reshimot* in *Malchut*. Know, that these five *Behinot* in the *Ohr Hozer* ascend and clothe the five *Behinot* in the *Ohr Yashar*.

(*Histaklut Pnimit*, Chap 2, item 2)

120. What changes in the *Ohr Hozer* before the *Ohr Yashar* clothes it and after the *Ohr Yashar* clothes it?

Any *Hidush Tzura* is regarded as an addition to the first *Tzura*. Thus, if *Behina Dalet* in *Malchut* was purified into *Behina Gimel*, then this is a different *Malchut*, additional to the first, because there is no absence in spirituality.

However, the force of the restriction in *Malchut de Behina Dalet* rides on the new *Malchut de Behina Gimel* too. Therefore the *Zivug de Hakaa* does apply to her, but she is still not regarded as *Malchut ha Mesayemet* as is *Malchut de Behina Dalet de Elyon* before the *Ohr Yashar* clothed her *Ohr Hozer*.

In other words, she expands to *Eser Sefirot de Guf* from her and within her and the *Ohr Hozer* descends to them from above downward with the complete measure of the level that clothed the *Rosh* through *Malchut de Malchut*, called *Tabur*. Only afterwards does *Tabur* become the ending point because the first *Tzimtzum* was only on the *Kli* of *Malchut* that has already clothed the *Orot*.

(*Histaklut Pnimit*, Chap 7, item 5)

121. What is the reason for the *Hitpashtut* of *Eser Sefirot de Rosh* to a state of *Guf*?

See above item 105.

(Part 3, Chap 8, item 1)

122. Are the four *Behinot Komot de Ohr Hozer* that limit ABYA from above downward, and why?

They certainly do from above downward because the *Ohr Hozer* from below upward places no *Gevul* (see item 112).

(Part 3, Chap 3, item 5)

123.   Why does the *Aviut* of *Behina Gimel* generate the level of *Hochma*?

Because the five *Reshimot KHB*, ZA, *Malchut*, in *Kli de Malchut* (see item 119) stand from below upward. That is because *Behina Dalet* is *Keter*, *Behina Gimel* is *Hochma*, *Behina Bet* is *Bina*, *Behina Aleph* is ZA and the purest of all is *Malchut*.

Because she lacks *Aviut de Behina Dalet*, even if she did receive the *Ohr* directly inside, she would not have a place to extend and receive the *Ohr* of *Keter*, for she lacks *Behina Dalet*.

Now too, when the *Masach* rejected and pushed that *Ohr* backwards, it only rejected from *Hochma* downward, namely the measure that she could receive. For that reason that *Ohr Hozer* cannot ascend and clothe *Keter*, but only from *Hochma* downward, as is its own level.

Similarly, if she has only *Aviut de Behina Bet*, the level of *Ohr Hozer* itself would lack the two *Sefirot Keter* and *Hochma*. For that reason it cannot clothe *Keter* and *Hochma de Ohr Yashar*, but only from *Bina* downward.

(*Histaklut Pnimit*, Chap 2, item 2)

124.   How do *Zivugim de Hakaa* occur in AHP?

Even though *Ohr AHP* is *Ohr de Hassadim*, there is still *Zivug de Hakaa* there because they necessarily have *He'arat Hochma*.

125.   Why are the *Eser Sefirot* that end the *Partzuf, Eser Sefirot de Ohr Hozer* without *Ohr Yashar*?

Because *Ohr Hozer* without *Ohr Yashar* hasn't any bestowal. For that reason it is called *Ohr Nekeva*, which only receives and does not give anything and therefore ends the *Partzuf*.

(*Histaklut Pnimit*, Chap 7, item 2)

126.   What is the *Hevel* that comes out of a degree?

Ohr Hozer that descends from above downward is called "*Hevel* that comes out."

(Part 3, Chap 11, item 7 and *Ohr Pnimi*, item 8)

127.   Why doesn't real *Hevel* come out from the eyes?

Because there is no *Hakaa* in *Behina Aleph* due to her frail *Aviut*.

(Part 3, Chap 11, item 5)

128.   What comes to be in the *Sefirot* as a result of the *Ohr* of *Histaklut*?

The *Ohr Yashar* and the essence of the existence of the *Ohr Hozer* come from *Ohr Histaklut*, meaning *Ohr Hochma* that expands from *Ein Sof*, called *Keter* (see item 116).

The essence of the existence of the *Kelim* is also from the *Ohr Histaklut*, for they are generated by the *Ohr Hozer*.

(Part 3, Chap 11, item 6)

129. What comes to be in the *Sefirot* as a result of the *Hevels* of the AHP?

The *Aviut* in the *Kelim*, which appears from the *Masach* downward (see item 122), is made of *Hevels* that extends from the *AHP*.

(Part 3, Chap 11, item 7)

130. Why isn't any reality made of *Orot AHP*?

Because *AHP* is only regarded as *Malchut*. *Malchut* that rose to *Behina Gimel* of the *Rosh* is called *Hotem* and *Malchut* that rose to *Behina Bet* of the *Rosh* is called *Awzen*. Thus, they do not have any *Ohr Yashar*, but only descending *Ohr Hozer*, called "exiting *Hevel*". They only create the *Aviut* in the *Kelim*, and that is why no reality came from them (see item 29).

(Part 3, Chap 11, item 7 and *Ohr Pnimi*, item 8)

131. A. What does it mean that there is no *Masach* at all in *Olam Atzilut*?

There is no *Masach* in *Olam Atzilut* because *Masach* means rejection of the *Ohr* from clothing the *Kli*. Wherever there is a *Masach*, it stops the *He'arah* of *Ohr Elyon* from shining.

You can therefore see that the real *Masach* in only at the *Sium Raglin* of every *Partzuf*, for it stops the *Ohr* and the *Partzuf* ends and its degree. However, the screens above the *Sium Raglin* of the *Partzuf* are but acts that rise from the *Masach de Sium Raglin*. In *Peh de Rosh* it performs a *Zivug de Hakaa*, and at the *Chazeh*, it stops the *Hitlabshut* of *Ohr Yashar*.

The *Behinot* of *Hizdakchut* of the *Masach* referred to the *Partzuf* are not actual screens, for they do not stop the *He'arah* of the degree of the *Partzuf*. They are rather operations that eventuate by the power of the *Aviut* and the *Kashiut* in the *Masach de Sium Raglin*. We only call them screens to simplify the issue.

B. What is the difference between *Ohr* of *Atzmut* and *Ohr* of *Tolada?*

The *Ohr Yashar* clothed in *Ohr Hozer* that ascends to them from below upward is the *Atzmut* of the degree. *Ohr Yashar* that is clothed in *Ohr Hozer* that descends from the *Masach* downwards, called *Eser Sefirot de Guf*, is called *Ohr* of *Tolada* from the *Eser Sefirot de Rosh* (Chap 8, item 9).

Ohr that extends to the *Tachton* because it bestowed upon the *Elyon* is called *Ohr* of *Tolada* and also *Guf*. Also, the three lines of ZA that extend because "three extend from one," are also called *Ohr* of *Tolada*, and *Guf*.

132. **Why is every level of *Eser Sefirot* named only after its uppermost *Sefira*?**

Because the smaller *Orot* are completely nullified in the greater ones and do not count.

133. **Why are the two *Orot* of ZON on the same level?**

Since they come from *Eser Sefirot* of the same level.

(Part 3, Chap 7, item 2)

134. **How is the *Zivug de Hakaa* performed for the purpose of the *Eser Sefirot de Beria* and *de Yetzira*?**

The *Eser Sefirot de Beria* came out by *Zivug de Hakaa* in *Karka de Atzilut*, and the *Eser Sefirot de Yetzira* came out by a *Zivug de Hakaa* in *Eser Sefirot de Beria*.

(Part 3, Chap 2, item 2 and *Ohr Pnimi*, item 3)

135. **How does *Ein Sof* shine in *Atzilut*?**

By *Hitlabshut* of *Ohr Ein Sof* in *Hochma*, meaning from a *Zivug* on *Masach de Behina Gimel*.

(Part 3, Chap 3, item 4)

136. **Why doesn't *Atzilut* receive above *Hochma*?**

Because *Ohr Hozer* that is rejected from *Malchut* doesn't have *Ohr de Keter*, but only from *Hochma* downwards (see item 123). For that reason it doesn't have anything with which to clothe the *Keter de Ohr Yashar* and receive from it.

(Part 3, Chap 3 and *Ohr Pnimi*, item 3)

137. **In which clothing does *Olam Atzilut* receive *Ohr Ein Sof*, and *Olam Beria*, *Olam Yetzira* and *Olam Assiya*?**

Atzilut receives in clothing, meaning *Ohr Hozer* from *Behina Gimel*, called *Hochma*. *Beria* – by a clothing of *Behina Bet*, called *Bina*, *Yetzira* – by a clothing of *Behina Aleph*, called ZA or *Tifferet*, and *Assiya* receives through *Malchut de Yetzira*.

(Part 3, Chap 3, item 2 and item 3)

138. **Why is *Hitnotzetzut* from *Elyon* to *Tachton* called Seal and Imprint?**

The *Ohr Hozer* that clothes all the *Behinot* from the *Masach* upwards to the *Orot de Rosh*, also brings them when it expands from the *Masach* downward to the *Eser Sefirot de Guf*, not a thing missing. For that reason, this *Ohr Hozer* that descends from above downward is exactly like a Seal. Every thing that is engraved in it is copied to the imprint, being the *Eser Sefirot de Guf*. It is like that also from every *Elyon* to *Tachton*.

(Part 3, Chap 8, item 9 and *Ohr Pnimi*, item 8)

139. Where do the *Kelim* come from?

The *Kelim* come primarily from the *Ohr* of *Histaklut* (see item 128), though their *Aviut* and *Tzura* were formed by the *Ohr Hozer* that descends from *Awzen, Hotem, Peh* downwards (see item 129).

(Part 3, Chap 11, item 7)

140. Why did the *Orot* come before the *Kelim*?

It is because when *Ohr Ein Sof* expanded to create the *Kelim*, there were four *Behinot* of *Ohr Yashar* there. We know that three *Behinot*, HB and ZA are regarded as *Orot*, and only *Malchut* is considered to be a *Kli*. It is because of that that the *Orot* come before the *Kelim*.

(Part 3, Chap 12, item 5 and *Ohr Pnimi*, item 2)

141. How are *Kelim de Rosh* made?

By the *Ohr Hozer* from the *Masach* upward.

(Part 3, Chap 12, item 4)

142. How are *Kelim de Toch* made?

By the *Histaklut* in AHP. During the *Hizdakchut* of *Tabur* to *Behina Gimel*, the *Ohr* leaves from the place between *Tabur* and *Chazeh* because the *Behina Gimel* of *Guf* is called *Chazeh*, and because of this *Hizdakchut Malchut de Rosh* rose from *Peh* to *Hotem*.

It is so because *Behina Gimel de Rosh* is called *Hotem*, and there was a *Zivug de Hakaa* there, on *Behina Gimel*, and the *Ohr Hozer* that descends from the *Hotem* down expanded to the *Chazeh*.

Afterwards, when *Malchut de Behina Gimel* purifies to *Malchut de Behina Bet*, the *Ohr* leaves from the place of the *Chazeh* as well, until *Shibolet ha Zakan*. That is because *Behina Bet de Guf* is found there, and because of this *Hizdakchut Malchut de Rosh* also ascends from the *Hotem* to the *Awzen*, which is *Behina Bet de Rosh*. Then there is a *Zivug de Hakaa* there, on *Masach de Behina Bet*, and the *Ohr Hozer* that descends from the *Awzen* downwards expands all the way to *Shibolet ha Zakan*.

Afterwards, because *Malchut de Behina Bet de Guf*, called *Shibolet ha Zakan*, was purified to *Aviut de Behina Aleph*, the *Ohr* left from *Shibolet ha Zakan* almost to the *Peh*. Because of that, *Malchut de Rosh* ascended from the *Awzen* to the *Eynaim*, meaning to *Behina Aleph de Rosh*, where there is no *Hakaa* (see item 127). For that reason there is also no *Ohr Hozer* there, which comes down and therefore no *Kli* was made for the *Ohr Hochma*.

369

Similarly, when she was purified to *Behinat Shoresh* and *Malchut* rose from *Eynaim* to *Galgalta*, namely *Keter de Rosh*, there was also no *Hakaa* there and that is why there was no descending *Ohr Hozer* there. For that reason the *Kli de Keter de Guf* does not emerge.

Hence, the *Guf* does not have *Kelim* for *Haya*, which is *Ohr Hochma*, or *Yechida*, which is *Ohr de Keter* because of the absence of *Hakaa* there during the *Hizdakchut* of *Malchut*. It turns out that there are only three *Kelim* here, namely *Malchut* - from *Chazeh* to *Tabur*, ZA - from *Shibolet ha Zakan* to the *Chazeh* and *Bina* - from below the *Peh* to *Shibolet ha Zakan*. You should know that there is no *Zivug de Hakaa* in *Malchut de Guf*, but in *Malchut de Rosh*, meaning from the *Peh* upwards.

(*Histaklut Pnimit*, Chap 6, item 5)

143. How are *Kelim de Sof* made?

Since *Malchut de Guf* cannot receive any *Ohr Yashar* but only *Ohr Hozer*, and *Ohr Hozer* without *Ohr Yashar* does not expand and bestow, for that reason the *Partzuf* ends.

(*Histaklut Pnimit*, Chap 7, item 5)

144. Why must every *Partzuf* consist of three degrees - Rosh, Toch, Sof?

Because first, there must be a *Zivug de Hakaa*, which uncovers the *Ohr Hozer* from below upward to the *Eser Sefirot* of *Rosh* and the roots of the *Kelim*. Afterwards, in order to expose the complete *Kelim*, the *Ohr Hozer* must expand from the *Masach* downwards (see item 142).

After that the *Eser Sefirot* that end the *Partzuf*, which are *Eser Sefirot de Sof* are needed. Thus, a degree is not completed but only in the three *Behinot* – Rosh, Toch, Sof.

(*Histaklut Pnimit*, Chap 5, item 4)

145. What is the ascent of *Malchut* to the *Maatzil*?

Ascent means purification. When *Malchut de Guf* purifies to *Behina Gimel*, it is regarded as *Malchut* ascending to ZA. When she purifies to *Behina Bet*, it is regarded as *Malchut* ascending to *Bina*, and when she purifies to *Behina Aleph* it is considered that she rose to *Hochma*. When she purifies to *Behinat Shoresh*, it is considered that she rose to *Keter*, called the *Maatzil*.

(*Histaklut Pnimit*, Chap 10, item 7)

146. Who causes the ascent of *Malchut* to the *Maatzil*?

Ohr Makif that remains outside the *Partzuf* and wants to shine in the *Pnimiut* is the cause of the *Hizdakchut*.

147. **When does *Ohr Ein Sof* clothe the *Kelim*?**

After the second *Histaklut* in *Orot AHP* (see item 142), which makes all the *Orot* from *Eser Sefirot de Guf* leave, there was a new *Zivug* and a second *Hitpashtut*, which shines once more and fulfills those *Eser Sefirot de Guf*. It also generates a new *Partzuf* that is clothed in that same place.

(see item 168)

148. **Why aren't the *Eser Sefirot de Rosh* regarded as *Kelim*?**

Because the *Aviut* in *Malchut* cannot ascend from where she is generated even one bit. For that reason, the *Ohr Hozer* that ascends from her upwards is regarded as *Ohr*, but with regards to the *Ohr Yashar* it is regarded as a *Kli*. Consequently, it is only enough to be caught in the degree and become a *Shoresh* for the *Kelim*.

149. **How were the *Kelim* formed one above the other?**

See above item 142.

150. **Why wasn't a *Kli* generated from the *Eynaim*?**

See above item 142.

151. **Why do the first three *Behinot* of *Ohr Yashar* not have the *Behina* of a *Kli*, but only *Behina Dalet*?**

Because the *Kli* consists primarily of the *Aviut*, meaning the will to receive in the *Ne'etzal*, which appeared in a sufficient amount only in *Behina Dalet*. The first three *Behinot* do not have a sufficient amount, but they are regarded as the generators of *Behina Dalet*. For that reason the first three *Behinot* are regarded as *Ohr*, and *Behina Dalet* alone is regarded as a *Kli*.

(Part 3, Chap 12, item 2)

152. **Why are *Neshama* and *Ruach* called *Ohr*?**

See above item 151.

153. **Where do the roots of the *Kelim* come from?**

From the *Ohr Hozer* that ascends from the *Masach* upward.

154. **Where do the complete *Kelim* come from?**

From the *Ohr Hozer* that descends from the *Masach* downward.

155. **How and where do the three *Kelim* of the *Guf*, *Bina*, *ZA*, and *Malchut* formulate?**

By *Hizdakchut Malchut de Guf* (See item 142).

156. **What are the names of the four *Behinot* of the *Aviut de Rosh*?**

Aviut de Behina Aleph de Ohr Yashar is called "reception through *Keter*." *Aviut de Behina Bet* is called "*Harchaka*." *Aviut de Behina Gimel* is called "*Halon* and narrow *Nekev*," and *Aviut de Behina Dalet* is called "*Halon* and narrow *Nekev* with *Harchaka*."

(Part 3, Chap 1, item 4)

157. **What is a *Hamshacha* and reception of *Ohr Yechida*?**

The *Hamshacha* is in *Aviut de Behina Dalet* and reception is in the totally pure, such as *Behinat Shoresh*.

158. **What is a *Hamshacha* and reception of *Ohr Haya*, *Ohr Neshama* and *Ohr Ruach*?**

For *Ohr Haya*, the *Hamshacha* is in *Behina Gimel*, and reception is in *Behina Aleph*. For *Ohr Neshama*, the *Hamshacha* is in *Behina Bet* and reception is also in *Behina Bet*. For *Ohr Ruach* the *Hamshacha* is in *Behina Aleph* and reception is in *Behina Gimel*, and for *Ohr Nefesh* the *Hamshacha* is by ZA and the reception is in *Behina Dalet*.

159. **Why do all the *Kelim* equalize in level in the *Zivug de Hakaa*?**

Because in *Ohr Yashar*, the purer is more important and higher, and the opposite is true in *Ohr Hozer*, meaning the *Av* is more important. Therefore, when clothing one another, their level becomes the same because the lower in *Ohr Yashar* is higher in *Ohr Hozer* and vise versa.

160. **Where are the five *Behinot* in the *Kli* of *Malchut* from?**

See above item 119.

161. **How can *Malchut de Rosh* expand from and within her to the extent of receiving *Eser Sefirot* from *Rosh*?**

See above item 121 and item 120.

162. **How far do *Eser Sefirot de Guf* expand?**

To *Malchut de Malchut*, called *Tabur*.

163. **Why are there no *Kelim* opposite *Haya* and *Yechida* of each *Partzuf*?**

See above item 142.

164. **What are these terms: *Shibolet*, *Chazeh*, *Tabur*?**

Shibolet is *Malchut de Bina de Guf*; *Chazeh* is *Malchut de ZA de Guf*; *Tabur* is *Malchut de Malchut de Guf*.

(See above item 142)

165. **When are the *Kelim* of one above the other filled with *Ohr*?**

In *Hitpashtut Bet*.

(See above item 147)

166. **Why does *Ohr Yechida* clothe *Galgalta* and not *Peh*?**

Because the giver gives in the more *Av* thing, and the receiver must receive in the more *Zach*.

167. **Why doesn't *Ohr Haya* clothe the *Hotem*?**

Because *Ohr Haya* is received only in *Behina Aleph*, which is *Ohr Eynaim*, as explained in item 166.

168. **How is AB emanated from *Partzuf Galgalta*?**

Every *Partzuf* must have two roots in its *Elyon*. Those are *Keter Malchut de Elyon*, called *Peh*, and *Malchut de Malchut de Elyon* called *Tabur*. It is so because by the ascent of *Tabur de Partzuf Keter* to its *Peh*, meaning when *Malchut de Guf* is purified from its *Aviut* and remains as pure as *Kli de Keter*, it is regarded as reaching the place of *Peh de Rosh*, being as pure as the *Peh*. That is because from above downward there is no *Aviut* in the *Peh*.

This *Peh* stands there and serves as *Malchut de Rosh*, which raises *Ohr Hozer* from below upward, and from below upwards it has *Aviut de Behina Dalet*. It turns out that the *Tabur* that rose there is also incorporated in that *Zivug* of the *Peh* from below upward, meaning mingled with the *Aviut* there.

However, *Tabur* cannot receive *Aviut de Behina Dalet* inside, as it is in the *Peh* because of the disappearance of its last *Behina* form it by the power of the purification. For that reason, *Tabur* receives only *Aviut de Behina Gimel* there.

Know, that this *Hitabut* that *Tabur* acquired from the *Peh* is called "descent to the place of *Chazeh de Partzuf Keter*". That is because after the *Tabur* (which is the *Behina* of *Malchut de Guf* from above downward) became *Av*, it became *Malchut de Guf* once more, called *Chazeh*.

Thus, by acquiring the above *Aviut*, *Tabur* left the *Behina* of *Peh* and descended once more near the *Tabur*, meaning to the place it was in before it purified, namely the place of the *Chazeh*. It didn't actually go down to *Tabur* because it did not become *Av* in *Behina Dalet*, but only in *Behina Gimel*, and the *Chazeh* is the place of *Malchut* of *Behina Gimel de Guf de Partzuf Keter*.

Thus, through its *Hizdakchut* and ascent to the *Peh*, the *Tzura* of *Tabur* has changed, because prior to its ascent, it had *Aviut de Behina Dalet*, and after the ascent back to its place, it received only *Aviut de Behina Gimel*. For that reason that *Tabur* is now considered to be a new *Kli* of *Malchut*. Therefore, it is regarded to have stepped completely out of the Upper *Partzuf*, namely *Partzuf Keter*.

Doing that, it became fit for *Zivug de Hakaa* and *Hitlabshut* of *Eser Sefirot de Rosh*, even though it stood in the place of the *Chazeh de Partzuf Keter*, even though the *Chazeh*, which is *Malchut de Guf* is unfit for *Hakaa* (see item 142). Because it comes from the *Behina* of *Malchut* after the *Ohr* clothed her from above downward (see item 120), that *Hitlabshut* does not concern that *Tabur* that rose and descended there. It is so because that *Tabur* is the new *Behina* of *Malchut*, where the *Ohr Elyon* has never yet clothed, rendering it fit for *Zivug de Hakaa* (see item 120 and item 210).

It is for that reason that *Ohr Ein Sof* expanded to the new *Behinat Malchut* of *Behina Gimel* that stands in the place of the *Chazeh de Elyon*. By the *Hakaa* in the *Masach* in her, the *Eser Sefirot de Ohr Hozer* came out and clothed the *Ohr Elyon* up to the level of *Hochma*, as it says in item 119, that the *Ohr Hozer* that rises from *Malchut de Behina Gimel* cannot clothe the *Keter*.

Thus, the *Eser Sefirot* of this new *Rosh* clothe *Partzuf Keter* from the place of *Malchut de Rosh*, meaning in *Chazeh de Partzuf Keter*, to the place of its *Peh*, for there is its Upper *Shoresh*, and they cannot transcend above their *Shoresh*. It turns out that the *Rosh de Partzuf Keter* remains uncovered.

After that the *Ohr Hozer* descends and expands from *Malchut de Rosh* downward to the *Eser Sefirot de Toch*, as it says in item 142, and *Eser Sefirot de Sof*, as it says in item 143. Thus, that *Rosh, Toch, Sof* is called *Partzuf AB* that is born and generated by its Upper *Partzuf*, called *Partzuf Keter*, or *Galgalta*.

(Part 3, *Histaklut Pnimit*, Chap 10)

169. How is SAG emanated from *Partzuf AB*?

It has already been explained that the primary cause of the birth of a *Partzuf* is that law of *Hizdakchut* that is always applied in the *Eser Sefirot de Guf* because of the clothing of *Ohr Elyon* inside them (see *Histaklut Pnimit* Part 2, Chap 10, item 1). Therefore, after the *Ohr Elyon* clothed the *Eser Sefirot de Guf de Partzuf AB* here too, it caused the *Hizdakchut* of the *Aviut* in its *Malchut de Guf*, called *Tabur de AB*. It was gradually purified from below upward until it became as *Zach* as *Shoresh*.

This is called the ascent of *Tabur de AB* to its *Peh*, where it acquired a new *Aviut* of *Behina Bet*. That is because the last *Behina* always disappears during the *Hizdakchut* (see previous item). Here in *AB*, whose *Aviut* is from *Behina Gimel*, the last *Behina* is

Behina Gimel, so that is what disappears through the *Hizdakchut*. Consequently, by its *Hitkalelut* with the *Peh*, *Tabur* now acquired only *Aviut de Behina Bet*.

The *Hitabut* of *Tabur* to *Behina Bet* is called "exit from the *Peh* and descent to the place of *Chazeh de AB*", which is the place of *Behina Bet de Guf*. *Tabur* is regarded as *Behina Gimel de Guf* there, and *Chazeh* as *Behina Bet*. For the reasons we have explained in the previous item, there was a new *Zivug de Hakaa* in this new *Malchut*, meaning in *Tabur de AB* that ascended and descended to the *Chazeh*.

For that reason, the place of the *Chazeh* became *Malchut de Rosh*. From the *Chazeh* upwards to *Peh de AB*, the *Eser Sefirot de Rosh* of *Bina*'s level expanded. From the *Chazeh* downwards, *Eser Sefirot de Toch* and *Eser Sefirot de Sof* expanded, as was explained in the previous item. Thus, the *Rosh, Toch, Sof* of this *Partzuf*, whose level is only up to *Bina*, is called *Partzuf SAG*.

170. **What causes the *Hizdakchut* of the *Aviut* of *Malchut*?**

The *Hitlabshut* of the *Atzmut* in the *Kelim* always causes *Hizdakchut* of the *Aviut* of *Malchut*.

(Part 3, Chap 10)

171. **Why did the *Zivug de Hakaa* become the *Eser Sefirot de Rosh de Tachton* in the place of the *Chazeh de Elyon*?**

Because the last *Behina* always disappears due to the force of the *Hizdakchut* and the ascent to the *Peh*. That is why *Tabur* that ascends there and receives the new *Aviut* always loses the last *Behina* it bad prior to its *Hizdakchut*, being its previous *Malchut* that always stands from *Tabur* to *Chazeh* of each *Partzuf*.

Thus, when it leaves the *Peh* and returns to its former location, it descends only to the place of the *Chazeh* and makes the new *Zivug* there for its other *Partzuf*, the lower one (see item 168). That is why we have the rule that *Chazeh de Elyon* is *Malchut de Rosh de Tachton*, called *Peh de Tachton*.

172. **Why is the *Shoresh* of every inferior *Partzuf* in the *Peh* of its superior?**

See above item 210.

173. **What does *Rosh de Partzuf AB* clothes from *Peh* to *Chazeh* in *Partzuf Galgalta*?**

See above item 168.

174. **Why can't *Rosh de AB* clothe above *Peh de Galgalta*, and also SAG with regards to AB and so on?**

375

Because the Upper *Shoresh* of every *Tachton* is the *Peh* of the *Rosh de Elyon* (see item 169). It therefore cannot transcend above its *Shoresh*.

175. What do the names *Shoresh, Neshama, Guf, Levush, Heichal* refer to?

They are appellations of these *KHB, ZA,* and *Malchut. ZA* and *Malchut* separated from them and became the surrounding *Kelim*, indicating the lack of *Haya* and *Yechida* there.

176. Why where *Levush* and *Heichal* separated from the inner *Kelim* and became surrounding?

Because of the association of *Midat ha Rachamim* with *Din*, meaning the ascent of *Malchut* and her restrictive force into *Bina*, and their *Hitkalelut*. Because of that the previous *ZA* and *Malchut* went below the point of the *Tzimtzum* and could not receive any *Ohr*. Consequently, they became *Makifim* (surrounding) that receive the *Ohr* but from a distance.

(Part 3, Chap 10, item 2)

177. What do the five *Behinot* implied in the names *Shoresh, Neshama, Guf, Levush, Heichal* relate to?

They imply specifically to *ZA* and *Malchut de Behina Dalet* that were separated and became *Makifim*. Because of that, the inner *Haya* and *Yechida* became absent in every *Partzuf* from *Olam ha Nekudim* onward.

178. Why do NRN, which are inferior, clothe *Shoresh Neshama* and *Guf*, which are superior?

Because the *Ohr* is always received in the purer *Kelim*.

179. What are the five *Behinot* in the *Neshama* called?

NRNHY.

(Part 3, Chap 5, item 3)

180. What are the five *Behinot* in the *Guf* called?

Moach, Atzamot, Gidin, Bassar and *Or.*

(There)

181. What are the five *Behinot* in the *Levush* called?

Ktonet, Michnasayim, Mitznefet and *Avnet* (shirt, trousers, miter and a girdle – respectively).

(There)

182. **What are the five *Behinot* in the *Heichal* called?**

Bait, Hatzer, Sadeh, Midbar (house, yard, field, desert – respectively).

(There)

183. **Why is each of the *Behinot* of the SNGLH (*Shoresh, Neshama, Guf, Levush, Heichal*), mingled with all other four?**

Because of the *Hizdakchut* of the *Masach* in each of their degrees.

184. **What *Behinot* of ZA and *Malchut* are there after *Tzimtzum Bet*?**

ZA and *Malchut de Bina*.

(Part 3, *Ohr Pnimi*, Chap 10, item 1)

185. **How do SNGLH of *Atik de Atzilut* clothe AK?**

Shoresh, Neshama, Guf de Atik clothe *Shoresh, Neshama, Guf de AK* because *Levush* and *Heichal de BON de AK* were separated from the inner of AK and became *Makifim*. It is so in every *Partzuf* from there onwards.

(Part 3, Chap 10, item 3)

186. **At which *Olam* does the *Shoresh* for the *Tachtonim* begin?**

At *Partzuf BON de AK* onwards, where the beginning of the association of *Midat ha Rachamim* with *Din* was.

187. **Which *Partzuf* in AK is regarded as the *Shoresh* of the inclusive *Eser Sefirot*?**

Partzuf BON de AK. However, the previous *Partzufim*, which come from the real *Behina Dalet*, stand alone for they haven't the association of *Midat ha Rachamim* with *Din*, as in the collective *Eser Sefirot*.

188. **Why do we sometimes mention four *Behinot* and other times five?**

The truth is that they are only four *Behinot*. However, when we also count *Shoresh* with them, which is called *Keter*, they are considered five *Behinot*.

(Part 3, Chap 7 item 9)

189. **Why do the *Eser Sefirot* not begin with *Keter*?**

Because *Keter* itself consists only of the roots of the four *Behinot* HB TM, and it too begins from *Hochma*.

(Part 3, Chap 8, item 9)

190. **What are the inclusive *Eser Sefirot*?**

BON de AK, *Atzilut, Beria, Yetzira Assiya*.

(Part 3, Chap 8, item 1)

191. **What are the many *Olamot* above *Atzilut*?**

They are all included in the five *Partzufim* of AK. That is because AK is regarded as the first *Eser Sefirot* that emerged in the *Rosh* after the *Tzimtzum*.

192. **What is the difference between the inner NRNHY in each *Partzuf* and the five *Partzufim* AB, SAG, MA, BON in each and every *Olam*?**

The inner *NRNHY* that are clothed in the *Sefirot KHB ZON* of each *Partzuf*, are generated by *Zivugim de Hakaa* on the path of the purification of *Malchut*. For that reason they stand one above the other.

However, the four *Partzufim*, AB, SAG, MA, and BON emerge by the ascent of *Tabur* to *Peh*, where she acquires a new *Aviut* and went back down to her place (see item 168). For that reason *Chazeh de Elyon* became the *Peh* of the *Tachton*, and they stand one below the other.

(Part 3, *Histaklut Pnimit*, Chap 13, item 1)

193. **What is the difference between the five *Partzufim* and the five *Olamot*?**

There are many differences among the *Olamot*, as will be explained in the coming lessons, which is not the case among the *Partzufim*.

194. **How are the *Eser Sefirot de Ohr Yashar* and *Ohr Hozer* that emerge through a single *Zivug de Hakaa* called?**

They are *Eser Sefirot* of even level, called – *Or, Bassar, Gidin, Atzamot, Mocha*.

195. **The five levels that emerge one on top of the other are called by whose name?**

They are called *NRNHY*, or *KHB ZON*, meaning after the highest *Sefira* on the level.

196. **Why are the five *Partzufim* called AB, SAG, MA, BON?**

Will be explained in later parts.

197. **Why is the *Guf* called "Seven lower *Sefirot*"?**

Because there are *Kelim* only for *Bina* and ZON, called *Shibolet, Chazeh* and *Tabur*. It turns out that from the *Shibolet* downwards, where the *Guf* begins, there is only the *Kli de ZA* and the *Kli de Malchut*, which are seven *Sefirot*. ZA contains *HGT NHY* and along with *Malchut* they are seven *Sefirot HGT NHYM*.

198. **Is there any difference between AK and ABYA from the perspective of the four *Behinot* of *Ohr Yashar*, and why?**

There is no differentiation of degrees from the perspective of the four *Behinot de Ohr Yashar*, for they are always *Behinot* of *Hitpashtut* from *Ein Sof*. That is because there isn't any *Hidush* of *Ohr* in the *Olamot* that does not extend from *Ein Sof*.

199. Why are ABYA denominated by the four Otiot HaVaYaH?

It is so because the four Otiot HaVaYaH imply HB TM, and the upper Sefirot in the four Olamot ABYA also imply HB TM. Thus, each Olam is named after its highest Sefira.

(Part 3, Chap 8, item 1)

200. Why are all the Behinot in Atzilut called Neshamot (pl. for Neshama) and in Beria Gufim (pl. for Guf)?

When we want to compare the Olamot that are associated with Midat ha Rachamim with the Partzufim of AK where there isn't this association of Midat ha Rachamim, we call the Sefirot, KHB TM, Shoresh, Neshama, Guf, Levush, Heichal. All its Behinot of AK are regarded as Shoresh, all the Atzilut as Neshama and all the Beria as Guf.

When we relate to the Olamot themselves, we call them NRNHY; Yechida is in AK, Haya, which is Ohr Hochma, is in Atzilut, Neshama is in Beria, Ruach in Yetzira and Nefesh in Assiya. You already know that with regards to the SNGLH, all the Olamot of BYA lack Yechida and Haya (see item 177). Consequently, Atzilut does not have more than Neshama, and that is why it is called here Neshama.

(Part 3, Chap 8, item 1)

201. What is the difference between a Nekuda and a Sefira?

The Masach and the Malchut before the Zivug de Hakaa is called Nekuda. After the Zivug de Hakaa and the clothing of the Eser Sefirot Ohr Hozer to Eser Sefirot de Ohr Yashar they are called Sefira.

(Part 3, Chap 5, item 1 and Chap 7, item 2)

202. What is the difference between a Sefira and a Partzuf?

See above item 192.

203. How many Behinot of Eser Sefirot must emerge to complete one degree?

Eser Sefirot of Rosh, Eser Sefirot of Toch (see items 141 and 142), and Eser Sefirot of Sof.

(See above item 143)

204. Why is the Keter called Ein Sof?

Because Malchut de Rosh, called Keter, does not end and places a Sof on the Ohr. Quite the contrary, it becomes the beginning of all the Orot in the Partzuf.

(Part 3, Chap 1, item 4)

205. Why is Keter called "middle" between the Maatzil and the Ne'etzal?

Because it has the force of the Maatzil and the force of the Ne'etzal (see item 210).

(See above item 210)

206. **Why are all the *Roshim* (pl. for *Rosh*) of the degrees called *Ein Sof*?**

Because *Malchut de Rosh* does not end the *Ohr*. Quite the contrary, it becomes a beginning for the *Ohr* through the *Ohr Hozer* that ascends from her.

(See above item 204)

207. **What is the meaning of *Hitlabshut Ein Sof* in *Keter*, in *Hochma*, in *Bina*, in *ZA* and in *Malchut*?**

When the *Eser Sefirot de Ohr Yashar* clothe the *Ohr Hozer* that ascends from the *Zivug de Hakaa* in *Masach de Behina Dalet* that clothes the *Ohr Yashar* up to *Keter*, it is called *Hitlabshut Ein Sof* in *Keter*.

If the level of *Ohr Hozer* is from *Behina Gimel*, it is called *Hitlabshut Ein Sof* in *Hochma*. If it is from *Behina Bet*, it is called *Hitlabshut Ein Sof* in *Bina*. When it clothes *Behina Aleph*, it is called *Hitlabshut Ein Sof* in ZA or *Tifferet*. Although there are *Eser Sefirot de Ohr Yashar* and *Ohr Hozer* in any *Hitlabshut*, still, any *Hitlabshut* is named only after its highest *Sefira* of the level.

(Part 3, Chap 3, item 4)

208. **What is the need for a "middle" *Behina* between Creator and creature?**

It is because they are as far apart as heaven from earth, and cannot stem from one another if not through an intermediate that connects them.

(Part 3, Chap 6, item 4)

209. **Why is *Keter* not part of the *Eser Sefirot* and is not implied in the *Otiot* of HaVaYaH, but only in the tip of the *Yod*?**

Because from the perspective of the *Nitzotz* of the Creator in it, it contains nothing of the *Behina* of the *Tachton* (see following item).

210. **What is the *Shoresh* of the four potential *Behinot*?**

The rule is that when the *Tachton* ascends to the place of the *Elyon*, it becomes exactly like the *Elyon* and they both become as one body. Thus, the whole difference and spiritual separation occurs as a result of the *Shinui Tzura* between them. It is that *Shinui Tzura* which divides them into two.

When you say *Tachton* and *Elyon*, it refers to a *Zach* degree and an *Av* degree, like *Tabur* and *Peh*. Because of the *Shinui Tzura* of the *Aviut* in the *Tabur* and because it is from above downward, it is separated from the purer degree, called *Peh*, and is lower. For that reason it is called *Tachton* compared to it.

When you say that *Tabur* climbed to *Peh* it means that it purified completely, like the *Peh*. By that they become once more as one, for there is no difference between them that would make them two separate *Behinot*. However, because of this *Hitkalelut* and unification, *Tabur* too is incorporated in this *Aviut*, meaning the *Aviut* from below upward that is found there (see item 168) since they are one body.

At that point the *Reshimot* that remained in the *Tabur* from before the *Hizdakchut* awaken. These *Reshimot* are from above downward and they join and mix with the *Aviut* from below upward in the *Peh* itself. From that a *Tzura* is born in *Tabur* that is different and much lower than the *Tzura* in the *Peh*.

It is so because the *Aviut* from below upward in the *Peh* is regarded as *Ein Sof* (see item 206), because *Behina Dalet* had not developed an approach of clothing to the *Ohr Yashar* (see item 220). However, *Aviut* from above downward means that *Behina Dalet* has already become clothed, and thus the force of the *Tzimtzum* rides firmly over it (see item 220).

When the *Reshimot* in the *Tabur* are silent, meaning when they are completely purified of their *Aviut*, they are regarded as nonexistent there at all. However, now that the *Tabur* is incorporated with the *Peh* and grew more *Av* than it, though it is merely *Aviut* from below upward, the silent *Reshimot* that rest in *Tabur* are awakened by it. Consequently, the *Behina* of from above downward in the *Tabur* becomes somewhat evident once more. That creates a certain *Shinui Tzura* between the *Peh* and the *Tabur*, as its inferiority becomes apparent. This is called "descent from the *Peh* downwards" to the place of *Behina Gimel de Guf* (see item 168).

Thus, even after the descent of *Tabur* from *Peh* downwards to its place in the *Guf de Elyon*, there are necessarily two entities in it: its *Aviut* and its *Reshimot*. This *Aviut* is completely from the *Peh de Elyon*, meaning the *Aviut* from below upward, that *Tabur* acquired and took from it by the incorporation with it into one *Guf*. However, the existence of the *Reshimot* in it is the part of *Tabur* itself, meaning of the *Tachton* himself.

Know, that these two entities are called: the "*Nitzotz* of the Creator", and "the *Nitzotz* of the creature". The existence of the *Aviut* in it is called "*Nitzotz* of the Creator", since it comes entirely from the *Peh de Elyon*, for the *Elyon* is always regarded as the Creator, or the *Maatzil* of the *Tachton*. The existence of the *Reshimot* in it is called "the *Nitzotz* of the creature" in it, for the *Tachton* is regarded as *Ne'etzal* or creature with regards to the *Elyon*.

The above *Nitzotz* of the Creator is regarded as the *Shoresh* of the *Tachton* in potential, but not in actual fact. It is so because it is certainly the primary *Shoresh* of the *Tachton*, for without that *Aviut* in *Tabur*, there would not be any *Zivug de Hakaa* after it has been completely purified. However, once it received the *Aviut* from the *Peh*, it became fit for *Hakaa* and emergence of *Eser Sefirot* in a new level for the lower *Partzuf* (see item 168).

Thus, though the above *Nitzotz* of the Creator is the entire *Shoresh* of the *Tachton*, it is still not regarded as the actual *Shoresh*. That is because the essence of the *Tachton* comes from the *Tabur* that rose to the *Peh* and came back down from it and outside it (see item 168).

For that reason, only the *Nitzotz* of the creature in it, meaning the *Reshimot* of the *Tabur* that awakened and grew *Av* because of the *Aviut* in the *Peh* are regarded as the *Shoresh* of the actual four *Behinot*. That is because they are the actual essence of the *Tachton*.

(Part 3, Chap 5, item 6 and Chap 6, item 4)

211. **What is the *Shoresh* of the four actual *Behinot*?**

Explained thoroughly in the above item.

212. **Why did *Malchut de Malchut de Atzilut* become *Atik* in *Olam Beria*?**

Karka de Atzilut is regarded as *Peh de Rosh* of the *Elyon* with regards to creation. There is also the matter of the ascent of *Tabur* to *Peh*, which gained *Aviut* in that *Peh*, and came back down to its place to become *Malchut de Rosh de Beria*. In other words, a *Zivug de Hakaa* was made on it and *Hitlabshut* of *Eser Sefirot de Ohr Hozer* to *Eser Sefirot de Ohr Yashar* (see item 141).

You can therefore find these two entities here as well (see item 210), being the "*Nitzotz* of the Creator" and the "*Nitzotz* of the creature". The *Nitzotz* of the Creator is the *Aviut* from below upward from the *Peh de Elyon* (see item 210). It is regarded as *Malchut de Malchut de Atzilut* that came down and became *Atik* to *Beria*, a potential *Shoresh*. The *Nitzotz* of the creature is the *Reshimot*. They are considered to have become *Arich Anpin de Beria*, which is the *Shoresh* of the actual four *Behinot*.

213. **From which perspective is *Keter* regarded "I am the last"?**

From the perspective of the *Nitzotz* of the Creator it is called "I am the last."

(Part 3, Chap 7, item 10)

214. **From which perspective is *Keter* regarded as "I am the first"?**

From the perspective of the *Nitzotz* of the Creator it is called "I am the first."

(There)

215. Where does *Keter de Beria* receive from and who is considered to be his *Shoresh*?

Malchut de Elyon gives the entire *Eser Sefirot* to the *Tachton*. However, it is still regarded that every *Behina* takes its exact corresponding *Behina* in the *Elyon*. *Keter de Tachton* extends from *Keter de Elyon*; *Hochma de Tachton* from *Hochma de Elyon*; *Bina de Tachton* from *Bina de Elyon* etc. Despite that, it is *Malchut de Elyon* that takes and brings them to each *Tachton*, through its *Ohr Hozer*.

(Part 3, Chap 8, item 10)

216. Why are all the *Behinot* of AK regarded as *Keter* to the *Behinot* of ABYA?

Since it has *Aviut de Behina Dalet*, the level of its *Ohr Hozer* rises and clothes the *Keter de Ohr Yashar*.

(Part 3, Chap 9, item 6 and item 8)

217. Why are HGT de AA regarded as *Rosh*?

This will be explained in later parts.

218. Why isn't the *Behina* of AA recognized in every *Olam*?

Because it is regarded as *Keter* and *Rosh*, and its *Guf* is concealed and clothed in the four *Partzufim* AB, SAG, MA, BON.

(Part 3, Chap 10, item 5)

219. Why is *Malchut* called "A mirror that has nothing of its own"?

Because she was restricted and does not receive any *Ohr Yashar*. It is known that *Eser Sefirot de Ohr Yashar* are the *Atzmut* and the essence of the *Orot*. Hence, it is considered that she does not have any *He'arah* from her *Shoresh* and *Atzmut*, from the perspective of her being *Malchut de Ohr Yashar*.

It is only by the *Zivug de Hakaa* that she becomes *Keter de Ohr Hozer*. For that reason it is called "a mirror that has nothing of its own", meaning from her *Atzmut*. It means that from the perspective of her being *Malchut de Ohr Yashar*, she does not have any *He'arah* from there.

(Part 3, Chap 7, item 2)

220. What is the meaning of the *Nekuda* that descends from an Upper *Olam* to a lower *Olam*?

The *Behina* of *Nitzotz* of the Creator that descends to become *Atik* in the *Tachton* (examine item 210 above carefully) is the *Nekuda* that descends from the *Elyon* to become a *Rosh* for the *Tachton*.

(Part 3, Chap 7, item 2)

221. **How did the moon diminish, meaning *Malchut de Atzilut*?**

Will be explained in later parts.

222. **What is the *Nekuda* that descends from *Olam* to *Olam* regarded as in and of herself?**

See above item 210.

223. **Why does the *Nekuda* that descends sucks from all the *Elyonim* although she is the smallest of them?**

Because she is regarded as *Malchut de Elyon*, meaning the *Peh* that raises *Ohr Hozer* and clothes the entire *Eser Sefirot de Ohr Yashar* and catches them in the *Partzuf*. It is a law in the Upper Ones that any degree that generates any additional *Ohr* in the Upper Ones, that additional *Ohr* is returned to the degree that generated it.

Therefore, because *Malchut*, through her *Ohr Hozer*, catches the *Eser Sefirot de Ohr Yashar* in the *Partzuf*, these *Eser Sefirot* return and are given back to that *Malchut*. Thus, although *Malchut* is the lowest in the *Eser Sefirot*, she still receives and sucks from all those *Eser Sefirot* (see *Histaklut Pnimit* Chap 9, item 2).

(Part 3, Chap 6, item 6)

224. **Why does the *Ohr Yashar* in all the degrees extend from *Ein Sof*?**

Because there is not a *Hidush* of *He'arah* in the *Olamot* that does not extend from *Ein Sof*.

225. **Why is there no differentiation in the four *Behinot* of *Ohr Yashar* from the *Rosh* of the *Kav* to the end of *Assiya*?**

Because in all the degrees, wherever they are, they extend evenly from *Ein Sof*.

(Part 3, Chap 2, item 3)

226. **Why can't *Ohr Yashar* reach below *Tabur*?**

Because it is regarded as *Malchut* from above downward, which is already regarded as clothing for the *Orot*. That is why the force of the *Tzimtzum* rides on her and she cannot receive any *Ohr Yashar*.

(See above item 120)

227. **Why is the Upper Degree always regarded as the *Maatzil* of its lower degree?**

Because it is emanated and caused by her. That is how all the degrees concatenate from *Rosh de Kav* to the end of *Assiya*, by way of cause and consequence; each is born from the one above her. That is why every *Elyon* is called *Maatzil*, or Creator of the *Tachton*, and the *Tachton* is called *Ne'etzal* or creature (created by the *Elyon*).

(Part 3, Chap 7, item 10)

228. What are the two roots of every *Behina*?

Besides *Malchut de Elyon* being the *Shoresh* of every *Behina* in the *Tachton*, every *Behina* in the *Tachton* extends very accurately from its corresponding *Behina* in the *Elyon*. *Keter de Tachton* from *Keter de Elyon*; *Hochma* from *Hochma de Elyon* (see item 215). Thus, each *Behina* in the *Tachton* has two roots: one *Shoresh* in its corresponding *Behina* in the *Elyon*, and a second *Shoresh* in *Malchut*, which is the general *Shoresh* of the *Tachton*.

229. What is the name given to *Eser Sefirot* of the same level?

They are called: *Or, Bassar, Gidin, Atzamot, Mocha*.

(Part 3, Chap 5, item 2)

230. Why is the *Mador Klipot* (Shell Section) between the *Levush* and the *Or*?

Because that is the place of the darkness, as it is written in item 65.

(Part 3, Chap 10, item 2)

231. Why is the *Ohr Pnimi* in the *Or* worse than in the *Basar, Gidin, Atzamot* and *Mocha* in the *Partzuf*?

Because the *Or* does not receive inside from the *Ohr Yashar* in the *Partzuf*, because of the *Tzimtzum* on her.

(See above item 65)

232. Why does every thing in *Kedusha* leave an imprint?

Because there is no absence in spirituality. When *Kedusha* appears once in some *Behina*, it never moves from there again.

(Part 3, Chap 7, item 3)

233. How high can one reach?

One can reach even higher than *Nefesh de Atzilut*.

(Part 3, Chap 10, item 4)

234. Why is *Nefesh de Elyon* regarded as *Ruach* for the *Tachton*?

Because any *Elyon* is necessarily one degree higher than the *Tachton*. Thus, if the *Tachton* has *Nefesh*, and *He'arah* from *Nefesh de Elyon* is added to it. This *He'arah* is higher than it by one degree, and one degree above *Nefesh* is *Ruach*.

(Part 3, Chap 10, item 6, and *Ohr Pnimi*, item 4)

235. Where do the NRNHY *de Nefesh* come from?

All the *Orot* of *Malchut* are called *Nefesh*, even the *Yechida* in her.

236. **What are the differences between Olam, Partzuf, Sefira, Nekuda?**

See above items 193, 201, 202.

237. **What are the differences between Eser Sefirot de Ohr Yashar and Eser Sefirot de Ohr Hozer in the same level, the Eser Sefirot where one is above the other, and Eser Sefirot where one is below the other, Eser Sefirot de Rosh, Eser Sefirot de Toch, and Eser Sefirot de Sof, the five Behinot of Kli de Malchut, the five Behinot of potential Kelim, and the five Behinot of actual Kelim?**

Eser Sefirot de Ohr Yashar are the four *Behinot* of *Hitpashtut* of *Ohr Ein Sof*. The *Eser Sefirot de Ohr Hozer* are the rejected *Orot* that are returned from *Malchut* (see item 119). The *Eser Sefirot* of even level are the *Eser Sefirot* of *Ohr Yashar* that clothe the *Eser Sefirot de Ohr Hozer* out of one *Zivug de Hakaa* (see item 194).

The *Eser Sefirot* one above the other come from the four *Zivugim de Hakaa* in *Malchut* as it purifies, meaning when she ascends from *Malchut* from *Tabur* to *Peh* (see item 142). The *Eser Sefirot* one below the other come from the five *Zivugim de Hakaa* in *Malchut* after she comes to the *Peh* and receives a new *Aviut* (see item 168).

The *Eser Sefirot de Rosh* are from *Malchut* upwards before she is clothed (see item 141), and the *Eser Sefirot de Toch* are from *Malchut* downwards (see item 142). The *Eser Sefirot de Sof* are *Ohr Hozer* without *Ohr Yashar*. That is because they are from *Malchut* downwards after she had clothed the *Orot*. That is why they end the *Partzuf* (see item 143).

The five *Behinot* in *Kli de Malchut* are from the *Reshimot* from *Ein Sof* that remained in *Malchut* after the *Tzimtzum* (see item 119). The four *Behinot* of roots for potential *Kelim* come from the *Nitzotz* of the Creator (see item 210). The four *Behinot* of roots for actual *Kelim* are from the *Nitzotz* of the creature (see item 210).

Regarding the *Eser Sefirot* one above the other, know that they are the inner *Eser Sefirot* in each *Partzuf*. There aren't *Kelim* for *Haya* and *Yechida* there because these *Eser Sefirot* emerge by a *Zivug de Hakaa* as *Malchut* purifies (see items 95 and 142).

Aviut of *Behina Aleph* is very frail. Because of that she doesn't really perform a *Zivug de Hakaa*, as she doesn't raise sufficient *Ohr Hozer* to clothe the *Ohr Yashar*, so that its from above downward would become a *Kli*. Needless to add, there is no *Zivug de Hakaa* when she is completely purified, as is *Keter*.

Thus, there are only three *Kelim* there, from *Behina Bet*, *Behina Gimel* and *Behina Dalet*, but there are no *Kelim* from *Keter* and from *Behina Aleph* there. The *Orot*

Haya, *Yechida*, should clothe the *Pnimiut* of the *Neshama*, namely the *Ohr* of *Bina* (see item 163).

You should distinguish between the *Hamshacha* and the reception here, which are found in every *Sefira* (see items 157 and 158). Thus, our above statement that there are no *Kelim* for *Ohr Yechida* and *Ohr Haya*, means only vessels of reception. However, she does have a *Kli* for *Hamshacha*, for the *Kli de Hamshacha* for *Ohr Haya* is *Behina Gimel*, and the *Kli de Hamshacha* for *Ohr Yechida* is *Behina Dalet*. These *Behinot* are complete in the *Partzufim* of AK, hence our statement that there are *Orot Haya* and *Yechida* there, though they are clothed in *Neshama*.

Midat ha Rachamim incorporated with *Midat ha Din* from *BON de AK* onward (see item 176). When *Behina Gimel* and *Behina Dalet* were reduced from the *Partzufim* and became surrounding, called *Levush* and *Heichal*, the *Kelim* for *Hamshacha* for *Haya* and *Yechida* were reduced from every *Partzuf* as well.

It turns out that *Orot Haya* and *Yechida* are also absent from the *Partzuf*, because there isn't a *Behina Dalet* to draw *Yechida* and *Behina Gimel* to draw *Haya*. Remember that and know that this absence of ZON only relates to AK, whereas for themselves, they certainly do have *Eser* complete *Sefirot*.

PART FOUR

The Ten Sefirot of Akudim, containing six chapters

CHAPTER ONE

Explains the Rosh and Guf of Adam Kadmon down to the Tabur. There is still no actual vessel in the ten Sefirot of Rosh, and in the ten Sefirot of the Guf there is one vessel called Keter. The Ten Sefirot in this vessel are discerned by their distance from phase four. Since they are in a single vessel, they are called Akudim [bound]. Contains eleven issues:

1. We do not have the strength to study prior to the world of Atzilut. 2. The Ten Sefirot of Atzilut are lights and vessels. In order to connect to their root above we must speak in a gradual order from Rosh to Sof. 3. The lights of the Guf of AK from Peh to Tabur are called Akudim. 4. The HaVaYot of the vessels were born from the mutual striking of the surrounding light and inner light outside the Peh. 5. There are no vessels prior to Akudim, meaning in the ten Sefirot of Rosh of AK. A single vessel for the ten Sefirot was made in Akudim. 6. The vessel of Akudim is Keter. Ten vessels KHB TM emerged below Akudim. 7. There is the force of ten Sefirot in the upper light. 8. It drew the light of Akudim from the Peh to the Tabur and departed back to its origin in the Peh. 9. A record that remained after the departure of the light became a vessel. 10. Since the light departed all at once, only one vessel was made, and it is called Keter. 11. Ten Sefirot are discerned in this vessel, according to their distance from phase four, meaning according to the four phases in the upper light.

We do not have the strength to study prior to the world of Atzilut.

1. You already know that we have no strength to study prior to the emanation of the ten Sefirot, or imagine any image and shape whatsoever (1). However, to simplify matters we do need to speak allegorically (2). Therefore, even if we speak of a picture that is up there, it is only to simplify matters.

Inner Light

1. Because all these phases we discern in the worlds stem and emerge from the world of Atzilut downward, meaning from the world where ten Sefirot and the correction of the lines have already appeared as Hesed, judgment and mercy.

However, above the world of Atzilut, meaning before the ten Sefirot appear, we have no grasp there, sufficient to discern any similarity and disparity of form between one Sefira and another. That is because attainment begins from the clothing of the ten Sefirot in ten vessels, meaning from the world of Atzilut downward.

That is why the ARI writes, "**we have no strength to study prior to the emanation of the ten Sefirot, or imagine any image and shape whatsoever.**" It is so because prior to the emanation of the ten Sefirot that appeared in the world of Atzilut, the ten Sefirot were regarded as light without a vessel suitable for it, and it is known that we have no attainment in the light without a vessel.

2. It means that from the world of Atzilut downward we can hint at the discernments in the spiritual upper roots above, as an allegory and metaphors taken from the reality or from the conducts of this world. All the details of the created beings and their modes of conduct in this world cascade and are extended from the upper worlds. It is just like the relation between the seal and its imprint, where all the details in the seal are copied and transferred to its imprint, none are missing.

Our sages wrote, "There is not a single blade of grass below that does not have an appointed angel above that strikes it and tells it, 'Grow!'" (Bereshit Raba, Parasha 10, omissions from Part 1, item 1). This tells us that there is not even a tiny detail in this world that does not have a root in the upper world. This root operates on it in all its forms and inclinations, in everything it does here before us in this world.

Thus, the sages have devised a special language to convey their attainment of the upper worlds orally and in text from generation to generation: They take the branches in this world, and with them, explain the reality of the upper worlds which relate to these branches.

The above relations of root and branch begin only from the world of Atzilut downward, meaning after revealing the complete ten Sefirot, and not at all before that. It is therefore obvious that it is impossible to imply the existence of the upper worlds using the corporeal branches, as these branches do not have a direct relation to them, qualifying them to explain these concepts.

The ARI writes there that here, too, he is speaking allegorically only to appease the ear. In other words, it is to give us some grasp, so as to show us the roots of the world of Atzilut. Thus, we must first understand the branch as it relates to its root in Atzilut, and then we can relate this root to its earlier root in the worlds that precede Atzilut.

The ten Sefirot of Atzilut are lights and vessels. In order to connect to their root above, we must speak in a gradual order from Rosh to Sof.

2. However, you should know that the ten Sefirot of Atzilut are two matters (3): The first is the expansion of spirituality, and the second is the vessels and organs, where the self expands. All this must have a root above, for these two phases, and therefore we need to speak of the order of degrees from Rosh to Sof.

Inner Light

3. They are the matter of spiritual expansion, called NRNHY, and the matter of vessels and organs called KHB, HGT, NHYM, or five Partzufim: AA, AVI, and ZON in which the NRNHY clothe. Each of these matters is a separate study in itself, meaning its conducts of cascading and manifestation differ from the other.

Moreover, they are completely opposite from one another, from one end to the other, since in the vessels, the upper vessels appear first. Keter appears first, then Hochma, and finally Malchut. The lights are the opposite: in them the lower ones appear first, beginning with the appearance of Nefesh, then Ruach and finally Yechida. Also, they are opposite in all their appearances and phases.

Thus, if we do not thoroughly know the reasons for the matters, from their root, we will not be able to avoid confusion in this wisdom. The ARI wrote, "**Therefore we need to speak of the order of degrees from Rosh to Sof.**" It means that then we will thoroughly know the reasons for every single matter at its root. We will be able to understand and distinguish in each degree, the proper conducts and the orders in the vessels, and the proper conducts and the order in the lights, and we will not replace the terms of one with the other.

The lights of the Guf of AK from the Peh to the Tabur are called Akudim

3. It is written "And saw in a dream, and, behold, the he-goats which leaped upon the flock were Akudim [streaked], Nekudim [speckled], and Brudim [grizzled]. (4)" It is also written, "For I have seen all that Laban is doing to you."

This verse implies all these phases that we discuss here. Laban is the upper whiteness that precedes all this Atzilut and makes all these phases, namely Akudim, Nekudim and Brudim, for the purpose of Atzilut that will emanate after them.

It is called by the name Yaakov [Jacob] and began with Akudim as they are the lights that come out from the Peh of Adam Kadmon. The manifestation of the HaVaYot of the vessels began in them, since the ten inner and surrounding lights

are tied and connected together in a single vessel. For this reason, it is called Akudim [bound], from the words, "and bound Isaac," meaning tied.

Inner Light

4. These are names of the first three worlds that cascaded down from one another until the ten Sefirot were emanated properly. It refers to ten lights, called: Nefesh, Ruach, Neshama, Haya, Yechida, clothed in ten vessels, called: Keter, Hochma, Bina, Hesed, Gevura, Tifferet, Netzah, Hod, Yesod, and Malchut.

In the beginning, only one vessel was emanated, called the vessel Malchut. All the other ten lights were clothed and tied to that single vessel. Thus, that first world is called the world of Akudim, from the words bound and tied, as we will discuss henceforth.

It is also called "one line," or the world of Adam Kadmon. It is called one line because the light is clothed in but a single vessel, and it still does not have the three lines of governance called Hesed, Din [judgment], Rachamim [also mercy]. This vessel is called the quality of judgment, which is the vessel of Malchut.

However, afterwards there was the association with the quality of mercy. It means that Malchut, called the quality of judgment, was incorporated and associated with each and every Sefira of its previous nine Sefirot, called the qualities of mercy.

Through this association, a vessel was made in each and every Sefira, at which time the ten Sefirot were completed properly. Then the three lines of governance are formed in the ten Sefirot, called: Hesed, judgment, mercy.

Our sages wrote: "In the beginning it came upon the thought to create the world in the quality of judgment; He saw that the world does not exist, preceded the quality of mercy and associated it with the quality of judgment" (*Beresheet Rabbah*). This verse seems unbecoming; are His thoughts like the thought of flesh and blood, who first want to do thus, but regret for some reason and do otherwise?

However, we have already explained (Part 1, explanation of the words "Before" and "After"), that "Before and After" in spirituality mean cause and consequence. The cause is called first, and the consequence that is extended from it is called "after."

Our sages tell us that the first cause for the emanation of the worlds, called the "first world," was emanated and emerged as only the vessel of Malchut, called the quality of judgment. However, "He saw that the world does not exist," meaning it does not have that wholeness desired from the creation of the world, and so He "associated it with the quality of mercy."

In other words, it therefore became the element that causes the association of the quality of mercy with judgment. As a result, ten Sefirot of lights and vessels, in the three lines, Hesed, judgment, mercy, emerged and were emanated. Our sages also implied that same matter in another place in different words (*Avot* 285): "The world was created in ten utterances. Could it not have been created with one utterance? But to avenge the wicked, who destroy the world that was created in ten utterances, and give a good reward to the righteous, who keep the world that was created in ten utterances."

Ten utterances refer to the ten Sefirot. They ask: "Since the first world of Hesed had been created in a single utterance, meaning with a single vessel, the vessel of Malchut, why then did ten Sefirot cascade and emerge from it?" They answered: "To avenge the wicked, etc., and to give a good reward for the righteous, etc."

In other words, the thought of creation to delight His created beings does not happen in another way, but by a conduct of reward and punishment, meaning the ten Sefirot, which is the governance in three lines, Hesed, judgment, mercy. Thus, the first world, where there was only the vessel of Malchut, had to cascade from state to state until the ten Sefirot were emanated, meaning the association of the quality of mercy with judgment. That, in turn, manifests the governance of reward and punishment that brings that benefit incorporated in the thought of creation.

The beginning of the above association occurred in the world of Akudim itself by the refinement of the coarseness in the screen. As a result, three Partzufim emerged and cascaded there, called Galgalta, AB, SAG. Even though they are all still regarded as Akudim, still the association gradually occurs in them.

Afterwards emerged, Partzuf BON of AK, called the world of Nekudim, where the three lines Hesed, judgment, mercy were emanated in the ten Sefirot of the first three, KHB, called Rosh. However, in the lower seven, the ten Sefirot still emerged in one line, and in that world was the matter of the breaking of the vessels.

This breaking of the vessels became the cause for the matter of the association of the quality of mercy with judgment to be completed as three lines Hesed, judgment, mercy and ten complete vessels also in the seven lower Sefirot HGT NHYM that are in the following world, called the world of Brudim and the world of correction, since the correction of the world, according to the thought of creation, begins specifically in that world and not before.

Now we have learned the difference between the three worlds, mentioned in the words of the ARI: the world of Akudim means that ten lights were bound and tied in a single vessel. However, in the world of Nekudim, in its upper three, KHB, there was already the association of the quality of mercy with judgment.

Only in the world of Brudim, called the world of Atzilut, was the association of the quality of mercy with judgment corrected completely, in the seven lower Sefirot as well. Thus, we have here a clothing of ten lights inside ten vessels, and from that world begins the distinction of ten Sefirot in actual fact.

The HaVaYot of the vessels were born from the mutual striking of surrounding light and inner light outside the Peh

4. In the bonding of the inner lights with the surrounding lights, they are connected inside the Peh (5). Consequently, when they emerge together outside the Peh, bound together (6), they strike one another and clash with each other (7), and the HaVaYot of the vessels are born from their striking.

Inner Light

5. You already know that the Peh is the Malchut of the Rosh of AK where the screen of phase four had been erected. It detains the upper light from expanding and clothing the fourth phase, as the upper light has the conduct of expanding in phase four also, and filling the entire reality as before the restriction. However, the screen established in the Peh detains it and does not receive it. This is called coupling by striking.

The entire measure of the upper light that is suitable for clothing in phase four, which (as was said) she does not receive, this upper light returns backwards to its origin and becomes a clothing over the first nine Sefirot of direct light (see above Part 3, Chapter 12, and in Inner Light there). It turns out that all the lights that are destined to come into the worlds after their correction, called surrounding lights, are included in that reflected light that clothes the first nine Sefirot of direct light of the Rosh of AK.

It is so because this is the upper light that is not received in phase four. Hence, it does not fill the entire reality as it was prior to the restriction. However, through all the couplings and the reflected light that are destined to appear in the worlds by raising MAN through the acts of the righteous, phase four becomes corrected until she becomes fit to receive the light as it was in Ein Sof before the restriction. It is written in *The Zohar*: "Ein Sof does not bring down His unification upon her until He is given his mate," which is the correction of phase four.

Now we have clarified that all the surrounding lights are included in the screen and reflected light in the Peh of the Rosh of AK, along with the inner lights, which are the nine Sefirot of direct light that are connected with it. The ARI writes, "**The inner lights with the surrounding lights are connected inside the Peh**," meaning Malchut, by the power of the screen of phase four that is established there.

6. Both the inner light and the surrounding light are connected in phase four. The upper nine Sefirot of direct light are connected and clothed in her reflected light, which are called inner light, but the lights that are destined to come until the end of the correction, called surrounding lights, are also included in that reflected light. It is so because they are the essence of the reflected light, thus destined to manifest bit-by-bit over six thousand years and after that until the end of correction.

7. Because when the two lights descend and expand from the Peh down into the Guf of AK, the surrounding lights cannot clothe inside the Guf because of the force of the screen there, which detains that light (see Part 2, Table of Questions, item 4). Because they are connected and incorporated there, they too want to expand in the internality of the Partzuf. Hence, they refine the coarseness in the screen, meaning that force of detainment that does not let them clothe there.

However, because of their clash with the coarseness of the screen, for which the screen is refined, it causes the departure of the inner lights from the Guf. It is so because as it becomes refined into the coarseness of phase three, the reflected light is shortened and clothes only the level of Hochma, and the light of Keter disappears from the Guf.

When phase three is also refined into the coarseness of phase two, the reflected light is shortened to the level of Bina, and the light of Hochma also disappears until all the coarseness is refined and there is no more coupling by striking there. Then, the entire inner light disappears from the Partzuf. When the ARI writes, "**they strike one another and clash with each other**," meaning that one rejects the other because the measure of the inner light is as the measure of the coarseness in the screen.

Hence, in a greater coarseness it grows stronger, and vise-versa, the detainment of the surrounding lights that cannot clothe is only because of the coarseness and limit in the screen. For this reason, it refines the coarseness, and for this reason they clash with each other until they both depart.

There are no vessels prior to Akudim, meaning in the ten Sefirot of the Rosh of AK

5. Prior to the existence of Akudim (8)**, the upper light could not clothe any vessel. That is because the vessels could not tolerate it** (9)**, and the light did not clothe**

the vessel until the expansion of that great light reached the phase of Akudim (10). Then, the existence of a single vessel for that great light has been made, and there began a certain limitation of the light in Atzilut (20), which could not have been done thus far (30).

Inner Light

8. Akudim are regarded as the ten Sefirot of the Toch of the first Partzuf the reality that follows the first restriction, called Adam Kadmon. Prior to that there weren't any Rosh, Toch, Sof in the upper light, but rather the upper light filled the entire reality (study closely in Part 1).

The ARI writes, "**Prior to the existence of Akudim**," meaning in the ten Sefirot in the Rosh of Adam Kadmon that precede the ten Sefirot of Toch of Adam Kadmon, called Akudim, "**the upper light could not clothe any vessel.**" It is thoroughly explained in Part 3, that there is no discernment of a vessel in the ten Sefirot of the Rosh, but only roots for the vessels.

9. The reflected light that rises from Malchut upward is not regarded as a vessel for reception of the upper light, but only as a root for a vessel of reception. Thus, as much as Malchut of the Rosh expands and broadens to ten Sefirot from her and within her by, the reflected light that overturns and descends from above downward, there are still no vessels there at all (see Part 3, Chapter 2, Inner Light, item 3).

It is so because the reflected light rises there from below upward, and any clothing from below upward indicates departure from reception. The reason we call it clothing is that the ten Sefirot connect there and become a root for the clothing. This is why the ARI writes, "**The vessels could not tolerate it.**"

10. Until Malchut and the reflected light with her extend the ten Sefirot of the Rosh to the Toch from above downward. Then a single vessel was made, meaning the vessel of Malchut. She expanded, broadened and received the entire amount of light inside it. Her reflected light clothed the ten Sefirot of the Rosh (see Part 3, Chapter 2, Inner Light, item 3). These ten Sefirot that descend from the Rosh downward and clothe the vessel of Malchut that had expanded are the ones called the ten Sefirot of Akudim, or the world of Akudim.

20. Because Malchut in the Sof of that vessel, which is regarded as Malchut of the vessel of Malchut, limits the upper light on its path from expanding from her downward. The force of that limitation is called Tabur, or Chazeh.

397

30. Meaning that although Malchut of the Rosh also limits the upper light, which is why a coupling by striking occurred there, and the raising of the reflected light (see Part 3, Chapter 1, Inner Light, item 70), nevertheless this limitation and this reflected light of Malchut of Rosh are not regarded as an actual limitation, only as a potential limitation. As the ARI writes in *Tree of Life*, gate 42, Keter is like a primeval substance, containing the root of all four elements, but in potential, not in actual fact. It is therefore possible to call it Ein Sof and Emanator, referring to the ten Sefirot of the Rosh, called Keter.

These words of the ARI are indeed profound, and we must understand them, for they pertain to the very root of the wisdom and its beginning. We must determine the difference between "potential" and "actual" that the ARI speaks of. He divides between the ten Sefirot of the Rosh that clothe the reflected light from below upward, and the ten Sefirot of the Guf that clothe the reflected light from above downward. It is for that reason that the ten Sefirot of the Rosh are sometimes called Ein Sof and Emanator to the ten Sefirot of the Guf.

There is a great difference and distance between the reflected light that rises from the screen in Malchut upward, clothing the ten Sefirot of the Rosh, and the reflected light that descends with the direct light from the ten Sefirot of the Rosh down to the Guf. It appears that they are opposite from one another because the reflected light that rises from below upward, not only is it not regarded as a vessel of reception for the clothing direct light, but it even has in it resistance to reception.

It is so because any "from below upward" means that the light turns to the Emanator and not to the receivers. However, the ascending reflected light still becomes a clothing for the upper light. In other words, it becomes the root for the attachment of the upper light to the emanated being, since the vessel of Malchut of the Rosh, which raised that reflected light, is expanded and broadened by it, from her and within her, and becomes a vessel of reception called the Guf of the Partzuf (see Part 3, Chapter 2, Inner Light, item 3). It is so because the ten Sefirot of the Rosh descend from above downward and expand and clothe within her.

You see that although from the perspective of their own quality, the ten Sefirot of the Rosh depart from coming into the vessel of reception, as this is the meaning of reflected light that rises from below upward, meaning to the Emanator and not to the emanated beings, as was written above, nevertheless, all the light that is actually received in the Guf is only from the ten Sefirot of the Rosh that expand in it from above downward, as explained in item 30.

For this reason, the ten Sefirot of the Rosh are considered to have ten potential Sefirot, but not actual. It means that the actual clothing of the light in the vessels is not at all in the Rosh, but only the potential and the root from which this clothing will be extended. That is why the Rosh is called Ein Sof, or Keter.

The ARI wrote, "**Then,**" meaning after the light expanded in the Guf of the Partzuf, called Akudim, "**the existence of a single vessel for that great light has been made, and there began a certain limitation of the light in it, which could not have been done thus far.**"

It means that before the Akudim, meaning in the Malchut of the Rosh, there could not be any limitation there because when Malchut limits and raises reflected light in the ten Sefirot of the Rosh, this limitation is actual bestowal, since the greater the limitation, the greater the measure of bestowal. The limitation of phase four extends the level of Keter, and a smaller limitation, meaning only on phase three, extends only the level of Hochma. Thus, no limitation is discerned in the Rosh whatsoever.

The vessel of Akudim is Keter. Ten vessels KHB TM emerged below Akudim and in Akudim a single vessel was made for the ten Sefirot

6. **However, first the entire light was of the parts that reach Atzilut. They were all concealed in but a single vessel, and that vessel had the phase of the vessel of the upper Keter in it. Afterwards, the light expanded further down from that phase, called Akudim, and then ten vessels were made.**

There is a force of ten Sefirot in the upper light

7. **Let us begin to clarify the existence of Akudim, what it's about. Know that the upper light is the part that is fitting to clothe Atzilut. It has the force of the ten Sefirot, although they are as yet not apparent as ten lights, but only after the completion of Akudim (40). However, certainly the force of these ten lights was there to begin with (50), but since the light was not limited inside the vessel (60), it was still not apparent that they are ten (70).**

Inner Light

40. Meaning only after the two Partzufim AB and SAG of AK emerged and were revealed. When the light entered and departed the vessel ten times, and these entrances and exits created and distinguished the ten separate lights.

50. This is before they expanded to Akudim, meaning in the ten Sefirot of Rosh where the ten Sefirot are only in potential and not in actuality (see this chapter, item 30).

60. This limitation begins to manifest only through a coupling by striking and the ascents of reflected light from below upward in the second look that comes after the clothing of the light in the emanated being, meaning after Akudim. However, the light is not limited by the first look in Malchut of the Rosh: remember that.

70. Even in the expansion from the Rosh downward it was still not apparent that they are ten lights, because the ten lights are regarded as a single light. It is so because all the differentiations in the lights are from the perspective of the vessels in which they clothe. Since here there is only one vessel, the ten lights are also regarded as a single light.

It drew the light of Akudim from Peh to Tabur and departed once more to its origin in the Peh

8. What did the upper emanator do when He wished to create that vessel called Akudim? He extended His light downward until a sufficient measure for the creation of Akudim had existed, which from the Peh to the Tabur $_{(80)}$, and after He extended it $_{(90)}$, that light departed upward and returned to its origin in the Peh $_{(100)}$.

Inner Light

80. Malchut of the Rosh is called Peh, and Malchut of the Guf is called Tabur. The first nine Sefirot of the Guf begin to expand from the Peh, meaning from Malchut of the Rosh, and end at the Tabur, which is Malchut of the Guf.

The entire place from the Tabur down to the Sium of the Guf is regarded only as the Sefira of Malchut. Even though there are ten Sefirot from the Tabur down, they are regarded as reflected light, and female light, and as receivers that cannot bestow. Thus, the expansion of direct light from the Peh down is considered to extend only through the Tabur, where it stops because of the screen in Tabur.

90. Meaning as the second look, as the ARI wrote (Part 3, Chapter 12) that it comes after the light is drawn to the vessel and not before (see Inner Light, Chapter 7, item 60).

100. It is Malchut of the Rosh, called Peh. It is regarded as the origin of the entire light that expands in the Guf of the degree because she extended it through the first look that is done in her (Part 3, Chapter 12).

A record that remained after the departure of the light became a vessel.

9. It is known that when the upper light expands and disappears once more, it necessarily leaves a record below. That light is the record that remains below. When the upper light departs and becomes concealed in its origin, the light of this record remains below, without that upper light. Then, a vessel is formed by the distancing [of the] remaining light. The expansion of the light and its departure later caused the making of a vessel (200).

Inner Light

200. The vessel is made primarily through the record that remains after the departure of the light, as explained here in the words of the ARI. Hence, both are equal in the making of the vessel. Therefore, two couplings are needed here, called: the first look and the second look. The first look is for the expansion of the light, while the second look is for the departure of the light.

It is by these two phases of couplings that the vessels of reception of the degree are completed, as it is written, "as the Lord rejoiced over you to do you good ... so the Lord will rejoice etc." Rejoicing means coupling. There is an upper coupling to destroy, meaning the departure of light, as there is an upper coupling to do good, meaning expansion of light. For that reason they are both called rejoicing.

Since the light departed at once, only one vessel was made, and it is called Keter

10. When the first light departed once more, it departed at once, in a single moment (300). Hence, all the remaining light became one vessel. It is called a vessel, called Keter, since the upper light had not yet been distinguished in ten Sefirot, for their being ten Sefirot had not yet become apparent. The reason it is called Keter and not some other Sefira is that Keter is always close to the Emanator.

Inner Light

300. Although couplings by striking are done there along the departure of the light, and because of it, four levels of ten Sefirot emerged one above the other, it is still regarded as a single departure at a single moment. It is so because the upper light copulates with the screen as it becomes refined and concealed, therefore, these couplings are not regarded as expansion.

The ten Sefirot in this vessel are discerned according to their distance from phase four, meaning according to the four phases in the upper light

11. However, although we have explained above that there are the vessels of Malchut and Yesod etc. in this vessel, they are still not called ten vessels since they are still not recognized as ten Sefirot, and also because the light departed together. The thing is that it is like one long vessel, whose parts are not equal, according to the distance of these parts from end to end (400).

Inner Light

400. You will understand that from what is written in Part 1 (Inner Light, item 50). There are four phases in the upper light itself: HB TM, even before it expands for coupling by striking. Because of it, the single vessel, too, was impressed by the same four phases HB TM in the light. Thus, these ten Sefirot are also discerned in that single vessel, according to the distance of these four phases from end to end.

However, since there is but a single vessel here, which is Malchut, the light is therefore regarded as a single light as well, without the discernment of ten Sefirot. It is so because we have no perception of the light, if not through the evaluation of its clothing in the vessels, and since the vessel is one, we also have a single light.

Chapter Two

Explains the records that remain after the departure of the lights and the reflected light that descends during the departure. Contains ten issues:

1. When the lights ascend and depart, they draw reflected light from above through couplings by striking. 2. The departing light leaves a record in its place. 3. Every upper light to its lower one is as the relation of a father to a son. 4. When the light of Keter departs, it leaves a record in its place to shine for Hochma. 5. When the light of Hochma departs, it leaves a record in its place to shine for Bina. 6. Malchut does not leave a record. 7. All the Sefirot leave records in their place after they depart, except for Malchut. 8. Since Malchut does not leave a record, she is called poor, for she has nothing of her own. 9. Two kinds of light remain in the vessel after the departure: a) reflected light, which is judgment; b) the records, which are direct light and mercy. 10. The coarse light that does not depart becomes a vessel, and the reflected light and the records remain in it.

When the lights ascend and depart, they draw reflected light from above through couplings by striking.

1. We must now let you know by a different approach, which includes all the worlds, regarding the matter of the return of the lights to the Emanator. Besides what we have explained elsewhere, although they ascend and depart, they draw from above downward (1), from the Emanator, the discernment of light called reflected light.

Inner Light

1. During the departure of the light of Keter because of the ascent of Malchut to ZA, to phase three, there was a coupling of upper light in the screen of phase three, and ten Sefirot of direct light and reflected light on the level of Hochma were extended. In this way, couplings were done in all the degrees along the ascent of the screen for its refinement (see Inner Observation, Part 2). The ARI writes, "**although they ascend and depart, they draw from above downward, from the Emanator, the discernment of light called reflected light,** since every coupling by striking draws

reflected light from the upper light, as that part of the light that is rejected from Malchut is called reflected light.

The departing light leaves a record in its place

2. There is yet another great and very beneficial discernment: Even though they depart, they never completely depart from all of their own phases and ascend. Instead, they leave of their strength and of themselves some illumination below, in the place where they first stood. This illumination is never uprooted from there, even when they ascend upward. This illumination is called a record (2), as it is written, "Set me as a seal upon thy heart," mentioned at the end of *Parashat Mishpatim* in Saba (114, 71).

Inner Light

2. The record is like a seal. After the seal leaves the place it was once attached to, it leaves its entire form there, nothing missing. So is the manner of the upper light: If it expands into some place, even when it departs from there, it leaves there its entire form, not a single impression missing. In the end, it shall return and manifest in the full measure, as in the beginning.

Every upper light to its lower one is as the relation of a father to a son.

3. The reason is that the upper lights are to the lower lights as a father to his sons; he always wants to bestow upon them, as is explained regarding honoring the father and the mother. A single spark is extended from the father to the son and never moves from there. Similarly, here in the ten Sefirot, the upper ones leave some illumination in the first place, called a record, so that illumination would be drawn from there to the lower ones (3).

Inner Light

3. This applies to both the light and the vessel, to the general and to the particular. The Rosh, Toch, Sof of the second expansion of AK, called Partzuf AB of AK, were born and emerged from the records that were included in the Tabur of the first expansion of Adam Kadmon that ascended to its Peh (see Table of Topics, item 210).

It is the same in the particular. A record that remains in the vessel of Keter of the first expansion becomes a male in the vessel of Keter of the second expansion. The record that remains in the vessel of Hochma of the first expansion becomes a vessel of a male in the vessel of Hochma of the second expansion. From their coupling emerged the males in the rest of the Sefirot, as the ARI wrote in *Tree of Life*.

Also, the females of the second expansion are made of the records that remain of the four levels that emerged during the first departure, called sparks, or letters. The incorporation of Malchut in ZA is made of the sparks that fell from the level of phase three, namely ZA, into the vessel of Malchut, namely phase four. Afterwards, in the second expansion, when the light of Malchut clothes the vessel of ZA, it finds there the vessel of Malchut that belongs to it.

Thus, the force of the sparks that fell from the reflected light of the level of phase two, which is Bina, caused the incorporation of ZA in the vessel of Bina. Later on in the second expansion, when the light of ZA came and clothed the vessel of Bina, it found its vessel there, and so on similarly (see Inner Light, Chap 3, item 80).

Thus, all the phases in the lower Partzuf are extended only from the records that its upper Partzuf left. The ARI writes, "**The upper lights are to the lower lights as a father to his sons.**" It means that a lower Partzuf is extended from an upper Partzuf as a son from a father. In other words, it cascades from the self of the lights in its upper Partzuf by the records that remain in the vessels of the upper Partzuf from its lights.

The ARI writes, "**the upper ones leave some illumination in the first place, called a record, so that illumination would be drawn from there to the lower ones.**" Remember this in all the places, for this is the key to the cascading of the degrees by cause and effect, from the beginning of the line to the end of Assiya.

When the light of Keter departs, it leaves a record in its place to shine
for Hochma.

4. It turns out that when the Keter ascends and departs, it leaves one record in its place, in its own vessel (4), to shine for Hochma, which is below it, after it ascends and departs. After it ascended and departed, an illumination was extended to the light of Hochma from that record (5) that the Keter left in its vessel. Although afterwards the light of Hochma will also ascend and depart to the emanator, nevertheless, the record that remains in the vessel of Keter does not move from it, even after the light of Hochma ascended to the emanator.

Inner Light

4. We might ask: In item 9 he says that the existence of the vessel was made from the record, and here he says that there is a vessel even before the record and before

the departure of the light! The thing is that there are two kinds of vessels in each Partzuf, which are: Vessels that are drawn from the first look in the Malchut of Rosh. This Malchut expands by the force of the reflected light in her, which she raised from below upward and expanded from her and within her into ten Sefirot from above downward. They are considered the vessels of reception for the first expansion. There is yet another phase of vessels in the Partzuf, which are drawn by the second look in Malchut of the Guf of the Partzuf, which causes the departure and return of that light to the emanator. The records that remain after that departure become complete vessels (see Part 3, Chapter 12, Inner Light).

All these records of the second look are drawn to all the phases, meaning to its lower Partzuf. It is said, **"The upper lights are to the lower lights as a father to his sons."** It means that the lower Partzuf is extended from the upper Partzuf like a son from a father, meaning by the records that remain inside the vessels of the upper Partzuf from its lights.

The ARI writes, **"the upper ones leave some illumination in the first place, called a record, so that illumination would be drawn from there to the lower ones."** Remember that thoroughly for it is the key for the cascading of the degrees by cause and consequence from the beginning of the line to the end of Assiya, where each lower one is caused by the records of its upper Partzuf.

5. Afterwards, when Malchut rose to phase three, where ten Sefirot come out on the level of Hochma, it is impossible for this light to begin in the Sefira of Hochma. It is so because any expansion of light must begin from the Keter. It therefore needs an illumination of a record of Keter, by which the light becomes adhered and tied to the root.

Also, when Malchut rose to Bina and ten Sefirot come out on the level of Bina, an illumination of the records of Keter and Hochma necessarily remains there, and so on likewise for the above reason. Remember this in every place, for it is impossible for any degree to lack the upper Sefirot altogether. Rather, when the upper Sefirot are regarded as mere illumination of a record do we say that they are absent there, for they do not shine there.

When the light of Hochma departs, it leaves a record in its place to shine for Bina.

5. Afterwards, when Hochma rises to the emanator, she leaves a record in his vessel, to shine from him to Bina, after he himself departs. Even after Bina rises to the emanator, the record of Hochma does not leave the vessel of Hochma, and likewise all of them until the Yesod.

Malchut does not leave a record.

6. However, when the light of Malchut departs, she does not leave a record in her vessel, for there is no Sefira beneath her to receive from her (6). Although there will be other worlds beneath her, receiving from her, it is not their kind and she has no adhesion with them (7), as there is adhesion with the ten Sefirot of each and every world in and of itself.

Inner Light

6. Because it is female light, receiving for herself and not bestowing. Because of it, her ten Sefirot end the degree, as it is only reflected light. Hence, she does not leave a record, as a record is only the remains of the expansion of direct light that remains there, as the ARI says. Also, there is no cessation in the upper light here, for the lower one is completely dependent on the upper one, but the upper one does not need the lower one.

7. Because they come in a renewed form of coarseness, she has no adhesion with them, as adhesion means equivalence of form, while separation and difference mean disparity of form (see Part 3, Table of Questions, item 210).

All the Sefirot leave records in their place after they depart, except for Malchut.

7. It turns out that all those Sefirot leave a record in their place and in their vessel when they want to depart and ascend. However, the light of Malchut does not leave a record in its vessel, only the record that the light of Yesod left in its vessel. The illumination is extended from there to the vessel of Malchut after the departure of her light.

Malchut is called poor since she does not leave a record, for she has nothing of her own.

8. There is another reason why Malchut is called "poor for she has nothing of her own", and also, "a mirror without light" (8). It is because her vessel does not shine at all when she ascends and the light leaves her, as no light remains in her, even as a record. Even the sustenance of that vessel does not come from her own light, but from the record that remains in the vessel of Yesod. From there it sustains and shines in the vessel of Malchut. That is why it is said, "She has nothing of her own."

8. The ARI has already written why Malchut is called "without light". It is because in the second expansion, ten Sefirot were extended only on the level of Hochma, and the light of Keter remained concealed in the Peh.

It turns out that the light of Hochma comes in the vessel of Keter, the light of Bina in the vessel of Hochma, the light of ZA in the vessel of Bina and the light of Malchut in the vessel of ZA. Thus, the vessel of Malchut is left without light, hence the name "a mirror without light". He adds another reason here—that Malchut did not leave a record behind her in the first expansion.

We might ask: If the light of Keter disappeared from the second expansion, the vessel of Keter should have remained there without light. Why were the lights switched, and the light of Hochma came in the vessel of Keter until the vessel of Malchut remained without light? It has already been explained in the Inner Observation (Part 2, Chapter 8) that the conduct of the lights is to clothe only in the most refined vessels in the Partzuf. Even if there is only the light of Nefesh there, it clothes only the highest vessel, namely Keter, while the lower nine remain without light.

Two kinds of light remain in the vessel after the departure: a) reflected light, which is judgment; b) the records, which are direct light and mercy

9. We have now learned by these two introductions how the vessels of the Sefirot, even when their lights return and depart to the emanator, still have two kinds of lights (9): The first is called reflected light, and it is judgment. The second is the light that remains in the vessel, called a record. This is direct light and mercy because it remains there from the phases of the lights that emerged from above downward as direct light.

9. The first expansion, extended by the broadening of Malchut from her and within her to ten Sefirot down to the Malchut of the Guf, is extended from above downward as clothing, and it is called direct light and mercy. Also, all the records that remain of these ten Sefirot after the departure of that light are also direct light, mercy, but as a small illumination called a record.

However, these levels that emerge through a coupling by striking as Malchut ascends and refines from below upward degree-by-degree until all the light departs, all these levels are called reflected light, judgment, since the levels gradually diminish until they depart completely.

The coarse light that does not depart becomes a vessel, and the reflected light and the records remain in it.

10. It turns out that in that world of Akudim, although at that time, the making of the vessels had not been completed, nevertheless, the phases and existence from which they were made, which is coarse light that is connected with refined light, had already been there [10]. When the refined light returns upward, the coarse light remains below, and this is the phase of the vessels themselves. There, in that coarse light [20], which is the phase of the vessels, the refined lights left the above two phases: 1 - direct light, a record; 2 - reflected light.

Inner Light

10. When the light expands from Malchut of the Rosh down to the Guf, that light consists of direct light and reflected light, as they clothe one another in the Rosh. This direct light is called refined light and reflected light is called coarse light since it is extended by the force of the coarseness and restriction in the screen of Malchut of the Rosh.

There is no recognition of coarseness above, in the Rosh, since it ascends and clothes the upper nine from the screen upward, and the force of the coarseness cannot operate above the place of its manifestation and existence even a bit. However, afterwards, this reflected light expands and descends once more with its direct light from Malchut of the Rosh downward. Then the coarseness in the screen is certainly in it, though it is not at all regarded as a drawback, for its entire merit is connected with the coarseness, as there wouldn't have been any light in the Partzuf without it.

Indeed, when the light finally departs from the Partzuf and the coarseness is emptied of that direct light that is clothed in it, then the full demerit and ignobility of that coarseness, compared to the direct light, is revealed.

The ARI writes, "...**remains below.**" It means that after the refined light had been emptied of the coarse light, meaning once the direct light departed and was pulled out of the reflected light that clothed it, the coarse light remained below. In other words, the demerit of the reflected light compared to the direct light was revealed. That is why it is said that after the return of the refined light upwards, the coarse light that remained below "**is the phase of the vessels themselves.**"

In other words, this reflected light that had been emptied of direct light after its first expansion is the entire substance of the vessels in that Partzuf, called the first expansion of AK, or Partzuf Galgalta of AK. The record and the sparks of the descending reflected light clothed inside it. We shall now see that these records and the sparks of reflected light became and were corrected as the vessels of the following Partzuf, called the second expansion, or AB.

20. Meaning the reflected light that remains after the departure of the direct light from within it. Yet, we need to thoroughly understand the above matter of the ascent of the lights, and know precisely: what ascended, what was refined, and what remained below and became vessels.

You already know that the screen means a "detaining force over the upper light so that it does not expand into the four phases of coarseness in phase four, called Malchut."

In the matter of the ascent of Malchut to ZA in the ARI's words below, know that it pertains only to the screen and reflected light in her. In the words of the ARI, these two are called the light of Malchut. They are called light, as there is no other light in Malchut from the restriction onwards.

However, the vessel of Malchut herself cannot rise to ZA, since ascent means refinement, and that can only be in the screen, but not in the vessels. This matter of refinement does not apply to the vessels whatsoever. Rather, that measure of coarseness that exists in the phase of the vessels in each and every Partzuf remains permanent and exists forever until they receive their correction. This has already been explained (Part 2, Table of Questions, item 43).

The matter of the refinement of the screen from phase four to phase three means that because of the clash of the inner light with the surrounding light in the screen, the last phase of the coarseness that is included in its force of detainment disappeared and was lost. From now on it detains the upper light from expanding further than phase three of the coarseness, which remains in it. It is so because phase four within phase four is no longer included in it, so it only detains and returns the upper light from the three phases of coarseness that remained incorporated in it from phase four.

The reflected light that is returned from these three phases is sufficient only to clothe the direct light up to Hochma, and its clothing does not reach Keter. It therefore naturally turns out that the light of Keter disappears from the Partzuf because the light is not captured in a Partzuf without a garment and a vessel (see Inner Observation, Part 2, Chapter 7).

It has been thoroughly explained that the ascent and the refinement relate to the screen and not at all to the vessels. The vessels that remain in their place after the departure of the direct light (which the ARI calls coarse light) are the four phases of coarseness incorporated in that reflected light that has already been clothed. They clothe the ten Sefirot of the Guf, which have now been emptied of their lights.

CHAPTER THREE

Explains four kinds of light: tastes, dots, tags, letters. Those are: 1. The first expansion from the Peh to the Tabur, namely tastes; 2. The levels that emerge during the departure are called dots; 3. The records are called tags; 4. The light that is born by the striking of the records and the descending reflected light on one another is letters. Contains thirteen issues:

1. When Yesod rises, it leaves a record in its place to illuminate to Malchut. 2. The record is a residue from the first light of Akudim that is extended from above downward through the straightness, which is mercy. 3. The first expansion of Akudim illuminated to the receivers from above downward, and the levels that emerged with their departure illuminated from below upward. 4. When the Keter ascended to the emanator, it illuminated through its back to the emanated beings. 5. The lights of the face are mercy, and those of the back are judgments, called reflected light. 6. Hochma receives from one posterior of Keter, Bina from two posteriors, and Malchut from nine posteriors. 7. There is yet another change, according to the quality of the Sefira, because Tifferet receives from the posteriors of Gevura, which are hard posteriors. 8. According to the changes in the phases of the Sefirot, so will be the light that is extended: weak judgment, medium or strong. 9. Three phases of lights: a) the first expansion of Akudim from the Peh to the Tabur; b) the records that remained from this the first expansion, which is mercy; c) the levels of the reflected light that are extended from the emanator during the departure of the lights, which is judgment. 10. The clash of the light of the records and the reflected light with one another engenders a fourth light, called sparks. 11. The first expansion of Akudim is called tastes; the level of the reflected light is called dots; the records are called tags; the sparks are called letters. 12. The sparks, called letters, are the vessels, called Guf. 13. The sparks merely mixed with the vessels, similar to the 288 sparks that remained in the broken vessels of Nekudim.

When Yesod rises, it leaves a record in its place to illuminate to Malchut

1. We shall start to explain them from Yesod, which is the last one to leave a record. It is said that during its ascent from Yesod to the place of Hod and upward, it leaves a record for Malchut in the place where Yesod was (1). That

record never leaves there, even when Malchut returns and rises to the emanator. All the other Sefirot do the same, excluding Malchut.

Inner Light

1. It has already been explained that Malchut of Akudim is called Tabur, and her emanator, which is Malchut of the Rosh, is called Peh. When the screen in Malchut of the Guf was refined from all the coarseness included in it and remained refined, in complete equivalence with Malchut of the Rosh, which is his emanator, it is considered that Malchut returned upward to the emanator. It is so because when they are both even in their measure of refinement, they are in adhesion and incorporated in one another like a single phase.

It is known that disparity of form is the measure of the difference and separation in the spirituals, and equivalence of form is the adhesion and the unification in the spirituals. Thus, when Malchut of the Guf and Malchut of the Rosh are equal in their measure of refinement, they are regarded as being in adhesion with one another and incorporated into a single phase.

It is said, "**that record never leaves there, even when Malchut returns and rises to the emanator.**" By this he tells us that even when the screen has been refined of all its coarseness until it remains equal to the refinement of the emanator, the screen is still incorporated with the records in the ten Sefirot of the Guf. Only phase four is excluded, as the last phase does not leave a record, because these records are of direct light and the last phase does not receive direct light inside her, and there is only reflected light in her.

Know that these records that remained incorporated in Malchut even when she is incorporated in the emanator, they are the nucleus for the birth of a second Partzuf. It is so because all the lights and the vessels are extended to the second Partzuf from these records, as written above (and see Inner Observation here, item 52).

It is so because the screen of Malchut of the Rosh is never refined, and the coupling by striking in phase four there is regarded as a never-ending coupling. Thus, when Malchut of the Guf rises there and is incorporated in the screen of the Rosh, she is also incorporated in the coupling of the Rosh. This, in turn, causes the awakening of the coarseness included in the records in her, as she receives from the coarseness from below upward that is incorporated there in the screen of the Rosh.

However, as soon as the records in her return to their coarseness, it is inverted in them into coarseness from above downward because they come from the ten

Sefirot of the Guf that were already there as clothing from above downward. By this, the phase of the Guf in the screen that ascended reappeared there, which is the coarseness from above downward, being Guf and not Rosh. This manifestation is regarded as descent and separation from Malchut of the Rosh because it returned to its previous state, to Malchut of the phase of the *Guf*, but not to phase four, called Tabur, but only to phase three, called Chazeh. There, a coupling by striking was done again, eliciting ten Sefirot on the level of Hochma in Rosh, Toch, Sof (RTS), called Partzuf AB, and this matter has already been explained (Part 3, Table of Topics, item 210), and study it there.

The record is a residue from the first light of Akudim that is extended from above downward through the straightness, which is mercy

2. This record is from the first light(2), which descended through straightness. A light that comes in straightness is mercy, and a light that comes on the way back up is reflected light, and it is judgment (3). The record is through straightness, which is why it is mercy.

Inner Light

2. From the first expansion, which expands from Peh to Tabur of AK. It consists of direct light and reflected light clothed in one another. Direct light is called refined light and reflected light is called coarse light (see Inner Light, Chapter 2, item 10). The residue that remains from the refined light after its departure is called a record. It is mercy because it is the remains of the direct light that is extended from above downward into the phase of clothing in the Partzuf. The reflected light that has been emptied of direct light after its departure is regarded as the vessels inside which the records that remained of the direct light clothed, as the ARI says above (item 10).

3. Meaning light that comes and is extended from the emanator because of the coupling by striking that is performed on the screen during the degrees of its refinement. At that time the levels gradually diminish until the light disappears entirely and returns to its root above, to Malchut of the Rosh. These levels are called reflected light, judgment, since they appear during the departure.

The first expansion of Akudim illuminated to the receivers from above downward, and the levels that emerged with their departure illuminated from below upward

3. It is known that when the Sefirot of Akudim came, their faces were downward(4) because the purpose of their coming was to shine downward. Therefore,

their faces were through the receivers. However, when they returned upward, they turned their faces upward toward the emanator and their backs downward (5).

Inner Light

4. There is no movement whatsoever here; no posterior and no anterior. As has been explained in previous parts, any change of form is called "spiritual movement" (see Inner Observation Part 1, item 33). Know that bestowal of lights or extension in the vessels is called face or anterior, and it is known that any giver gives in the coarser thing. Thus, the coarser the screen, the higher the level of ten Sefirot that is imparted there.

Therefore, the lights of mercy are regarded here as being imparted as clothing in the Partzuf, with their face downward, for the word face means bestowal. Downward means greater coarseness. "**Their faces were downward**" means that the bestowal is captured in the greater coarseness in the degree.

5. It has already been explained that the state of bestowal is called face. It is therefore understood that the state of departure from bestowal is called back. It has also been explained that "**downward**" means the coarser phase there. "**Their backs downward**" means that the lights depart and retire themselves from the coarseness, so that a greater departure will be in the phase with the greater coarseness.

When the Keter ascended to the emanator, it illuminated through its back to the emanated beings

4. When the Keter rises to the emanator, there is no doubt that the light of the emanator never stops even for a moment from the receiving emanated beings (6). The only difference is that at that time, when the Keter rises upward, that light that descends from the emanator descends from it to the Sefira through its back, since he turned his face upward and his back to the emanated beings, and it is judgments. The other Sefirot operate similarly as they return and ascend.

Inner Light

6. This is a great rule in the wisdom: The upper light flows and pours incessantly, without any changes whatsoever, as it is written, "I the Lord do not change," as we have written in length (Inner Light, Chapter 2, item 2). Also, during the departure, meaning during the refinement of the screen, the departure was instantaneous and at once. However, because the refinement necessarily ascends in the order of degrees

in the four phases of coarseness, it is necessarily refined to phase three first, phase two next, then phase one and then the phase of Keter.

It is therefore considered that the light of the emanator that does not stop expands to it and couples with it during its ascent and arrival from phase to phase. It elicits a new level of ten Sefirot in each phase according to the measure of its coarseness. When it comes to phase three, it elicits the level of Hochma; when it comes to phase two, it elicits the level of Bina, etc., until it is completely refined and the upper light stops due to the absence of reflected light to clothe it, for there is no manifestation of light without a vessel and clothing.

The lights of the face are mercy, and those of the back are judgments, called reflected light

5. It turns out that even during the ascent of the lights they extend downward light that descends from the emanator to the lower ones by them and through them _(7)_, although at that time, it is then extended through their back. It is known that face is mercy and backs are judgments. The descending light is now called reflected light, since it descends when the upper lights return to rise to their root and emanator, and that is why this light is judgment.

Inner Light

7. It means that light descends from the emanator to the lower phases that were made in each and every Sefira as the screen ascends and becomes refined. Every place to which the screen of Malchut rises becomes the lowest phase. It means that it stops the light of the emanator and detains its expansion from her downward. Thus, the light of the emanator ends at that place. This is why we call the place to which the screen comes by the name "the lowest phase."

The ARI makes this precision: "**to the lower ones by them and through them.**" It tells us that the light is extended from the emanator only by the lowest phases and through the lowest phases, meaning through the screen that raises reflected light as it ascends and is gradually refined. When it comes to phase three, which is ZA, phase three becomes the lowest phase that strikes the upper light and detains it from expanding from it downward.

It turns out that the entire measure of light that was suitable to be received in it had been rejected and pushed back as reflected light, and it extends ten Sefirot on the level of Hochma, and so on likewise. Thus, you find that the extension of light always comes from the lowest phase that has been initiated, and the light that she did not receive became reflected light.

Hochma receives from one posterior of Keter, Bina from two posteriors, and Malchut from nine posteriors

6. It turns out that when Keter returns and rises to the emanator (8), before all the Sefirot, that light that descends from the emanator to the Sefira below Keter is extended and passes through the posterior of the Keter, and it is judgment. It is likewise during the ascent of the other Sefirot, though there is one difference, which is that Hochma receives only from the posterior of Keter (9). Bina receives from two posteriors, making it more judgment, and it is likewise in all of them, until you find that Malchut receives from nine posteriors, making it more judgment than all the other Sefirot above her (10).

Inner Light

8. Meaning because of the refinement of the screen from phase four to phase three, when the reflected light that ascends from phase three does not come to clothe the light of Keter. It therefore returns and ascends to its root, as there is no manifestation of light without clothing. This departure of the light of Keter is called the "the posterior of the Keter". It is because anterior means bestowal and expansion, and posterior means departure from bestowal.

9. Posterior means departure. In the first expansion all the Sefirot emerged on the level of Keter. It follows that all the Sefirot received from the face of the Keter, since they were with it on an equal level, unlike during the refinement, since when it was refined to phase three and the level of Hochma emerged and the light of Keter remained concealed in the Peh, it follows that now Hochma receives from the posterior of the Keter. In other words, she suffers and feels the great lack from the concealment of the light of Keter. It is said that "Hochma receives from the posterior of the Keter," meaning the state of judgment because she feels the lack of its illumination. It is likewise in the rest of the Sefirot.

10. The rule is that all the forces of the upper one are always present in its lower one, which necessarily receives all the posteriors of its upper one. When it is refined to phase three and the level of Hochma emerges and receives the state of judgment that appears in her due to the lack of illumination of the light of Keter, the Sefirot below Hochma receive the same posteriors, too, since they, too, received from the

anterior of Keter in the first expansion, as did Hochma, for all of them were there on the same level, up to Keter.

Now, on the level of phase three, they all lack the light of Keter and have only the light of the face of Hochma. Similarly, when it is refined from phase three to phase two and the level of Bina emerges, Bina, too, suffers from the departure of the light of Hochma. Then, she receives two posteriors into her. These are the posterior of Keter that she has already received when she was on the level of phase three, and the posterior of Hochma that she receives now.

Thus, the Sefirot below Bina also suffer from the same posterior of Hochma in addition to the posterior of Keter that they received during the appearance of the level of phase three, etc., similarly. When it is refined to the phase of Keter, where only the level of Malchut emerges and all the upper nine are missing, Malchut receives from nine posteriors.

It is so because when she was on the level of phase three, she received the posterior of Keter; when she was in phase two, she received the posterior of Hochma; and when she was in phase one, she received the posterior of Bina. Now that she has only her own light, she receives from the posterior of ZA, too, which are the six Sefirot HGT NHY. Thus, Malchut received nine posteriors.

There is yet another change, according to the quality of the Sefira,
because Tifferet receives from the posteriors of Gevura, which are
hard posteriors

7. There is yet another discernment: Tifferet receives her light from the posterior of the Sefira of Gevura. They are hard posteriors and very strong Gevurot. The other Sefirot above are not like that.

According to the changes in the phases of the Sefirot, so will be the light that is
extended: weak judgment, medium or strong

8. It turns out that, according to the difference between the phases, so will be the difference in the light that is extended: weak judgment, medium judgment, or strong judgment. However, the equal side in all of them is that they are all judgments, because they are through the posterior, as we have said, and the pen has no power to elaborate and detail all these details in this matter.

Three phases of lights: a) the first expansion of Akudim from the Peh to the Tabur; b) the records that remained from this the first expansion, which is mercy;

c) the levels of the reflected light that are extended from the emanator during the departure of the lights, which is judgment

9. It turns out that there are three phases of lights here: The first light is the first light among all of them, called Akudim. They descended and expanded from the Peh outwards and down to the (Chazeh) Tabur (20)**.**

The second light is the light of the record that the first light left of that light itself that came through straightness (30)**, and it is mercy.**

The third light is [reflected light]. It is a light that was extended from the emanator to the Sefira, and it was extended when the lights ascended and returned from below upwards (40)**. This light is judgment, since it is extended through the posterior.**

Inner Light

20. Meaning the first expansion, when the coupling by striking emerged on phase four, called Peh, which is the phase of Malchut of the Rosh. After that this Malchut expanded into ten Sefirot from her and within her down to her Malchut. These ten Sefirot are called Guf, and Malchut of the Guf is called Tabur, and the ten Sefirot of this Rosh and Guf were at the level of Keter.

30. See the words of the ARI above (Chapter 2, item 10). He wrote that two lights remained after the departure of the first expansion: The first is the light that remains of the direct light. The second is coarse light, meaning reflected light that has been emptied of the direct light it clothed during the first expansion, remained below, and its coarseness manifested. This coarse light is the vessels, and the refined light that remained from the direct light is called a record. This record remained clothed within the coarse light.

40. "Ascended" implies refinement from the coarseness in order to reach equivalence of form with its upper one, namely the emanator. "Returned" implies departure of the light after its expansion, regarded as returning to its root.

It is said: **"light that was extended from the emanator to the Sefira, and it was extended when the lights ascended and returned."** Explanation: The upper light is extended through a coupling by striking during the refinement of the screen and its coming into the degrees on the path of its refinement. At that time, the levels gradually diminish until it is completely refined and equalizes its form with the emanator, meaning Malchut of the Rosh. This issue is always called "the ascent of the lights to the emanator", and remember that.

The clash of the light of the records and the reflected light with one another engenders a fourth light, called sparks

10. There is indeed a fourth light born from the aforementioned lights. It is so because the third light, called reflected light, is extended and descends downward to shine in the Sefira(50). At that time, it encounters the second light, called record, which remains below. However, they differ in their nature, for one is direct light and mercy, while the other is reflected light and judgment (60).

Hence, they strike and clash with each other, especially since the light of the record wishes and yearns to ascend to its source (70), which is the first light. Although it does not actually ascend, as the record remains forever below, it nonetheless wishes and yearns to ascend.

However, the reflected light descends below(80), and as they are of opposite nature, they strike each other, for there is clashing and striking only when the lights differ in their nature. Then, through their striking on each other, they generate sparks of light as reflected light, which is judgment, and worse than the light of the record, which is mercy. These sparks are the fourth light we have mentioned.

Inner Light

50. As the ARI has said (Chapter 3, item 3), the degrees relate to each other as father to sons. Hence, during the ascent of the lights to the emanator, when the screen of phase four had been refined to phase three, there was a coupling in phase three, and phase four remained emptied of her light. At that time, phase three bestows upon phase four from the illumination of her coupling.

Afterwards, when phase three becomes refined into phase two, and the coupling is in phase two, phase three remains emptied of light, and phase two bestows her illumination from the coupling upon phase three, and so on similarly. From the perspective of the extension of the lights, phase four is regarded as Keter and phase three as Hochma. However, from the perspective of the vessels themselves it is the opposite: phase three is regarded as ZA and phase four as Malchut. Because phase four is emptied of light, only the vessels themselves are discerned here, and it is the same manner in all of them.

It is written, "**the third light, called reflected light, is extended and descends downward to shine in the Sefira.**" The third light refers to the light of the levels that emerge during its refinement. That light is extended and descends below the place of the coupling as well, to shine to the Sefira below it. In other words, when the coupling is in phase two, the illumination of the coupling is extended to the Sefira below it, namely to phase three, which is empty of light.

It is known that the lights left records in the Sefirot after their departure from there. Thus, when the illumination of the coupling of phase two is extended to phase three, it encounters the light of her record there.

It is said, "**At that time, it encounters the second light, called record, which remains below.**" It means that the light of the coupling in the upper phase is extended and descends to the lower phase, which is emptied of her light, and meets the record there. The ARI will henceforth refer to that light that descends from the illumination of the coupling downward, as "the descending reflected light".

60. It means that the record is from the direct light that remains from the first expansion, reaching up to Keter, since the coupling by striking occurs there in the screen of phase four. Because of that, the coarseness of phase four is regarded as its face, as it is from her that it gets its entire level, and the coarseness of phase three and above is regarded as the posterior side of its vessel and does not shine in it.

Its opposite is the reflected light descending to it from the illumination of the coupling of the upper phase. For example, when the illumination of the coupling of phase two descends to a Sefira of phase three that has been emptied of its light, that descending reflected light comes from a coupling by striking performed in the screen of coarseness of phase two, whose level reaches up to Bina. The coarseness of phase two is regarded as its face, meaning its maximum height.

It leaves coarseness of phase three and phase four as posterior, meaning ignobility and a flaw. Because they do not shine in it, it lowers them and brings them down. In other words, the disparity of form in them becomes the separator over the light, meaning the opposite of the record where the coarser phase four draws and connects with the greatest light.

It is said, "**they differ in their nature, for one is direct light and mercy, while the other is reflected light and judgment.**" It is so because the records that remain in all the Sefirot come from direct light and mercy, meaning from the first expansion, when the coupling on the screen of phase four emerged, where the coarser it is the better, for it is all mercy.

However, the descending reflected light from the illumination of the couplings that emerge during the refinement, all these levels are regarded as reflected light and judgment since they depart from the coarseness, bring down and lower the coarseness to a state of posterior.

Thus, the reflected light that descends from them is in contrast with the records, in which the coarser is more important. It turns out that what is regarded as face for the record, is regarded as back for the descending reflected light. Likewise, what is regarded as face for the descending reflected light, is regarded as back for the record, and it is for the reason that they strike and clash with each other.

70. Since she is the part that remains after the first expansion, when she has already departed and disappeared to her origin, that yearning and desire becomes imprinted in the record as well. It is said: **"Although it does not actually ascend, as the record remains forever below, it nonetheless wishes and yearns to ascend."** In other words, even though the record is destined to remain in the vessel and never rise to her origin, she nonetheless has the desire to ascend, as the force of the light in general necessarily remains imprinted in her.

80. It means that it is extended and comes from the emanator through a new coupling, and descends to clothe inside the Guf because all these couplings that emerge on the degrees of his refinement are done in the Rosh, and from there they are extended from above downward to the Guf. However, because they emerge during the refinement and will not continue to exist, it is regarded as reflected light and judgment.

It is said, **"However, the reflected light descends downward."** In other words, if we consider only the time of the coupling, you find that it expands and descends temporarily for clothing in the Guf. The record, however, wishes to depart from the Guf and ascend to its origin.

Know that because of that, the reflected light that descends from the illumination of the coupling overpowers the light of the record when they strike and clash with each other. As a result, sparks spread from this reflected light and clothe inside the vessel that is emptied of light. Thus, the light of the record is rejected from within her and rises above that vessel, as tags on top of the letters.

As the ARI writes later (Chapter 4, item 4) that the two of them cannot be in a single vessel, for they are opposites. Know that the above striking and clash is done above the empty vessel, for the record strikes the reflected light and does not let it expand, and the descending reflected light strikes the record in order to clothe and shine in the vessel, until sparks spread from the reflected light and descend and come into the vessel.

The first expansion of Akudim is called tastes; the level of the reflected light is called dots; the records are called tags; the sparks are called letters

11. Now you can understand what we have said, that there are four phases in these lights of Akudim: tastes, dots, tags, letters. This is what they are about: The first light among them is called tastes, and the third light, called reflected light, is called dots, since dots are discerned as judgment. The second light, called record, is called tags, and the fourth light is the falling sparks, and they are called letters.

The sparks, called letters, are the vessels, called Guf

12. This fourth light, which is the sparks, called letters, are themselves the discernment of vessels(90), as it is known, for the letters are called Guf. This explains where the vessels were made.

Inner Light

90. Afterwards, the light returned and expanded in them a second expansion on the level of Hochma. Keter remained concealed in the Peh, and the light of Hochma clothed in the vessel of Keter, light of Bina in the vessel of Hochma etc. until Malchut remained without light. Know that these sparks have been prepared as vessels for these lights (see above in Inner Light, Chapter 2, item 3).

The sparks merely mixed with the vessels, similar to the 288 sparks that remained in the broken vessels of Nekudim

13. It appears to me that I had heard from my teacher that there were phases of vessels in them to begin with(100), but these sparks mixed and connected with them and were in them as the 288 sparks that remained inside the vessels of the world of Nekudim when they were broken, etc. (200).

Inner Light

100. The ARI explicitly wrote above (Chapter 2, item 10) that the coarse light that remained after the departure of the light of the first expansion are the phases of the vessels of the Partzuf themselves, in which the above two lights came. These are called "the second light," a record, and "the fourth light," the falling sparks, which are called letters.

It is said, "there were phases of vessels in them to begin with, but these sparks mixed with them." It means that two phases of vessels must be prepared for the second expansion, for there is male and female in every Sefira. Thus, of these phases of vessels that were in them to begin with, meaning from the above coarse light, the vessels for the male lights of the second expansion were made. The vessels for the lights of the females of this expansion were made of the sparks that fell inside them and mixed with them.

It is said, "**mixed**" to tell us that the phases are not equal. Sparks of phase three came into phase four, and sparks of phase two in the vessel of phase three, and sparks of phase one in the vessel of phase two etc. and that is why this connection is regarded as a mixture.

200. It is a great thing that he tells us here: it is known that the 288 sparks that remained in the vessels after they were broken and died were the cause of the revival of the vessels. It is so because these sparks were an association of mercy with judgment.

Thus, here the sparks that fell from the descending reflected light are also from the association of the quality of mercy with judgment. However, it is as a beginning, for every upper phase is regarded as the quality of mercy toward the phase below her. Because the sparks of the upper phase fell, mixed and connected with the lower phase, it is regarded as mixing the quality of mercy with judgment, the same as the above 288 sparks.

Know that this is the whole merit of the departure of the first expansion. It is because of her that the above sparks descended and the root for the association of the quality of mercy with judgment was formed. The ARI writes below about this departure, that it is regarded as "corruption in order to correct", meaning like the breaking of the vessels, which also occurred in order to revive. It means that it refers to the association of the quality of mercy with judgment, from which comes the revival and from which comes the entire correction of the world.

CHAPTER FOUR

Explains the striking and the clash between the descending reflected light and the records, which occurred during the departure of the lights to the emanator. The vessels, which are the letters, were made from the sparks that emerged by the striking. The tags are from the records. Contains eight issues:

1. Malchut is called a mirror without light because her light did not come back down into her vessel. 2. A second reason that Malchut is called a mirror without light is that she did not leave a record in her vessel. 3. A coupling by striking between the descending reflected light from Yesod to Malchut and the first light of the ascending Malchut. 4. The vessel of Yesod was made from the sparks that fell from the striking of light that comes through its posterior in the record, and the tags were made of the record that shines from afar. 5. Three discernments in the ten Sefirot: Keter, the other Sefirot, and Malchut. Keter left a record and not a vessel; the other Sefirot left records and vessels; and Malchut left a vessel and not a record. 6. After all the departure, the lights returned to their place in the Partzuf AB of AK, except for the light of Keter. Then there was a clash between the record of Keter and light of Hochma on each other, and two vessels emerged, one for Keter and one for Hochma, which are male and female in the Rosh of AB of AK. 7. The refinement and the departure in Akudim are somewhat similar to the revoking of the Melachim in the world of Nekudim who died and were revoked. 8. The difference between them is that here there was corruption in order to correct, while in Nekudim there was actual breaking and death.

Malchut is called a mirror without light because her light did not come back down into her vessel

1. *Know that when all nine lights rose back up, they left a record in their place. However, Malchut rose in her entirety, leaving no record in her place. This is the meaning of what is written in the Zohar and the Tikkunim, that Malchut is called "a mirror that has no light of its own". This matter has already been explained above regarding the vessel of Malchut, whose light did not come back down into her vessel, but remained in the vessel of Yesod (1).

Inner Light

1. In the second expansion, when the coupling emerged only on the level of Hochma, by which the lights were swapped, where the light of Hochma came in the vessel of Keter, and the light of Bina in the vessel of Hochma etc., and the light of Malchut in vessel of Yesod. Thus, vessel Malchut remained without light (see Inner Light, Part 4, Chapter 2, item 8).

A second reason that Malchut is called a mirror without light is that she did not leave a record in her vessel

2. There is another reason: when her light rose, it did not leave any record in her at all. However, the record that remained in the vessel of Yesod for its own need illuminated from there in the vessel of Malchut too.

A coupling by striking between the descending reflected light from Yesod to Malchut and the first light of the ascending Malchut

3. *When the light of Malchut rose to Yesod, Yesod illuminated in the vessel of Malchut through the posterior of Yesod (2) as reflected light. Then the descending reflected light in the vessel of Malchut encounters the first ascending light of Malchut herself (3), one clashed with the other, and sparks came down from the descending reflected light (4) into the vessel of Malchut (5).

Inner Light

2. It has already been explained that all the levels that emerge on the path of refinement are regarded as reflected light and judgment, though there is direct light in them as well. However, because they are extended through the posterior, meaning on the path of the refinement of the coarseness, called anterior, the direct light is also regarded as judgment.

It is said, "**Yesod illuminated in the vessel of Malchut through the posterior of Yesod**," where all these ten Sefirot of direct light and reflected light together are discerned as posterior and judgment.

However, we must still understand that the entire reflected light that descends from Yesod to the vessel of Malchut is only reflected light without any direct light. It is so because since the place of the coupling and the screen is in the vessel of Yesod, meaning in phase three, that screen detains the direct light, so that none of it will expand from phase three downward. Thus, all that descends from Yesod to the vessel of Malchut is only reflected light and not direct light, hence the ARI's precision, "**as reflected light.**"

3. This light is on the level of Keter. It regards the greater coarseness as anterior, and the descending reflected light lowers the great coarseness of phase four, preferring the more refined phase three, which is in contrast with the ascending light of Malchut. This is the reason they clash with each other (see Part 4, Chapter 3, item 9).

4. They are called sparks because of the similarity to the sparks that emerge from under a hammer, which shine and burn out instantly, as it is written in *The Zohar*. However, the analogy is not quite the same as the lesson: the sparks that emerge under the hammer shine for a moment and instantly vanish, and their place remains unknown.

Conversely, these sparks here, as well as the 248 sparks, although they instantly burn out because of the departure of the coupling to the higher phase, being phase two, nevertheless, they do not vanish from there, as it is known that there is no absence in the spiritual. Their self and reality remain there, and later regain their strength when the second expansion reaches there.

5. It is the coarse light that remains below after the departure of the first expansion, which is the essence of the vessels that belong to the first expansion of Akudim. This is where the lights placed their records and this is where the sparks from the reflected light fell (see Part 4, Chapter 2, item 10).

The vessel of Yesod was made from the sparks that fell from the striking of light that comes through its posterior in the record, and the tags were made of the record that shines from afar

4. When Yesod rose, it placed a record in its place. When the light came through its posterior, it struck that record, sparks fell from it, and the phase of the vessel of Yesod was made of them (6). That record illuminated in that vessel from afar, and did not enter it. This is the meaning of the tags (7).

Inner Light

6. For the second expansion, which comes afterwards, called Partzuf AB of AK, though the vessel of Yesod of Akudim here was made of the coarse light that remained below after the departure of the first expansion.

7. Study the words of the ARI thoroughly (Part 4, Chapter 3, item 9 and Inner Light, item 80). Know that after the coupling in the upper vessel had stopped and rose above it, the illumination of the coupling from the lower vessel necessarily stopped, as well. At that time, the sparks that descended there are put out, too, and the record, which was above the vessel, can therefore clothe the vessel once more as in the beginning (see above Inner Light, Chapter 3, item 80).

However, that illumination from afar, called tags, did not stop from the vessel afterwards, for there is no absence in the spiritual, as it says, "the Shechina never moves, etc."

Three discernments in the ten Sefirot: Keter, the other Sefirot, and Malchut. Keter left a record and not a vessel; the other Sefirot left records and vessels; and Malchut left a vessel and not a record

5. So did all the Sefirot do except for Keter $_{(8)}$, which left the record for Hochma. However, he did not make a vessel $_{(9)}$, since when the rest of the Sefirot rise up by striking in what is above them $_{(10)}$, and the striking of the record $_{(20)}$ became the vessels $_{(30)}$, but the Keter had no one to strike his record as he rose $_{(40)}$. For this reason, his vessel was still not completed. Thus, Keter left a record and not a vessel, while the rest of the Sefirot left a record and a vessel, and Malchut left a vessel and not a record.

Inner Light

8. It means that that record became the phase of vessel of the male of the light of Hochma in Keter of the second expansion, called AB of AK. The ARI writes, **"for Keter, which left the record for Hochma. However, he did not make a vessel."** This means that it did not make a vessel for the female of the light of Hochma in the vessel of Keter of the second expansion.

9. The ARI has already written (Chapter 2, item 10) that the essence of the phase of vessels of Akudim was made of the coarse light that remained from the light of departure itself. You can therefore see that this does not refer to the vessel of Keter itself but to the vessels of the second expansion, which come after the current departure, where there are the phase of male and the phase of female in the vessel of Keter. It is the same in the vessel of Hochma, Bina, Yesod and Malchut, as the ARI writes below (item 6).

The vessels of the males from there were made of the records that remain in the vessels of Akudim, and the vessels of the females were made of the sparks that fall from the reflected light that descends into the vessels of Akudim here.

It is said, "**Keter, which left the record for Hochma,**" meaning the vessel of the male of the ight of Hochma in the vessel of Keter of the second expansion. "**But did not make a vessel,**" meaning for the female there.

10. Reflected light is extended and descends to the emptied vessel by the coupling by striking in the phase above the vessel that has become emptied of light, meaning after the light departed from the vessel of Malchut. This is so because the screen of phase four has been refined into phase three, which is Yesod, and the coupling was done in the vessel of Yesod. At that time, reflected light descends from this illumination of the coupling to Malchut, which has been emptied of the light. This is the meaning of "**through striking of what is above them**" was the reflected light drawn to the vessel.

20. The record that remained in the emptied vessel strikes the reflected light that descends to its own vessel because it is opposite to the descending reflected light. Sparks were born and spread from the descending reflected light as a result of that striking, fell into the vessel that had been emptied, and the vessels were made out of these sparks.

30. Meaning the vessels, for the purpose of the vessels of the second expansion. However, the vessels of Akudim of the first expansion were made of the coarse light, as the ARI said in chapter 2, item 10 and Inner Light, chapter 2, item 100.

40. When the screen reaches complete refinement, like the state of the emanator, its power ceases and there is no coupling by striking in it any longer that will bring down reflected light in the vessel of Keter after the light has been emptied. "**For this reason, his vessel was still not completed,**" for there are no sparks of the descending reflected light there, as has been explained.

> After all the departure, the lights returned to their place in the Partzuf AB of AK, except for the light of Keter. Then there was a clash between the record of Keter and light of Hochma on each other, and two vessels emerged, one for Keter and one for Hochma, which are male and female in the Rosh of AB of AK

6. **Indeed, after the reception of these Sefirot from the emanator, they returned to their place** (50), **except for Keter** (60). **The vessel of Keter was made only on the return** (70) **because when Hochma reentered him, light of Hochma struck the record that Keter placed in his place** (80).

These were double strikes (90), **for since the record of Keter is a higher phase than Hochma, it therefore strikes Hochma and elicits sparks. Likewise, since Hochma**

is now coming from above, she stands on the record and is higher than it. As a result, he now struck the record and elicited other sparks.

Hence, two vessels were made now, one for the record of Keter and one for the Hochma that has now come $_{(100)}$. We have already discussed at length in a different place $_{(200)}$ how there is male and female in Keter, which are the two we mentioned here, namely the record and the Hochma.

Inner Light

50. We must thoroughly understand this matter of reception that the Sefirot received from the Emanator after their ascent to Him. You will understand this matter after you thoroughly know the matter of departure of the ten Sefirot of the Guf and their ascent to the Emanator.

Know that all this is drawn from and connected with the light of Malchut only, meaning the screen and reflected light in Malchut. That is because there is no other light in Malchut, for she never receives any direct light.

Thus, all the light in her is but the reflected light extended through a coupling by striking in her screen. The coarseness of phase four is the vessel of Malchut, and the screen that detains the upper light from expanding to the coarseness of phase four, along with the reflected light that ascends because of it, are regarded as the light of Malchut.

You can therefore see that the essence of the issue of the ascent of the lights to the Emanator is connected only to the ascent of Malchut. Ascending means refining and equalizing the form with the upper one. The equivalence of form with the upper one brings him to and connects him with the upper one.

Thus, the issue of the refinement of the coarseness pertains only to Malchut, where there is coarseness. Conversely, there is no discernment of a vessel whatsoever in the first nine Sefirot, and they are regarded here only as complete light (see Part 4, Chapter 1, item 11). Thus, how can we refer to a refinement of the coarseness in them?

Indeed, the matter of the ascent and the refinement refers solely to Malchut. This does not pertain to the vessel of Malchut since the vessels are never refined from their coarseness (see Part 2, Table of Questions, item 43). Instead, it pertains to the screen installed in the vessel of Malchut (see above Inner Light, Chapter 2, item 10).

You already know the issue of the four levels that are emerge through a coupling by striking on the screen from the beginning of its refinement until it is refined into the state of the Emanator. Know that these levels that gradually diminish are the very Sefirot of which the ARI says that they rose to the Emanator. Though there are ten Sefirot on each and every level, they are still recognized by the name of the highest Sefira on their level.

Though the level of phase three has ten Sefirot that only reach the level of Hochma, she is still regarded as light of Hochma entirely, after the name of the highest Sefira on the level. Similarly, the ten Sefirot of the level of phase two, reaching Bina, is only called Bina. Phase one is called ZA and the phase of Keter and root is called Malchut.

You should also know that all these records that the lights of Akudim placed in their vessels after their departure remained only in the vessel of Malchut. It is so because she is the designated vessel for all ten Sefirot of Akudim.

This is the coarse light that the ARI refers to above (Chapter 2, item 10), which is the phase of the vessels of Akudim themselves. Also, this is where the lights placed their records. It is therefore necessary that it is the phase of Malchut alone, for there is no coarseness in the upper nine.

It has been clarified there in inner light, that this coarse light is the reflected light in Malchut that expanded with it from her and within her to clothe the ten Sefirot of direct light from above downward, called Guf. Thus, it is clear that all the records that remained from the first expansion after her departure, necessarily remained only in Malchut.

It has been clarified that Malchut includes all the records that remained of the first expansion. Hence, after the screen rose to Malchut of the Rosh, meaning when the screen had been refined from all its coarseness and it came into equivalence of form with Malchut of the Rosh, it is discerned that the screen that rose also includes all the records that remained in Malchut, except for the record of phase four, as the last phase does not leave a record (see Part 4, Chapter 3, item 1). Now you understand the ARI's words here, who says, **"after the reception of these Sefirot from the emanator, they returned to their place, except for Keter."**

In other words, after the ascent of the screen of Malchut of the Guf to Malchut of the Rosh, called the phase of emanator of the Guf, which occurred because of the equivalence of form with it, you therefore find that it was connected and incorporated with the screen in Malchut of the Rosh as a single phase. Since the screen in Malchut of the Rosh is in a perpetual coupling by striking there, as there is no refinement in the Rosh, then the screen of the Guf that rose and was incorporated in it works along with it for the coupling by striking and for raising reflected light from below upward that is done in the Rosh, since it was incorporated in the same coarseness that exists in the screen in Malchut of the Rosh.

You already know that these records that remained in Malchut of the Guf are included in the screen that rose to the Rosh, which are only up to the coarseness of phase three, since no record was left of the coarseness of phase four.

Thus, once the screen of the Guf was incorporated and came into the coupling on the screen of the Rosh, and received from it the coarseness from below upward that is included in it, the records included in it from Malchut of the Guf reawakened and regained their initial coarseness, meaning coarseness from above downward as it is in the Guf.

Accordingly, initially, the screen was first incorporated in Malchut of the Rosh, and gained the coarseness from below upward that is in the Rosh. Subsequently, the records incorporated in the screen also awakened and gained coarseness, and the coarseness in them was inverted and became the state of from above downward.

You should understand the great difference between the coarseness from below upward and the coarseness from above downward. From below upward implies resistance to clothing, and at any rate, there is no clothing there whatsoever. For this reason, she is the phase of Rosh, called Keter or Ein Sof.

Its opposite is the discernment of coarseness from above downward, meaning a state of complete clothing on the direct light. For this reason, it is called Guf or emanated being, and is never called Ein Sof or emanator. This distinction applies to the Rosh and Guf of all the Partzufim in the worlds.

The screen had been completely refined from its coarseness and equalized its form with the phase of Malchut of the Rosh, which is completely clean from the coarseness from above downward. Naturally, the records included in it were completely silent, and were regarded as nonexistent. Then the screen of the Guf became incorporated in the screen of the Rosh with the coarseness from below upward.

However, since the screen has gained coarseness, though it is only coarseness from below upward, still, those silent and resting records incorporated in the screen awakened and were revived because of that, meaning they, too, gained coarseness. However, since these records came from the Guf, where they had already been clothed, the coarseness was naturally inverted in them into the state of from above downward, into the state of Guf. Consequently, the screen acquired a disparity of form that is very far from the Rosh, as the measure of the difference between the discernment of Rosh and the discernment of Guf.

It follows that the moment the coarseness from above downward appeared in the screen that is the state of Guf, it is discerned that the screen returned, departed from the Rosh and descended to the Guf. However, not to phase four of the Guf, called Tabur, but only to phase three of the Guf, called Chazeh. This is so because the screen could gain coarseness only up to phase three, as phase four did not leave a record in the screen.

You therefore find that the screen that rose to the emanator acquired two phases of coarseness there: coarseness from below upward, by the power of the initial incorporation in Malchut of the Rosh, and coarseness from above downward that reawakened and returned to the records incorporated in it.

Thus, when the screen departed from Malchut of the Rosh to the place of the Chazeh in the Guf, it first elicited a coupling by striking of the phase of ten Sefirot of Rosh from the Chazeh upward, by the force of the coarseness from below upward included in it, meaning only on the level of Hochma, as it has only the coarseness of phase three. Afterwards, it expanded from the Chazeh downward, to the phase of ten Sefirot of the *Guf*, because of the coarseness from above downward included in it. This is called the second expansion.

It is said: **"after the reception of these Sefirot from the emanator,"** meaning after the screen of the Guf had been refined entirely, regarded as having risen to the emanator, which is Malchut of the Rosh, it received there once again the power to and expand once more for clothing ten Sefirot, as in the beginning. In other words, the coarseness reawakened in the records in it, up to phase three, at which time it returned to its place in Malchut of the Guf as in the beginning. In that state the second expansion occurred in the ten Sefirot of Rosh and Guf as in the beginning, and ZA "returned to their place," meaning the place of Malchut of the Guf.

60. It is because the screen did not become coarser than phase three by its incorporation in Malchut of the Rosh, as phase four did not leave a record. The expansion on the screen of phase three is only up to the level of Hochma, lacking the light of Keter.

It is said: **"they all returned to their place, except for Keter."** It turns out that the light of Hochma clothes in the vessel of Keter, the light of Bina in the vessel of Hochma, the light of ZA in the vessel of Bina and the light of Malchut in the vessel of ZA. Thus, Malchut remained without light.

70. Meaning the vessel of Nukva of the Keter, which is light of Hochma clothed in the vessel of Keter, which is missing here for the above reason (this chapter, item 4, and Inner Light there).

80. The light in the level of Hochma that comes to clothe the vessel of Keter resembles the nature of the above-mentioned descending reflected light (see Chapter 3, item 9 and Inner Light there). It is in contrast with the light of the record and they strike each other.

90. Since the record that remains from the first expansion is higher than Hochma, as her level is up to Keter, it is in contrast with the light of Hochma that comes now, whose level is only up to Hochma (Inner Light, Chapter 3, item 60). Also, there is merit to the light of Hochma for it now comes from above downward to clothe in the vessels. However, the record is imprinted with the desire to depart from clothing although she does not actually ascend (Chapter 3, item 9 and Inner Light there, item 70).

100. It means that the coarse light, which fell from the record by the striking of the light of Hochma in it, became a vessel for the light of the record, which is discerned as the male of the vessel of Keter. The vessel for the light of Hochma in the vessel of Keter, discerned as the female of the vessel of Keter, was made of the sparks that fell from the light of Hochma by the striking of the light of the record in it. Although there is already a vessel for the male of the vessel of Keter, nevertheless, by the striking of the light of Hochma, it is ended and renewed, as will be elaborated on it in part 5.

200. See *Tree of Life*, Gate Present and Not Present, Chapter 3.

The refinement and the departure in Akudim are somewhat similar to the revoking of the Melachim in the world of Nekudim who died and were revoked

7. Now you can understand how in the world of Akudim there is also revoking of the kings [Melachim], similar to those kings who reigned in the land of Edom, died and were revoked, as mentioned in the study of the world of Nekudim. After all, the matter of the concealment of the lights Akudim and their ascent to their emanator (300) is also the revoking of the kings here.

Inner Light

300. Both were through the ascents of the lights to the emanator, meaning the refinement of the screen, and so their ways are equal too. This is elaborated on in

my book *Panim Meirot uMasbirot* about *Tree of Life*, regarding the breaking of the vessels.

The difference between them is that here there was corruption in order to correct, while in Nekudim there was actual breaking and death

8. However, the difference between them is that here in Akudim, the corruption was in order to correct, and ruins in order to build $_{(400)}$, as the prime intention was to rise in order to make vessels. However, in Nekudim, there was actual revoking and death. Yet, because from Akudim, the vessels began to be revealed a little, therefore, here, too, there was some revoking.

Inner Light

400. The levels in the screen gradually diminished by the refinement in the screen, and sparks fell from each higher phase to the phase below it. This is the beginning of the association of the quality of mercy with judgment, because the sparks of the upper phase are as the quality of mercy from the perspective of the lower one. It is known that the association of the quality of mercy with judgment is the foundation for the existence of the world (see Inner Light, Chapter 1, item 4).

It is written "**in Akudim, the corruption was in order to correct, and ruins in order to build.**" This is like the breaking of the vessels, where the sparks fell in order to revive them with the quality of mercy, and the only difference between them is that here there is only corruption, and there was "**actual revoking and death.**"

CHAPTER FIVE

Explains the inner and surrounding lights of Akudim. Contains eight issues:

1. The lights of Akudim have ten inner Sefirot and ten surrounding Sefirot. They shine in the anterior and also sideways, and all around AK. 2. The inner light shines at half the coarseness of the wall of the vessel from the inside, the surrounding light from the outside, and the vessel shines and is refined through both of them. 3. Since the surrounding light is much greater than the inner light, the externality of the vessel where the surrounding light clothes should be more refined and better than the internality of the vessel where the inner light is clothed. 4. There is a second reason: if the externality of the vessel had not been refined, the surrounding light would not have been able to connect with the inner light. 5. The internality of the vessel is more refined than the externality of the vessel as the inner light is limited in her and receives complete illumination. The surrounding light, however, shines from afar in the externality of the vessel. 6. The lower the worlds, the more incomplete they are. 7. Until the world of Nekudim, there were five inner and five surrounding, and the changes were according to the proximity of the surrounding to the inner. 8. From Nekudim and below, there are no more than five inner and two surrounding, and there cannot be less than that.

The lights of Akudim have ten inner Sefirot and ten surrounding Sefirot. They shine in the anterior and also sideways, and all around AK.

1. The ten inner Sefirot and ten surrounding Sefirot (1) emerged from the Peh of Adam Kadmon. They are extended from opposite the anterior to opposite the Tabur of this Adam Kadmon (2). This is the main light, but it also shines through the sides and all around this Adam.

Inner Light

1. We should not think that this contradicts what is written later (Chapter 6, item 18) that from the Peh of AK emerged only five Partzufim and two surrounding, as there he speaks of the general surrounding, but in the particular, you have no light that does not have internal and surrounding.

2. It means that there are two phases of lights are discerned in a complete Partzuf: the first is called light of Hochma, and the second is called light of Hassadim. Correspondingly, we discern two illuminations in each Partzuf: "right" and "left"; "anterior" and "posterior". "Right" and "left" relate to the illumination of the light of Hassadim, "anterior" and "posterior" relate to the illumination of the light of Hochma.

It is known that the first restriction was primarily on the light of Hochma to prevent it from appearing in phase four. For this reason, the Partzufim were divided into anterior and posterior: the phases above phase four that receive the light of Hochma are called anterior, and those included in phase four, which cannot receive the light of Hochma, are called posterior.

There is right and left in both the anterior and the posterior. The phases that receive the light of Hassadim abundantly are called right, and the phases that do not receive the light of Hassadim abundantly are called left. You should also know that the names anterior and posterior relate primarily to the Tabur. From the Tabur up it is called anterior, and from the Tabur down it is called posterior, as the Malchut of the Guf is called Tabur.

It is written, "**they are extended from opposite the anterior to opposite the Tabur.**" This means that the expansion of these ten Sefirot from the Peh of AK downward is extended and shines primarily in the anterior of the Partzuf, which is above phase four called Tabur. However, from the Tabur down it does not shine because of the restriction on phase four.

However, he tells us, "**this is the main light, but it also shines through the sides and all around this Partzuf,**" to its posterior too, though it reaches it through the sides, from the right side and left side. It is so because through the reflected light that phase four brings in the Partzuf, which is light of Hassadim, she receives illumination of Hochma, as well, though it is discerned as female light, only reception and not bestowal.

2. **You should not wonder at what we have written above, that the externality of the vessel was made from the light of the left Ozen that enters the Peh, and the internality of the vessel was made from the left foramen of the Hotem (3). Though the surrounding light is greater and better than the inner light, the internality of the vessel is still greater than the externality of the vessel as is apparent with the sense of sight.**

It is not so with the phases of lights, for the great light that the vessel cannot draw and receive within shines on the outside as surrounding light, and the scant light remains within, unlike the vessels. Thus, how will the phase of Ozen, which is the upper one, be the externality of the vessel, and the Hotem, which is the lower one, be the internality of the vessel (4)?

Inner Light

3. Know that there are necessarily two phases in every vessel. These are the phase of extension and the phase of reception (see Part 3, Table of Topics, items 157, 158). It is so because the coarser phase is better for the extension of lightה and vise-versa regarding the reception and clothing of light. That is because in it, the more refined is better, as it must be in equivalence of form with the light that is received in it.

These two phases are sometimes called upper one and lower one and sometimes called internality and externality, and you must know the difference between them. The thing is that when we speak of a complete degree, which has the phase of extension and the phase of clothing, they are regarded as upper one and lower one, since the coarser its internality, the vessel of extension, the higher the level it draws.

For example, if its internality is phase four, it clothes up to the level of Keter. It turns out that from the perspective of the extension it is lower, coarser. However, because the light of Keter must have a more refined vessel to clothe in, it is thus higher from the perspective of the clothing, more refined. In other words, it has the most refined vessel, like none other, fitting for clothing the light of Keter. Thus, when speaking of a complete level, these four phases are regarded as one above the other, the more refined is higher.

However, when we only speak from the perspective of the vessel of extension, these four phases are regarded as the walls of a vessel having four layers one atop the other to its width. The abundance in it is received and measured only in its inner layer, and does not touch the three external layers at all. These serve merely as support of the interior layer in the wall.

Likewise, we discern four phases in the vessel of extension, clothing one atop the other. The coarser is more internal, and phase four, the primary one that draws the upper light through coupling by striking, where the upper light is measured exactly according to the level of the reflected light that she raises - is regarded as the internality of the vessel.

The other three phases are regarded as the externality of the vessel, they do not touch the light at all and do not serve it. Rather, they are the reasons that cause phase four, as she cannot manifest without them.

It is written, "**the externality of the vessel was made from the light of the left Ozen,**" which is phase two, "**and the internality of the vessel was made from the left foramen of the Hotem,**" which is phase three. It means that the coarser is more internal, as has been explained.

4. He poses two questions: 1. Since the surrounding light is greater than the inner light, the externality of the vessel should have been more important than the internality of the vessel, as it serves a greater light. However, in reality we see the opposite: the internality of the vessel is the entire importance in the degree, as its level and sustenance entirely depend on it, and the externality of the vessel is not so important. 2. The second question is: if the internality of the vessel is indeed far more important than the externality of the vessel, it should have extended from a more important root, from phase two of the Rosh called Ozen, and the externality of the vessel from a lower root, phase three. Why then is it the opposite?

> The inner light shines at half the coarseness of the wall of the vessel from the inside, the surrounding light from the outside, and the vessel shines and is refined through both of them.

3. **The answer is this: know that the light is in complete evenness** (5). **When it wanted to enter and be limited inside the vessel** (6), **then that light that cannot enter the vessel remained outside as surrounding** (7). **The inner light shines from within the vessel and the light passes through half the coarseness of the walls of the vessel from within** (8).

The surrounding light shines from outside the vessel and passes through half the coarseness of the walls of the vessel from without. The vessel shines and is refined through these two lights.

Inner Light

5. This means there is no discernment in the light in and of itself, but only from the perspective of the vessel.

6. It means that the measure of the illumination is limited and depends on the measure of the vessel, not more and not less, since the coarseness of phase four draws the level of Keter, and of phase three only Hochma, and of phase two only Bina, etc.

7. The rule is that everything received that is in the Partzuf is called inner light. Everything that is not received yet but is destined to come into the Partzuf is called surrounding light. Ein Sof is the first surrounding light, surrounding only AK. It is so because the coupling by striking on the screen of phase four of the Peh of AK and the great reflected light that rose there and clothed the ten Sefirot of the Rosh of AK up to the Keter, which is adjacent to and in adhesion with Ein Sof, that reflected light contains the surrounding light of Ein Sof.

The of reflected light is the entire measure of the light rejected from Malchut by the power of the screen. The measure of that rejected light is the whole difference between Ein Sof that filled the entire reality and AK, which is regarded as one thin line compared to Ein Sof. Thus, all this great light of Ein Sof is regarded as the surrounding light of AK.

Also, every Rosh is regarded as surrounding light to the ten Sefirot of its Guf; as the coupling by striking in the screen at the Peh of the Rosh of that Partzuf detains the upper light from expanding into the Malchut of that Partzuf. Thus, the entire light that does not enter the vessel of Malchut becomes the reflected light clothing the ten Sefirot of the Rosh of the Partzuf. Consequently, that reflected light that stands at the Rosh consists of all that light that cannot enter the Partzuf, called surrounding light.

8. It has already been explained above that the four phases in the Peh of the Rosh, discerned as a vessel of extension, are distinguished in internality and externality there. It is like the wall of a vessel that has four layers one atop the other, where only the interior layer touches and receives the abundance within her.

Likewise, in Malchut of the Rosh, called Peh, the coarser phase there is regarded as the internality, meaning as drawing the upper light. The more refined ones are regarded as externality, without direct connection to that light that is received there. Instead, they only serve as surrounding light.

It turns out that the inner light is connected and shines only from the perspective of the internality of the vessel and does not touch the externality of the vessel at all; and the surrounding light appears gradually only by the externality of the vessel. It has no contact with the internality of the vessel.

Moreover, the internality of the vessel is what prevents the surrounding light from entering the vessel, since it is the coarseness that the screen detains. Also, the externality of the vessel is the posterior of the inner light, as it diminishes its level.

Since the surrounding light is much greater than the inner light, the externality of the vessel where the surrounding light clothes should be more refined and better than the internality of the vessel where the inner light is clothed

4. We need the external half of the vessel to shine because of the surrounding light. Yet, the surrounding light is indeed great and its illumination would not pass and become absorbed and shine within the walls of the vessel (9), for there is a great distance and difference and disparity between them. Hence, it was necessary for the internality of the worse vessel to equalize with the worse inner light, and one would shine in the other (10). Likewise, the finer surrounding light would shine in the externality of the finer vessel; otherwise the externality of the vessel would remain without illumination (20).

Inner Light

9. Because the light does not clothe in the vessel unless they are in equivalence of form. As long as there is an apparent form in the vessel with respect to the light, that disparity of form rejects and separates the light and does not let it pass inside it and become absorbed in the vessel. It is written, **"for there is a great distance and difference and disparity between them,"** the disparity of form is what separates and distances the spirituals.

10. All the greatness and merit of the inner light is in the worse and greater coarseness. It therefore follows that the internality of the vessel, which is coarser and worse, completely equalizes with the measure of the inner light, which is worse than the surrounding light.

20. Because it is completely devoid of the coarseness of the vessel that is required for the drawing of the light. This does not apply to the Surrounding Light, and therefore relates only to the more refined phase in the vessel so as to have equivalence of form with it; that is needed for the clothing of the light.

There is a second reason: if the externality of the vessel had not been refined, the surrounding light would not have been able to connect with the inner light

5. There is yet another reason, very close to the first reason: the Surrounding Light yearns and wants to bond with the inner light (30). Thus, if the outer half of the wall of the vessel had not been more refined, the surrounding light would not have passed through it (40). Consequently, the inner light would have been lacking the reception of the surrounding light inside it. However, since half the

vessel of the outer wall is refined, the surrounding light can pass through half the inner thickness of the wall. In that state, they shine in one another, and though the inner half of the wall will not be refined, it is not a cause for concern since the inner light passes and shines in it through half its inner thickness though it is not more refined.

Inner Light

30. That is, it yearns to clothe in the internality of the vessel and shine along with the inner light, as much as it can. It is so because it will ultimately be entirely clothed in the vessel. Inner light means what is already clothed in the vessel, and surrounding light means that which is destined to clothe the vessel afterwards, over time, until the end of correction.

40. He adds a precision about it, that if it did not have the more refined externality, which is better suited to the surrounding light, the surrounding lights would never be able to clothe in the Partzuf even a bit, for **"the surrounding light would not have passed through it. Consequently, the inner light would have been lacking the reception of the surrounding light inside it."**

The reason for this is that the inner light is always extended from above downward to the Guf from the corresponding phase in the Rosh. For example, the inner light of Malchut of the Guf is extended from Malchut of the Rosh, which, like her, is phase four. The inner light of the vessel of ZA of the Guf is extended from the phase of Hotem of the Rosh, which is phase three, like him. Also the inner light of the vessel of Bina of the Guf is extended from the Ozen of Rosh which is phase two, like her, etc., likewise.

However, the surrounding light is always extended from the Sefira above the corresponding phase, since the surrounding light of Malchut of the Guf is extended from the Hotem, which is phase three, and the surrounding light of ZA is extended from the Ozen, which is phase two, and so on likewise.

This is in the first expansion of Akudim, where the screen in Malchut is phase four. In the second expansion where the screen in Malchut is phase three, the inner light is extended to that Malchut from the Hotem which is also phase three, like her. The Surrounding Light for that Malchut is extended from above from the corresponding phase, from the Ozen which is phase two, etc., likewise.

Now we thoroughly understand that Malchut cannot receive the surrounding light unless she also has a vessel from above its corresponding phase in the Rosh. She acquired this through her ascent to ZA, as he writes, **"from the light of the left Ozen, etc."** This means that in Partzuf AB, whose Malchut is phase three, the internality of the Peh is from the Hotem, which is phase three, and the externality of the Peh is above her phase, from phase two which is the Ozen.

The internality of the vessel is more refined than the externality of the vessel as the inner light is limited in her and receives complete illumination. The surrounding light, however, shines from afar in the externality of the vessel.

6. Should you say that we can still ask and say, "We see that with our sense of sight that the internality of the vessel is more refined than the externality" (50)**. The answer is as follows: Although the inner light is smaller than the surrounding light, nevertheless, because it is confined inside the vessel** (60)**, the vessel receives complete illumination from it. However, although the surrounding light is a great light, still, because it is not in adhesion with and restricted within the vessel, it does not shine that much in the externality of the vessel as the inner light shines in the internality of the vessel** (70)**. That will put everything in its proper place.**

Inner Light

50. He asks: In the end, we find the externality of the vessels to be less important than the internality of the vessels, and they do not shine like they do. However, if they receive the externality of the vessels from the surrounding light, which is a greater light than the inner light, it should have been the opposite.

60. In other words, since the level of the light is measured and limited in the greater coarseness of the vessel, in a way had its coarseness been less, its measure of light would have been less. Therefore, the coarseness in the vessel receives complete illumination, as the coarseness does not dim the light whatsoever. On the contrary, it increases it. For that reason the internality of the vessel is very refined even though the light is small.

70. that there is no vessel of extension there to draw this light as coupling by striking. Therefore, the light does not clothe in its internality. Thus, that light is not adhered with the vessel, since the little coarseness, which is necessarily present in the externality of the vessel, as well, has disparity of form from to the light which is completely refined.

Thus, the measure of coarseness in the externality of the vessel diminishes the light. Had it been more refined, it would have received a greater surrounding light.

Hence, any external vessel is not so refined, for its coarseness is distinguished as a great demerit, separated from the light and not connected with it. Thus, although her light is great, it does not shine in the externality of the vessel as much as the inner light shines in the internality of the vessel.

The lower the worlds, the more incomplete they are. Until the world of Nekudim, there were five inner and five surrounding, and the changes were according to the proximity of the surrounding to the inner

7. **Know that in the upper worlds, the lower they are in degree from each other, the more incomplete they are compared to each other (80). Thus, until the world of Nekudim you find that there were five phases of inner lights and five revealed surrounding lights (90). However, the differences between them are that in some, the surrounding were nearing the inner, and in others, they were growing further.**

Inner Light

80. They gradually diminish because of the refinement of the screen, since in the second Partzuf of AK, where there was only coarseness of phase three in the screen, the light of Keter was diminished and its level reached only that of Hochma. In the third Partzuf, where there was only the coarseness of phase two, the light of Hochma was also diminished and its level reached only that of Bina, etc. similarly. It is likewise in the worlds as well (see Part 3 above).

90. precisely in the Roshim (pl. for Rosh) of the Partzufim from Malchut of Rosh upward. However, from Malchut of Rosh downward, even in the first Partzuf of AK, there were no more than five inner and two surrounding, as the ARI says below in chapter 6, item 18.

From Nekudim and below, there are no more than five inner and two surrounding, and there cannot be less than that

8. **However, from the world of Nekudim downward, which is the world of Atzilut, there is one drawback (100): Not more than five inner lights and two surrounding lights, which are the surrounding of Yechida and the surrounding of Haya, manifested in all their details. However, the other inner three do not have the phases of NRN of surrounding lights, but only the phases of Yechida and Haya (200), which surround everyone and not their own phases. They do have other disparities and drawbacks according to the order of the Partzufim and the worlds,**

but the rule in them is that there cannot be less than five inner and two upper surrounding lights.

Inner Light

100. This means that even in the Roshim (pl. for Rosh) of the Partzufim after the world of Nekudim, we do not find more than five inner and two surrounding. It is so because of the ascent of the lower Hey to the Eynaim, which is the association of the quality of mercy with judgment that was done there.

Because the place of the coupling was in Hochma of the Rosh, which is the Eynaim, because of it, Bina, ZA and Malchut of Rosh went outside the Rosh, to the state of from above downward, which is the phase of the Guf. Thus, all that remains in the phase of the Rosh is only Keter and Hochma.

200. This means that the two surrounding lights, Yechida and Haya, surround the three lower lights NRN, as well, though not from the phases of NRN but from the phases of Yechida and Haya. Know that all this refers to the general surrounding lights, though there are always five internal and five surrounding in the particular surrounding lights, for there is no light that does not have internal and surrounding

CHAPTER SIX

Explains the return of the lights to the emanator to receive their completion. Contains twenty-two issues:

1. In the first expansion of Akudim the lights did not emerge complete. Hence, they returned to their root to be completed and thus a vessel was made. 2. In the first expansion the refined light, which is direct light, and the coarse light, which is reflected light, were mixed in one another. However, in the departure to their root, the coarse light remained below, as it could not ascend, and its coarseness increased and it became a vessel. 3. Though the light returned to its place in the second expansion over the screen of phase three, the coarse light was still not revoked from being a vessel, since the light of Keter was missing in the second expansion. 4. The first expansion of Akudim emerged only in the phase of Nefesh. 5. In Akudim, the vessels emerged from below upward: the vessel of Malchut first, and Keter last. It is the opposite of Nekudim, where the vessels emerged from above downward. 6. First, Malchut emerged in the phase of Nefesh. Later, when Yesod emerged in the phase of Nefesh, illumination of Ruach was added from him to Malchut. 7. The light of Ruach came from VAK of ZA. Hence the light of Ruach began to manifest in Yesod, and was completed with the coming of Hesed of ZA. 8. There are five Hassadim, HGT NH, corresponding to the five phases KHB TM. Yesod is not an inner Hesed, but contains all five Hassadim HGT NH. 9. When Yesod of ZA emerged, the general Nefesh of ZA manifested, and when Hod emerged, one edge of Nefesh of ZA appeared etc., until all six edges were completed. 10. Each and every edge of the HGT NH provided the general illumination of Nefesh in Yesod when they emerged. However, in the five phases themselves, none adds anything to another. 11. When Bina emerged, she was Nefesh for herself, Ruach for ZA, and Neshama for Malchut. When Hochma emerged, she was Nefesh for herself, Ruach to Bina etc. When Keter emerged, He was Nefesh for Himself and Ruach to Abba etc. 12. When Keter emerged, He only had Nefesh, and that phase, too, did not remain in him, for she departed to the emanator. 13. When Keter came, Malchut had NRNHY and the rest of the Sefirot were absent and had to return to the emanator. 14. Keter emerged last and returned first; Malchut emerged first and returned last. 15. When Keter disappeared, Malchut rose to the place of Yesod, and thus Malchut received the surrounding light of Haya, ZA received Yechida, Bina

Haya, and Hochma Neshama. 16. When Hochma rose, Yechida was added to Bina, ZA received the surrounding of Haya, and Malchut the surrounding of Yechida. 17. When Bina rose, the surrounding of Yechida was added to ZA. ZA and Malchut did not gain more than that. 18. Each and every phase has ten Sefirot contained in five, both in the inner and in the surrounding. 19. There are five inner lights and five surrounding lights in the ten Sefirot of Rosh, but there are only five inner and two surrounding, Yechida and Haya, from the Peh of AK downward. 20. During the ascent of Keter to the emanator, the manifestation of Yechida departed from Malchut. 21. When Keter concluded his ascent to the emanator, the manifestation of Yechida returned to Malchut. 22. During the ascent of Hochma to the emanator the manifestation of Haya from Malchut departed, and when Hochma concluded her ascent, the manifestation of Haya returned to Malchut.

In the first expansion of Akudim the lights did not emerge complete. Hence, they returned to their root to be completed and thus a vessel was made

1. Let us explain the emergence of these lights, called Akudim: Know that when they emerged, they did not emerge complete (1). The reason for it is that the intention of the emanator was to now make the beginning of the HaVaYot [pl. for HaVaYaH] of the vessels to clothe the light for the receivers, so they could receive. Thus, since they emerged incomplete and unfinished, they returned to their root above to be corrected and completed, and thus a vessel was made (2).

Inner Light

1. As we have written before, this is because only Malchut received the complete five Partzufim NRNHY, but the other first nine Sefirot were deficient. ZA lacked Keter, Bina lacked Hochma, too, Hochma lacked Neshama, as well, and Keter also lacked Ruach. The outer vessels for the surrounding lights were absent there altogether.

2. The surrounding lights and inner lights were clashing with each other (Part 4, Chapter 1, Inner Light item 7), and thus became refined and rose to their root, to the Peh, where they received their completeness.

In the first expansion the refined light, which is direct light, and the coarse light, which is reflected light, were mixed in one another. However, in the departure to their root, the coarse light remained below, as it could not ascend, and its coarse-ness increased and it became a vessel

2. The thing is that the phase of vessels was certainly in potential (3), though it was not actually inside the light, since it was in the phase of light that was coarser and cruder (4), though it was well connected with the essence. Consequently, its phase remained concealed (5).

It is so because when the light emerged through the Peh outwards, it all emerged mixed together (6). When they returned to ascend and be completed (7), then, certainly, through the emergence of the light outside the Peh, that light of the phase of the vessels, which is coarser, now acquired more coarseness.

Thus, it too cannot return to its origin as in the beginning (8), and the refined light expanded from it and rose to its source. In that state, further coarseness was added to the coarseness of the above coarse light, and the phase of the vessel was completed and remained (9).

Inner Light

3. Relates to the ten Sefirot of the Rosh, where the reflected light clothes from below upward. This is only potential clothing, but not actual clothing (Part 4, Chapter 1, Inner Light item 30).

4. It means that the phase of reflected light that clothes and receives for the ten Sefirot of the Rosh from below upward is regarded as the phase of "potential" vessels there. With respect to the ten Sefirot of direct light there, it is called coarse and crude light, since it is regarded as light of departure, meaning light that is not received in Malchut because of the power of the detaining screen.

This reflected light expands the vessel of Malchut of the Rosh into ten Sefirot from her and within her and expands with her from the Peh down to actual clothing, called Guf. After the departure of this expansion from within the reflected light that clothes her, this reflected light remains below as actual coarse light.

5. Because the reflected light in the Rosh is connected to the essence of the direct light and is as refined as it, without any difference whatsoever. Even though it is the light of departure, which is judgment, it is nevertheless manifested only to the vessels of reception. However, in the Rosh, where there is no clothing whatsoever (see Part 4, Chapter 4, Inner Light item 30), it is not at all regarded as judgment.

Moreover, it is regarded as the very source of mercy, for it extends and connects the ten Sefirot of direct light until it brings them from above downward into the Guf. For this reason, it is connected to the essence of the direct light, and there is nothing to distinguish between them.

6. It means that even afterwards, when the reflected light exited the Rosh and expanded with the direct light from above downward for clothing inside the Guf, there is still no apparent difference between the direct light and the reflected light that clothes it, which is the vessel. Rather, they are seemingly mixed together.

The reason for it is that the coarseness that appears in the reflected light as it expands from above downward has no lowliness and demerit at all. It is not at all darker than the direct light that is clothed in it, as the coarseness is its entire merit and the height of its level. Had it lacked some of its coarseness, its level of light would have been deficient. Hence, they are of equal importance and regarded as mixed together.

7. It means that its coarseness is regarded as demerit and lowliness. The quality of judgment included in it while it is in the Rosh is apparent, meaning what is regarded as the light of departure and judgment. Until now it was not apparent because of the importance of the extension and clothing that the reflected light performs. However, now that the direct light has departed and expanded from it, the quality of judgment in it has appeared.

8. In order to be included in the reflected light of the Rosh, like the direct light. The reason is because this reflected light, which expanded and descended from above downward, is in complete oppositeness to the reflected light of the Rosh that stands there from below upward, meaning it departs from clothing (see above Part 4, Chapter 1, Inner Light, item 30). For this reason, they are distant from each other from one end to the other, and it remains below.

9. Meaning, besides the coarseness included in it from the beginning of its formation, meaning it is light of departure and judgment, further coarseness has been added to it. It is so because it remained below without light, and this darkness is regarded as new coarseness that was not included in it before it expanded from above downward. Know that above, this new coarseness was called posterior (the ARI's words, Chapter 3, item 6).

Though the light returned to its place in the second expansion over the screen of phase three, the coarse light was still not revoked from being a vessel, since the light of Keter was missing in the second expansion

3. If you say that when the refined light descends once more and expands in the vessel, the vessel will be refined again, as in the beginning, and will stop being a vessel," (10) **the answer to this is that not all the ten Sefirot that rose to their**

source descended again. Rather, only the lower nine descended, and the highest one, namely Keter, always remains with the emanator.

By this now find that it is the light of Hochma that returned to clothe in the vessel of Keter $_{(20)}$. It is likewise in all the other Sefirot, and now the vessels can receive from it the diminished light from what they had in the beginning.

Inner Light

10. Because once the direct light expanded in it once more and was limited inside its coarseness as in the beginning, you find that the measure of coarseness draws a greater light. Thus, once more there is no apparent demerit in the coarseness, for the light and the vessel are mixed together. Therefore, from where did the distinction between the light and the vessel later appear?

20. It turns out that each Sefira is deficient of the filling of its appropriate illumination, for the light of Hochma does not fill the vessel of Keter, and the light of Bina does not fill the vessel of Hochma etc. Thus, each vessel is left with some measure of coarseness that does not clothe the light, since the excessive coarseness that it had acquired during the first departure has not stopped there. Hence, there is a great need for the light in the vessel, which remains apparent.

The first expansion of Akudim emerged only in the phase of Nefesh

4. Know that they all emerged as mere Nefesh $_{(30)}$. This is the meaning of the verse, "The Lord has sworn by Himself," for Atzilut is called Nekudim, as we have said, and He who is called HaVaYaH, has sworn by He who is greater than Him, which is the world of Akudim that emerged as mere Nefesh. Delve in this and see how deep His thoughts are, as even the highest, world of Akudim, is merely the phase of Nefesh.

Inner Light

30. Here there are three things we must know first:

1. The order of the arrival of the lights is that the lower ones come first. At first, Nefesh comes into the vessel of Keter. When the light of Ruach comes into the vessel of Keter, Nefesh descends to the vessel of Hochma, and Ruach clothes in the vessel of Keter. When the light of Neshama comes into the vessel of Keter, Ruach descends to the vessel of Hochma, Nefesh into the vessel of Bina, and so on likewise until Yechida comes in the vessel of Keter and Nefesh in the vessel of Malchut.

2. The measure of the light depends on the number of vessels that the light has: if it has one vessel, it has only Nefesh. If it has two vessels, it has two lights: Nefesh and Ruach. Finally, when it has five vessels, it has NRNHY.

3. Each lower one that passes through the upper one leaves its root there. Thus, any light that comes to Keter is but the Nefesh of that light. For example, if Nefesh comes to the vessel of Keter, it is merely Nefesh of Nefesh; if Ruach comes to Keter, it is merely Nefesh of Ruach. The same applies to Nefesh of Neshama and so on.

It is so because at that time, it then has only one vessel, which receives only Nefesh. If Ruach comes to Keter and Nefesh descends to Hochma, you find that she has left her root in Keter and it shines the phase of Ruach of Nefesh to her. In that state, Nefesh has two vessels, Keter and Hochma, and she has Nefesh Ruach of Nefesh.

Similarly, when the light of Neshama reaches the vessel of Keter, it is Nefesh of Neshama because it is a single vessel. Nefesh descends to Bina, and Ruach with the root of Nefesh, which is Ruach of Nefesh, descends to the vessel of Hochma.

Then the root of Nefesh, which has not departed from Keter, grows into Neshama of Nefesh and now Nefesh has NRN and three vessels. Ruach has two vessels: the root in the Keter is Ruach of Ruach, and in Hochma it is Nefesh of Ruach.

Neshama has a single vessel and Nefesh of Neshama. It is the same in all the others until Nefesh came to Malchut. Then she acquired five vessels and has NRNHY of Nefesh: Nefesh from her own place, and YHNR from the vessels she passed through.

Similarly, when the light of Ruach comes to Keter it is merely Nefesh of Ruach, though when it comes to its place, it has Nefesh in its place and HNR from the three vessels it passed through etc., similarly. Thus, when all five lights of NRNHY are in their own place, they are regarded as mere Nefesh, and they receive the rest of the lights from the vessels they passed through and left their root there.

In Akudim, the vessels emerged from below upward: the vessel of Malchut first, and Keter last. It is the opposite of Nekudim, where the vessels emerged from above downward

5. All ten Sefirot emerged, but not all of them emerged together. First the phase of Malchut from the world of Akudim emerged, the opposite of the world of Nekudim.

First, Malchut emerged in the phase of Nefesh. Later, when Yesod emerged in the
phase of Nefesh, illumination of Ruach was added from him to Malchut

**6. This Malchut first emerged as merely the phase of Nefesh (40), for there is no
Sefira that does not have NRN. Rather, now they emerged only in the phase
of Nefesh. Thus, Malchut first emerged in the phase of Nefesh. Then, when
the phase of Yesod emerged, only the phase of Nefesh appeared (50) in Yesod
for itself, but illumination was added in Malchut, where the phase of Ruach
appeared (60).**

Inner Light

40. Meaning, in the world of Nekudim the vessels preceded the lights. It is so
because the vessels of KHB ZA and Malchut first emerged from the records of the
Partzuf SAG. Afterwards all the lights came to Keter. He gave Hochma nine lights,
Hochma gave to Bina eight lights etc., until Malchut received her light last.

However, in Akudim the vessels were made by the refinement as in the second
look, when phase four was refined first and became the vessel of Malchut. After
that phase three was refined and became a vessel for ZA etc. Thus, the vessel of
Malchut emerged first.

50. Though the light of Yesod is Ruach, it still has only a part of Nefesh of Ruach
because when each phase comes to Keter, there is only Nefesh in it. Also, each phase
has only Nefesh of its own phase in its own place, and receives the rest from the
vessels it passed through.

60. When Ruach is drawn to the degree, it is drawn in the vessel of Keter. Then
Nefesh descends to the vessel of Hochma and the root that she left in Keter becomes
Ruach of Nefesh for her.

Ruach has six edges, as it is regarded as ZA. Therefore, Ruach too is divided into
six degrees HGT NHY. When Yesod comes from VAK of Ruach to the vessel of
Keter, Nefesh acquires the general Ruach of Nefesh.

He says that when the light Yesod came out to the Guf, "illumination was added in
Malchut, where the phase of Ruach appeared." Also, afterwards, when the light of
Bina comes to the Guf, you find that Malchut receives from it the light of Neshama,
and ZA receives from it only Ruach.

The light of Ruach came from VAK of ZA. Hence the light of Ruach began to
manifest in Yesod, and was completed with the coming of Hesed of ZA

7. The reason for it is that since Ruach comes from VAK. Therefore, when Yesod came, the phase of Ruach began to manifest in Malchut. It is not entirely completed before all the VAK emerged (70), meaning from Yesod to Hesed, at which time the entire phase of Ruach of Malchut is completed. When each of them comes, one edge from the phase of Ruach appeared in Malchut, as it is written in *The Zohar*, Portion *Truma*.

Inner Light

70. ZA is but one phase of the above four phases, namely phase three. However, there are six edges in it, called HGT NHY. Thus, the light of Ruach is completed only after its clothing in these six vessels. It is said that the illumination of Ruach that Malchut receives from ZA is not completed before all its six edges appear, as then ZA is completed.

There are five Hassadim, HGT NH, corresponding to the five phases KHB TM.
Yesod is not an inner Hesed, but contains all five Hassadim HGT NH

8. It is already known that Yesod is not a part of VAK, for there are only five Hassadim from Hesed to Hod (80), but Yesod does not take a particular Hesed for himself (90); rather, all five edges are included in him. Thus, the general phase of Ruach is what appeared in Malchut when Yesod came. Yet, when Hod or Netzah emerged, or any of the other Sefirot, the actual edges of Ruach appeared in Malchut.

Inner Light

80. There is an original concept here that we must thoroughly grasp: indeed, there are no more than five phases in every ten Sefirot. These are the root, called Keter, and the four phases Hochma, Bina, ZA and Malchut.

These five phases are discerned even in the direct light itself, as is written in Part 1. We distinguish six Sefirot HGT NHY here, not because there is any addition here to the five phases, but because they are a special discernment of these five phases, in terms of their incorporation in ZA. The three Sefirot KHB, contained in ZA, are diminished in him into the three Sefirot HGT. The Sefira Netzah in him is his own phase, and the Sefira Hod in him is the incorporation of Malchut in ZA.

The reason for the double discernment of five phases specifically in ZA is very interesting: the entire light received in the Partzufim is regarded as two phases, light of

Hochma and light of Hassadim, and the difference between them is indeed great (see Part 1, Chapter 1, Inner Light item 5).

They are also called light of GAR and light of VAK because the light of Hochma is only distinguished in the three upper Sefirot Keter, Hochma, Bina, which are Yechida, Haya, Neshama. However, in Ruach Nefesh, which are ZA and Malchut, there is merely light of Hassadim, even in their GAR, as it is written in the Zohar (*Mishpatim*, item 520): "The head of the King is corrected in Hesed and in Gevura."

Since the first three Sefirot of ZA, KHB, are merely light of Hassadim, we therefore have a special distinction of the first three phases, as they are merely light of Hassadim. It therefore turns out that we have two kinds of the first three phases, either from the light of Hochma, or from the light of Hassadim.

When the first three phases are discerned as light of Hochma, they are discerned by the names Keter, Hochma, Bina. From the perspective of their being discerned as light of Hassadim, they are discerned by the names Hesed, Gevura, Tifferet, meaning in ZA.

Thus, at one time we call the five phases KHB, ZA, and Malchut, when the first three are light of Hochma. Another time, we call them HGT NH, or five Hassadim, when the first three are regarded as mere light of Hassadim. Remember that in all the places.

However, these five Hassadim HGT NH are not regarded as five phases of coarseness like the general five phases, because the light of Hassadim itself is merely phase three, called light of Ruach. Hence, there is no difference in the measures of the coarseness among the six Sefirot HGT NHY.

90. As there are no more than five phases here. Indeed, the Sefira Yesod is the third distinction of the five general phases, meaning from the perspective of the incorporation and the association of the quality of mercy with judgment, brought above (Part 4, Chapter 1, Inner Light item 4).

Thus, each of the five phases HGT NH are in themselves mercy and judgment. From the perspective of mercy, they are called five Hassadim, and from the perspective of judgment, they are called five Gevurot (pl. for Gevura).

The Sefira Yesod is the place of the association of the quality of mercy with judgment. These five Hassadim and five Gevurot are incorporated in each other there and sweetened together, and from here they are imparted to Malchut. This is why it is said, "**but Yesod does not take a particular Hesed for himself, rather, all five edges are included in him**".

When Yesod of ZA emerged, the general Nefesh of ZA manifested, and when Hod emerged, one edge of Nefesh of ZA appeared etc., until all six edges were completed

9. All this concerns the phase of Malchut. However, what concerns the six edges of Zeir Anpin is in the following manner: when Yesod emerged, the general five edges of Zeir Anpin appeared only in the phase of Nefesh. But when Hod comes, the first edge of Nefesh of Zeir Anpin appears, and so on until all six edges are completed.

Each and every edge of the HGT NH provided the general illumination of Nefesh in Yesod when they emerged. However, in the five phases themselves, none adds anything to another

10. There is yet one more difference between Yesod and the five other edges (100): when Hod came, he gave his general force in Yesod anew, but only in the phase of Nefesh. So did all of them, until Hesed emerged and he too gave his general force in Yesod when he emerged. However, this is not so with the other five edges, for when one came, it added nothing whatsoever in the other, for they are all equal. Only when all six were completed, was Zeir Anpin completed in the phase of Nefesh.

Inner Light

100. Yesod is but the incorporation of the five edges. For this reason, it must be imparted by them. Hence, when each and every edge comes, it is filled and completed. However, the five edges themselves are five separate phases, like the five general phases, and therefore one does not add anything to another, for each is fenced in its own phase.

When Bina emerged, she was Nefesh for herself, Ruach for ZA, and Neshama for Malchut. When Hochma emerged, she was Nefesh for herself, Ruach to Bina etc. When Keter emerged, He was Nefesh for Himself and Ruach to Abba etc.

11. Afterwards Bina emerged merely in the phase of Nefesh for herself, the phase of Ruach for Zeir Anpin, and the phase of Neshama for Malchut (200). Then Hochma emerged in the phase of Nefesh for herself, the phase of Ruach for Bina, the phase of Neshama for Zeir Anpin and the phase of Haya for Malchut. Then Keter emerged in the phase of Nefesh for himself, the phase of Ruach for Abba,

the phase of Neshama for Ima, the phase of Haya for Zeir Anpin and the phase of Yechida for Malchut.

Inner Light

200. It is so because when she comes to Keter, she has but one vessel, which can only receive Nefesh. Then Ruach descends to the vessel of Hochma, and its root, which remains in Keter, becomes Ruach for ZA, and Ruach of Nefesh descends along with him to the vessel of Hochma. The root of the Nefesh that remains in Keter becomes Neshama of Nefesh since there is no absence in the spiritual. Hence, now Nefesh has NRN, Ruach has NR and Neshama has Nefesh.

Also, when Hochma emerged and came in the vessel of Keter, she has only Nefesh of Haya there. Then Nefesh of Neshama descends to the vessel of Hochma with the Neshama of Nefesh and with the Ruach of Ruach. The root of Nefesh, which remained in Keter, now becomes Haya of Nefesh, and the root of Ruach, which remained in Keter, now becomes Neshama of Ruach. Finally, the root of Neshama, which remained in Keter, now becomes Ruach of Neshama. Now the degree has Nefesh of Haya, NR of Neshama, NRN of Ruach and NRNH of Nefesh.

Also, when the light of Yechida emerged in the vessel of Keter, she has only her own Nefesh, as she has only one vessel. Then Haya descends to the vessel of Hochma, and along with her the Ruach of Neshama with the Neshama of Ruach and with Haya of Nefesh.

The root of Haya that remained in Keter becomes Ruach of Haya and the root Neshama that remained in Keter becomes Neshama to Neshama, and so on similarly.

We might ask: but the ARI says (in Part 3, Chapter 12, item 7) that the reflected light that ascends in Akudim and clothes the direct light equalizes all the vessels on the same level, and the level of each and every one reaches up to Keter (Inner Observation there, Chapter 3, item 4).

The thing is that KHB TM length-wise and KHB TM width-wise emerge here, meaning five times KHB TM these over those width-wise, without any difference between them whatsoever. However, in the length-wise KHB there are certainly differences, as the Keter in it has but Nefesh of Keter, Hochma only NR of Hochma, and Bina only NRN of Neshama etc.

When Keter emerged, He only had Nefesh, and that phase, too, did not remain in him, for she departed to the emanator

12. Thus, when Keter comes, being the last of all of them, he emerged only as Nefesh. This is the meaning of the verse, "The Lord has sworn by His soul." Even this phase of Nefesh of Keter did not remain in the world of Akudim (300), for it was once more concealed and remained adhered to her place in her emanator.

Inner Light

300. That is because the level of Keter is drawn only through phase four. Phase four was no longer renewed in a coupling by striking after having been refined in the departure of the first expansion of Akudim, since phase four did not leave a record behind her, as the ARI said. Hence, that great light disappeared from all the Partzufim and the worlds from here on.

When Keter came, Malchut had NRNHY and the rest of the Sefirot were absent and had to return to the emanator

13. Indeed, when Keter comes, Malchut is complete with all five inner lights, which are NRNHY. Now all the Sefirot were still deficient, for they emerged deficient and incomplete. This was indeed intentional, and this is why they had to return and rise to the emanator to receive their completion from him.

Keter emerged last and returned first; Malchut emerged first and returned last

14. Now, going back, Keter returned before all of them (400). It follows that he departed last and entered first. Malchut is the opposite: she left first and entered last (1). This is the meaning of the verse, "I (Ani) am the first and I am the last." The explanation of this verse is correct both in the Sefira Keter and in the Sefira Malchut, though one is the opposite of the other. It is known that Ani (I) is an appellation for Malchut, and its opposite, Ein (absence), is an appellation for Keter.

Inner Light

400. This has already been explained above. It is because in the first refinement from phase four to phase three, the level of Keter instantly disappears from the Guf. It is so because the coupling by striking that occurs on phase three elicits only ten Sefirot at the level of Hochma, and the light of Keter disappears to its origin.

1. For she disappeared only after the screen had been refined from all its coarseness and equalized its form with the emanator.

When Keter disappeared, Malchut rose to the place of Yesod, and thus Malchut
received the surrounding light of Haya, ZA received Yechida, Bina Haya, and
Hochma Neshama

15. When Keter disappeared to his origin (2)**, Hochma rose to the place of Keter,
Bina to the place of Hochma, and all of them similarly. In the end, Malchut was
in the place of Yesod, and by this ascent to the place of Yesod, light was added
in her, and she had one surrounding light opposite the inner phase of Haya** (3)**.**

**Zeir Anpin, too, rose by one degree, and the phase of Yechida from the inner
lights was added in him. Now all his five inner lights have been completed** (4)**. An
inner phase of Haya was added in Bina** (5)**, and the inner phase of Neshama was
added in Hochma** (6)**.**

Inner Light

2. As it is written above, the ascent of Malchut to the place of Yesod means that
the screen of phase four, which is the phase of the vessel of Malchut, rose and was
refined to phase three, which is the phase of the vessel of Yesod. Then the upper
light, which never stops, copulated with the screen of phase three and ten Sefirot
at the level of Hochma emerged. When Keter disappeared to his origin, the light of
Hochma rose to the place of Keter and Bina to the place of Hochma etc., similarly.

3. For now, Malchut has acquired a sixth vessel from the level of phase three,
through her ascent to Yesod, regarded as an external vessel in relation to phase four,
and the surrounding light of Haya clothes in her in this an external vessel.

4. For now he gained a fifth vessel, and since he has a fifth vessel, five lights of
NRNHY expand in them in completeness.

5. For she acquired a fourth vessel and has a place for the light of Haya.

6. For she acquired a third vessel and has a place for the clothing of the light of
Neshama of Haya.

When Hochma rose, Yechida was added to Bina, ZA received the surrounding of
Haya, and Malchut the surrounding of Yechida

16. After that Hochma rose in the emanator and Bina rose to the place of Keter
(7)**, and an inner phase of Yechida was added in her, thus completing her with
all five inner lights** (8)**. A single surrounding light was added in Zeir Anpin, corresponding to the inner Haya** (9)**, and a higher surrounding light was added in
Malchut, corresponding to the inner Yechida.**

7. It means that screen of phase three, too, has refined to phase two, ten Sefirot at the level of Bina emerged, and the light of Hochma disappeared as well and rose to its origin to the emanator. It is then considered that Malchut rose to Bina, the place of the coupling in Malchut, ZA to the place of Hochma, and Bina to the place of Keter.

8. For she acquired a fifth vessel and has a place for the clothing of Yechida.

9. Meaning that during the coupling of phase two, when the level of Bina emerged, Bina came in the Keter, ZA in Hochma, and then ZA acquired a vessel for the surrounding light of Haya from the level of Bina. Malchut acquired from this level of phase two the surrounding of Yechida.

When Bina rose, the surrounding of Yechida was added to ZA. ZA and Malchut did not gain more than that

17. Afterwards Hesed rose to the place of Keter, for Bina rose to her emanator (10). Hence, the phase of the second surrounding upper light was added in ZA, corresponding to the inner Yechida (20). From there on Zeir Anpin and Malchut did not gain any more and no additional light was added in them (30).

Inner Light

10. It means that the screen of phase two was refined into phase one, which is called Malchut that rose to Hochma. At that time the ten Sefirot diminished to the level of ZA, and the light of Bina disappeared from the Partzuf and rose to its origin, to the emanator. It is written, "**Hesed rose to the place of Keter,**" meaning ZA in the place of Keter and Malchut in the place of Hochma.

20. Meaning, when the level of phase one emerged, which is the level of ZA that came in the vessel of Keter, and Malchut in the vessel Hochma, ZA acquired the surrounding light of Yechida from this new vessel. Bear in mind that the surrounding light always wants to shine to the Partzuf, as every refinement is performed for this reason. However, since it needs a vessel, when they attain a sixth vessel and a seventh vessel, the surrounding lights of Haya and Yechida immediately shine in them.

30. The reason is that the reflected light of the coupling by striking done in phase one of the Rosh, called Eynaim, is very small, since the coarseness of that screen is faint. This is why it is called a thin look. See the above words of the ARI (Part 3, Chapter 11, item 6) who says that the vapor of the Eynaim does not expand downward, but

remains in its place in the Rosh (see Inner Light item 4). The meaning of vapor is reflected light that emerges by coupling by striking.

Therefore, only ZA that now stands in Keter can receive from the illumination of the coupling of the Eynaim. Even though its illumination does not reach below the Rosh, still, because Malchut of the Rosh became Keter to the Guf, ZA is therefore close to the phase of Rosh and can receive from the Eynaim. However, Malchut, which now stands in Hochma, is already completely below the Rosh and cannot gain anything by the coupling of phase one, for she cannot receive any surrounding light from the illumination of the Eynaim, as we have explained.

Afterwards, when Malchut rose to Keter and the level of ZA disappeared in the emanator as well, the coupling by striking stopped entirely. It is so because the screen that is refined into the phase of Keter no longer has sufficient coarseness for striking and does not raise reflected light. Thus, the illumination of Malchut that is received there is very small and is not regarded as surrounding light to Malchut.

It is written, **"Zeir Anpin and Malchut did not gain any more and no additional light was added in them."** It is so for the above-mentioned reason that Malchut cannot receive even from the Eynaim, as they do not shine below the Rosh.

After ZA received the second surrounding light, he is already in his origin in the emanator. Hence, they have no more than five inner and two surrounding. [Second version: It follows from the manuscript of Baal HaSulam that this commentary is redundant since there are no more than five inner and two surrounding, as the ARI said here in item 19].

Each and every phase has ten Sefirot contained in five, both in the inner and in the surrounding

18. The thing is that there is one foreword you should know, which is that it has been clarified above that there are ten Sefirot in each and every phase, in each and every world and every Partzuf, no more and no less.

There are ten inner lights and ten surrounding. However, the inner ten are contained in only five, corresponding to the five phases of the Partzufim that they have, as mentioned elsewhere. These are AA, AVI and ZON, and in themselves they are called the general NRNHY of each and every particular world. Similarly, the surrounding lights are the same, meaning ten contained in five (40).

Inner Light

40. This is very simple, as there are no more than five phases here, upon which five levels emerge, called KHB, Zeir Anpin and Malchut, or five Partzufim, AA, AVI and ZON. However, the phase of ZA, meaning phase three, has six Sefirot HGT NHY, and there is no difference of level among them, for they all have one phase of coarseness. For that reason there are no more than five inner lights and also five surrounding lights.

There are five inner lights and five surrounding lights in the ten Sefirot of Rosh, but there are only five inner and two surrounding, Yechida and Haya, from the Peh of AK downward

19. However, you should know that in all the lights, worlds, and Partzufim from the Hotem of Adam Kadmon upward (50), in every Partzuf, these phases are always complete. They are: five inner lights, consisted of ten inner Sefirot, and five surrounding lights, consisted of ten particular Sefirot.

Yet, from the Peh of Adam Kadmon down to the end of all the worlds there are only five inner lights and two upper surrounding lights (60), corresponding to Haya and Yechida, not more, as the light was diminished from there onward. Thus, in the world of Akudim, which are the lights that emerge from the Peh of Adam Kadmon outwards, there were only five inner lights and two surrounding lights, and not more. Remember this foreword.

Inner Light

50. Meaning in the ten Sefirot of the Rosh of AK, where reflected light rises from Malchut of the Rosh upward, and clothes the nine upper Sefirot. Malchut of the Rosh, where the screen of phase four stands, is called Peh, and ZA of the Rosh, from which begins the direct light of the Rosh, is called Hotem.

60. Meaning in the ten Sefirot of the Guf that are extended from above downward for clothing in the vessels, there are not more than two upper surrounding, which are Haya and Yechida. The reason for this is the absence of the external vessels required for the surrounding lights of NRN.

The externality of the vessels for the reception of the surrounding lights emerges by the couplings by striking, which are done during the refinement of the screen and its ascent to the emanator (see above in this chapter, item 1, and Inner Light there).

461

Since there is no coupling by striking from phase one upward, no more than two outer vessels could emerge, one for Yechida and one for Haya.

During the ascent of Keter to the emanator, the manifestation of Yechida departed from Malchut

20. *Know that when Keter rose to the emanator, in the same measure and duration of its ascent, the apparent phase of Yechida departed from Malchut (70), which is the light that was extended to her from Keter. Because Keter ascended and departed, he did not intend to shine in her, hence she was left with merely the record (80).

Inner Light

70. After phase four was refined and before the coming of the screen to the coupling of phase three, the Partzuf was then without any illumination. That is because the level of phase four, which is the light of Keter, departed, and the level of phase three hasn't come yet.

80. We should not say that this contradicts what is written above, that Malchut did not leave a record behind her. It is because there he speaks precisely of the records of direct light, included in the screen when it comes to the emanator, over which emerges the coupling for the second expansion, called AB. Here, however, he speaks of the record ascribed to the light of Malchut, which is the phase of reflected light.

When Keter concluded his ascent to the emanator, the manifestation of Yechida returned to Malchut

21. When Keter concluded his concealment and Malchut concluded her ascent to the Sium of Yesod (90), the emanator shone the phase of Yechida in her once more, as in the beginning. It is so because after Keter rose to the emanator she too rose in Yesod, and was one degree closer to the emanator. Now she received from him what she would previously receive from Keter (100).

However, as long as Keter did not complete his ascent, Keter was interfering between her and her emanator, and Keter himself also did not shine in her (200). It is similar in the phase of Haya that receives from Keter, and similar also in Hochma, Bina and so on.

90. It has been explained above that Malchut means the screen in her. The completion of her ascent to Yesod means that Malchut of the Rosh, too, rose to the Hotem, and a coupling by striking on the level of Hochma emerged there. This is regarded as the completion of the ascent.

100. As he explains, after she rose in Yesod, meaning the screen was refined and received the coarseness of phase three. At that time the screen in the Peh of the Rosh also rose to the Hotem, which is phase three of the Rosh, the coupling by striking on the level of Hochma emerged there and was extended from there down to the Guf.

It turns out that now she is "**one degree closer to the emanator.**" It means that she now receives from above, from her corresponding phase in the Rosh. This is so because now she receives from the coupling in the Hotem, and the emanator shines the phase of Yechida in her once more, but on the level of Hochma, which is the phase of Haya of Yechida, and this Haya of Yechida became the surrounding light of Haya in her.

It is written, "**Now she received from him what she would previously receive from Keter.**" It means that she now receives from the Hotem through the Keter of ZA as she received before through her own Keter.

200. After phase four was refined and Keter began to be concealed, as long as there was no coupling in phase three, the concealment of Keter interrupted the illumination in the Partzuf. This is because there is no coupling from phase four, and phase three still does not shine.

During the ascent of Hochma to the emanator the manifestation of Haya from Malchut departed, and when Hochma concluded her ascent, the manifestation of Haya returned to Malchut

22. Also, when Hochma rose up in her emanator, the part that would come to Malchut from him departed from her, and only a record remained in her until Hochma completed her ascent to her emanator, at which time the light returned as in the beginning. You can also deduce from this to all the others, as there are many divisions.

It is so because when Hochma began to ascend in Keter, her illumination departed from everything below her (300). When she already rose in Keter, it returned as in the beginning. When it returned to ascend in the emanator a second time, the light departed a second time, and when the ascent was completed, the light regained its strength. The reader will understand the other divisions similarly regarding the surrounding lights of ZON that take during their ascent and departure upward.

Inner Light

300. When Keter began to ascend to the emanator, all the ten Sefirot in the level were drawn and rose after Him. Each and every one began to ascend to the phase above her. When Keter completed his ascent, meaning the coupling in phase three arrived, they all completed their ascent; Hochma came to Keter, Bina to Hochma etc.

INNER OBSERVATION

The Sefirot of Akudim, contains six chapters

Explains six topics: 1. The matter of couplings by striking and clashes. 2. The matter of reflected light. 3. The matter of records. 4. The matter of vessels. 5. The matter of the screen. 6. The matter of direct light.

1. All of the words of the ARI here are fundamental, as the whole foundation of the wisdom is built on them. There is not a single matter in all the worlds of ABYA that does not have, in the general and in the particular, the results of all the matters that are brought here in the ten Sefirot of Akudim. Moreover, any slight change and tiny innovation here branches in the Partzufim of ABYA into numerous profound matters.

It is known that all the forces and the new forms in the upper ones must be present in every lower one, without a single detail missing. This applies throughout the cascading of the Partzufim and the worlds to the Sof of Assiya. It is even more so here, where we are still concerned with the first line that is extended from Ein Sof to the place of the restriction, which is the first Partzuf of Adam Kadmon.

Hence, every single word here is a precious gem that must be understood in its entire breadth and true definition. It must be memorized and remembered throughout the rest of the wisdom.

Thus, here I have come to arrange the topic headings brought in this part in a useful order for remembering, and also to distinguish each issue of the primary discernments that the ARI brings here, and define each matter as much as possible. The purpose is that the reader will be able to beware of taking an issue out of its true definition, as a slight error in these places will completely stop the understanding throughout the rest of the wisdom.

CHAPTER ONE

Five kinds of coupling by striking and clash

2. There are five kinds of coupling by striking and clash that we find here in the ARI's words in the first expansion of AK, which are:

a. The first look, which is coupling by striking of the upper light in the screen in the vessel of Malchut for the phase of vessels of the Rosh (see Part 3, Chapter 12, item 4).

b. The striking and clash of the inner light and the surrounding light with each other, as they exit the Peh of AK, which the ARI introduces here (Chapter 1, item 3).

c. The second look, which is coupling by striking of the upper light in the screen in the vessel of Malchut to make vessels for the Guf (see Part 3, Chapter 12, item 5).

d. Striking and clash of the record and the descending reflected light with each other (see here Chapter 3, item 9).

e. The clash of the light of Malchut with the descending reflected light (see Chapter 4, item 3).

The first coupling by striking makes only the roots of the vessels. The second – the vessel and the light are mixed, and the third makes complete vessels

3. The root of everything is the coupling called the first look. All the light in the Partzuf is extended from it, and its issue has been thoroughly explained in the ARI's words (Part 3, Chapter 1, item 1 and Chapter 12 items 2 and 3). However, it is sufficient only to elicit the roots for the vessels, called "potential clothing," not "actual," because here the reflected light clothes from below upward, which means resistance to the clothing in the coarseness of the vessel. This is why the ten Sefirot in the Rosh are called Ein Sof, or Keter, as the ARI wrote (Part 3, Chapter 6, item7).

Moreover, even afterwards when the ten Sefirot from Malchut of the Rosh expand down into the Guf through the Tabur, they are still not distinguished as vessels in and of themselves. Rather, it is as though the light and the vessels are mixed together, as the ARI wrote here (Chapter 6, item1). The manifestation of the HaVaYot of the vessels begins primarily in the second look done on the screen in the vessel of Malchut during the refinement, meaning the four levels that emerge in the degrees of its refinement.

The third coupling by striking is performed by the surrounding light and the inner light. The surrounding light refines the screen and the upper light makes a coupling by striking on the screen in the degrees of its refinement, eliciting four levels HB TM

4. This matter of refinement is done by the striking of the inner light and the surrounding light on each other, as the ARI wrote here (Chapter 1, item 3, and see there in Inner Light). It explains there that the surrounding light refines the coarseness in the screen until it becomes as refined as the screen in Malchut of the Rosh.

Indeed, this whole refinement is done instantaneously and at once, as the ARI says (Chapter 1, item 9). However, the upper light does not stop shining even for a minute. Thus, the upper light makes a coupling with it in the four degrees to which the screen comes during its refinement. It elicits four levels of ten Sefirot there, which are Hochma, Bina, ZA, and Malchut, as it is written in Inner Light (Chapter 1, item 7).

The completion of the manifestation of the vessels is only through the second look

5. The difference between the three kinds of coupling by striking has been explained: the first look, though it is the root and the origin of all the lights and the vessels in the Partzuf, still has no ability to actually manifest. The entire manifestation is only through the second look, done in the degrees of the refinement of the screen. This matter of refinement is done by the striking and the clash of the inner light and surrounding light with each other.

The last two couplings through striking are for the following Partzuf

6. All these three kinds of striking are the purpose of the Partzuf itself. However, the striking and the clash of the record and the reflected light with each other is for the vessels of the following Partzuf (see Inner Light Chapter 2, item 3). Similarly, the striking of the light of Malchut on the record is for the purpose of the vessel of Malchut of the following Partzuf. Thus, it has been clarified how the first three kinds of striking are for the purpose of the Partzuf itself, and the two final strikings are for the purpose of the following Partzuf.

CHAPTER TWO

Twelve kinds of reflected light

The general reflected light rejected from Malchut becomes the surrounding light

7. We find twelve kinds of reflected light in the ARI's words; here they are:

The first is the reflected light rejected from phase four during the first look when the screen detains the upper light and does not let it expand there. The light returns backwards and clothes the ten Sefirot of direct light.

There are two kinds of reflected light to discern here: the first is all of the light that was rejected from clothing in the vessel of Malchut. There is a great measure of it, especially in the first Partzuf of AK that we are concerned with. It contains the entire difference from Ein Sof, which filled the entire reality, to Partzuf AK, which is but a thin line of light, in relation to the light of Ein Sof. Know that this reflected light incorporates all the surrounding light in all the worlds.

The reflected light that clothes the direct light is an outcome of the first reflected light, rejected from Malchut

8. The second kind of reflected light included here is the reflected light that ascends from below upward, and clothes the ten Sefirot of direct light. There is great depth in that, as there is existence in the reflected light rejected from phase four, meaning the actuality of the light that is rejected from there.

We must discern the negation in it, which is the force of the striking itself, generating a great light because of the withdrawal from the light. It is a correlation between the light that is rejected back, and phase four, which is left empty of that light.

This reflected light, which is born by the withdrawal from the light, is the second kind of reflected light, rising and clothing the ten Sefirot of direct light. Hence it is considered an outcome of the first kind of reflected light, especially from the negation, but through the correlation, as explained above.

There are two kinds of reflected light: inner light and surrounding light. A great difference between HB TM of inner light

9. The above two kinds of reflected light are considered the inner light and the surrounding light of the ten Sefirot of the Rosh. It is so because that reflected light

clothing the ten Sefirot of direct light is a very small part of all the reflected light that is rejected back, as it is but an outcome and correlation of the vessel of Malchut and the rejected light.

You already know that there are four phases of direct light one above the other, called HB ZA and Malchut, and Keter is their root. The differences between them are indeed great and very vast. Hence, the outcome born from the correlation of the rejected light with the phase of Malchut is not like the outcome born from the correlation between the rejected light and the phase of ZA, let alone with the phases above ZA.

NRNHY are born and emerge from the correlation between the rejected reflected light and the KHB TM of direct light

10. Now you can understand the birth of the five lights, called: Nefesh, Ruach, Neshama, Haya, Yechida. The outcome of the correlation of the reflected light with the phase of Malchut is called the light of Nefesh. The outcome of the correlation between the reflected light and the phase of ZA is called the light of Ruach. The outcome of the correlation between the reflected light and the phase of Bina is called the light of Neshama. The outcome of the reflected light with the phase of Hochma is called the light of Haya, and the outcome of the reflected light and the phase of Keter is called the light of Yechida.

If the clothing reflected light is a result of the correlation between the rejected reflected light and Malchut, it is considered the light of Nefesh

11. Now the clothing reflected light over the ten Sefirot of direct light was an outcome of the reflected light with the phase of Malchut. Hence, the light that is drawn into these ten Sefirot is called the light of Nefesh. It is discerned as inner light of these ten Sefirot, and the general rejected reflected light is the surrounding light of these ten Sefirot. Thus we have explained two kinds of reflected light.

The third reflected light is that which is clothed in Malchut of the Rosh. It is the origin and the Keter for both the ten Sefirot of reflected light in the Rosh, and the ten Sefirot in the Guf

12. The third kind of reflected light is the reflected light that remains permanently present in Malchut of the Rosh, as the origin and the emanator of all the lights and the vessels in the Guf. You have nothing in the Guf that is not extended from that origin. Since Malchut, with the amount of reflected light that she raises, clothes

all the lights of Rosh, she is therefore regarded as the phase of Keter and a root for both the lights of the Rosh, and the lights of the Guf. There is no hold at all of the light without a vessel, and since she begets the reflected light that clothes the lights, she is also regarded as begetting the lights themselves.

The fourth reflected light expands from the Peh to the Tabur, becoming vessels over the direct light, though incomplete

13. The fourth kind is the reflected light that expands the vessel of Malchut to ten Sefirot from her and within her from above downward, called from Peh to Tabur. Malchut of the Rosh is called Peh, and Malchut of the Guf, which is the tenth Sefira of Malchut of the Rosh, is called Tabur.

Indeed, this reflected light becomes actual vessels over the ten Sefirot of direct light that descend inside it from above downward. This is why these ten Sefirot are called the "Guf of the Partzuf," although they do not seem as such because of the great importance of the coarseness in it (see Inner Light Chapter 6, item 5).

The fifth reflected light is the reflected light in Malchut of the Guf called Tabur

14. The fifth kind is the reflected light in Malchut of the Guf, called female light. This is actually illumination from the direct light, but it is a small illumination, having only the quality of reception, without any power of bestowal. This is why it is called reflected light, and remember that.

The sixth reflected light is the one that expands from Tabur downward

15. The sixth kind of reflected light is all that expands from Tabur of the Guf downward. It is entirely the phase of Malchut of the Guf alone, as the first nine Sefirot of the ten Sefirot that expand from the Peh to the Guf end at the Tabur. Malchut in them occupies the entire place from Tabur to the end of the Partzuf. Although she is only Malchut, for herself, she is still regarded as expanding into ten Sefirot. This is from the perspective of the end of each and every Sefira distinguished in this place.

That which emerges in the coupling by striking in the Rosh is discerned only in the Guf. The expansion to Malchut is regarded as being from Peh to Tabur, and the rejection from Malchut is considered to be from Tabur down

16. You must understand here that we have no perception in the ten Sefirot of the Rosh. It is so because they are the state of Ein Sof, and everything we discern in

the ten Sefirot of the Rosh is only their expansion into the Guf, and the upper one is studied from the lower one.

We say that the upper light expanded up to Malchut and the screen in the vessel of Malchut struck the light and did not let it enter the vessel of Malchut and pushed it back, and this reflected light clothed the ten Sefirot of direct light. This clothing of the first nine Sefirot and this rejection from expanding in Malchut are discerned by us because this is how they operate in the Guf on the Tabur.

The first nine Sefirot from Tabur up are received and clothed inside the reflected light, and the light that belongs to the Sefira of Malchut is rejected. It is not received in Malchut of the Guf, which is the entire place from the Tabur down.

Since that Malchut had clothed all ten Sefirot when she was in the state of Ein Sof, prior to the restriction, hence the light filled the entire reality, as written at length (Inner Observation, Part 1, Chapter 1 and Chapter 2). For this reason, we also discern ten hollows in the Malchut that has been restricted, meaning in the place from Tabur downward, which have been emptied of the light that they had had in the state of Ein Sof. Now there is only reflected light inside them.

Hence, we discern ten Sefirot in and of themselves in Malchut of the Guf, as they carry the entire deficiency that appeared because of the restriction. For this reason, the place from Tabur down is called posterior, due to the lack of direct light. The place from Tabur up is called the anterior of the Partzuf because it is the place of all the light in the Partzuf.

The seventh reflected light is what remains in the Partzuf after the departure of the direct light from it

17. The seventh kind is the reflected light that remains in the Guf below, after the departure of the direct light from there. It is brought in the ARI's words (Chapter 2, item 10). When the direct light returns up to its root, the reflected light does not ascend with it, as the very essence of the reflected light is the light of departure.

It has been explained above in item eight that it comes from the withdrawal of phase four, which does not receive the light because of the force of the restriction and the screen that rides over her, regarded by its origin as coarseness and judgment. But when it becomes a vessel that draws and clothes the upper light, the coarseness and judgment are inverted to complete refinement and mercy until it is no longer regarded as lowly and dark compared to the upper light that is clothed in it (see item 14).

However, during the departure, when the upper light expands from it and rises to its root, its importance expires and nothing more than its own essence remains of it, meaning coarseness, restriction and judgment. It is therefore clear that during the departure, when the direct light returned to its root, the reflected light could not ascend with it. Moreover, now its descent below has been revealed, meaning that the judgment and the coarseness in it became apparent as it is according to its own essence, and for this reason, it is called coarse light.

From now on, the difference is regarded in advance between the vessels that clothed the light, meaning the reflected light, and the light clothed in it, which was not at all apparent prior to the departure (see item 13). This is why the ARI says there that this coarse light is the phase of the vessels of the Partzuf.

The eighth reflected light is the above reflected light, after having acquired additional coarseness to its own coarseness

18. The eighth kind is the above reflected light from the perspective of its reception of additional coarseness to its own coarseness, as the ARI says (Chapter 6, item 2). It is so because besides the coarseness that appeared in it, from what it is according to its own essence, the impression of a new judgment that it acquired by the current departure, which left it in the dark, has been added to it. Because of this, it is in double coarseness.

The ninth reflected light rises from the coupling by striking on the screen during the degrees of its refinement

19. The ninth kind is the reflected light that ascends through the coupling by striking performed on the screen in the degrees of its refinement. The levels that emerge in these couplings are generally regarded as reflected light, even the direct light in them. This is because the couplings emerge during the judgment, meaning during the departure of the lights to the emanator.

20. We might ask: but there is expansion of direct light from above downward into the Guf in each and every level, and it is known that all that is extended from above downward is mercy. The thing is that, indeed, there is nothing more than a matter of refinement here.

Even those couplings made of the upper light are also included in the departure of the lights, as this is the conduct of refinement. It must pass and come through the four phases during its refinement, as the upper light, which does not stop for even a minute, makes a coupling with it on its way.

It is like a person who walks out of the house: even though he takes, for example, four steps on his way out of the house, we still don't regard them as being four rests in his walk; this is completely unthinkable. It is impossible for him to exit the house except through steps as that is the conduct of walking.

So is the issue before us: Even though the screen passes four phases during the departure, and the upper light makes a coupling with it on its way, it is still not regarded as expansion of the upper light into the Partzuf, as mercy. Rather, it is considered judgment because the time is a time of departure, which includes the expansions on its way, as well, as this is the usual manner of departure, and remember that.

21. It has been explained that even though there is a complete level of RTS (Rosh, Toch, Sof) in each and every coupling, which emerges during the refinement of the screen, they are still not regarded as direct light, mercy, but as reflected light and judgment. However, all of this relates to the self of the Partzuf in general, suffering from the departure of the lights from inside it. Hence, it pays little regard to the levels that emerge during the refinement and the departure of the light.

Nevertheless, regarding the values of the levels, meaning as the levels are in and of themselves, we have an inverse relation: Every level that emerges by a closer coupling to the emanator is better (see items 9, 10). That is because in phase four, only the light of Nefesh emerges, and when it is refined into phase three, the light of Ruach emerges. When that is refined into phase two, the light of Neshama emerges, etc.

22. This above matter of inverse relation must be thoroughly and clearly understood, as it is the whole connection and the entire difference between the light and the vessel. Hence, not knowing it will fail us every step of the way throughout the wisdom before us.

The thing is that there is a vessel for the reception of the upper light on the part of the direct light, which are the five phases KHB ZON, or NRNHY, and there is a vessel for reception on the part of the reflected light, which are the levels that are also called KHB, ZA and Malchut. They are completely opposite from one another because from the same coupling by which the level of Keter of reflected light emerges, meaning the greatest vessel, the phase of Nefesh of direct light emerges, too, which is the smallest light.

23. The origin of these two values has already been explained. The value of the four phases of direct light is extended so from the light of Ein Sof. The first three phases are still not considered vessels of reception, as the distinction of disparity

of form is still not apparent in them. The difference between them and the upper light is only in that they cause the cascading of phase four, which is known to be the phase of absolute reception.

Each more refined phase is therefore considered greater because it has greater adhesion with the upper light clothed in it. Hence, Keter, which is the farthest cause from phase four, is the root of the entire expansion, and phase one, which is the nearest cause to phase four, from Keter, is regarded as a smaller light than Keter. Besides being a consequence and an outcome of Keter, there is also a fine difference in it from the light that is clothed in it, in that it is a second cause and closer to phase four.

In phase two, which is a third cause and closer to phase four, the light clothed there is smaller, and so on similarly. Finally, phase four itself has no light at all because of the disparity of form in it, and on which there was the restriction. All this is known from previous parts and there is no need to elaborate.

24. The differences in values of the above phases are called by the names: Nefesh, Ruach, Neshama, Haya, Yechida. There is a great difference between them, which pertains primarily to the proximity and distance from phase four, over which there is the force of restriction.

There is yet another difference between them, that of cause and consequence. Keter is the cause of Hochma; Hochma of Bina and so on. The merit of the cause over its consequence is indeed great in the spirituals, unlike any cause and consequence in corporeality. It is so because here they are all eternal and all the lights attained by the consequence must pass to it through its cause.

Moreover, most of this light that passes remains in the cause, and only a small branch of it is imparted and comes to the resulting lower one, although the light belongs solely to the consequence, and there are many other discernments too. Thus, the distance between the cause and its consequence is immeasurably great.

Besides all this, there is a great difference between these four phases according to the kind of light in the essence. Even though the upper light is entirely even, there is a matter of a correlation here between the upper light and the phase of direct light in which it is clothed. Thus, the light of Haya is the self, the light of Neshama is primarily light of Hassadim, and there are other differences that will be explained in their place.

25. Know that all the above-mentioned values in the four phases of direct light are extended so from Ein Sof, since they come to shine from the restriction down. Also,

all the above discernments apply to the ten Sefirot of circles, as well, since they come this way from Ein Sof before they enter into the coupling by striking and the clothing of the reflected light. You already know that the whole difference between the ten Sefirot of circles and the ten Sefirot of straightness is only with regard to the coupling by striking, which does not apply to the circles.

26. Now we shall explain the second term, meaning the five levels of reflected light, which is an entirely different matter. It has already been explained in Inner Observation Part 2 (Chapter 6) that from the restriction down the reflected light became the vessel of reception for the upper light instead of phase four (see there, Chapter 2).

It is because that reflected light that was rejected from Malchut, which Malchut does not receive due to the detainment in the screen, became a vessel and a receptacle for the light, as phase four was in Ein Sof. Thus, no light is received in the worlds except by way of the reflected light, see there.

27. Therefore, if the coupling by striking performed on the screen of phase four, which is the primary receptacle in Ein Sof that clothed all the light up to Keter, which is the meaning of the light filling the entire reality, now, however, when all that great measure has been rejected from her and has risen up as reflected light, that reflected light also clothes the entire height of the light up to Keter.

However, if it is refined to phase three in her, and the measure of phase four disappears from there, then the screen that rejects the upper light from clothing in her rejects only the measure of three phases. Thus, even if the light had clothed this vessel of phase three, she would only receive from it up to Hochma. Hence, the level of the rejected reflected light is also short and clothes only up to Hochma, etc., similarly.

28. Just as the difference between Keter and Hochma of direct light is indeed great, precisely so is the difference between the level of Keter and Hochma of reflected light immeasurably great. Even though in the reflected light the coarser is greater, this pertains to the vessels of extension, meaning the screen and the Malchut in which the coupling by striking is carried out.

However, they need the more refined vessels for the clothing of light, as it is necessary for the light to have equivalence of form with the vessel. The light is greater in the phases of direct light because it is more refined (see item 22). It is therefore obvious that when it comes to be clothed in the vessel of reflected light, that vessel must equalize with it.

Consequently, it is necessary that if the level of reflected light reaches Keter, then there is a refined and clear vessel there, fitting to clothe that great light of clear Keter. However, the level of phase three, whose level reaches only up to Hochma, the merit of the vessel that clothes the light of Hochma is immeasurably lower than the vessel of Keter on the level of phase four, etc., similarly.

29. We might ask: if only the coarseness of phase three remains when the coarseness of phase four is refined, it turns out that the phase of Malchut disappeared from there and only the first three phases KHB and ZA remained. In that case, that level should have been cut off from Malchut, as that part of reflected light is missing there. Why then was the reflected light cut off from clothing in Keter, while that phase is not absent from there?

The thing is that the matter of the two directions in the ten Sefirot has already been explained in Inner Observation Part 2 (Chapter 9). The ten Sefirot of direct light are regarded as from above downward, and the reflected light is the opposite, regarded as from below upward. Thus, below, in the place of Malchut of direct light, there is the Keter of reflected light, and in the place of ZA of direct light there is Hochma of reflected light etc. Finally, in the place of Keter of direct light, there is Malchut of reflected light.

30. Now you can understand what is written in *Sefer Yetzira* (*Book of Creation*), that "Its end is embedded in its beginning, and its beginning in its end." Phase four, which is Malchut, is the end of all the Sefirot, and through the striking of upper light on the screen in her, she draws the light of Keter into her, meaning she binds it to shine in the Partzuf.

Thus, she is literally embedded in its beginning, meaning Keter, the beginning of all the Sefirot. Since Keter is drawn to the reflected light of phase four, all ten Sefirot are drawn along with it, since Keter contains all of them.

Thus, Malchut is regarded as Keter of reflected light, meaning the actual measure of Keter. Phase three is called ZA of reflected light, which is second to her, attributed only to the Sefira of Hochma, as she is second to the place of the coupling at the level of Keter and one degree more refined. It continues similarly until the Keter in her, which is the fifth from the place of the coupling, regarded only as Malchut. Thus, the end of the direct light, namely the Sefira of Malchut, is embedded in the beginning of the reflected light, namely Keter of the reflected light.

31. Now you can simply understand the question we raised: If it is refined to phase three, then it lacks only Malchut. Why then was the reflected light so shortened

that it cannot clothe up to Keter but only from Hochma down? Now this is clearly understood, since there is an inverse relation here: phase four is regarded here as Keter, phase three as Hochma and so on, the complete opposite of the direct light.

32. However, we must still consider the measure of the reception of the direct light explained above (items 22, 24). Although its end is embedded in its beginning and Malchut draws the light of Keter for herself and becomes the Sefira of Keter, it does not mean that Malchut draws the actual light of Yechida for herself.

It is utterly impossible for the light of Yechida to come through the drawing of the vessel of Malchut, but only through the drawing of the vessel of Keter of direct light. Moreover, how can the relation of the phases of direct light with the upper light that are clothed and extended so from Ein Sof change? The difference of above and below in them is immeasurably great, as we have explained above (items 23, 24). However, they are kept in utter precision, and each phase does not move from the value of her merit even a bit.

33. The matter of its end being embedded in its beginning means that the light of Nefesh of Malchut, ascribed to her by the direct light, grows and attains its own phase, which is included in the Keter. It is so because Keter contains all ten Sefirot up to Malchut, and the lights in them are regarded as the five parts of Yechida, called NRNHY of Yechida. Hence, the light of Nefesh of Malchut now attains the root that she has in Keter, called Nefesh of Yechida. Indeed, she does not attain anything above her own phase.

34. You can see that although there is an inverse relation between the ten Sefirot of reflected light and the ten Sefirot of direct light, they still do not cancel or diminish each other even slightly. One does not touch the other at all, although they emerge simultaneously from a single coupling.

The level of ten Sefirot up to the actual Keter emerges from the coupling of phase four, though only up to Nefesh of Yechida. The ten Sefirot on the level of Hochma emerge from the coupling of phase three, though it does not attain the phase of Hochma, called Haya. It is so because phase three is the phase of ZA, which is the light of Ruach of direct light, and the light of Hochma is drawn only through Hochma of direct light.

Instead, it attains its own phase, rooted in Hochma, called the phase of Ruach of Haya. It is similar with all of them, as each one draws and attains only its own phase in the direct light, but the level of reflected light causes it to take its phase from a high place, according to the measure of the level.

35. We might ask accordingly, how is the light of Ruach, whose merit is many times greater than the Nefesh (see items 23, 24), found to be clothing a lower level than Nefesh? After all, the light of Nefesh is drawn by phase four and clothes in the level of Keter, and the light of Ruach must be drawn by phase three and is found to be clothed in merely the level of Hochma, which is much lower than Keter.

Indeed, in the world of correction, when the vessels were properly corrected, we always find that even though the light of Ruach is drawn by phase three, it is still clothed only in the level of Keter. This is because then Nefesh descends from the level of Keter and clothes the level of phase three, and the light of Ruach is clothed in the level of Keter.

It is the same with all of them, though here, before the vessels were corrected, they emerged here only by way of refinement. When phase three emerged and drew the light of Ruach, the vessel at the level of Keter was no longer in reality, as the screen had already departed from there. Hence, it had to come and clothe in a lower vessel than the vessel of Nefesh, and this is why the Partzuf could not receive from it the entire measure of its illumination.

The tenth reflected light is the one that descends from the four levels that emerge during the refinement of the screen into the empty vessel below them

36. The tenth kind is the reflected light descending from the four levels that emerge in the refinement of the screen from the place of the coupling down into the vessel below it, which is empty of light. It is brought here in the ARI's words (Chapter 4, item 3), that when phase four was refined into phase three, the light departed from phase four, the level of Keter disappeared, the coupling was done on phase three, and the level of Hochma emerged. At that time, the reflected light descends from the illumination of the coupling in phase three and comes into the vessel of phase four, which is empty of her own light. Also, when the place of the coupling departed from phase three and rose to phase two and phase three was emptied of her own light, the illumination of the coupling descended from phase two into the empty vessel of phase three, etc. similarly.

There are two flaws in this reflected light: 1. It comes from the refinement of the screen, which is judgment. 2. It is extended below the Tabur

37. This reflected light has two flaws:

1. It comes from the coupling that is done during the refinement. For this reason, that level is generally considered reflected light and judgment, as in the eighth kind of reflected light.

2. The second flaw is its being extended from the phase below the Tabur. When the screen was refined to phase three, Malchut of the Rosh rose to the Hotem, which was then regarded as the Peh of the Rosh. From there the light descends and expands from above downward into the Guf, reaching phase three of the Guf, which is now regarded as the phase of Malchut of Malchut of the Rosh, called Tabur. Also, when it was refined into phase two, phase two of the Guf is regarded as the phase of Tabur, etc., similarly.

Thus, the reflected light descending from the illumination of the coupling of phase three from the Guf to phase four of the Guf is regarded as reaching below the Tabur. It has already been explained that this reflected light is the quality of posterior and judgment (see items 15, 16).

The eleventh reflected light is reflected light born out of the striking of the record and the descending reflected light on each other, called sparks

38. The eleventh kind is the reflected light born by the coupling by striking of the record and the descending reflected light on one another brought in the words of the ARI here (Chapter 3, item 9), and is called there "fourth light." This is because the record and the reflected light naturally disagree and strike each other. As a result, sparks emerged from the above-mentioned descending reflected light and came into the empty vessel below the place of the coupling.

The twelfth reflected light is the above-mentioned reflected light after the cessation of the coupling, at which time it is extinguished and grows dark

39. The twelfth kind is the same reflected light as the eleventh kind, but after they are extinguished. After the illumination of the coupling stops from phase three, for example, the illumination of the coupling that was extended from there into phase four also stops along with it. Hence, the sparks that fell and came into phase four are extinguished, meaning they become darkened from their illumination, as do the rest of the sparks from the rest of the phases.

CHAPTER THREE

Twelve kinds of records

A record of extension and a record of clothing

40. The first kind is the record that remains of the lights after their departure, which come from the phases of clothing. The second kind is the record that remains of the lights after their departure, which comes from the phase of extension. It means that you already know that the greatness of the level is measured by the level of coarseness in the screen, where the coarser draws a greater level.

It is also known that we should always discern two ends in this, which stretch from one person to another. It is so because the greater the level, the farther are the ends. The greater level necessitates a greater coarseness in the screen and the vessel of Malchut, and also more refined vessels of reception. For example, phase four, which is the coarsest, draws the level of Keter, but at the same time needs the most refined vessel, fitting to receive the entire light of Keter inside her (see Inner Observation Part 2).

Records of extension remain in the vessels of extension, and of clothing remain in the vessels of reception

41. Thus, after every departure we discern two kinds of records: the first remains in the vessel of extension of that light, and the second is the record that remains in the vessel of reception of that light. Indeed, if we judge by the record for itself, they are almost one, though in their origin, they are as far from one another as the distance of the east from the west. The record of the phase of extension is from the lowest coarseness there is, and the record of the phase of reception is from the highest refinement there is. It is so because one is phase four and the other is the root phase.

The record of clothing is male and the record of coarseness is female

42. Know that they relate to one another as male and female. It is so because in fact both have the same level of light, meaning light clothed in a properly suited vessel. However, after the light departed from there and the coarseness in the vessel is regarded as lowliness (as the ARI says here in item 18), that great distance between

these two records appears. Still, since they are one to begin with, they are therefore regarded as male and female.

There is no record of coarseness left of the last phase after the refinement

43. Know that this record of the female phase did not remain after the departure of the light from there. Though she is not lost, as there is no absence in the spiritual, she remains silent and completely inactive until the end of correction.

In chapter 2, item 6 the ARI writes that the last phase does not leave a record, and only the record of the male phase remains there. In chapter 2, item 4, the ARI writes that when the Keter rises and departs, it leaves one record in its place in that vessel, to shine from it to Hochma below it, after it rises and departs. See Inner Light there.

Records that clothe in their vessels

44. The third kind are records that clothe in the place of the general light that departed, meaning in the reflected light and the vessel of Malchut that expanded from her and within her into ten Sefirot. These clothed the ten Sefirot of direct light, and thus each and every one of the records that remained after their departure clothed according to its phase and share as well.

For example, Keter of direct light was clothed in Nefesh of reflected light during the expansion. Afterwards, when it departed from there, the record clothes in its place, meaning in Nefesh of reflected light, and also the record of Hochma in Ruach of reflected light, etc. However, they certainly did not need the entire measure of the vessel, as the record is a small part of the departing light, and occupied a certain measure of the vessel, according to its share. This is brought in the ARI's words here (item 18).

Records that do not clothe in their vessels but are above their vessels

45. The fourth kind is the records that do not clothe in their vessels. Instead, each and every one of them is found above its designated vessel, as tags over the letters (as the ARI says in Chapter 4, item 4). The reason for their exit from their vessels is this: Because of the striking of the descending reflected light and the record on each other, since the reflected light comes from the illumination of the coupling, it overpowers the record, regarded as a residue of the departure of the coupling.

Since the light of the record is opposite from the reflected light descending into her vessel, they cannot be together in the same carrier, meaning in one vessel. For that reason the record was forced to depart from her vessel and exit above her vessel.

Records that returned to their vessels

46. The fifth kind is the records that returned to their vessels after having left there. As a result of the departure of the coupling from the upper phase, too, the illumination of the descending reflected light departed too, and the sparks that fell into the vessel below it were extinguished. Then the record returned into its own vessel as before, for now there is no longer resistance from the reflected light inside its vessel, since it, too, is after the departure of its coupling. Hence, the record overpowers the reflected light once more.

The reason that the departure of the coupling is called "extinguishing the sparks" is that the illumination of reflected light is called sparks. Hence, the discontinuation of its illumination is called extinguishing, which is a term used for sparks of fire.

A record that consists of refined light and coarse light, a record from the refined light, a record from the coarse light

47. The sixth kind is a record that contains refined light and coarse light. The seventh kind is called refined light, brought by the ARI here (Chapter 2, item 10). The eighth kind is called the coarse light of the record.

As the refined light was mixed with the coarse light in the lights of the first expansion, so it is in the record that the first expansion left

48. Explanation of the words: Everything that is found in the light is also found in the record that remains of that light. Hence, the record is called a record of a seal (see Part 2, Inner Light, item 3).

For this reason, the records that remain from the lights of the first expansion contain light and vessel, like the lights from which they came (see item 44). However, as long as the record is clothed in its vessel, there is no distinction between the light and the vessel, similar to the lights of the first expansion where the lights and the vessels are mixed (see the ARI's words, Chapter 6, item 2, and Inner Light item 6).

Thus, in the record that comes from them there is also no distinction between the light and the vessel. Rather, they are mixed together. This is the above sixth kind, meaning the record that contains the refined light and the coarse light, although the coarse light is not apparent in it but mixed in it.

The coarseness in the vessel manifests after the departure of the record from the vessel

49. Now you will understand the above seventh and eighth kinds. It has been explained above (item 45), regarding the fourth kind of the record, that because of the striking of the descending reflected light on the record, the record departed and went out from its vessel, rising above it as tags over the letters.

Now, because of the departure of the record from the vessel, the difference between the vessel and the record has become apparent, as now the coarseness in the vessel becomes apparent. It is now regarded as coarse light, like the lights of the first expansion (Chapter 6, Inner Light, item 7). Also, you already know that everything that applies to the lights also applies to the records that come from them.

50. It has been explained that after the departure of the record from the vessel, the difference between the light of the record and the vessel of the record has become apparent. The vessel is now called the coarse light of the record, and you should know that the vessels of the males of the second expansion were made of the coarse light of the record. The light of the record is now called the refined light of the record, from which the lights of the males of the second expansion are made, and remember that.

The record of clothing that remains in Malchut

51. The ninth kind is the record of the light of Malchut, brought in the ARI's words here (Chapter 6, item 20). Know that this record is of the above-mentioned seventh kind, called refined light. It means that it does not have the phase of a vessel. It is written above (item 45), that the record from the phase of the extension had been lost. It means that the phase of the coarse light of this record, which is the eighth kind of the record but the refined light in her remained without a vessel, which therefore rose above its own vessel, meaning to Yesod (Chapter 4, items 2, 3).

The records incorporated in the screen after its refinement

52. The tenth kind is the records that were incorporated in the screen on its ascent to the emanator. The light of Malchut, which is the screen and the reflected light in her, is refined and rises from phase to phase until it reaches the emanator, meaning the Peh of the Rosh. As it passes in them, it also becomes incorporated with the records that the lights left there after their departure. Hence, when it reached the Peh, it was incorporated with all three phases of the records over which the

new coupling was done, from which the vessels and lights of the second expansion emerged (see Inner Light, Chapter 4, item 4).

The records that remained of the four levels that emerged during the refinement

53. The eleventh kind is the records that remain of the four levels that emerged during the refinement from the phase of the first nine Sefirot in them. Here the ARI speaks only of the records that remained from the first nine of the first expansion, before it began to be refined, called the first light, as the ARI says here (Chapter 3, item 8). However, the four levels that emerged afterwards, during the refinement, also left records in their vessels after they departed, meaning also from the first nine Sefirot in them, as it is known that the last phase does not leave a record.

The records of clothing that remained of the last phases in the above four levels

54. The twelfth kind is the records that remain of the last phases in the above four levels that exited during the refinement, meaning only the phase of refined light in those records. The coarse light in these records was lost from the last phases, as was clarified with the last phases of the records that remained from the first light (see above items 29 and 51).

55. Now we have clarified the twelve kinds of records, which are:

1. The records that emerge from the phase of clothing, explained in items 40, 41, 42, 43.

2. The records that emerge from the phase of extension, explained in the above items too.

3. The records clothed inside their vessels, explained in item 44.

4. The records that do not clothe in their vessels, but are as tags over the letters, explained in item 45.

5. The records that returned to their vessels after having left there, explained in item 46.

6. The records that include refined light and coarse light, and the coarse light is not apparent in them, explained in items 47, 48, 49.

7. The refined light of the records from which the lights of the males of the second expansion were made, explained in the above items, too.

8. The coarse light of the records, from which the vessels for the males of the second expansion were made, explained there too, as well as in item 50.

9. The record of the light of Malchut which is only from the phase of the refined light in this record, because the last phase does not leave a record, explained in item 51.

10. The records that were incorporated in the screen along its ascent to the eEmanator, where they were renewed in the coupling for the second expansion, explained in item 52.

11. The records that remained of the first nine Sefirot of the four levels that emerged during the refinement, explained in item 52.

12. The records of the last phases from these levels, explained in item 54.

CHAPTER FOUR

Ten kinds of vessels

The root of all the vessels is phase four

56. The first kind is phase four of the four phases of direct light, which is the root of all the vessels in the worlds. This is Malchut of Ein Sof where the first restriction was performed. Prior to the restriction, she clothed all four phases of direct light, which is the meaning of the upper light having filled the entire reality, and there was no other phase of reception but her.

Once she was restricted and corrected with a screen, she makes a coupling with the upper light in coupling by striking that raises reflected light. This reflected light now became the vessel of reception instead of her, as the ARI says (Part 3, Chapter 1, items 1, 2, 3 and Chapter 12, item 4).

After the restriction, phase four was incorporated in the screen, and the reflected light became the vessel instead of her

57. Know that the above phase four is the essence of the vessel after the restriction as well, meaning the phase of coarseness in her. However, this coarseness is no longer fit for reception from the restriction onward, unless incorporated in the screen. In that state the reflected light that she raises is actually measured in the coarseness in her, and according to the measure of the coarseness in her, so is the measure of light that she raises. This reflected light became the vessel of reception for the measure of the height of the level of the upper light (see Inner Observation Part 2).

The expansion of the light and its departure caused the existence of the vessels

58. Here the ARI sets a great rule for us: **"The expansion of the light and its latter departure, caused the making of the vessel"** (see here, Chapter 1, item 9). However, we should understand his words, since the first expansion, too, requires a vessel, even before it departed, as there is no light without a vessel.

We should explain his words according to what he wrote above (Chapter 6, item 2), that when the first expansion emerged from the Peh of AK, it emerged all mixed together. In other words, the light and the vessel were mixed in one another, and the vessel was indistinguishable before the departure, though it was necessarily there.

The expansion and the departure are equal factors in the making of the vessel

59. This explanation is a little far-fetched because the term "**caused the making of the vessel**" does not sit well, the words imply that before the departure, the vessel does not exist at all, but we must delve deeper into his words. Indeed, his words are prudent, for he did not say that the departure of the light caused the making of the vessel. Rather, he says that the expansion of the light and its departure caused the making of the vessel. It means that both of them, the expansion and the departure, are equal factors in the making of the vessel.

The first substance of the vessel is phase four

60. His words become clear with the above explanation (items 56 and 57), that the first substance of the vessel is phase four, over which there was the first restriction, meaning the great will to receive incorporated in the light of Ein Sof, called Malchut of Ein Sof. She was completely indistinguishable in Ein Sof and the beginning of her manifestation was after she had been restricted and became a vacant space.

In that state, the great will to receive became apparent as oppositeness of form from the upper light, which is all bestowal, and has nothing of the will to receive whatsoever. By this she was separated and descended, and became distanced from the upper light from end to end.

It is so because disparity of form is the differentiation in the spiritual, and oppositeness of form is complete separation in the spiritual from one end to the other. Hence, from then on, this great will to receive in the restricted phase four is considered the great coarseness in the worlds compared to the upper light, which is regarded as the ultimate refinement in reality.

This is only from the perspective of the cleanness from the will to receive, for all of it is to bestow. We have no further attainment in the upper light in and of itself, as we have already discussed at length in Part 1 (Inner Light and Inner Observation) and we need not elaborate further here.

After the restriction, phase four is incorporated in the screen, and the reflected light that rises through both of them becomes a vessel of reception

61. Despite all the distant separation in phase four from the upper light, there is no other vessel of reception but her, though she needs the correction of a screen. As she received prior to the restriction according to the measure of the drawing, to the same extent she now receives according to the measure of the rejection. Meaning she

receives according to the measure of the light she could have received, had she not been limited in the restriction and the screen [see Part 2, Table of Questions, item 43 for a thorough understanding of the meaning of the words restriction and screen].

The departure of the light from phase four was the reason for the emergence of the screen

62. It has already been explained in Part 2 that Malchut of the circles, over which there was the restriction, is the root and the reason for Malchut of straightness and the screen in her. It is so because after the light from Malchut of the circles departed from all four phases in her, she drew the light once more to the three phases in her, over which there was no restriction.

This desire is the meaning of the correction of the screen so that the light would not expand to phase four in her, but only to the three phases and not more. This happened to her because of the departure of the light from all four phases in her, and her remaining completely empty of light. Thus, you find that the departure of the light was the reason for the creation of the screen.

Phase four is a consequence of the expansion of the upper light. Thus, the expansion and the departure caused together the making of the vessel, since phase four and the screen emerged from them

63. Phase four, in and of herself, is a consequence of the expansion of the light, as she is phase four of the direct light, which is the meaning of Malchut of Ein Sof. However, the light departed from her afterwards because of the above restriction. thus, phase four is actually a consequence of the expansion of the light, and the screen is a consequence of the departure of the light.

It is explained, in item 61, that from the restriction on, both of them, meaning phase four and the screen, join into the phase of the vessel of reception. Beside them there are no vessels of reception in the worlds.

Therefore, you see how right were the words of the ARI when he said, **"The expansion of the light and its latter departure, caused the making of the vessel."** It is so because phase four herself, meaning the coarseness in her, is extended from the expansion of the light, and the screen that is established in her, without which she is unfit for reception whatsoever, is extended from the departure of the light.

The beginning of the forming of the vessel comes from the expansion and departure. Hence, every vessel must first have these two forces

64. It is known that all the forces in the upper ones must be present in their lower ones. Hence, since the beginning of the forming of the vessel in Malchut of straightness, which is the Peh of the Rosh of AK, comes because of the expansion of the light and its departure, from then on, every vessel must first have these two causes, meaning the expansion of the light and its departure. No vessel can be formed in the worlds without them.

The substance of the vessel is the coarseness, and the form is the screen

65. Now we have thoroughly explained the fundamental substance and the form of the vessel, which are the coarseness of phase four—the substance—and the screen established in her is the form. From these two, all the kinds of vessels in general and in particular cascaded in all four worlds ABYA.

The second kind is the reflected light that rises from the Peh up and clothes the ten Sefirot of direct light

66. The second kind of vessels is the reflected light that rises from below upward through the coupling by striking of the upper light with the screen established in the vessel of Malchut, called the first look. It is written above, in item 61, that from the restriction on, the measure of the upper light that the degree receives is dependent on and allotted by the measure of the reflected light that rises because of the coupling by striking in the screen. It is so because this reflected light connects and clothes the ten Sefirot of direct light.

The reflected light of the Rosh is not an actual vessel, but a root for the vessels

67. You must remember all that is explained here in Inner Light regarding this matter of the clothing of reflected light on the ten Sefirot of the Rosh. Especially, that this is not considered actual clothing, as it ascends from below upward, meaning as resistance to clothing in the coarseness of the vessels. Nevertheless, this reflected light expands the vessel of Malchut of the Rosh into ten Sefirot from her and within her, and they became actual vessels of reception, as we have elaborated on it (Inner Light, Chapter 1, item 30).

The third kind of vessels is the reflected light that is inverted from the Peh downward and clothes the ten Sefirot of the Guf to the Tabur

68. The third kind of vessels is the one brought above (item 65), that the reflected light of the Rosh, which is the above-mentioned second kind, though it is not at

all clothing in and of itself, it is nonetheless inverted and becomes an actual vessel of reception. This third kind is always called the Guf of the Partzuf, and the above-mentioned second kind is always called the Rosh of the Partzuf.

The fourth kind is the vessels from the Tabur down

69. The fourth kind is the vessels below the Tabur, regarded as ten Sefirot of reflected light that have no direct light. The issue of the above-mentioned third kind applies only through the Tabur, the place of the first nine Sefirot of the Guf. However, from the Tabur down, which is the place of Malchut of the Guf, they are not regarded as vessels of reception.

The rejection and the clothing that the screen caused in the Rosh in potential manifested in practice in the Guf, the clothing from Peh to Tabur, and the rejection from the Tabur down

70. The reason is that the Rosh and the Guf are regarded as the relation of the "potential" to the "actual," where everything that is included in the Rosh as potential manifests in practice in the Guf. Hence, these two operations that the screen causes in the ten Sefirot of Rosh, namely the detainment of the upper light so it does not expand into phase four, which is Malchut, and the clothing it performed by the force of the ascending reflected light, where both only in "potential" in the Rosh.

However, the place of the manifestation of these two operations is in the Guf. The potential clothing that was in the Rosh manifests in practice above the Tabur of the Guf, and the phase of detainment into Malchut manifests in actuality below Tabur of the Guf.

The fifth kind is the vessels of the first expansion, called coarse light

71. The fifth kind is vessels that were emptied of the upper light, called coarse light. After the ten Sefirot of the Guf expanded from the Peh of AK to the Tabur as the third kind (see item 68), the upper light departed from within them once again, and the vessels remained empty of light.

There is a big difference here. Although in the above first expansion they are discerned as actual vessels of reception (item 68), they are nevertheless not regarded as real vessels yet because of the great importance that the vessels have there, as is written here in Inner Light (Chapter 6, item 5). This is why the ARI says there that the vessels and the light within them are mixed. However, after the light departs from there, their coarseness becomes apparent, and a difference is made between the light and the vessel. That is why these vessels are called coarse light.

The sixth kind is vessels that were emptied of their lights, and the records that remained sustain them

72. The sixth kind is vessels that were emptied after the departure, and records from the lights that departed remained in them. The records sustain and revive the vessels to make them suitable to acquire their lights as in the beginning. Also, they shine to the Partzuf after them, as the ARI says here (Chapter 2, item 1 and item 8, and Chapter 4, item 2).

The seventh kind is vessels that were emptied and no records were left in them

73. The seventh kind is vessels that were emptied after the departure and no records of the lights that departed were left in them. They are the last phases of every Partzuf and expansion, because the last phase does not leave a record, as the ARI says (Chapter 2, item 6). This is the same as has been explained above (item 43).

The eighth kind is vessels that were qualified for the purpose of the next Partzuf, which follows it

74. The eighth kind is the phase of vessels that were prepared and qualified in the Partzuf for the purpose of the next Partzuf, which follows it, brought in the ARI's words (Chapter 4, item 6). Even the vessel of Keter, which the ARI says there that it was not made in the first Partzuf, but only in the following Partzuf, the phase of the vessel of Keter from the male phase was nevertheless prepared from the first Partzuf, as is explained in the Inner Light.

The above kind of vessels is the male vessels in the next Partzuf

75. This above-mentioned eighth kind is the male vessels for the purpose of the next Partzuf. They come from the records that the lights left in the vessels after their departure. The male vessels were made from the coarse light contained in these records (see Inner Light, Chapter 2, item 3).

The ninth kind is vessels that were prepared in the Partzuf for the female vessels for the following Partzuf

76. The ninth kind is the vessels for the females that were prepared in the first Partzuf for the purpose of the following Partzuf. They were made of the sparks that

fall into the empty vessels after the light departed from them, which come from the illumination of the coupling in the upper phase of the empty vessel, as the ARI says (Chapter 4, item 3).

In the next Partzuf, the lights change, and the light of Hochma comes in the vessel of Keter, the light of Bina in the vessel of Hochma, and the light of ZA in the vessel of Bina, etc. Hence, they needed vessels there that will be equal to their own phase. For this reason, these sparks had been prepared. The sparks that fell from the level of Bina into the empty vessel of the level of Hochma became the vessel for the light of Bina, which comes in the vessel of Hochma. Similarly, the sparks that fell from the level of ZA into the vessel of the level of Bina became a vessel for the light of ZA, which comes in the vessel of Bina, and so on similarly.

The tenth kind is the external vessels for the surrounding light

77. The tenth kind is the external vessels for surrounding light. No surrounding light is received in a degree unless it is received from its upper phase, from its opposite phase in the Rosh.

Hence, it needs a vessel suitable for this light, meaning the vessel should also be from the upper phase, from its opposite phase in the Rosh. If the degree is from phase four, it needs a vessel that will be from phase three; if it is from phase three, then it needs a vessel that will be from phase two, etc. Therefore, the vessels of surrounding light were called "external vessels" because from the perspective of the vessels, it is always considered that the more refined is more external (see Inner Light, Chapter 5, item 15).

The above vessels come into the degree during the refinement

78. These external vessels are attained in the degree only by ascending to the degree above it. This is done during the ascent of the lights to the emanator, as the ARI says here (Chapter 6, item 15), see there in Inner Light.

CHAPTER FIVE

Seven discernments in the screen

79. We've already discussed the matter of the screen (items 62, 63). It is explained there that the screen is the boundary made after the restriction to receive the light only in the first nine Sefirot and detain the light from expanding into phase four, meaning Malchut, as it says, "You shall come thus far, but no further."

This screen is a consequence caused by the restriction, meaning by the departure of the light. It is so because after the light departed completely from all four phases that are there, although the restriction was only on phase four, because of it, a new form of desire was initiated in Malchut of Ein Sof, to once more draw the light by the force of the boundary, meaning only from phase four and above, and not from phase four and below.

This boundary that was initiated is called a screen. Since this boundary primarily applies only to phase four, which is Malchut, it is therefore considered that the screen is present and established inside the vessel of Malchut.

The boundary and the coarseness in the screen come in it as one

80. There are seven primary discernments that we should make here in this screen: the first discernment is that the boundary and the coarseness are incorporated and come in it as one, without distinguishing between them whatsoever. Since the boundary in it applies only to the coarseness of phase four, we find that it does not limit and detain the expansion of the light from a degree that doesn't have this measure of coarseness.

Thus, the coarseness and the boundary come as one, and both together are called screen. It is impossible to speak of and distinguish the screen in and of itself, meaning when it is not incorporated with coarseness, for then it does not exist in reality at all, so there is what to discern in it.

There is coarseness without a screen and there is no screen without coarseness

81. However, there is much to discern in the vessel of Malchut in and of herself, meaning when she is not corrected with a screen. First, we should know that Malchut of circles is not corrected with a screen at all, for there is only a screen in

the Sefirot of straightness. This has already been explained in Part 2, and there are many other discernments that will be explained in their place. When we speak of Malchut alone, it means that we speak only of the coarseness, without the correction of the screen. Thus, there cannot be a screen without coarseness, but there can be coarseness without a screen.

The force of detainment in the screen of the Rosh is potential, not actual

82. The second discernment is the discernment of "potential detainment" inside the screen. There is "potential" and "actual" in the detainment of the screen on the upper light, meaning the difference between the Rosh and the Guf.

We say that the upper light expands until it hits the screen in the vessel of Malchut, the screen pushes the light back, and this reflected light clothes over the ten Sefirot of the Rosh. However, all this is only in potential, not in actual fact (see above item 16). Hence, you should know that the boundary and the detainment on the light in the screen in Malchut of the Rosh is only potential detainment, not actual.

The potential force of detainment in the screen is called Peh, and the actual is called Tabur

83. The third discernment is the actual detainment in the screen. That clothing and that detainment that are done in "potential" in the Rosh, come and actually manifest in the Guf. It is so because Malchut of the Rosh expands from her and within her to ten Sefirot from above downward, generally called Guf. Malchut of these ten Sefirot is called Tabur, where the entire force of detainment on the upper light in the screen of the Rosh manifests. It does not let the upper light clothe, but only from the Tabur up, and detains it from clothing from the Tabur down.

Know that these two names, Peh and Tabur, relate to the above-mentioned two discernments. It is so because the potential detainment of the screen is called Peh, and the actual detainment in the screen is called Tabur.

The incorporation of the screen in the first three phases through its refinement

84. The fourth discernment is the incorporation of the screen in the coarseness of the first three phases, which comes because of the refinement of the screen (see item 4). It is done by the striking and clash of inner light and surrounding light with each other, as the ARI wrote (Chapter 1, item 3). This is something that should be thoroughly understood as it is the pole on which the entire wisdom hangs.

The incorporation of the screen in the first three phases means the first three phases of phase four

85. We have already elaborated on that matter, in Inner Light, and this is not the place to expand on it. However, we must understand in this regard, that this above incorporation in the screen does not mean that the first three phases themselves have now been restricted, as phase four was restricted before. Rather, this entire refinement occurred only in phase four herself.

It has already been explained in Inner Observation of Part 2, that phase four herself consists of four phases because she comes from Ein Sof. Hence, the screen established in her also consists of all of these four phases (see item 80), as the entire coarseness in Malchut is included in the screen.

Now you can see that when it says that the screen rose to ZA, to phase three, it means that phase four within phase four was refined from the screen, and only the coarseness of phase three within phase four remained in her. It turns out that her form had been equalized with the phase of ZA.

You know that equivalence of form is unification in the spiritual, and thus it is considered that she rose and united with ZA, as if she herself was the phase of ZA, for there is nothing to tell them apart. This is called being incorporated with ZA.

You can similarly understand the rest of the incorporations that were said about the screen until it rose and was incorporated in the Peh of the Rosh, meaning it equalized its form as the potential screen, and it was not at all apparent in it that it is an actual screen, and understand this well.

If the screen departs from the vessel, the light departs from it

86. The fifth discernment is the cessation of the operation of the screen from the vessel because of its exit from there. In other words, when the screen was refined from phase four to phase three, discerned as the screen exiting the vessel of Malchut and ascending to the vessel of ZA, Malchut was seemingly liberated from the force of detainment and boundary that was on her, and now she can receive the upper light without delays. However, this is not the case. On the contrary, Malchut remained completely dark because of the exit of the screen from her. It is so because from the first restriction on, Malchut is no longer fit to receive any light, but only through a screen.

Thus, the two operations—the reception of the light and the rejection of the light—are both connected with the screen. As it rejects the light from the last phase, so it connects and clothes the lights from her and above.

A screen that acquires the coarseness of the Rosh after its refinement

87. The sixth discernment is the coarseness of the Rosh, acquired anew in the screen after its refinement, meaning by its ascent and coming into Malchut of the Rosh, where it is incorporated, as written elaborately in Chapter 4, item 50, and in Inner Light.

The screen that acquires the coarseness of the Guf after its refinement

88. The seventh discernment is the coarseness of the Guf, acquired in the screen anew after its refinement. After the screen of the Rosh received the coarseness from below upward, all the records with which the screen of the Guf was incorporated on its way through the Sefirot of the Guf up to the emanator awakened. These records are from the phase of coarseness from above downward, meaning from the phase of the Guf. It turns out that this coarseness that they receive from the Rosh in the phase of from below upward becomes inverted in the records of the Guf into coarseness from above downward, as it is written above in Inner Light.

CHAPTER SIX

Six discernments in the direct light

The upper light is completely even, and all the above changes relate to the receivers

89. First and foremost, we must know and remember that the upper light is completely even, and the multitude of changes we find in the worlds are all done on the part of the receivers. Moreover, they come by a necessary order of cause and consequence from the first receiver, namely Malchut of Ein Sof (see Part 1 Inner Light and Inner Observation).

After all that, no change occurs in the upper light, and it does not undergo changes even with respect to the receivers. It means that its simple light will finally appear to the receivers as it was apparent in the first receiver, meaning in Malchut of Ein Sof before the restriction, without any change, as it says, "I the Lord do not change."

The knowledge of the wisdom depends mostly on knowing the order of the cascading of the Sefirot and the Partzufim and the worlds in an order of cause and consequence

90. Know that knowing this wisdom depends mostly on knowing the order of the cascading of the Sefirot, the Partzufim, and the worlds from one another by absolutely necessary cause and consequence. The sages of *The Zohar* explained this in the manner of *sod* (secret), but no one understood their words until the ARI came and revealed the matters.

Know also that the whole innovation in the Kabbalah of the ARI, with respect to previous interpreters, is primarily in the disclosure of the ten Sefirot of reflected light. Although the ten Sefirot of reflected light in general were revealed to all the prior Kabbalists, their primary attainment and understanding was only according to the conducts in the ten Sefirot of direct light. When the ARI came and explained to us the knowledge in the ways of the reflected light in their every detail, he thus opened before us the hidden treasures, locked in *The Book of Zohar*.

All the discernments in the reflected light are extended from the direct light

91. However, we must know that all these many discernments observed in the reflected light are extended from the ten Sefirot of direct light. Thus, you haven't

even a tiny innovation in the reflected light that is not extended from the direct light. For this reason, they are also called by the same names as those of the direct light. Not only are they extended from them, but their attributes are the same as well. The only difference is in the inverse relation between them, as one is a light and one is a vessel.

The ARI spoke very little about the ten Sefirot of direct light

92. Indeed, the ARI spoke very little of the ten Sefirot of direct light, and even that was very concisely, since he relied in that on the prior Kabbalists whose words were only from the direct light. Hence, he found no reason to elaborate on them, and we must admit that we very much need his clear knowledge of the ten Sefirot of direct light; it is an immeasurable absence.

93. There are six discernments here in the ten Sefirot of direct light that we must always remember during the engagement in the wisdom. They are: The first discernment is that the upper light is completely even, while the phases discerned in the ten Sefirot of direct light are the garments over the upper light. However, they become apparent only by clothing in the reflected light.

The number ten Sefirot is only in direct light, but in reflected light, they are five phases

94. The second discernment is that the number ten Sefirot is primarily in the direct light, but in the reflected light there are but five phases, as the ARI says here (item 63).

The ten Sefirot of direct light are considered a single illumination. They are separated from one another only when they clothe in the reflected light

95. The third discernment is that the ten Sefirot of direct light in and of themselves are not separated degrees from one another as when they are clothed in reflected light. Rather, they are regarded as a single illumination. However, when they clothe inside the ten Sefirot of reflected light, great and enormous differences appear between them.

There are distances in the ten Sefirot of direct light in terms of themselves, although they are as one illumination

96. The fourth discernment is the distances in the ten Sefirot of direct light from the perspective of the self of each and every Sefira as written in Part 1, Inner Light item 50 and Inner Observation there.

Everything that exists in the consequence, it receives from its cause. The illumination remains primarily in its cause, and only a branch of it is imparted to the consequence

97. The fifth discernment is the measure of the distance between the cause and the consequence, and that all that exists in the consequence, it receives from its cause. It cannot receive anything from any degree above its cause if not through its cause. As much as the cause imparts to the consequence, most of the illumination remains in the cause, and only a small branch of it is imparted and reaches the consequence, although the illumination comes primarily for the consequence (see item 24).

All that is closer to phase four is regarded as coarser

98. The sixth discernment is the discernment of the proximity to phase four. The closer it is to phase four, the lower and coarser it is considered (see item 23). This discernment begins in the ten Sefirot of direct light only from the restriction downward, when phase four became a vacant space and was corrected with a screen. Hence, this discernment does not apply to the circles, since there is no screen there.

99. All these above discernments, except the last, apply to the ten Sefirot of direct light even before the restriction. Even though we have no attainment whatsoever prior to the restriction, nevertheless the upper one is still studied from the lower one. Remember these discernments well and let them not move from before your eyes when you engage in the study of the wisdom.

Made in the USA
Monee, IL
31 December 2024

75761708R00275